A Path of Reason for America

Phillip Scanlan

Cover designed specifically for *A Path of Reason for America* by Ric Borum
© 2019 Copyright to Phillip Scanlan

A Path of Reason for America is self-published through Amazon Kindle Direct Publishing.

ISBN   978 168 805 137 9

Book Availability and Pricing

Book Type and Source	Price
Amazon Kindle eBook	$7.95
Paperback from Amazon.com and Affiliates	$19.95+Shipping
Paperback from Independent Book Sellers	$19.95+Service Charge

DEDICATION

A Path of Reason for America is written with the hope that it will help to improve the quality of life for the next generation in America.

This book is dedicated to my children: Walter, Maureen, Michelle, and John

My grandchildren: Trevor, Travis, Lauren, Sarah, Isabelle, Meara, Charlie, Jack, Pat, and Reagan

My great-granddaughter: Elaina Leia

and

All future generations of Americans.

ACKNOWLEDGEMENTS

Thanks to my former employer, AT&T, for giving me the opportunity during the last dozen years of my career to help lead their quality improvement efforts; an opportunity where I learned from many.

Thanks to the State of New Jersey (NJ), in particular Dave Rosenblatt, for allowing me to work with him to assist the state of NJ in applying quality methods to help resolve the NJ shore ocean pollution crisis, another learning opportunity.

Thanks to Phil Sterner, who ran a week-long workshop on how to be a useful sage. This workshop was run at "The Mountain," a retreat center in Highlands, NC, atop a beautiful forested mountaintop. This workshop gave me the nudge I needed to get started on writing this book, to share what I have learned.

Thanks to Lorelei Jacobs for her suggestion to add my personal stories to show the impact that each U.S. crisis can have on an individual and how we might also have a small impact on each crisis.

Thanks to Gregg Kaufman, the facilitator of a forum course on democracy at the University of North Florida. The forum class enabled me to gain a better understanding of the barriers that inhibit citizens' support of improvements to reduce crises. I learned that most citizens want our elected officials to work with the experts on each crisis and eliminate them.

Thanks to the subject matter experts who gave me their comments on the crisis analysis examples: Carl Bazarian, Don Hughes, Peter Johnson, Pete Onstott, Munsell McPhillips, Robert Prager, Roger Rufe, Joe Simon, and the Ocean Conservancy staff.

Thanks to Ric Borum, graphic artist, who designed the jacket cover used on *A Path of Reason for America.*

Thanks to Nancy Dickson for helping edit the writing style used in this book. Her recommendations helped me to make this data-heavy book more readable.

Thanks to Nancy Freedman, for editing my sentence structure, punctuation, terminology consistency, and for checking references.

Thanks to Leah Ward-Lee, author of *$1,000 Start-Ups,* for her advice on publishing and marketing a self-published book.

Thanks to Cheyenne Grooms, General Partner of Aerial Social Media Marketing, for her help in developing marketing plans for this book.

Thanks to all four of my children: Walter Scott, Maureen Imelda, Michelle Ann, and John Phillip for their comments and encouragement.

Most of all, thanks to my fiancée, Judy Comley, for keeping me healthy (eating right and walking the beach) and keeping me stress-free by bringing daily fun and love into my life, while writing this book about how to eliminate our national crises.

Contents

DEDICATION i

ACKNOWLEDGEMENTS ii

PREFACE 1

Chapter 1 – GOALS 9

Citizens' Views of Government 9

Why Goals Are Needed 16

A Proposal for Goals 17

Chapter 2 – CRISES 22

Historical Analysis 22

Changes Contributing to Crises in America 25

Progress on Resolving U.S. Crises 27

Reducing Crises 64

Chapter 3 - BARRIERS, FOLLIES and VALUES 68

Removing Barriers 68

Removing Follies 78

A Proposal for Adding Values 84

Chapter 4- UNFIXING WASHINGTON 88

Success Examples 88

A Quality Check 91

The Swamp in Washington 95

A Proposal for Unfixing Washington 100

Proposal for House Crisis Action Teams (House CATs) 104

Chapter 5 –QUALITY APPROACH 115

Quality Improvement 115

Bloom's Taxonomy of Knowledge 118

Plan, Do, Check, Act (PDCA) Cycle 119

Chapter 6: A PATH OF REASON FOR THE WORLD 128

World Crises and Organizations 128

Democracy and Autocracy 130

World Homicide Crisis 132

Preface for the Second Half of the Book 139

Chapter 7: FINANCIAL CRISES 154

National Debt Crisis 155

Wall Street and Corporate Debt Crisis 176

Trade Balance Crisis 184

Infrastructure Maintenance Crisis 192

Chapter 8 – WORKER CRISES 197

Worker Skills Crisis 197

Worker's Fair Pay Crisis 205

College Education Debt Crisis 216

Social Media Crisis 224

Chapter 9 - HEALTH CARE CRISES 229

Use of Drugs Crisis 230

Diabetes Crisis 236

Cancer Rate Crisis 243

Gun Violence Crisis 251

Health Care Costs Crisis 259

Chapter 10 – ENVIRONMENT CRISES 268

Land , Air & Fresh Water Crisis 268

Oceans Crisis 276

Climate Change Crisis 284

Chapter 11 – SECURITY CRISES...295

    Nuclear Arms & Waste Crisis....................................295

    Cybersecurity Crisis 305

    Border Security Crisis 316

    Defense Cost Crisis 327

Chapter 12 –DEMOCRACY CRISES....................................337

    Election Campaign Crisis 337

    Government Crisis 349

    Political Party Crisis 356

SUMMARY of – A PATH OF REASON FOR AMERICA.............................365

    Appendix A – First 100 Days – Of President elected in Nov. 2020....369

    Appendix B – Second 100 Days –of President elected in Nov. 2020 371

    Appendix C – Third 100 Days of President elected Nov. 2020 374

    Worksheet to Tally Primary Responsibility for Government Follies: 384

REFERENCES...386

GLOSSARY of TERMS 418

    INDEX 424

LIST OF TABLES

Table 1: Change in U.S. Crises' Results over Time   29

Table 2: Crisis Cost Estimates by Category   32

Table 3: Administration Policy Impact on Crises   62

Table 4: Decisions of Folly, Improvements, and   66
Budget Reductions by Crisis

Table 5: Types of Repeated Follies   83

Table 6: The Swamp – Washington Governance Process   96

Table 7: Comparison of Critical Thinking Levels and Quality   118
Changes that Facilitate Follies

Table 8: Nation Government Type Changes   132

Table 9: Gross Crisis Cost (GCC) by Primary Responsibility   142

Table 10: U.S. Debt-to-GDP Ratio History   160

Table 11: Past Surpluses in the Federal Budget   168

Table 12: 2 + 2 Balanced Budget Plan   169

Table 13: Minimum Wage by State   212

Table 14: Least Expensive College Costs by Country   219

Table 15: Teenage Average Screen Time   225

Table 16: Body Mass Index Categories   237

Table 17: Obesity by Country   238

Table 18: U.S. Obesity and Diabetes Increases   239

Table 19: Highest Gun Deaths by Country   251

Table 20: Lowest Gun Death Rates by Country   252

Table 21: How We Deal with Cars and Guns Differently   256

Table 22: Nuclear Weapons States   297

Table 23: Nuclear Countries Who Have Not Signed the NPT   297

Table 24: Nuclear Power Countries   301

Table 25: Military Expenditures by Country   329

Table 26: Presidential Election Expenditures   339

Table 27: Congressional Election Expenditures   339

Table 28: Party Political Policies versus Solutions to Root Causes   359
          Of Crises

PREFACE

In the past, most Americans believed that their children would be better off than they were, thus justifying their hard work and efforts on behalf of their offspring. This belief was often called the American Dream; however, in March of 2019, The Pew Research Center completed a poll of Americans showing that only 20% of Americans expect families to fare better financially in the future than they are today. The majority of Americans have lost hope in the American Dream; they believe that Washington has let them down and that Washington needs to be fixed (Parker et al. 2019).

To fix Washington, Americans have been voting for candidates who promise change. In 2008, Barack Obama was elected President for two terms on a message of change. In 2016, Donald Trump was elected President, also on a message of change. America elected two very different candidates who had only two things in common: very little political experience and a promise of change. In the 2018 congressional election, a number of candidates with little political experience were elected in the House of Representatives, also calling for change. Voters from both parties are dissatisfied with the current state of affairs in America, and they want Washington fixed in order to reduce the crises they are facing daily, and to improve their hope for America's future.

Most politicians and elected officials have been calling for change in what is being done in Washington; however, the change politicians are usually pushing for is their predetermined political party programs. Those predetermined political party positions have been pushed for decades and they are not addressing the root causes of our multiple crises. We need to identify and eliminate the root causes of the multiple U.S. crises that are causing the loss of hope in the future of America.

The most significant common root cause of all the U.S. crises is intentional decisions of folly over reason. Folly generally means a lack of good sense. The word folly in this book refers to decisions that are made for greed and selfish ambition intended to benefit a few rather than making decisions based on reason to benefit the many.

These decisions of folly may be dishonest, unethical, immoral, corrupt, and unscrupulous, but they are legal. The system in Washington has been changed to increase follies, not decrease them, in order to benefit special interests over the common good.

Officials are elected to make decisions for the benefit and welfare of all, but too often they have used their power to make decisions instead for their own selfish ambition and to benefit a few; usually the few that helped finance their election campaigns. Furthermore, over the past 20 years, the Washington governance process has been fixed in favor of special interests over the common good, which is what is facilitating all these decisions of folly.

A bipartisan use of a quality approach to identify root causes of our U.S. crises can help to reduce our follies and crises, and help restore hope in America. The phrase "quality approach" is used throughout this book and refers to a simple Plan, Do, Check, Act (PDCA) process for reducing a problem or crisis.

One way to get to root causes of a problem, or a crisis, is to repeatedly ask "Why" until you reach the root cause. For example:

The overarching crisis in America is that the majority of Americans have lost hope that the future in America will be better for the next generation; Americans have lost hope in the American Dream.

1st Why: Why have Americans lost hope in the future of America? America is facing multiple crises and disasters that are affecting the daily lives of Americans and their hope for a better future. Those crises have not been adequately resolved, and collectively they have become such a burden that they have affected hope in the future of America.

2nd Why: Why does the U.S. have unresolved crises?
Increased decisions of folly have contributed to the number and size of our crises. Affordable solutions to most crises are available, but choices of folly to benefit a few are being chosen instead of decisions to reduce the crises for the benefit of many.

3rd Why: Why does America have decisions of folly contributing to increased crises?

Changes in how Washington operates have facilitated decisions of folly over reason. Washington has been fixed in the wrong direction. It has been fixed to benefit the few over the many, and those changes need to be identified and reversed. In addition, changes need to be made in Washington in order to be able to reduce our multiple increasing crises. Our crises can be solved using critical thinking problem solving skills contained in a quality approach, if they are used in a bipartisan manner with decisions of reason for the common good.

4th Why: Why has Washington made systemic changes to the Washington governance process that facilitates decisions of folly over reason? Increasingly, special interest groups' campaign money is controlling elected officials' decisions, thus making changes in Washington that facilitate decisions of folly over reason. About 27 changes have been made to our Washington governance processes that have resulted in a government that favors special interests over the common good. Washington has been fixed to favor special interests.

This book has two sections. The first half of this book (Chapters 1 through 6) analyzes the lack of measurable goals to reduce our crises, the current status of our crises, the decisions of folly (decisions for the greed and selfish ambition of a few) that have contributed to each of 23 U.S. crises, a proposal for unfixing Washington, and how the steps and tools of a quality approach can be used to reduce our crises and restore hope in America. The final chapter in the first half describes how this approach could also be applied to reduce world crises.

The second half, Chapters 7 through 12, provides examples of how the quality planning approach can be used to reduce each of our 23 crises. These analyses identify the root causes and decisions of folly that have created our crises. These examples can be used as a starting point for government action to address our crises using a quality approach. To reduce our crises, government needs to lead the way; however, businesses and individual citizens also have a significant role.

Each crisis analysis includes an estimated cost of the crisis in 2020. I have referred to the annual crisis cost for all 23 crises as the U.S. Gross Crisis Cost (GCC), which is estimated to be about $9.1 trillion dollars per year in 2020; that is about 42% of the U.S. annual Gross Domestic Product (GDP). This GCC is the financial burden placed on U.S. citizens that has caused a loss of hope in the future. This annual GCC estimate does not include a value for the lives lost from these crises or the burden that places on America.

We can't eliminate all these crisis costs, but we can reduce them. A 10% reduction in annual crisis costs would save about $900 billion per year, just about the amount of the annual federal budget deficit. This book contains proposals about how to reduce our U.S. crises, reduce our crises' costs, and get to a balanced federal budget at the same time. Currently, with the existing government approach, most of our crises are still growing larger.

What is different about the approach in this book that could lead to the change needed in Washington to reverse the decline of hope for the future?

- It provides the historic background of the disastrous impact of follies and crises on past governments, and it shows that we are facing similar follies and crises in the U.S. today. This similarity should motivate an effort to make the changes needed.

- It provides a comprehensive analysis of 23 crises and offers an understanding of how these crises are interrelated. It is the collective impact of both follies and crises that have caused the loss of hope in the future of America – loss of hope in the American Dream.

- Many specific crises have been analyzed individually and in depth by subject matter experts; however, the collective impact of all our crises on America have not been comprehensively analyzed. When the multiple U.S. unresolved and increasing crises are looked at collectively, it becomes clear that the future of America depends on resolving all these interrelated crises. While many decisions have been made to help special interests (decisions of folly), the collective enormous impact of all these decisions of folly on America has not been analyzed and understood previously. Those making decisions for the benefit of special interests need to know that the collective impact of their decisions is causing the loss of hope in the American Dream. When citizens understand the collective impact of our decisions of folly and our crises, they will demand, and vote for, the change we need.

- A common bipartisan quality approach is proposed, with examples, to resolve each crisis. Using a common approach to address each of the U.S. crises can help gain support for solutions from both elected officials and citizens. This approach is based on using agreed-to credible facts and critical thinking skills to address our crises. Bipartisan agreement on the crises we need to reduce, and agreement on the common goals for reducing these crises, is a needed first step.

Decisions of folly have not only been made by government; businesses and citizens have also made significant decisions of folly. The specific follies associated with each crisis are identified, and hopefully they will be reversed. In addition, process and system changes are recommended to avoid future decisions of folly.

This book is analytical, not political. It is based on facts and reason to address our problems. This book uses a quality approach to identify root causes of each crisis and develop efficient and effective improvement plans to eliminate those specific root causes. It also includes proposals on how to change government in Washington in order to use common sense, and to support choosing paths of reason over paths of folly. This book does not support any political party's predetermined positions of what to do; that is what has helped get us into this mess.

Over the past 20 years, we have lost our democracy to special interests. We now need to recover our democracy by reversing the changes that were made to serve special interests. Every day that goes by without establishing goals, creating a plan, and formulating actions to reduce our growing crises allow our crises to become more disastrous, more overwhelming, and harder to resolve. Such a delay increases the risk that our political parties could make the mistake of moving toward right-wing fascism or left-wing socialism as a solution to our crises, which will make things worse for the U.S. and the world.

H.L. Mencken, one of the most influential American writers of the 20th Century, observed, "For every complex problem there is an answer that is clear, simple, and wrong." In the U.S., we get it wrong because of our tendency to oversimplify complex problems. Too many politicians pick someone to blame, or pick one cause of a crisis to address, when there are multiple causes that need to be addressed. We then are misdirected to spend our time blaming others, or arguing about which single cause of a crisis we should be addressing, while addressing *none* of the real causes.

While this goes on, our crises continue to grow. Our crises are complex, with multiple root causes. A critical thinking (quality) approach can be used to identify the multiple root causes of each crisis and, having done that, prioritize common sense, efficient, and effective solutions to the root causes of each crisis. A common approach can make resolution of our large number of complex crises relatively simple, and doable; without oversimplifying.

We need to focus on four things:

- Establishing a bipartisan goal to restore trust in Washington and hope in the American dream

- Unfixing the Washington governance processes that have been fixed to serve special interests instead of the common good

- Reversing the decisions of folly that were facilitated by the actions of the Swamp in Washington

- Reducing all our U.S. crises, which have been fueled by fixed government processes (the Swamp in Washington), using a common quality approach and values in government

At the time of this book's publication (October 2019), the Leader of the House of Representatives announced that a formal inquiry into impeachment of the President of the United States will begin, as a result of a whistleblower complaint that the U.S. Department of Justice Inspector General found to be credible.

The whistleblower complaint that led to the decision to launch an inquiry into impeaching the President was labeled "urgent concern" for action. "Urgent concern" is a term used for issues that are viewed to be an abuse of power, not just a politically different viewpoint. The complaint charged that the President withheld military defense funding for Ukraine, to request that Ukraine do a political favor which could help the President's 2020 political re-election campaign. This was done during a time that Ukraine was under attack from Russian military intervention.

Using a medical analogy, there are 155 urgent concerns in this book (a combination of 27 process changes, 105 government follies, and the 23 U.S. crises) that constitute a cancer on our Democracy; they are life-threatening and growing. We need to eliminate every one of these cancer spots (i.e., the urgent concerns) to get America into remission, and we need to establish the necessary treatment to prevent the cancer from returning.

This entire book could be considered an "urgent concern" complaint, with proposals for solutions.

This book includes the need to address the following 155 urgent concerns:

- 27 process changes that have created "The Swamp" in Washington, by prioritizing special interests rather than the common good

- 105 government follies (i.e., decisions to serve special interests over the common good) are listed in Appendix C. Government folly #88, which is part of our Election Crisis, states, "Encouraging foreign countries to interfere in our elections." This happened in the 2016 Presidential election. On the July 25, 2019 telephone call between the U.S. President and the President of Ukraine, the "favor" requested by the U.S. President could be considered another instance of this same folly, but it is encouraging interference in a *future* election, the 2020 Presidential election. Repeated follies are a significant part of our nation's crises. A table of a dozen "Types of Repeated Follies" is included in Chapter 3.   If we were to add folly #88 to this table, the number of repeated follies would increase to 13.

- 23 unaddressed national crises that collectively have caused the loss of hope in the American Dream

The combination of these three categories above adds up to 155 "urgent concern" complaints. What is different about these 155 "urgent concerns," is that this book also includes proposals for what to do about all 155 of them.

A *Path of Reason for America* is like a Global Positioning System (GPS) for our democracy. Our vehicle GPS uses data from 24 satellites to provide the necessary information to navigate from point A to point B. *A Path of Reason* uses data from 23 national crises to provide the necessary information to navigate from point A (our current crises results measures) to Point B (our goals for crises results measures). Many no-cost and low-cost improvements are identified to improve our estimated time of arrival (ETA) at our goals. Of course, like with our vehicle GPS, it is up to each of us and each of our leaders to use this GPS guide along the path of reason to restore our democracy and hope in the American Dream, or not.

This book shows how a quality approach can be used to address our crises. We can do it, and we must do it. For those who want to know what we need to do, Appendix A, B and C specifically address what needs to be done to address these three areas during the first year of the President who takes office in January 2021.

Chapter 1 – GOALS

The first step in a quality approach is to establish a customer-driven goal for what is to be done by the organization; in this case, the organization is the U.S. government and the customers are American citizens. Our country needs a goal to provide motivation and direction for improvements. Nothing gets better without having a goal to get better; without that goal, things get worse. To help make that goal a citizen-driven goal, we need to know citizens' views. Surveys of citizens can provide us with those views of how well our government is doing.

Citizens' Views of Government

Citizen trust in government remains near historic lows. Only 17% of Americans today say they can trust the government in Washington to do what is right, either always or most of the time. This compares to 75% in the early 1960s under President Eisenhower and President Kennedy (Pew Research Center 2019).

U.S. government leadership should have a goal to improve this 17% rating and an action plan to reach that goal. For example, a goal could be to improve to the 75% of the early 1960s, in the first 4-year term of the next President. If the recommendations in this book are implemented by our government, our government could return to that 75% confidence level.

A Harvard University poll in the spring of 2019 showed that only 20% of millennials believe America is heading in the right direction (Harvard Kennedy School Institute of Politics 2019). In addition, that poll showed that 64% of young Americans have more fear than hope about the future of democracy in America. 77% of millennials believe politicians, not outside forces, were responsible for existing U.S. problems. The Washington swamp presents the greatest threat to our nation. "Young Americans are deeply concerned and fearful about our country's future," said Institute of Politics Polling Director John Delta (Harvard Kennedy School Institute of Politics, n.d.).

It is up to us to fix the way things are being done in our government, and not simply blame others for our problems. Specific reasons for the low citizens' view of the U.S. future cited in the Harvard University poll included poor economic policies and a heated political divide. Those are two very big reasons for our problems, and they must be addressed to improve things. Many believe that America is financially unable to address our crises, and the country lacks a long-term financial plan to address this very credible fear. The analysis of our crises in the second half of this book confirms that fear; this book will provide a plan to address our financial crisis.

Fear of the future was found to be the number one stressor in a poll conducted by the American Psychological Association (American Psychological Association 2017). Roughly two thirds of Americans said they are stressed about the future of our nation, and that number increased in a second poll conducted the following year. The concern over the future of America was the highest source of stress for all Americans. Furthermore, 59% of those polled said this was the lowest point in our nation's history that they could remember (American Psychological Association 2017).

For the Gen Z generation (born between 1995 and 2005), 75% see mass shootings as their source of most stress: three quarters of this country's children should not have to live in fear of being shot. The same survey found that 69% of parents with children in school agreed that school shootings were a significant source of stress. Stress is a significant cause of health issues, which contributes to the U.S. Health Care crisis (American Psychological Association 2018).

Americans of all generations reported experiencing stress at the highest levels in a decade, according to a Gallup Poll of more than 150,000 people around the world. 55% of Americans experienced "a lot of stress" compared to only 35% for those in the rest of the world. Americans are the most stressed people in the world (Ray 2019).

In an HBO Special, Dr. Sanjay Gupta looked deeper into our national stress crisis in the documentary "One Nation Under Stress." Significant findings include:

- Stress contributes significantly to many of our health crises
- The U.S. average life expectancy has dropped every year for the last 3 years [Centers for Disease Control and Prevention (CDC)]

- The middle class is the most stressed

- Inequality is a major stressor, creating anger about unfairness

- Chronic stress is causing an epidemic of self-destructive behavior, including suicide and drug use

- Stress causes changes in the brain that reduce the capability for having empathy for others, and it increases primitive behaviors focused on self-survival

- Social support from family, friends, and community is the opposite of stress and helps people deal with stress

- We are in a destructive negative spiral with increasing stress causing decreasing compassion; but sadly, compassion is needed to deal with many of our crises that are causing the stress

- Leaders addicted to power and money are making decisions to benefit the rich and powerful; these decisions increase stress on the middle class

The combined effects of multiple U.S. crises are significantly increasing stress on Americans. This increased stress is making Americans less willing and able to support efforts to deal with our common crises, and more focused on their own individual survival. To help individuals understand the connection between individual stress and these national crises, an example of how a personal crisis can be caused by each of the national crises has been included in Chapters 7 through 12. Each crisis analysis includes a personal story of how my life has been connected to, and affected by, these 23 U.S. crises.

Well over half (64%) of young voting-age citizens (18-29) are more fearful than hopeful about the future of democracy. There is agreement among both young Democrats and Republicans that money in politics is a major cause of America's poor outlook on the future: 75% of Democrats and 63% of Republicans blame money in politics for their fear of the future (Harvard Kennedy School Institute of Politics, n.d.).

These collective polls of Americans show that the country needs to improve citizens' hope in the future of America by:

- Developing a responsible financial plan for the future of the U.S.

- Reducing money in politics

- Reducing divisiveness in politics

- Reducing mass shootings and gun violence

- Providing more affordable education, health care, and housing

According to the Dalai Lama, the spiritual leader of the Tibetan people, "If the situation, or problem, is such that it can be remedied, then there is no need to worry about it. In other words, if there is a solution or way out of the difficulty, you do not need to be overwhelmed by it" (Goodreads, n.d.). But Americans today can see no way out of our crises, and we are overwhelmed. Stress on Americans today is not just from the crises we are facing, but also from the fact that there is no credible approach to developing solutions to them. If the government were to agree to use a proven bipartisan approach to address the above crises, that step alone would be enough to reduce Americans' stress significantly, and increase hope for the future. This book is written not simply to analyze our crises, but to provide a credible approach to addressing them. When that credible approach is successfully implemented by our government on the first few crises, it will begin to reduce stress in America by showing that we have a credible approach in place to address all our crises.

U.S. goals to reduce our crises need to be bipartisan in order to be effectively supported over the long term through changing administrations. A simple place to start would be for the government to agree on a bipartisan goal to improve hope in the future of America. In order to reach this goal, each U.S. crisis that contributes to the loss of hope in the future of America would also need a goal for improvement, and a plan to reach that goal. The second half of this book will propose improvement goals for each of our 23 U.S. crises. Some readers may want to add additional crises to my list of 23, and I would encourage that. However, 23 is the limit for what I could address in one book. Hopefully, those who review these 23 crises can then determine how to use the same approach on additional crises. My selection of these 23 crises was based on my understanding of the crises that were having the most impact on the overarching U.S. crisis, which is the loss of hope in the future of America.

When we establish goals for our country, we should not only consider the current views of citizens, we should also consider the vision and goals set for our country in our Declaration of Independence and the preamble to the Constitution.

The Declaration of Independence starts with the words: "We hold these truths to be self-evident, that all men are created equal, that they are endowed by their Creator with certain unalienable Rights, that among these are Life, Liberty and the pursuit of Happiness."

Thirteen years later, when our country had achieved freedom from Great Britain, our new country needed a Constitution. Ours starts with: "We the people of the United States, in order to form a more perfect Union, establish Justice, insure domestic Tranquility, provide for the common defense, promote the general Welfare, and secure the Blessings of Liberty to ourselves and our Posterity [future generations], do ordain and establish this Constitution for the United States of America."

Two hundred and thirty years later, our country is facing multiple crises that are negatively impacting American citizens' ability to achieve the goals set forth in our Declaration of Independence and Constitution: goals for life, liberty, happiness, justice, tranquility, defense, and general welfare, for both ourselves and our posterity (National Archives, n.d. Declaration of Independence) (National Archives, n.d. Constitution). While America has never quite met these goals, in the past it had continued to move towards meeting those goals generation after generation. Over the past two decades however, America has lost this continuous improvement and in fact has slid backwards.

Simply having a democratic form of government is not sufficient to make America great. In order to achieve greatness, America needs continued improvement toward the goals set forth in our Declaration of

Independence and Constitution. America's continued improvement in the past toward those original goals is what has made America a role model, and it is the primary reason for the significant increase in democratic countries in the world.

At the end of 2016, 97 of 167 countries (58%) with populations of at least 500,000, were democracies; only 21 (13%) were autocracies. The remaining 26% exhibited elements of both democracy and autocracy. This is a significant change over 40 years since 1976, when only 24% of countries were democracies and 62% were autocratic (DeSilver 2019). That is a significant improvement for democracy in the world, thanks in part to successful democracy role models.

Democracy spread rapidly after the Soviet Union crumbled between 1989 and 1991. The economic failure of the Soviet Union and the economic success of the United States and European democracies was a signal that many in the world followed, in order to achieve a better quality of life. The percentage of countries that are democracies has more than doubled in the past 40 years, because those countries decided to follow economically successful democratic role models.

While it is good to see the increase in democracy in the world, a study by Pew Research in the prior year showed that 51% of citizens in democracies are dissatisfied with how democracies are working. Therefore, while democracies may be the best form of government in the world, they still need improvement.

America can't impose democracy on other countries with money, CIA operatives, or military force; we should know that by now after seeing many failed attempts for regime change in other countries. America can lead by example, however, by being a role model economy with a great quality of life. To continue leading the world as a democracy, America needs to ensure continued improvement toward meeting its original goals. Unfortunately, we have lost that continued improvement as a result of multiple unaddressed crises. Let's take a quick look at some of those unaddressed crises.

For the past few decades, our government has allowed mass murderers to have military assault weapons to slaughter our children and adults in schools, houses of worship, and other public places. Multiple surveys show our children are living in fear of being killed, and America has not taken adequate actions to address this crisis and reduce their fear. More than 80% of Americans want some simple preventive changes made to ensure America has responsible gun ownership, but elected leaders continue to support the NRA by not addressing our U.S. gun violence crisis. The reason our leaders refuse to act is simple: the NRA provides election campaign funding and lobbying to ensure no improvements are made. This is an example of a decision to follow a path of folly for the benefit of a few, rather than a path of reason for the majority.

While the current gun crisis prevents Americans from enjoying "life," our economic crises interfere with their ability to pursue "happiness." Over the past few decades, America has seen an increase in the number of working poor, many of whom have lost their hope for a better life and a better life for the next generation. Those graduating from college have had to start their career with enormous college debt, creating a burden and a barrier to their success.

The debt crisis interfering with our pursuit of happiness is not just the debt accrued by individuals. The U.S. federal government has created an enormous financial debt (over $22 trillion as of 3/1/19), creating a future burden for our children and grandchildren. Due to the enormous and increasing national debt, future generations know they will have fewer benefits and higher taxes, contributing to their loss of hope for the future.

It took a decade, $800 billion in government loans to Wall Street, and trillions in increased U.S. deficits to recover from the 2008 economic crisis. The next recession will be even more difficult to recover from, given the increased U.S. government financial debt crises.
This debt crisis is exacerbated by the pay inequality between the top leaders in business and the average worker – an inequality that has never been greater.

Rapid technology shifts require a reskilling of workers to meet job openings and to obtain adequate pay, but America is not keeping up with the reskilling required by these technology shifts.

Historically, America welcomed immigrants; in fact, this country was built by the hard work of immigrants. All of us, except Native Americans, are descendants of immigrants. However, America has recently begun incorrectly blaming immigrants for our problems and then mistreating those seeking asylum in America: separating young children from their parents at the border, sending military forces to confront those families seeking asylum here, having very long processing times for immigrants, and dramatically reducing the allowed number of immigrants seeking asylum to be accepted legally into America.

The above provides a quick review of several areas where America is now falling short of meeting the goals of the Constitution to promote the general welfare for ourselves and our posterity.

Why Goals Are Needed

Without a goal, any path will do. Goals are needed to guide all potential and proposed improvements, so that approved improvements move the organization in the same direction: toward the goal. The goal is a quantitative long-term measure of achievement, with annual measurable objectives for improvement. The U.S. lacks bipartisan agreed-to goals for the future, and without agreed-to goals, bipartisan improvement efforts cannot be expected.

In order for all government employees and citizens to make decisions on what they can do to help improve America, they need to understand the improvement goals America is trying to reach. Goals empower decision making at all levels. Without an agreed-to bipartisan goal, only the top leaders can make decisions, because only they know their own goals which could be based on personal ambition, political party power, or greed. America needs a much broader involvement of empowered citizens to address the crises that have caused their loss of hope in the future. To achieve this much broader empowered citizen involvement, agreed-to goals are required to provide direction for our improvement efforts.

To help understand the importance of goals, I will share a story from my efforts to help the state of New Jersey deal with what was then the worst ocean pollution crisis in the nation. After a few years working with the state of New Jersey to resolve the 1988 Jersey shore ocean pollution crisis, I asked the New Jersey Department of Environmental Protection (DEP) Manager, Dave Rosenblatt, what he thought was the key to our success. He did not hesitate, saying, "Setting a citizen-driven goal was the key." The goal we had set was for zero Jersey shore beach closings due to pollution. Prior to setting that goal, there had been no government teamwork among the responsible agencies: the federal Environmental Protection Agency (EPA), NJ State DEP, five County Health Departments, and 44 Jersey shore beach towns (Dave Rosenblatt, telephone conversation, January 2019). Over the entire Jersey shore (about 140 miles), there were 803 beach closings due to pollution in the 1988 summer season. Seven years later in 1995, by using a quality approach to identify root causes and make improvements, New Jersey had successfully reduced that to only 4 beach closings – a reduction of 99.5%. Since then, New Jersey has maintained its ocean water quality improvement. This is an example of the impact that can be obtained by using a quality approach in government to reduce a crisis.

My first book, *The Dolphins are Back – A Successful Quality Model for Healing the Environment,* describes this approach used in New Jersey (Scanlan 1998). The book was written to share this quality approach with the 30 U.S. states that have ocean, gulf, or Great Lake shore beaches, and with people interested in how to obtain excellent pollution-free beach water quality. However, this approach can be used to address any type of crisis, which is the purpose of writing this, my second book, A *Path of Reason for America.*

A Proposal for Goals

Today America lacks the common bipartisan goals which are needed to pull us together and make the type of improvement that was achieved with the Jersey shore crisis. Instead, we have partisan political platforms that pull us in different directions. While each political party may have their different predetermined political platforms, they also need to come together on needed bipartisan goals for America, and work as one to achieve them.

A proposed American goal could be to revive hope for a better future for our children, and to restore hope in the American Dream. To achieve that goal, America also needs to set a goal to be crisis free, by establishing a process to set goals and develop plans to resolve each crisis.

This book will explain how a quality approach can be used in government to reach a goal of improved hope in the future of America and resolution of the U.S. crises that have caused that loss of hope. This proposal will also include a plan to balance the budget, since the growing deficit is one of the crises that must be resolved.

The U.S. government can use the improvement methods used by business to improve both the effectiveness and efficiency of government in order to reduce the crises America now faces. However, there are barriers to using this business approach in government that must be recognized and overcome. Chapter 2 – Crises, will review 23 unresolved U.S. crises that we are facing and failing to reduce. Chapter 3 – Barriers, Follies and Values, will describe the barriers government must overcome to use a quality approach in government, in order to reduce our crises.

Many improvements are possible, requiring zero or minimal funding, to address these crises. However, without an agreed-to goal to reduce these crises, there has been insufficient bipartisan support for even approving no-cost or low-cost improvements. With an agreed-to goal for improvement, the U.S. government could prioritize implementation of the least costly improvements first, and make decisions to implement them as soon as possible in order to start reducing our crises. Every day that we take no action, our crises are growing larger, which means it will get harder and harder to resolve them.

In most cases, multiple improvement options to address each U.S. crisis have already been developed by non-profits, research universities, states, leading U.S. communities, or other countries. However, these improvements are not widely implemented due to the common cause of folly identified by Barbara Tuchman in her book *The March of Folly*. A decision of folly is a choice of a path for the greed or selfish ambition of a few, over a path of reason for the common good (Tuchman 1984). These decisions of folly, being made too often by our government leaders, keep us from implementing low-cost solutions that would reduce our crises.

Many non-profits (the points of light referred to by President George H. W. Bush) have been formed to help America address a particular crisis. These non-profit efforts are voluntarily funded by citizens who want a particular crisis to be addressed and reduced. They have also identified proven best practices for reducing crises in communities, which can then be used on a national scale to address our crises. We should look to proven best practices, research university studies, and citizen-funded non-profits, instead of large corporations' recommendations, if we want to choose the path of reason, over the path of folly.

Most people in government at federal, state, county, and city levels want to do better, and they can do better if they use a quality approach to continuously improve our governance system. To improve results, you must improve the processes and systems that produce the results. That is how the quality approach has been used in successful businesses, and a similar approach can be used in government. To improve government results, the government processes and systems that produce those results must be improved, which requires a willingness to commit to continuous improvement. Based on my experience helping government improve, I know that citizens can help government use a quality approach to make significant improvements. In fact, citizen involvement may be necessary to get our multiple levels of government, and our political parties, to work together to improve our government. I believe our forefathers designed a government in which they expected significant citizen involvement to ensure it did not drift into serving special interests. However, as our government has grown in size, that citizen involvement has been made increasingly difficult. Government and citizens working together can revive hope for the future of the next generation in America. Non-profits focused on specific crises are our best opportunity to gain the citizen involvement needed to reduce our crises. However, these non-profit groups need a seat at the table – a seat currently taken by special interests.

The historic ability of America to make the country even greater for each generation has unfortunately been lost. On July 4, 2019, America was 243 years old. As we have gotten older, America has slowly fallen into decline, like many large old corporations that do not continuously improve rapidly enough to keep up with change and competition. A sure way to be outdated as a corporation, or a country, is to fail to keep up with rapidly changing technologies.

America now has multiple large unresolved and growing crises that collectively are putting increasing pressure on the U.S. and its citizens. As these crises continue to increase the pressure on America, they also increase the loss of hope for a better future in America. The increasing pressure from these crises is also increasing the divisiveness in our country. In turn, this increasing divisiveness is making it harder to resolve the crises being faced. This negative loop needs to be broken, and it can be broken by using a quality approach with bipartisan support.

Some will say we cannot afford to address all our crises. However, it is actually too costly *not* to address them. Our country can begin saving money as the disasters created by our crises are reduced. The resources exist, and are in place now, to solve our crises if our government does the following:

- Works as a bipartisan team

- Learns and utilizes a quality approach

- Makes use of non-profits, research universities, investigative studies, and best practices of other countries, to agree on the facts about each crisis

- Develops a common understanding of the root causes of our crises

- Identifies and prioritizes the most effective and efficient solutions to root causes of our crises

- Makes decisions for a path of reason for the common good, instead of a path of folly for the greed of a few

- Recognizes continuous government system and process improvements are needed, rather than continuous change of elected partisan officials

The information in this book offers a common sense approach to problem solving, which our government can use in a bipartisan way. However, using this approach will take some improvements in our government system and processes, which will be covered in Chapter 4 – Unfixing Washington.

Summary

America needs to establish bipartisan goals to return citizen hope for the future of America; in order to accomplish that, bipartisan goals are needed to reduce each and every U.S. crisis. Without goals, any path will do.

Chapter 2 – CRISES

Before we can move forward in solving the many crises the U.S. faces, we need to look to the past to see how we got here. This chapter includes an historical analysis of the crises that caused the collapse of past civilizations. These historic crises that caused the failure of other civilizations are eerily similar to the crises our country faces today, and we need to learn from those past mistakes.

We need to understand how we got into this mess, in order to figure out how to get out of it. The many changes over the past 20 years that have contributed to the creation of our current U.S. crises will be described. Promised quick fixes, or silver bullets, are false promises and waste our limited time. It is possible to begin to reverse our growing crises and begin to make continuous annual improvements right away, but we will need to be persistent over many years to reverse 20 years of damage done by the swamp that has been created in Washington.

This chapter will also analyze 23 national crises that are causing repeated disasters that negatively affect the daily lives of all citizens today, and impair the hope for a better future for America. A more in-depth analysis of these crises, and how to reduce them, will be covered in chapters 7 through 12.

Finally, this chapter will include a proposal for using a quality approach in government to reduce our crises, and to return hope for the future of America.

Historical Analysis

A 2019 study by Luke Kemp, a researcher at the Centre for the Study of Existential Risk at the University of Cambridge, found that 87 ancient civilizations collapsed between 3,000 BC and 600 AD, and they had an average life of only 336 years. It takes hard critical thinking work to deal with crises in order for governments to live as long as possible. Kemp defined a civilization as a society with its own geographical region, agriculture, cities, military dominance, and a continuous political structure. His study, which is part of a BBC Future series about the long-term prospects of humanity, looked into historic causes of government collapse, and found they were linked to the accumulation of unresolved crises – many of which are similar to those the U.S. is now facing. The study's researchers hoped that these findings could help current civilizations deal more effectively with the crises that have caused the collapse of governments in the past. Kemp states, "Great civilizations are not murdered, they take their own lives" (Kemp 2019).

This book is an attempt to help our government deal more effectively with our crises, and thus avoid a collapse of our government by addressing our crises using a critical thinking approach. Corporations and governments do collapse as they age, if they do not continuously improve, and when they focus on government leaders' greed, instead of citizen needs. This is what has caused the collapse of governments in the past.

The causes of collapse of these past civilizations were attributed to the collective impact of crises, which include the following:

- Climate change that resulted in crop failures and the creation of deserts

- Environmental degradation that resulted in deforestation, water pollution, and soil degradation leading to famine

- Inequality that resulted in social distress, political divisiveness, and violence

- Unresolved health epidemics

- Decline in competitiveness with other countries

- Military conflicts

The Kemp study also reported that a society's resilience may be able to delay, or prevent, collapse. That resilience includes things such as:

- Economic diversity, with less reliance on a few industries

- Increase in trading partners, to be less reliant on a few partners; many trading partners are better than a few
- Learning from past failures and using critical thinking problem solving skills to resolve all crises as quickly as possible

Jared Diamond, a noted historian and environmentalist, found similar causes of government collapse, in his book *Collapse*. Diamond warned, "Even the richest and technologically advanced societies today face growing environmental and economic problems that should not be underestimated." He warned collapse can happen quickly and is almost impossible to reverse once started. Collapse can also be simply a continued lowering of living standards (Diamond 2006).

In another book by Diamond, *Upheaval,* he states that although America is the military and economic world leader, we need to acknowledge key problems that America is facing and take actions to address them. Diamond suggests, "...acknowledgement of responsibility, painfully honest self-appraisal, and learning from models of other nations" would be a start (Diamond 2019).

A Path of Reason for America picks up where Kemp's studies and Diamond's books leave off. This book explains *how* we can reduce our crises using a quality approach (first half of this book) with examples of *how* to use that approach on our multiple crises (second half of this book). This book will also provide some painful self-appraisals of the declining situation in the U.S. over the past 20 years. Benchmarks will also be provided from models in other nations that we can learn from, along with many no-cost and low-cost improvements we can make.

While both Kemp and Diamond studied past civilizations and governments, this book studies the U.S. today. We may have already entered a collapse phase of our government by Diamond's definition, by simply having a continued lowering of living standards.

Kemp and Diamond both suggest that a key to avoiding collapse is to not deny the crises that are being faced, but instead use critical thinking skills to resolve them. Unfortunately, today, the U.S. has at least 23 crises which are contributing to the reduction in our living standards, and we are not dealing effectively with any of them. The approach proposed in this book is to use critical thinking problem solving skills to resolve our crises as soon as possible. Of course, first we have to admit we have them.

The well-known historian Barbara Tuchman provides another historical analysis in her book *The March of Folly*, which identified the underlying common reason for government crises: "the choice of decisions of folly for the benefit of a few instead of decisions of reason for the common good."

Kemp's, Diamond's, and Tuchman's historical studies of past government failures offer lessons for America today. Crises that can lead to government failure need to be resolved as soon as possible. Tuchman warns us that decisions of folly need to be avoided in order to prevent creating or increasing crises.

The proposals in this book can prevent decisions of folly, and resolve crises as soon as possible. It is up to citizens, in and out of government, to make the choice to address our follies and crises, or to continue with the status quo until these crises collectively create government failure; that is, a government unable to implement its responsibilities. Actually, our government is already unable to implement its responsibilities, as demonstrated by the number of unresolved crises we now face. If our government chooses to continue not addressing these follies and crises, that choice will be made by the few who are benefitting from decisions of folly. If government chooses to make the changes necessary to eliminate our crises and the follies that create them, that will probably be because enough citizens speak up, and vote for the political leaders who are willing to follow a path of reason and support the common good over greed for a few.

Changes Contributing to Crises in America

America is more than 240 years old, and an aging America has not been keeping up with changes in the world. Changes in America that have contributed to creation of our current crises include the following:

- The U.S. population is getting older, which means we have fewer workers and more retirees. Our population is also becoming less healthy and thus needs more health care services.

- World trade has become much more competitive, and world transportation costs have become much lower, so we are in competition on a grander scale than ever before.

- Technology shifts are happening more quickly, affecting large segments of the workforce such as: manufacturing automation, container shipping, internet shopping, and renewable energy; more shifts are coming in the future with artificial intelligence technology.

- Technology shifts leave large numbers of workers with insufficient skills for the jobs needed by the new technology. In 2018, for example, the U.S. had 6 million people unemployed and 6 million job openings. In April 2019, the U.S. had more job openings than people unemployed. Jobs are no longer the crisis; job skills are.

- In response to the 9/11 attack, the U.S. adopted a preemptive military policy changing our Department of Defense significantly. Adding this additional function costs a lot more than simply defending our borders. In 2018, U.S. military expenditures were greater than the next 7 countries combined: $649 billion for the U.S. military, compared to $609 billion combined for the military in China, Saudi Arabia, India, France, Russia, United Kingdom, and Germany (Stockholm International Peace Research Institute 2019).

- America's two major political parties have become very divisive, thus preventing the cooperation needed to address the multiple large crises facing our country. In 2018, a survey showed that 60% of the members of each political party believe members of the other party are ignorant. That is, each party believes the people in the other party are not aware of some basic facts. To reduce this problem, and reduce divisiveness, both parties need to work on developing a common understanding of the basic facts associated with each of our crises. Members of both political parties also need to be willing to address our crises without a partisan bias.

- In 2010, the Supreme Court allowed unlimited special interest money from unidentified businesses to be used in election campaigns through super political action committees (Super PACs), which in turn influences politicians' decisions. These Super PAC donations contribute to increasing decisions of folly for the benefit of a few that are the causes of multiple crises for the many.

- The Federal Government has had record high debt for an extended period, continues to spend more money than it is taking in, and lacks a financial plan to address this enormous financial crisis; this is a threat to our government's ability to address our other multiple crises.

- The current U.S. governance system has been changed over time to enable more decisions of folly, which are contributing to increasing the size and number of our crises. The multiple crises are causing repeated costly disasters.

Individually, each of these changes is significant; collectively they have created our current over-arching crisis, which is a loss of hope in the future of America.

Progress on Resolving U.S. Crises

Twenty-three unresolved crises in six categories (Finance, Worker, Health Care, Environment, Security, and Democracy) will be identified and analyzed using a quality approach in Chapters 7 through 12. These crises are a source of the repeated disasters that affect the daily lives of U.S. citizens today.

Many of these crises are also root causes of increases in other crises; therefore, working on all of them is essential to resolve them. Establishing a credible approach in Washington to resolve all our unresolved crises would reduce stress in America and begin to restore hope in the future of America. This book is a proposal to establish that credible approach in Washington to resolving our U.S. crises.

The next table, "Change in U.S. Crises Results over Time," shows that 21 of these 23 crises have been getting worse over the past two decades; it also provides a summary of the change in the results of each U.S. crisis over time, for all crises analyzed in Chapters 7 to 12. The only two crises that have been improved over the past 20 years are the Land, Air, and Fresh Water and the Border Security crises; however, the current administration's actions have resulted in making even those two crises even worse.

One of the reasons we have not effectively addressed our crises is that we have not agreed to goals and measures for our crises. Chapters 7 to 12 include proposed goals and measures for each of 23 U.S. crises, providing an assessment of our progress in dealing with our crises, based on the proposed crises' measures. The citizen surveys in Chapter 1 showed that citizens know America is not adequately addressing our crises; the following table provides a measurable assessment of each crisis that confirms the citizen survey results.

Table 1: Change in U.S. Crises' Results over Time

Crises	From	To	Measure	Change
Chp. 7-Financial				
National Debt	2000	2019	U.S. Debt	+ 290%
Wall St. & Corporate Debt	2000	2018	Corp. Debt	+ 35%
Trade Balance	2000	2018	U.S. Deficit	+ 67%
Infrastructure Maintenance	2001	2017	Invest. Gap	+ 54%
Chp. 8-Worker				
Worker Skills	2000	2019	Workforce Participation	-6%
Worker's Fair Pay	1995	2017	CEO ratio	+ 193%
College Education Debt	2008	2018	Student debt	+ 62%
Social Media	2008	2018	Screen time	+ 38%
Chp. 9-Health Care				
Use of Drugs	2000	2017	Deaths	+ 320%
Diabetes	2000	2015	Diabetes	+ 113%
Cancer Rate	1999	2017	+ 33%	+ 34%
Gun Violence	2000	2017	Deaths	
Health Care Costs	2000	2017	Costs	+ 133%
Chp. 10-Environment				
Land Air and Fresh Water	2000	2017	Infant deaths	-12%
Oceans	2016	2019	Proposed MPAs	-46%
Climate Change	2017	2018	Carbon emissions	+ 3%
Chp. 11-Security				
Nuclear Arms and Waste	2016	2019	Treaties	-50%
Cybersecurity	2006	2015	Intrusions	+ 900%
Border Security	2000	2016	Illegal arrests	-75%
Defense Costs	2000	2020	Costs	+138%
Chp. 12-Democracy Crises				
Election Campaign	2000	2016	Pres. camp.	+ 700%
Government	2000	2019	Follies	Worse
Political Party	2000	2019	Divisiveness	Worse

Crisis measure calculations are included in Chapters 7 to 12.

While the political party focus has been on increasing campaign donations and fighting for funding of favorite projects, our U.S. crises have been allowed to grow without a goal or a plan to reduce them.

When people look at these crises, they often believe that reducing one crisis will increase another. This "either/or" mentality, that we have to make a *choice* of what to do, is standing in the way of improvement. Indeed, the opposite is true. We need to develop a "both/and" mentality; that is, we can do both and we need to do both. Many of our crises are root causes of other crises; therefore, addressing all crises simultaneously will result in a faster reduction of them all. Because of the interrelatedness of these crises, as each crisis is allowed to grow, it contributes to the growth of other crises. Not only can we address them all, we have the capability to do so.

We simply need to decide to address these crises for the common good, instead of making decisions that serve the greed of a few. A brief review of the House of Representatives' 538 caucuses shows that 88% are focused on serving special interests; only 12% are focused on addressing our national crises. That needs to change if we are going to successfully reduce our national crises.

In Chapters 7 through 12, 130 follies have been identified that have contributed to the 23 crises; that is an average of 5 follies per crisis. Follies are not mistakes; they are intentional choices of decisions based on greed and selfish ambition for a few. When faced with temptation, humans frequently choose to make decisions of folly. Perhaps those making these decisions of folly, to help a few, have not realized the collective impact that many decisions of folly have had in creating the multiple crises in America. These decisions have collectively eroded the American Dream of a better life for every generation. The proposals in this book are aimed at reducing those temptations for decisions of folly, through the use of process improvements, a quality approach, deployment of agreed-to values, and exposure of decisions of folly.

America has had over 200 years of continuous improvement; however, that has been reversed over the past 20 years by an enormous number of decisions of folly and changes in Washington that facilitate decisions of folly to serve the greed of a few over the common good. We need to reverse that; we need to unfix Washington, and we need to focus on reducing our crises in order to serve the common good. The change that got us into this mess over the past 20 years now undermines our democracy; today we need another big change, a reversal, to restore our democracy's capability for continuous improvement.

These crises all have a cost, which I have tried to estimate. Many of these crisis cost estimates come from research universities, non-profits, or government organizations that have done the analysis of the annual cost for a particular crisis. In some cases, such as with the Health Care crisis costs of $1.5 trillion per year, I made a calculated crisis cost estimate based on our U.S. cost as a percentage of GDP compared to an average of other countries, using the cost we pay *above* the world average as our crisis cost. In the case of Border Security, I used a crisis cost estimate of zero, which is based on an assumption that we are spending about the same percentage of our GDP as the average of other countries; however, because I do not have the data on that crisis for other countries, I used zero as a crisis cost rather than overestimate our U.S. crisis costs.

The Gross Crisis Cost (GCC) table below shows the estimated 2020 annual crisis cost for each crisis, as well as the total GCC annual cost. The U.S. GCC for 2020 is estimated to be over $9 trillion, which is equal to 42% of the U.S. annual GDP. Because 21 of these 23 crises have been getting worse, this GCC will increase significantly in future years. In fact, recent changes by the current administration resulted in a reversal on the only two crises that were getting better. For those who say we can't afford to address these crises, the truth is we can't afford *not* to. Those who say we cannot afford to address our crises have not understood the cost of those crises. That is why I have included a crisis cost calculation for each of the 23 crises analyzed in Chapters 7 to 12.

Table 2: Crisis Cost Estimates by Category (2020)

Chapter 7 – Financial Crises	Crises Cost Est. (Billions $)
National Debt	175
Wall Street and Corporate Debt	80
Trade Balance	891
Infrastructure Maintenance	200
Chapter 8 – Worker Crises	
Worker Skills	1,000
Worker's Fair Pay	482
College Education Debt	75
Social Media	1,000
Chapter 9 – Health Care Crises	
Use of Drugs	1,000
Diabetes	327
Cancer Rate	160
Gun Violence	300
Health Care Costs	1,500
Chapter 10 – Environment Crises	
Land, Air and Fresh Water	535
Oceans	200
Climate Change	250
Chapter 11 – Security Crises	
Nuclear Arms and Waste	40
Cybersecurity	110
Border Security	0
Defense Costs	410
Chapter 12 – Democracy Crises	
Election Campaign	430
Government	N/A
Political Party	N/A
Gross Crisis Cost (GCC) in $ B	**$9,165**

This is probably the first time the total annual cost of our national crises' costs has been calculated. Our GCC is equal to about 42% of our GDP (which is forecast to be $22.1 trillion in 2020) just for these 23 national crises; and we do have more crises. Therefore, this Gross Crisis Cost (GCC) should be one of our key national economic indicators. We need to reduce this annual cost to the nation. For those who say we can't afford to address our crises, I say we can't afford *not* to. The key is to be willing to put our national interests and our common good ahead of special interests in our decision making.

Although some politicians campaign on a general platform of simply reducing regulations on businesses, we need to understand that some regulations, which are essential for our protection, have been put in place to prevent repeated decisions of folly by big business (i.e., the sort that led to the 2008 Wall Street crisis), or emissions that cause global warming. Eliminating those regulations simply increases the temptation for business to maximize their profits by making more decisions of folly.

Business is driven by one primary goal, which is bottom-line profit. Because of competition, individual businesses cannot resist opportunities to increase profit, even when these decisions may cause enormous harm to the common good. The common good of the country cannot be left to businesses, because executives must compete with other companies and maximize their profit, or be replaced by their Board of Directors. Business executives must do whatever the law allows, because if they don't do it, some other company will. Therefore, laws, or regulations, are needed to avoid repeated business follies and repeated crises that create great harm for the common good. Good executives and good companies understand and support this need for reasonable industry regulations to protect the common good.

Of the 130 follies identified with the 23 U.S. crises, 81% are government follies. The other 19% are business or citizen follies. Therefore, in order to reduce follies that are contributing to our crises and to the decline of hope in the future of America, government is a good place to start.

In Chapters 7 through 12, 172 possible improvements to reduce these crises have been identified; most of these proposed improvements come from non-profits and research studies that have subject matter experts focused on each individual crisis. 74% of improvement recommendations

(128 of 172) are identified as no-cost or low-cost to the U.S. government. These improvement recommendations are not new, so why haven't these no-cost or low-cost improvement recommendations already been made to help reduce these U.S crises? The answer to that goes back to the common cause of the growth of our U.S. crises over the past 20 years, which is the intentional choice of folly for the benefit of a few, over choices of reason for the benefit of many. The decisions to not implement these 128 no-cost or low-cost improvement recommendations could be considered additional decisions of folly being made to benefit a few.

What follows is a brief review of each of the 23 crises we face to assess how we are doing, including giving a letter grade to create a report card on our crises. This brief review is based on the more in-depth analysis of these 23 crises in Chapters 7 through 12. I will include a letter grade assessing performance on each of the 23 national crises covered here. The criteria used in establishing this letter grade for each crisis include the following:

- How U.S. performance compares to the world average

- How U.S. performance compares to established responsible standards

- Direction of change: increasing size is bad, and decreasing size is good

- Having goals and plans for improvement; a lack of goals and plans for improvement is bad

Financial Crises
Included in this category are the very high national debt, the very high and increasing trade deficits, continued Wall Street speculation, increasing corporate debt, and the lack of sufficient infrastructure maintenance.

National Debt Crisis
The U.S. national debt is out of control, at a debt-to-GDP ratio of 108%, with no plan to reduce it to a financially responsible 60% level, which is a

requirement for European Union (EU) countries. The debt-to-GDP ratio is obtained by dividing a country's total debt by its annual Gross Domestic Product (GDP). Germany, the largest EU country, has a 60% debt-to-GDP ratio. China has a debt-to-GDP ratio of 51% (World Population Review, n.d.).

The high U.S. debt weakens our ability to provide the financial resources to address all other crises and their ensuing disasters. Being above the responsible debt limit reduces the ability to borrow when needed, and annual interest payments on that debt reduce annual budget funds available for needed programs. The answer to why improvements can't be made to reduce U.S. crises and disasters is often, "We can't afford it," but unless we find the power to stop the ever-increasing national debt, all our crises will continue to spiral out of control, and our ability to implement needed improvements will decline.

Components of this crisis include:
- The U.S. budget deficit reached a new high of $985 billion in 2019.

- The U.S. budget has increased by 290% from 2000 to 2019. If it had increased at 3% per year, it would have increased by only 75%.

- The U.S. national debt reached a new high of $22 trillion in 2019. That debt is seven times the annual U.S. Federal Government revenue. Imagine if your credit card debt was seven times your annual salary.

- The U.S. debt-to-GDP ratio is 108% in 2019. Of the world's economic powers, the U.S. has the highest debt-to-GDP ratio (World Population Review, n.d.). The debt-to-GDP ratio indicates a country's ability to pay back its debts.

- This debt crisis is already affecting our government's responsibly to fund needed healthcare, infrastructure maintenance, and other programs.

Personal analogy

If your spouse continued to spend 30% more than your family's income, spent all your retirement savings, and built up enormous debts, you would probably consider a divorce in order to implement a sound financial plan for your family. What is even worse than that is this: our elected officials doing the same thing for our entire country, spending 30% more than income and all our savings, which affects us, our children, and our grandchildren in a negative and stressful way.

Grade for the National Debt Crisis   F

Wall Street and Corporate Debt Crisis

The potential inability of corporations and Wall Street to be able to meet debt payments, and potential speculation losses, still looms over the U.S. and could create another 2008-type recession that took a decade and trillions of dollars to recover from. One criterion for responsible debt levels is cash flow-to-debt ratio. In 2017, U.S. corporate cash flow-to-debt ratio was the lowest in 48 years, at only 12%. Another criterion for a responsible debt level is whether those being given loans can pass the financial tests to repay those loans. In 2018, the percentage of corporate loans made, that pass adequate financial tests to ensure a repayment capability, was only 20%; this was down from 75% in 2007.

From 2000 to 2017, the median corporate debt rating has dropped from A to BBB, which is only one step away from a junk rating. A junk rating means a high risk of bankruptcy. At the same time, corporate debt has increased by 35%. There is no U.S. goal or plan in place to improve these poor financial measures to where they should be, to reduce the potential for creating another national economic crisis or recession.

Adding to this crisis, the current administration is pushing for the same deregulation of Wall Street that was the root cause of the 2008 economic crash and the 2008 Great Recession.

Personal analogy

If your spouse decided to lend all your family's savings to distant cousins who were unlikely to repay those loans, that might be a reason to consider a divorce. What is even worse than that is this: the financial and banking system the country relies on, and bails out when necessary, is loaning money to corporations that can't pass reasonable loan standards; this risks the need for another bail out, and the potential for the negative impact and stress of another long recession.

The U.S. lacks a goal and a plan to reduce this crisis.

Grade for Wall Street and Corporate Debt Crisis   D

Trade Balance Crisis

The U.S. trade deficit in 2018, at $621 billion for goods and services, was the highest in the world. Our U.S. trade deficit (i.e., annual exports minus annual imports) has been steadily increasing since 2006 (Duffin 2019). When our exports are less than our imports, our trade deficit contributes to many other crises, including a decline in the standard of living for Americans and an increased U.S. budget deficit.

This trade deficit is an indicator of the increase in world competitiveness. A negative trade balance means that other countries are receiving more money for their products and services than we are receiving for our goods and services. Those other countries, with a positive trade balance, can invest that money in new enterprises to make them even more competitive, and allow them to make infrastructure improvements. Thus, a continued negative trade balance leads to a cycle where the U.S. falls further and further behind other countries in needed investments for the future. The U.S. trade deficit has increased by 67% from 2000 to 2019. By contrast in 2017, China had a trade surplus of $421 billion for goods and services.

A tariff war has been started to address this U.S. trade crisis. Many experts think that a tariff war is the wrong approach to deal with this crisis. In 2018, Midwest (e.g., Illinois, Indiana, and Wisconsin) farm bankruptcies had doubled from what they were in 2008 (the year of the Great Recession). This doubling of farm bankruptcies is a result of the current administration's trade wars; farm bankruptcies were also up significantly across the entire nation. In addition, U.S. farm debt reached $409 billion in 2018 (Pearce 2019). The end result of these trade wars has yet to be determined as of September 2019, when this U.S.-initiated trade war was escalating.

The U.S. lacks a trade balance goal, and a credible plan, to reduce this crisis.

Personal analogy

If your neighborhood had a weekly picnic for which your family brought most of the food, week after week, you might one day decide to stop supplying all that food. What is even worse than that is this: our country expecting the world will continue to supply most of the goods for our consumption, year after year, with us just borrowing more money to pay our part.

Grade for the Trade Balance Crisis   F

Infrastructure Crisis

Infrastructure maintenance is insufficient, resulting in unsafe bridges and roads that cause disasters. Deferred maintenance costs are increasing every year. Inadequate infrastructure has a negative impact on our economy that relies on the country's transportation network.

In 2017, 9% of U.S. bridges needed rehabilitation. While 9% may not sound like many, it is 55,300 bridges that carry 188 million vehicle trips per year. The cost of that backlog in bridge rehabilitation is estimated at $123 billion (American Society of Civil Engineers 2017).

Assessment of several other infrastructure categories has been done by the American Society of Civil Engineers (ASCE), and the total backlog in needed infrastructure funding is $2 trillion. The infrastructure funding backlog gap has increased by 54% from 2000 to 2018; this crisis is getting worse (American Society of Civil Engineers March 2017).

As of July 22, 2019, a two-year budget deal was reached that would raise spending by $320 billion over existing budget caps and allow the government to raise the debt limit to keep borrowing. This budget deal did not include a needed major infrastructure funding plan (Cochrane et al. 2019).

Personal analogy

If you gave your son a house and he did nothing to maintain it, letting it drift into disrepair and causing major damage to the asset, you would probably not simply fix it for him or buy him a new house. What is even worse than that is our elected officials letting our infrastructure drift into disrepair, polluting our water due to lack of sewage treatment facilities, and risking our lives on bridges that have not been maintained.

Grade for Infrastructure Crisis   D

Summary of Financial Crises

National Debt	F
Wall Street and Corporate Debt	D
Trade Balance	F
Infrastructure Maintenance	<u>D</u>

Average Grade for the Financial Crises   F+

Worker Crises

This category includes worker skills that are not keeping up with technology shifts, inadequate worker pay for a reasonable quality of life, growing debt for college graduates, and a social media addiction.

Worker Skills Crisis

U.S. worker reskilling/retraining has not kept up with the need to fill new job categories. Since the future will bring ever increasing technology shifts and increasing world trade competition, our workers must be enabled to keep up with the rapid technology shifts so they can earn a living wage and help us reduce our trade balance. It would have helped if the 6 million looking for work had the skills to fill our 6 million job openings. That would have also helped reduce our trade deficit and our government budget deficit.

The U.S. ranks 96th on the list of country workforce participation rate (i.e., the percentage of the population gainfully employed) at 63%. Our position in the world is worsening: our workforce participation rate declined by 6% points from 69% in 2000 to 63% in 2019. By comparison, China is 44th on the list, with 69% workforce participation; China has 4 times the population of the U.S., which means they have a lot more people working to produce goods than we do.

Increasing the U.S. workforce participation to 69% would provide a 10% increase in our workforce, which would significantly help reduce the trade deficit. America lacks a process for reskilling workers to help those hurt by a combination of swift technology shifts and Wall Street-based recessions, as well as a goal and plan to address this crisis.

Personal analogy

If you trained as a young adult to learn job skills for a career and there were no jobs for that career when you were middle aged, the quality of your life would probably be destroyed when the only job you could find paid half your prior job wages. What is even worse than that is this: our businesses and elected officials are planning new technology shifts that will put millions of people out of work, with no plans or established process to reskill them for the future. People sometimes just need a hand up, not a handout.

Grade for the Worker Skills Crisis   F

Worker's Fair Pay Crisis

Worker pay is insufficient to keep up with increases in health care, housing, and living costs. This creates an increasing number of working poor who need government assistance. The cost of supporting the U.S. working poor can only be reduced by reducing the number of working poor.

In the 1970s, the CEO-to-average worker pay ratio was 50 to 1.
In 1995, the CEO-to-average worker pay ratio was 123 to 1.
In 2017, the CEO-to-average worker pay ratio was 361 to 1.

The U.S. lacks a goal and plan to address this crisis.

Personal analogy

If you worked hard for 40 hours per week and could not afford to meet basic needs for yourself, and you could not afford to have a family, that would be a pretty sad life. What is even worse than that is that our business and elected leaders are getting richer while implementing practices and policies that increase the number of working poor.

Grade for Worker's Fair Pay Crisis   F

College Education Debt Crisis

College student debt is so high, it often requires a lifetime to pay it off. This results in an increasing burden to graduates and an increasing default rate on student loans. This increased debt of college graduates is an additional burden to the other crises young people will have to face, by limiting the savings and investment capability of the next generation to support their families and to prepare for their retirement.

In 2018, 69% of college students graduated with debt averaging $29,800. Student debt has risen by 62% in the last 10 years. The U.S. is the second most expensive country in the world in which to attend college (Student Loan Hero 2019).

Student loan debt is a burden that our next generation cannot afford, while they are also facing the expectation of increasing world competition, decreasing retirement employment benefits, and an increasing U.S. debt that will have to be paid by them. There are several ways that students can minimize the college debt they take on, and they need to be advised on these options before taking on more debt than they can afford.

If you were saddled with an enormous debt to pay, after obtaining a college education needed for your career, that might crush your dreams by keeping you from being able to buy a home. What is even worse than that is this: college costs are increasing so much that the number of students with enormous debt to pay off has doubled and is crushing the American dream.

The U.S. lacks a goal and plan to address this crisis.

Grade for the College Education Debt Crisis   F

Social Media Crisis
U.S. time spent on study and work has declined, as time spent watching TV and time on social media has increased. To stay competitive with the world, Americans will need to spend more time reskilling and working, and less time watching TV and on social media. In 2016, U.S. adults averaged 7 hours per day and teenagers averaged 11 hours per day on TV/Cable/Streaming and social media. In the last decade (2008 to 2018), TV and social media screen time has increased by about 38%.

Personal analogy

If you did not succeed in completing the education you needed for your career because of time spent on video games and social media, that would negatively affect the quality of your entire life. What is even worse is that the youth in our country are addicted to video games and social media which is negatively affecting their education and quality of life, as well as the future of America.

The U.S. lacks a goal and plan to reduce this crisis.

Grade for the Social Media Crisis   F

Summary of grades for Worker Crises:

Worker Skills Crisis   F
Worker's Fair Pay Crisis   F
College Education Debt Crisis   F
Social Media Crisis   F

Average grade for Worker Crises   F

Health Care Crises

The Health Care Crises category includes the growing drug epidemic fueled by Big Pharma, increasing obesity and diabetes fueled by manufactured food and junk food, a 38% lifetime chance of developing cancer fueled by carcinogens (cancer causing agents) in our air, water and food, acceptance of increasing gun violence and mass murders as normal, and soaring health care costs resulting from the declining health of U.S. citizens and the high prices for prescription drugs.

Use of Drugs Crisis

The drug epidemic in the U.S. has caused death and disruption of families. It has also added substantially to the Health Care Costs Crisis. For the families of drug addicts, chronic stress affects the lives of the children and non-addicted adults, which impairs their health and their ability to have a normal life. This epidemic is costly, with long-term consequences for the generation of children that grows up with a drug-addicted parent.

In 2000, the number of U.S. drug overdose deaths was 17,000. In 2017, there were 70,237 U.S. drug overdose deaths, which is a 320% increase in 17 years. The drug overdose deaths in 2017 were more numerous than the total U.S. troop lives lost in the 10-year Vietnam War. In 2017, 68% of drug overdose deaths came from opioid overdoses.

Personal analogy

If you, your spouse, or your child were given pain medication by a doctor which led to a drug addiction and destroyed your life and your family's life, that would be devastating. What is even worse than that is this: our government has authorized addictive pain medications, and our medical community is prescribing them to millions of Americans, creating a lethal epidemic that is killing thousands annually and destroying thousands of families' lives.

The U.S. lacks a goal and plan to reduce this growing drug crisis.

Grade for the Use of Drugs Crisis   F

Diabetes Crisis

Diabetes and obesity rates have been increasing dramatically, destroying the quality of life for millions of people, while driving up Health Care costs. The nation has to get healthier in order to have lower health care costs. Both food industry changes and individual changes are required to resolve this crisis. The U.S. incidence of diabetes increased from 4.4% in 2000 to 9.4% in 2015. Thirty million people had diabetes in 2015 (Centers for Disease Control and Prevention 2017).

The prevalence of diabetes is estimated to increase 54% to more than 54.9 million Americans between 2015 and 2030; annual deaths attributed to diabetes will climb by 38% to 385,000 per year. Total annual medical costs related to diabetes will increase by 53% to more than $622 billion per year by 2030 (Rowley et al. 2017).

Obesity is a significant factor in the cause of diabetes, and in 2016 the U.S. obesity rate was 40% for adults. Among high school students, the obesity rate increased from 10% to 15% between 2000 and 2017.

In 1900, the average consumption of sugar was close to zero; however, that has increased to about 150 lbs. a year per individual, which adds about 500 calories per day. The increase in obesity correlates with this increase in sugar (Gunnars 2017). People in the U.S consumed 2.5 times more sugar than what The World Health Organization (WHO) recommends (Food Pyramid 2015).

Personal analogy

If you or a family member gained a significant amount of weight from eating processed foods that were widely advertised as "good tasting," and those ads contained no warnings about the weight gain to be expected from eating these foods because of the added sugar and other fattening items, you might be upset when you later found out how easy it is to gain weight and how hard it is to lose it. What is worse than that is this: the food industry has created a 40% obesity rate in America, and it is continuing on the track toward 50%, or more. The impact of obesity on quality of life is a disaster for Americans, and the resultant health care costs are overwhelming.

The U.S. lacks a goal and plan to reduce the growth in this crisis.

Grade for the Diabetes Crisis   F

Cancer Rate Crisis

Today cancer affects most U.S. families. While the medical community is focused primarily on treatment, increased efforts are needed on prevention. A focus on prevention would require reducing known causes of cancer, carcinogens allowed in our air, water and food, lifestyle changes like stopping smoking and avoiding sunburns, and the use of new vaccines for cancer like the Human Papillomavirus (HPV) vaccine. Prevention will require increased efforts from the health care industry, the food industry, the Environmental Protection Agency (EPA), and from individuals in their choices.

From 1999 to 2017, the annual new cancer incidence rate increased by 34%. In 2018, there were 609,000 cancer deaths in the U.S. That is nine times the number of drug overdose deaths in 2017. If the drug crisis is an official CDC epidemic, we need a new name for this cancer crisis.

Over one third of Americans (38%) are expected to contract cancer in their lifetime, which means almost all families will be affected. This may be due, at least in part, to the more than 40 types of carcinogens allowed in our food and environment. Eighty million people in the U.S. have the cancer-causing HPV virus. Even though there is a vaccine for it as of 2017, only 50% of adolescents were up to date on the HPV vaccine (Centers for Disease Control and Prevention, n.d.).

Personal analogy

Using a personal analogy, if you, your spouse, or child were diagnosed with cancer as a result of being exposed to the over 40 chemicals allowed in our foods and environment, that would be a disaster. What is even worse is this: our elected officials are actively rolling back the regulations that limit carcinogens in our food and environment, which will sadly facilitate an increase in the already horrible 38% cancer rate in America.

The U.S. lacks a goal and plan to reduce this crisis.

Grade for the Cancer Rate Crisis   F

Gun Violence Crisis

Gun violence and public mass shootings cause loss of life and create elevated fear and health-damaging chronic stress levels in America. Gun violence is also responsible for causing disruption of the families of both the victims and the criminals. While police are doing their best to enforce laws being violated, we also must focus on preventing and reducing gun violence in America. The root causes of gun violence can be found in the lack of responsible gun management, the difficulty providing help to those in need of mental health care, and the increasing number of hate groups inciting mass shootings.

From 2000 to 2017, U.S. gun deaths increased 33%. For every 100,000 people in the U.S. in 2017, 12 per year died of gun violence. The world average is 3.4 per 100,000 persons, about one third of the U.S. rate.

The epidemic of public mass shootings in America has resulted in both children and adults living in fear. The 2nd Amendment can be protected while still enabling responsible use of guns. However, the U.S. has chosen an irresponsible approach to the use of guns that supports the right of anyone over 18 to own a military assault weapon. This facilitates continued mass murders and very high gun violence rates. A fundamental right in the Constitution is being violated: the right to life. Several non-profit organizations have studied this issue and developed recommendations for significant improvement, without violating the 2nd Amendment.

Areas of urban poverty, easy access to illegal drugs, and the easy availability of guns is unfortunately a perfect trifecta for the formation of gangs and gun disasters in many communities. This is an example of how our multiple crises feed the growth of all our crises.

The U.S. lacks a goal and plan to reduce this crisis.

Personal analogy

If your children were killed while in school by a young man with a military style assault weapon, that would be horrendous. What is even worse than that is this: our elected officials are facilitating more young men with mental health illness, and young men who are part of hate groups, having access to assault weapons, enabling a continuation of mass murders of our children while attending school.

Grade for the Gun Violence Crisis   F

Health Care Costs Crisis

Health Care Costs are exorbitant in part due to the above four health crises, but also due to high prescription drug prices and the overprescribing of drugs by physicians. In addition, medical procedures are more costly here than in other countries around the world. The U.S. Health Care industry needs to adopt best practices from benchmarks around the world that have better health care results at lower costs, and allow access to lower prescription drug prices from credible worldwide sources.

In 2016, the U.S. spent 18% of its Gross Domestic Product (GDP) on health care; by contrast, other high-income nations spent an average of

---

Personal analogy

Using a personal analogy, if you and your family members were charged ten times more than your neighbors for needed prescription medicines, that would be a rip-off. What is worse than that is this: our elected officials are not allowing Medicare and Medicaid to allow prescription medications from Canada that are 90% less expensive than the prices charged by U.S. Big Pharma; this increases the profits of Big Pharma.

11% of their GDP on health care. Based on this GDP comparison, the U.S. spends 64% more on health care costs than other high-income nations, and when compared to other high-income nations, health care is less available to U.S. citizens. From 2000 to 2017, U.S. health care costs increased by 425%. Grade for the Health Care Costs Crisis F

Summary of grades for Health Care Crises:

Use of Drugs	F
Diabetes	F
Cancer Rate	F
Gun Violence	F
Health Care Costs	F

Average grade for the Health Care Crises: F

Environment Crises:

This category includes the continued destruction and degradation of U.S. land, air and water, pollution and overuse of U.S. ocean resources, as well as climate change driven by the use of fossil fuels.

Land, Air, and Fresh Water Crisis

Land, air, and fresh water damage creates health and safety risks for all citizens who should be able to live on unpolluted land, breathe unpolluted air, and drink unpolluted water. Some U.S. states have already begun court battles to fight over our limited clean water supply. Lack of sufficient environmental protections results in very high costs for government clean-up efforts later. Florida alone has $625 million in their 2019 budget to address the algae bloom and red tide problems that have affected both the west coast Gulf and east coast Atlantic shore lines. These algae blooms and red tides are the direct result of pollution from sewage and agriculture fertilizer runoff. For both of these, prevention is less costly than cleanup. If you have a hole in your roof, you fix the hole; you don't spend years just cleaning up the mess after every storm. In this case, there are organic compost options that can be used and adequate buffers should be provided to prevent us from fertilizing our rivers with agricultural runoff.

The good indicator of a healthy environment is infant mortality rates. The U.S. infant mortality rate in 2014 was 5.8 deaths per 1,000. This rate is over 70% higher than the comparable average from other countries (Gonzales and Sawyer 2017). There were 23,161 U.S. cases of infant mortality in 2017 (Murphy et al. 2018).

The healthiest nations (including Japan and Finland) have an infant mortality rate of 2 or fewer deaths per 1,000. The U.S. is about three times worse than these best countries for infant mortality rates.

The U.S. has made significant progress over the past 50 years in improving the environment, thanks to policies like the Clean Water Act, the Clean Air Act, and other environmental protections. However, the current administration is rolling back environmental protections to increase short-term business profits, which is a path of folly decision.
The U.S. lacks a goal and plan to reduce this crisis.

Grade for the Land, Air, and Fresh Water Crisis   C

Personal analogy

If you and your neighbors became deathly sick from polluted water or land in your area, that would be dreadful. What is worse than that is this: elected officials are not adequately funding cleanup of polluted sites and adequate infrastructure to avoid polluting thousands of locations in America. 16% of American families live within 3 miles of a superfund toxic site (Environmental Protection Agency 2017).

Oceans Crisis

Ocean pollution and overfishing damage a healthy fish supply for current and future generations. Ocean resources are overfished; that is, the fish populations are being continually reduced, not maintained for future years. New fishing technology enables giant factory fishing ships to overfish the ocean resources and pay nothing for the resources they take. No generation should destroy or over-utilize limited environmental resources that will be required for the lives of future generations. Fishing can be done in a sustainable way, and it needs to be done that way in order to have fish for future generations.

In the U.S., the Magnuson-Stevens Act supporting fisheries management improvement has been helpful; however, there is a lack of similar fisheries management in the rest of the world. As a result, China is now using military force to take over fishing areas in Asia. Military force does not produce more fish; however, known sustainable practices can multiply the fish supply. It doesn't take a miracle to multiply fish; we know how to do it with sustainable practices.

Ocean pollution kills and wastes valuable fish and other marine resources. Untreated sewage is regularly dumped into the oceans by older cities with antiquated combined sewer and storm drain pipe systems. This reflects a lack of needed infrastructure improvements. We have a U.S. Clean Water Act that should be preventing this continued pollution; however, lack of funding for sewage system improvements has led to lack of enforcement of the Clean Water Act. In addition to sewage overflows and agriculture fertilizer runoff, we also have pollution in our storm water runoff from many other sources. Storm water runoff includes residential and commercial property fertilizer, pharmaceuticals, and chemicals. The sources of the pollution must be eliminated or reduced to reduce water pollution.

There is a growing dead zone in the Gulf of Mexico at the foot of the Mississippi River from agricultural fertilizer runoff. No fish can live in this dead zone. Billions of tons of plastics are flowing annually into oceans worldwide. The U.S. had protected a sizable portion of our oceans, but the current administration has proposed to roll back those protections.

Grade for the Oceans Crisis   D

Personal analogy

If you and your family owned property on a shoreline on our oceans, gulf, or Great Lakes, and that water was so polluted that it killed fish and was not swimmable, that would be tragic. What is even worse than that is this: our elected officials are continuing to allow shore water pollution, and they are promoting actions that lead to an increased risk of shore pollution.

Climate Change Crisis

Climate change, like several of the other crises on the list, negatively contributes to many other crises. Increased intensity of hurricanes and forest fires caused by climate change increases disaster recovery costs, and thus the national debt. It also increases infrastructure costs needed to create resilient coastlines. Denial of this crisis leads to increases in the size of other crises.

The U.S. is spending more than $250 billion per year for disaster recovery, and with further increases in global warming, that amount is projected to more than double. Our carbon emissions are 15% of the world's carbon emissions, even though our population is only 5% of the world's population; clearly the U.S. is contributing more than our fair share of carbon emissions. Therefore, we should be doing more to reduce our emissions.

In 2018, after our current administration withdrew from the Global Climate Agreement, the U.S. then had a 3% increase in carbon emissions.

Personal analogy

If the area you live in was flooded or burned as a result of climate warming, that would be tragic. What is even worse than that is this: in order to help the fossil fuel industry increase short-term profits, elected officials are taking actions that will **increase** climate warming, jeopardizing the lives of all citizens.

Grade for the Climate Change Crisis   F

Summary of the grades for the Environment Crises:

Land, Air and Fresh Water   C
Oceans   D
Climate Change   F

Average grade for the Environment Crises   D

Security Crises

This category includes insufficient nuclear arms control and nuclear waste management, uncontrolled cybersecurity threats, border security issues, and uncontrolled enormous military defense costs.

Nuclear Arms and Waste Crisis

A lack of success in the area of nuclear arms and waste will have devastating effects and result in disaster. Unfortunately, the good progress made over many decades has been set back recently with the current administration breaking nuclear arms control treaty agreements and the lack of a continued reduction in nuclear arms warheads, as had been agreed to by treaty.

The world had a strategy, under the Treaty on Non-Proliferation of Nuclear Weapons (NPT), with U.N. verifications, to work together to reduce and prevent the spread of nuclear weapons. That strategy is being trashed by the U.S. for a go-it-alone country-by-country confrontational approach, using our economic and military power to bully countries to drop their nuclear plans. However, history has shown us that a worldwide NPT alliance, with U.N. verifications, is a better strategy than U.S. one-on-one confrontations. Our one-on-one confrontations over nuclear weapons proliferation include the following countries: Iraq, Iran, North Korea, and Russia.

The U.S. lacks a goal and plan to reduce this crisis.

Personal analogy

If you and your family were exposed to radiation that caused cancer, that would be a tragedy. What is even worse than that is this: our elected officials are not storing nuclear waste in the safest possible manner. The tax money that was to be used for safe storage of nuclear waste was spent on other things; therefore, there is no plan for storing our nuclear waste as safely as possible.

Grade for Nuclear Arms and Waste Crisis   D

Note: Because of the very high risks, deficits in the ability to control nuclear arms and manage nuclear waste safely will always be a critical crisis if its letter grade is lower than an A.

Cybersecurity Crisis

Cybersecurity weakness should be high on the list of U.S. crises because America has become reliant on the internet and information technology, and our information technology is not secure; it is more like an open door. The entire U.S. economy and governance system is reliant on insecure information system networks. Beyond personal economic losses and identity theft, America lost trust in our election process in 2016 when Russians hacked campaign emails and used social media to create increased divisiveness in America in order to help their favored candidate get elected. More recently we have been informed that Russia also hacked into Florida's voting systems. The credibility of U.S. democratic elections was compromised by Russian cyber intrusions. Recently in 2018 and 2019, we have had major U.S. cities' IT systems hacked and held for ransom. The economic losses at risk in this area affect everything we do.

Cybersecurity, which is managed by the Department of Homeland Security, not the Department of Defense, is perhaps the biggest weakness in the U.S. defense system. Homeland Security is focused on handling immigration and building a wall on our southern border; in addition, Homeland Security does not have the resources of the Department of Defense.

The number of cyber incidents increased tenfold from 2006 to 2015. In 2015, just one intrusion resulted in the compromise of the records of 4 million government employees and affected 22 million people. This is by far the weakest aspect of our U.S. security, and it is getting worse faster than any other crisis area.

Grade for Cybersecurity Crisis   F

Personal analogy

If your bank was hacked and your financial account information was destroyed, or transferred to others, that would be traumatic. What is worse than that is this: having our cities' IT systems shut down for ransom, and having our leaders elected with the help of foreign adversaries. Our cybersecurity is our greatest security weakness, and it is being inadequately addressed.

Border Security Crisis

Security on the U.S. southern border has preoccupied the Department of Homeland Security (DHS) and Washington, which resulted in a Congressional bill to improve the southern border's security in February 2019. This congressional action and funding should help resolve the southern border security crisis.

Border Security Immigration

As part of the DHS, Southern Border Immigration measures the Total Interdiction Rate (TIR), which is the percentage of illegal border crossings that are stopped; it improved from about 50% in 2006, to about 75% in 2016 (Department of Homeland Security 2017, 4). This is a significant improvement.

In addition, arrests for illegal immigration on the Southern Border from 2000 to 2016 were reduced by more than 75%. This is the key indicator of success used by DHS. The Recidivism Rate, the percentage of illegal immigrants who, after being deported, tried for a second time to enter this country, dropped from 31% in 2005 to 12% in 2016. This is another significant improvement. On all three of the above measures, the DHS made significant improvements to the immigration crisis on the southern border between 2000 and 2016.

However, in 2019, the immigration problems on the southern border got a lot worse. There was an increase in immigration arrests as a result of increased asylum seekers and reduced legal immigration limits for asylum seekers. In addition, there was cruel separation of children and parents, and over-crowded caging of asylum seekers in cells for extended periods with inadequate provisions for health care. Policy changes by the current administration contributed to all these southern border immigration crisis problems in 2019, and an increase in this crisis that had previously been improving for years.

Personal analogy

If you had a family member who lived in another country, and that country was being controlled by gang violence, and that family member was not allowed to seek asylum in the U.S., that could be devastating. What is even worse than that is this: our elected officials are reducing the number of people being allowed asylum in the U.S, from about 100,000 per year to about 18,000 per year, while simultaneously deporting criminals and gang leaders, caught at our southern border, back to their country of origin, enabling them to continue the violence that is causing the increase in asylum seekers. In addition, our elected leaders are supporting more weapon sales to gangs in these countries in order to help gun manufacturers increase their profits, by dropping out of a UN treaty to reduce sales of guns to countries with high gang gun violence.

Southern Border Drug Smuggling

U.S. border security has reported that about 85% of drug smuggling goes through Ports of Entry (POE), and about 15% through open areas. Thus, the need for improved POE drug detection capability is much greater than the need for more walls in open areas. The 2019 congressional border security act passed by Congress addressed this need to improve POE security.

Grade for the Border Security Crisis

Border Security with respect to Immigration	C
Border Security with respect to Drug Smuggling	D
Average grade for Border Security Crisis	D+

Defense Costs Crisis

High defense costs are a crisis contributing to America's debt. Defense costs are currently higher than they have ever been, and they are increasing without control. In 2017, the U.S. defense budget was $610 billion, 260% higher than the next country, which was China at $228 billion. The U.S. is spending about 3.5% of its GDP on defense, while China is spending less than half that, or only about 1.5% of its GDP, on defense.

In March 2019, the current administration requested $750 billion for defense in the 2020 budget, a 23% increase over the 2017 budget. Our federal debt is a defense weakness and an enormous threat to our long-term ability to secure our country. In fact, overspending on military caused the Soviet Union's collapse. The U.S. is already unable to implement its government responsibilities due in part to our debt. A long-term strategy is needed to improve U.S. defense at a lower cost, while also improving our cybersecurity.

From 2000 to 2020, defense costs have increased by 138%. The U.S. lacks a goal and plan to reduce this crisis.

Personal analogy

If you had to spend 20% of your monthly income on a home-alarm security system and as a result could not afford to help your children pay their college tuition, that would be frustrating. What is even worse than that is this: elected officials are spending almost 20% of our federal income on our defense, while our inadequate cybersecurity system is like an open door to our adversaries, and we can't afford needed infrastructure maintenance.

Grade for the Defense Costs crisis: F

Summary of grades for Security Crises
Nuclear Arms and Waste   D
Cybersecurity   F
Border Security   D+
Defense Costs   F

Average Grade for the Security Crises   F+

Democracy Crises

The Democracy crises include the Election Campaign Crisis, the Government Crisis, and the Political Party Crisis.

Election Campaign Crisis

Unlimited funding in election campaigns is allowing special interests to determine who is elected in America, and that is facilitating decisions of folly for the interests of a few over the many. In recent elections, in 90% of U.S. Senate races and 80% of the U.S. House races, the candidate with the most money has won. This campaign funding crisis has gotten substantially worse since the 2010 Supreme Court decision allowing Super PACs.

Personal analogy

If you are facing multiple crises in your life and believe the future will only get worse, that could result in loss of hope and depression. What is even worse than that is this: elected officials are facilitating follies for the benefit of special interests who donate to their campaigns, instead of working for the common good.

Grade for Election Campaign Crisis   F

Government Crisis

Americans have lost hope in our future, the American Dream, because the cumulative effect of our crises is so burdensome to our day-to-day lives, and because these crises are not being effectively addressed by our elected leaders:

- For each crisis, we have an average of 5 follies, 4 of which are made by government

- The system in Washington has been fixed, or rigged, to facilitate more follies

- Simple no-cost and low-cost improvements to reduce our crises are not being implemented

- The national debt is twice the financially responsible level, with no plans to reduce it

- Washington has put special interests first and America's interests a distant second. We lack goals and plans to reduce our multiple and growing crises.

This high number of decisions of folly that have contributed to our crises is not an accident; there have been 27 changes in the governance processes in Washington that have helped facilitate this long list of follies.

Personal analogy

If you served your country in the military in time of combat, risking your life and seeing comrades in arms lose their lives to defend the American Dream, then when you finish that military service and find out there is no career for you, that could cause depression and even suicide. What is even worse than that is this: elected officials are squandering the American Dream for the future of all Americans, for campaign donations and the support of special interests.

Grade for Government Crisis   F

Political Party Crisis

Our political parties have become so divisive, they cannot work together to solve our crises. The increase in divisiveness is a result of the political parties shifting to the far right and far left, making it more difficult to find common ground.

Political parties are responsible for the majority of the government follies that have contributed to the creation of, and fueling the growth of, our crises. They have put party before country, contributing to our many crises and the loss of hope for the future of America.

Political parties have been applying their same predetermined political party policies to every problem and crisis, without success. Political parties have simply lied and made up their own facts to support their predetermined political positions on a crisis, or simply denied that a crisis exists when it does not fit with their agenda. The political parties have not come together to use a critical thinking approach to agree on the facts, and develop efficient and effective solutions to the root causes of our crises, apparently because that might conflict with their predetermined political platforms.

Political parties are contributing to the growth of all our crises, rather than reducing them. Both political parties need to change for our crises to be reduced and for hope to be restored in our democracy.

If you belong to a political party, have worked for campaigns, have donated to candidates, have voted for your party's candidates and then found out our political parties are a major cause of America's problems, that can be frustrating. What is even worse than that is this: the political parties we support are responsible for the follies that have caused the crises we face and the loss of the American Dream.

Grade for Political Party Crisis	F

Summary of Grades for Democracy Crises

Election Campaign	F
Government	F
Political Party	F
Average Grade for Democracy Crises	F

Summary of Grades for all 23 Crises

Financial	F
Worker	F
Health Care	F
Environment	D
Security	F+
Democracy	F
Average Grade for all Crises	F

This assessment shows that the U.S. is failing to adequately address the crises America is facing and is therefore failing to address the decline of hope in America's future.

We have failing grades (F) on 17 of 23 (74%) of our national crises, and an overall grade of F. If our children brought home this report card, we would call for immediate change. We probably would not throw out the child; instead, we would look for what changes need to be made to help the child. These grades should justify a national call for significant change in Washington; this book provides the changes necessary to help our elected leaders improve their failing grades. Of course, they need to be willing to change.

The change I am calling for is to apply a common business improvement approach that has been successfully used in leading companies, and in fact is encouraged by the U.S. National Quality Award. I am simply encouraging our government to use an approach that is being encouraged, by our government, for U.S. organizations to use to achieve excellent performance.

These 23 crises have developed over the past 20 years under three different presidential administrations: George W. Bush, 2001 - 2009; Barack Obama, 2009 - 2017; and Donald Trump, 2017 - present. We have a systemic problem in Washington that contributes to many decisions of folly, which is the primary cause of the failing grades on our crises. However, our leader's and appointed administration heads' policies can have significant impact on these crises. The table shown below, "Administration Policy Impact on Crises," provides an assessment of the impact of the three different presidential administrations' policies on each of these 23 crises.

Table 3: Administration Policy Impact on Crises

Impact: Crisis Increase (NEG), No impact (-), or Crisis Decrease (POS) Negative

Crises	Impact of Presidential Administrations		
	2001-2009	2009-2017	2017 – Present
Chp. 7 – Financial			
National Debt	NEG	NEG	NEG
Wall Street & Corp. Debt	NEG	**POS**	NEG
Trade Balance	NEG	NEG	NEG
Infrastructure Maint.	NEG	**POS**	-
Chp. 8 – Worker			
Worker Skills	-	-	-
Worker's Fair Pay	-	-	-
College Education Debt	-	-	-
Social Media	-	-	-
Chp. 9 – Health Care			
Use of Drugs	-	-	-
Diabetes	-	-	-
Cancer Rate	NEG	**POS**	NEG
Gun Violence	-	-	-
Chp. 10 – Environment			
Land Air and Fresh Water	NEG	**POS**	NEG
Oceans	NEG	**POS**	NEG
Climate Change	NEG	**POS**	NEG
Chp. 11- Security			
Nuclear Arms and Waste	NEG	**POS**	NEG
Cybersecurity	-	-	NEG
Border Security	**POS**	**POS**	NEG
Defense Costs	NEG	NEG	NEG
Chp. 12- Democracy			
Election Campaign	-	-	NEG
Government	-	-	NEG
Political Party	-	-	NEG
Crises Reduction Impact	**1**	**8**	**0**

The assessment in the Administration Policy Impact table indicates that over the past 20 years, we have only been able to reduce these crises in 9 of the 69 opportunities, or 13% of the time. We have had a negative impact 29 of 69 times, which is 42% of the time. That leaves 31 of 69 opportunities (45%) where the administration policies have not had an impact. The table does show that changing administrations can help, or hurt, our crisis situation. However, changing administrations alone is insufficient to reduce all our crises; we need systemic change to drain the swamp, resolve our crises, and restore hope in the future of America.

The thrust of this book is a proposal for the systemic change needed in Washington to make a continued significant reduction in all our crises all the time, and to restore hope in the future of America.

The 2001 to 2009 administration was focused on responding to the 9/11/01 terrorist attack and the bailout of Wall Street after the 2008 economic crash. Unfortunately, part of that response to 9/11 was a mistaken invasion of Iraq.

The 2009 to 2017 administration was focused on reducing five major crises we had during that time frame:

- The ISIS terrorism that evolved from the war on Iraq

- The 2008 economic crash that came from Wall Street deregulation

- The Great Recession and job losses that came from the 2008 economic crash

- The dramatic drops in the GDP and stock market from the 2008 crisis

- The need to expand affordable coverage of healthcare insurance

The current administration has been focused since 2017 on five major changes, primarily to help businesses' profitability:

- Major cuts in corporate taxes

- Rolling back environmental protections

- Deregulating Wall St., again

- Supporting the NRA and gun sales

- Nominating Supreme Court Justices who are supportive of businesses

While different administrations will perhaps focus on a half dozen priorities critical to them during their term in office, we need a systemic change in Washington to continually work on reducing all our crises during all administrations. We can do that with elected officials who are willing to make the changes needed.

Reducing Crises:

To reduce our crises, this book proposes our government use a quality approach that is used by the best businesses. It involves the following:

- Setting bipartisan goals to reduce each crisis

- Determining root causes of each crisis

- Learning from the best practices of others to reduce each crisis

- Implementing the most efficient and effective improvements.

This proposal is also consistent with the U.S. National Quality Award, which was established to encourage excellent performance in all U.S. organizations. Why not have the U.S. government use the quality approach they are encouraging all other organizations in the U.S. to use to achieve performance excellence?

The first half of this book explains the quality approach and how it can be used in government. Chapter 4 – Unfixing Washington provides a specific proposal for how to incorporate this approach in the U.S. government to reduce our crises. The second half of this book analyzes

23 U.S. crises using this quality approach, and provides examples of how this approach can be applied to reduce each of our crises. These example analyses propose improvement goals for each crisis and identify potential improvement recommendations to reach those goals.

The following table, "Decisions of Folly, Improvements, and Budget Reductions by Crisis" provides a summary of the number of decisions of folly that have contributed to the creation and growth of the 23 U.S. crises. Shockingly, there is an average of almost 5 decisions of folly per crisis, and these follies are root causes of the multiple growing crises the U.S. is now facing. The last half of the book identifies the follies associated with each of the 23 crises, and Appendix A includes a complete listing of the government follies.

Included in the following table is the number of possible improvements to reduce these crises, and an estimate of the 2024 federal budget savings that could be obtained by reducing these crises. The 2024 budget savings calculations are included with the analysis of each crisis in Chapters 7 through 12. This 2024 budget cost reduction, by reducing our crises, along with 2% annual revenue growth, would be sufficient to balance the federal budget in 2024.

Table 4: Decisions of Folly, Improvements, and Budget Reductions by Crisis

	Decisions of Folly Gov./Total	Improvement Recommendations Low-cost/Total	Budget Red. in 2024 ($ Billions)
Chp. 7 – Financial Crises			
National Debt	9/9	8/9	(40)
Wall Street and Corp. Debt	8/9	6/6	0
Trade Balance	3/5	7/8	0
Infrastructure Maintenance	3/3	2/3	0
	23/26	23/26	(40)
Chp. 8 – Worker Crises			
Worker Skills	4/4	4/7	50
Worker Fair Pay	1/4	6/6	120
College Education Debt	1/3	6/9	14
Social Media	2/5	3/3	50
	8/16	19/25	234
Chp. 9 – Health Care Crises			
Use of Drugs	1/4	4/11	0
Diabetes	2/4	4/7	7
Cancer Rate	2/4	5/6	10
Gun Violence	6/6	4/5	15
Health Care Costs	4/4	11/13	120
	15/22	28/42	152
Chp. 10 – Environment Crises			
Land Air and Fresh Water	7/8	12/12	0
Oceans	7/7	3/6	0
Climate Warming	3/3	4/6	0
	17/18	19/24	0
Chp. 11 – Security Crises			
Nuclear Arms and Waste	6/6	3/6	20
Cybersecurity	4/4	2/9	(15)
Border Security	3/6	5/9	10
Defense Cost	7/7	3/5	170
	20/23	13/29	185
Chp. 12- Democracy Crisis			
Election Campaign	5/5	8/8	100
Government	11/13	12/12	N/A
Political Party	6/7	6/6	N/A
	22/25	26/26	100
Total for 23 Crises	105/130	128/172	631
2%/year Revenue Increase	0	0	353
5-yr budget deficit reduction	0	0	984

Summary:

This chapter provided an historical overview of the crises that caused the collapse of past civilizations. We can learn from those crises that caused the collapse of past civilizations, since they are eerily similar to the current unresolved and growing U.S. crises.

A number of changes over time have contributed to the U.S. crises and are related to the aging of America and the increasing competitiveness of the rest of the world. In addition, a high number of follies, decisions to benefit special interests, are fueling our crises.

An overview of how we are doing on addressing the 23 U.S. crises was provided; the assessment is we have a failing grade. We also have a lack of goals and plans to reduce our crises that have collectively caused a loss of hope in the future of America.

Finally, a proposal was made for using a quality approach in our government to reduce the number of decisions of folly that have created our crises, implementing a number of no-cost and low-cost improvements to reduce all our U.S. crisis, and reducing the enormous annual Gross Crisis Cost (GCC) which can help to balance the federal budget. The U.S. government encourages organizations throughout the U.S. to use this approach in the National Quality Award criteria.

Chapter 3 - BARRIERS, FOLLIES and VALUES

A number of barriers to using a quality approach in government need to be removed in order to make the changes required to fix Washington. This chapter offers a proposal for how to reduce or eliminate each barrier to improvement. These barriers are very similar to the reasons most people would give for why Washington can't be fixed. Washington can be fixed, but it will require removing these barriers. America's future depends on fixing Washington in order to reduce the follies that are creating and fueling our crises.

This chapter will review the types of repeated follies that have created our crises, as well as the systemic process changes that have been made in Washington which are the cause of increased decisions of folly.

Finally, this chapter will propose that Congress agree on, and deploy, agreed-to values that support the common good over special interests, to be followed by employees in all parts of the U.S. government, including our elected leaders.

We need to push for these changes. The generation who fought in World War II and led the industrial boom has been characterized as America's "Greatest Generation." Their children's generation (of which I am a part) could be one day characterized as America's "Worst Generation" if the U.S. government system changes that have enabled increased decisions of folly, increased U.S. crises, and loss of hope for the future of America are not corrected.

Removing Barriers

Before tackling our multiple crises, leadership must be willing to remove the barriers to implementation of effective and efficient improvements needed to reduce our crises. Why figure out what to do if no one will implement decisions of reason? In fact, a significant number of reasonable no-cost and low-cost improvements to reduce our crises have already been proposed, but not implemented due to these barriers.

Barriers are easy to identify; everyone is an expert on why something can't be done. Those "why it can't be done" reasons are the barriers. A straightforward way to identify the barriers is to hold a brainstorming session and let each person share their view about why the improvement goal to reduce the crises *cannot* be accomplished. Capture all these barriers on an easel sheet so they can be addressed.

After identifying all the barriers, rank them in order of significance. The next step is to develop plans to address or reduce those barriers. Starting with the most significant barriers, brainstorm with the same individuals to determine what they believe needs to be done to reduce or eliminate the barriers. The people facing these barriers usually know what is needed to eliminate them; however, they usually do not have the authority to do so; that is where they need leadership help. Improvement cannot occur until the barriers to improvement are eliminated; it is the job of leadership to remove barriers to improvement.

After those barriers have been identified, plans can be implemented to reduce or eliminate them. Communication between leadership and management teams on efforts to eliminate barriers is needed to encourage the improvement efforts. Every improvement to reduce a crisis, of the hundreds that will be needed, should not have to overcome the same dozen barriers to improvement. The U.S. needs continuous improvement on 23 crises; those improvement efforts cannot be stifled by a dozen barriers to improvement.

Partisan politics may be the biggest barrier to improvement. Understanding the threat to America of continuing business as usual, while also agreeing to common goals for reduction of our crises, is the best way to eliminate partisan political barriers. In large part because of partisan politics, we lack goals and plans to reduce our crises. Chapters 7 through 12 propose specific goals to reduce each of 23 U.S. crises. Bipartisan agreement on these goals, and ones like them, will substantially reduce partisan politics.

Government organizations are significantly different than business organizations, and those differences can create a number of additional unique barriers to using a quality approach to improve successfully. The following identifies nine barriers to improvement in government and what can be done to eliminate each:

1. Too much money in campaigns

Politicians today need large and frequent funding from lobbyists who want their special short-term interests supported in exchange for this campaign funding support. A 2010 Supreme Court decision allowed businesses to use unlimited funding from unidentified sources to fund political attack ads through Super Political Action Committees (Super PACs). This Supreme Court decision facilitates what Tuchman refers to as "the impotence of reason in the face of greed" and undermines democracy in America.

The Supreme Court decision overruled earlier Federal Election Commission (FEC) rules on campaign financing which restricted funding and did not allow unidentified campaign funding. This 2010 Supreme Court decision needs to be reversed; it needs to be challenged on the basis that the decision has now been proven to cause significant harm to the U.S. government, which is an established and recognized reason for restriction of free speech by the Supreme Court. We now have evidence (which will be provided in Chapter 12 – Democracy Crisis) that the 2010 Supreme Court decision has facilitated increased decisions of folly, which have increased our U.S. crises, which has caused loss of hope in the future of America.

2. Lack of alignment of three branches of government

Two independent branches of government (Congress and the Supreme Court) are intended to provide needed checks and balances on the Executive Branch. These three branches of government can each drive the country in the right, wrong, or simply different directions. Our forefathers created these three branches to avoid having a president who acts like a king, because a king typically puts special interests before the common good.

The Executive Branch of government tends to use a partisan-driven approach, following their political party's platform. This branch is led by the President, and partisan-appointed heads of government agencies, who focus on implementing political parties' predetermined platforms and political campaign promises instead of addressing the root causes of the country's crises. The Executive Branch should instead focus on excellent execution of congressional bipartisan policies that address the root causes of our multiple crises with the most efficient and effective solutions.

Congress is often focused on making laws that set the bar for the minimum level of performance required to avoid legal penalties. Congress does not typically set the goals and establish the plans that are needed to reduce our crises and to compete in today's world. In order to reduce our crises, Congress must take a stronger role in establishing bipartisan goals and improvement plans for America. They have the opportunity to create bipartisan goals to reduce our crises that can unite the country on required improvement efforts.

3. Lack of alignment among our four levels of government

Federal, state, county, and city governments are separate entities, and each has independent goals and plans. Bipartisan goals and plans to reduce crises that affect all levels of government can help align state, county, and city goals. A lack of federal goals to reduce our multiple crises prevents that alignment.

While multiple levels of government increase the difficulty in solving a crisis, a common bipartisan goal and improvement plan can facilitate teamwork at all levels of government. The appropriate use of positive incentives and recognition is a good way to get alignment of the multiple levels of government, while allowing the necessary flexibility for each level of government to adapt improvements in the most effective manner.

The best solutions are made by those closest to the problem. States and communities should be able to choose from a variety of best practices to implement the most effective and efficient solutions for their state or community, with recognition and some funding support from the national level to encourage improvement.

4. Lack of education and experience in management

Elected leaders may not have the education and experience necessary to deal with large organizations and national crises. For example, when lawyers are elected to office, their approach to problem solving tends to be to make more laws and regulations. Inexperienced elected officials may be influenced by lawyers to also only pursue legal and regulatory solutions.

Laws and regulations provide the sticks needed for minimum performance, but government needs to use more carrots to encourage the excellence needed in today's competitive world. A carrot can be as simple as recognizing benchmark performance and best practices of a state or community; that recognition can then encourage replication nationally. Recognition is an underutilized, efficient, and effective way to encourage replication of improvements.

A business manager who becomes an elected official may not appreciate the differences between the approach needed in a large democratic government and an autocratic CEO-led business.

Newly elected officials may need training and education to gain the skills they need to perform their new job. Government leaders need to learn to use critical thinking skills, which are very similar to quality approach skills. They both include problem solving skills, process improvement skills, and organizational capability assessment skills.

Elected leaders and staff can learn the quality approach, and how to use it in government, by simply reading this book. Successful business leaders have had to learn this approach to continuously increase both efficiency and effectiveness. If high school graduates working in our factories have learned this approach on the job, then members of Congress can learn this approach on the job.

5. Divisiveness between the two parties

The two parties that control our government increasingly treat each other as the enemy. Fighting for political party power and winning elections has replaced doing what is best for the country. Negative political ads, bitter personal attacks, and name calling have increased dramatically over the past few decades. This negativity has spread to citizens who are now treating members of the other party as the enemy.

Even some family members do not talk to each other. This atmosphere of hatred and disgust with everything the enemy party says and does has disabled our ability to work together on needed bipartisan solutions to our crises. Political party leaders need to set an example by showing more respect for those in a different political party. The Golden Rule, "Do unto others as you would have them do unto you," does include those in another political party.

Fundamental differences between our two major parties should not inhibit cooperation, because often common ground can be found. For example, Republicans generally support businesses and Democrats generally support workers. That apparent dichotomy overlooks the fact that 75% of all businesses are comprised of a single person with no other employees. Thus, for 75% of businesses, the business and the worker are identical and should have the support of both parties.

Both parties should be able to support the 99.7% of all businesses that are small businesses, which are adding the majority of new jobs in the U.S. Small businesses contribute roughly half of the U.S. GDP (El-Najjar 2017). There are 30.2 million small businesses (i.e., fewer than 500 employees) in the U.S. Small businesses employ 58.9 million people, which makes up 47.5% of the country's workforce (Giese 2019). Since these small businesses are not strong enough to cause a national crisis, a reduction in the multiple government organizations regulating small businesses could be a good thing.

Large businesses in each sector provide the services, or products, to compete internationally and to help with our trade balance crisis. Government needs to support large business to help reduce the U.S. trade balance deficit crisis. Our government must consider, and support, our ability to compete in the world when dealing with large businesses.

However, there are very large businesses, particularly in the financial, energy, pharmaceutical, and social media sectors that need responsible regulation due to their power to have a major negative impact on the whole country. The U.S. does not want a repeat of the 2008 Great Recession, which was caused by the financial sector's irresponsible speculation with other people's money. That 2008 Great Recession was caused by the same type of Wall Street speculation that caused the 1930s Depression. We do not want to repeat the opioid crisis which was caused by the Big Pharma industry. Therefore, reasonable regulation of these large industries is needed to prevent significant harm to the nation.

My mother once told me, "The devil does not sin, the devil tempts." The government should not play the role of the devil by deregulating businesses such as Wall Street and tempting them to legally maximize their profits by taking high risks with others' money, putting the entire U.S. economy at risk again. Both parties can and should agree to reduce regulations on small businesses and maintain the needed regulations on large businesses, recognizing that large businesses are only 0.3% of all U.S. businesses. Both political parties also need to be willing to support both business and workers; business needs skilled workers and workers need high-paying jobs.

Over the past 20 years, our political parties have moved to positions that are more extreme, farther apart, and less helpful to America. At the extremes, the Republican Party is moving to become the business and Special Interest Party, and while some members of the Democratic Party are moving to support more socialist agenda. These movements to pull our two parties towards extremes, neither of which are good for the future of America, have also contributed to the increased political party divisiveness.

A phrase we often hear today is 'partisan politics.' Partisan is both an adjective, meaning biased, prejudiced, one-sided, discriminatory, unjust, unfair, and inequitable. But partisan is also a noun meaning adherent, devotee, fanatic, zealot. Given these descriptions, we should want to become less partisan.

6. Increasing financial pressures

The crises in the U.S. are becoming larger and causing increasingly costly disasters. Increased financial pressures on the government are causing increased fighting over the declining funds available for the favorite political programs of each political party.

The 2018 tax cut, primarily benefitting businesses, added to the annual national deficit significantly and reduced available funding to address our crises. This 2018 tax cut also included a smaller tax cut for individuals, but that smaller cut will expire in a few years while the larger business tax cuts will not expire. America is now spending about a trillion dollars more than it has coming in every year, which creates a trillion-dollar annual deficit. This annual deficit will worsen our already major debt crisis.

Worldwide, the average corporate tax rate has dropped from 46% in the 1970s to 23% in 2019. This major reduction in business tax rates, essentially cutting them in half, is due to increased global competition, and was done in response to large businesses relocating to low-tax countries. Countries worldwide are all cutting corporate taxes to compete in attracting businesses. However, that leaves countries with the problem of how to deal with the loss of those corporate tax revenues. Alternatives include raising taxes on citizens who are less willing or able to relocate, cutting government costs, or borrowing money to make up for the loss in corporate taxes. So far, the U.S. has chosen the borrowing option. We should expect this trend in worldwide reduction in corporate taxes, in order for countries to compete for businesses, to continue. Therefore, we need an approach, other than increasing our debt, to compensate for business tax revenue loss.

The U.S. needs money for new program funding, but we cannot afford to fund new programs because the 2018 U.S. tax rate cut (35% to 21%) for corporations reduces revenues for other programs. This is a tax cut that world competition forced, but one which the U.S., deep in debt, could not afford. As a result, we are borrowing from China to pay for a $1 trillion budget deficit each year. When you have to borrow from your adversary to compete, that makes you weak.

America needs a bipartisan plan to balance the budget and get to a reasonable debt-to-GDP ratio. To solve the national debt crisis, America also needs to resolve the crises that are causing repeated costly disasters. The preface to the second half of this book shows that the 23 crises in this book have an annual Gross Crisis Cost (GCC) of about $9.1 trillion per year, which is equal to 42% of the annual U.S. GDP.

7. Culture of reaction versus prevention

Americans respond enthusiastically to a disaster. We take great pride in helping those hurt in a hurricane or a mass shooting; First Responders are our heroes. When America faces an increase in the frequency or size of disasters, the knee-jerk reaction is to add more First Responders to deal with the increasing problems and more resources to help those hurt by the disaster. Politicians often also ask for prayers to prevent such crises from happening again. However, we seem to dislike the preventive planning work necessary to reduce disasters. This book is all about that preventive work that "second responders" (i.e., those responsible for reducing crises and disasters rather than responding to them) need to do in an effective and efficient manner. We do not need to spend billions or trillions more to reduce our crises; we can reduce our crises and reduce government cost. In fact, we need to do that, because government cost is one of our major crises.

Non-profits that have led efforts to reduce national crises with preventive measures, like Mothers Against Drunk Driving (MADD), are made up of people who want to prevent repeated unnecessary loss of life. Today's non-profits that are trying to reduce mass shootings, or reduce opioid overdose deaths, or respond to other crises, are made up of teams of dedicated individuals who would appreciate second responder teams taking preventive steps to reduce repeated disasters and loss of life. These are the non-profits government needs to listen to for the preventive actions needed to reduce our crises. Credible non-profits, working for the common good, need to be given a more significant voice in the people's House of Government. That voice is now being given to lobbyists who are working for special interests.

The most cost-effective solution to disasters is to reduce the crises that are creating the repeated disasters. We need to work to reduce the climate change driving the storms that are causing coastal flooding, instead of just repeatedly funding rebuilding in flood zones. We need to also work to change construction requirements for any homes being rebuilt, so they will be resilient to future flooding. Today, we are doing neither. Instead, our government helps to fund repeated rebuilding in flood zones of homes that are not resilient.

The creation of House Crisis Action Teams (House CATs, which will be defined in Chapter 4) could begin reducing crises and begin saving costs; that initial success could increase belief in the benefit of using a preventive approach rather than relying only on expensive reactive approaches.

8. Short-term versus long-term planning

Another cause of not addressing crises is that the country's attention span seems to be growing shorter and shorter. The stock market is focused on the next quarter, not the next several years. We now even have stock market day-traders, who are gamblers not investors.

Government leaders are elected for 2, 4, or 6 years. Therefore, they tend to focus on what can be done before the next election, while they are also campaigning for that next election. This leaves them little time to address our long-term crises that take time to resolve. The government operates on annual plans with last-minute, or late, budgets, rather than 5-year or 10-year plans. A longer planning view is needed to help America address our long-term crises; one that requires persistence and bipartisan improvement efforts through multiple political party administrations' terms.

Government elected leaders often appeal to voters' short-term interests and their emotional desires and fears, rather than focusing on the long-term interests of America. Voters frequently do not have the opportunity or time to analyze complex issues, so their tendency is to look for who to blame for our crises, rather than finding and addressing the root causes of our crises. In order to get votes, politicians often try to place the blame for a problem on their opponent, a minority group, or another country. Unfortunately, many voters then believe this misplaced blame.

Establishing bipartisan teams and goals that address the root causes of our U.S. crises is essential to eliminate the decline of hope in America.

9. Confirmation bias

This is the barrier created when people make up their mind about an issue, and then put up a barrier to accepting any new information that may require a change to that predetermined belief or opinion and accept only information that confirms their preset ideas. To change this, people need to be open to using critical thinking skills in a bipartisan manner to address our crises. People also need to have respect and trust in credible bipartisan information sources. This confirmation bias effect is stronger for emotionally charged issues and deeply entrenched beliefs. Confirmation biases contribute to overconfidence in personal beliefs, and result in poor decisions.

Removing Follies

Decisions of folly must also be eliminated in order to reduce our crises. Barbara Tuchman's analysis of several historic follies, which occurred over a 500-year period, concluded that decisions of folly were a common cause of government failures. She found that decisions of folly were not an error, but the intentional rejection of decisions of reason that would benefit many, in order to satisfy the greed and selfish ambition of a few. Tuchman's historic analysis provides a lesson the U.S. should have learned, but unfortunately, we did not.

In analyzing the root causes of our national crises, 130 decisions of folly were identified that contributed to the creation of 23 crises. 105 of those 130 decisions (81%) were U.S. government decisions. Making decisions of folly that create and fuel crises is a systemic problem in Washington; that systemic problem needs to be understood and fixed. Chapter 4 – Unfixing Washington will address this systemic problem.

In addition to these 130 decisions of folly that have been made, an equal number of opportunities to implement decisions of reason for the common good have *not* been made. In the second half of this book, the 23 U.S. crises are analyzed, and in that analysis, 172 improvement recommendations are identified which include 128 (74%) that are no-cost or low-cost to the Federal government.

Over 100 decisions of folly made by government have contributed to 23 crises that are causing repeated disasters affecting the daily lives of all Americans. These unresolved crises and repeated disasters have collectively caused loss of hope in the future of America. The first half of this book explains how a quality approach can be used to unfix the government system that creates and fuels crises, and how to apply a quality approach to reduce our multiple crises.

Decisions of folly, in the face of reason, occur when emotions overrule reason in order to pursue human desires for greed and selfish ambition; that greed has a much greater cost to many. An approach to develop reasoned solutions to crises, based on credible research into root causes and prioritized ranking of the most efficient and effective improvements, is useless if repeated decisions are made to pursue folly over reason.

Future decisions of folly must be eliminated, and past decisions of folly should be corrected in order to reduce our crises. To eliminate decisions of folly, four changes are needed:

- Establishment and deployment of a set of government-wide values that support decisions for the common good over special interests

- Election of public officials who have demonstrated virtues (e.g., telling the truth) that align with government values that support the common good over special interests

- Establishment of a process to identify and publicize decisions of folly and proposed paths of folly; sunshine on decisions of folly can help reduce them

- Unfix Washington, which has been fixed to facilitate follies (this will be covered in Chapter 4)

Greed and selfish ambition cause follies. Greed is an intense desire for wealth or power; a desire to possess more than one needs. A folly is a decision made to achieve that greed and selfish ambition, in spite of knowing that it will cause a much greater cost to the common good. These decisions of folly are legal, but they are not in the interest of the common good that officials are elected to support. They are legal, they are wrong, and they are a cause of our crises.

Most people would like to be rich and famous; there was even a TV show called "Lifestyles of the Rich and Famous." There is nothing wrong with being rich and famous, if you become rich and famous without cheating and damaging others. If the path to being rich and famous includes cheating, damaging others, and damaging the nation, that may be legal, but it is wrong. I say that, recognizing that some of our leaders believe that anything that is legal is also right.

There are many rich and famous people who are ethical and helping others through their work and contributions to society. However, if their fortunes are made by risking the savings of others, by causing drug or gambling addiction, by declaring bankruptcy to avoid paying workers and suppliers, or by destroying the environment that we all need to live, then that is destructive to the common good. It may be legal, but it is a folly that is contributing to the loss of hope in America. We need to reduce these follies that collectively are destroying America.

Unfortunately, some elected leaders actually believe that follies, if legal, are the smart and clever thing to do to maximize their wealth or fame, or their friend's wealth. However, elected leaders are elected to serve the common good, not maximize the wealth of special interests and themselves. We have the right to expect government decisions to benefit the common good, not special interests.

Many politicians have been calling for change; however, the change that has actually occurred in Washington has been to facilitate more decisions of folly, which is clearly the wrong type of change. Washington is being "fixed"; however, it is being fixed for the rich and greedy and those with selfish ambitions. Those changes to facilitate folly in Washington must be eliminated in order to recover our democracy that was created to serve the common good, not special interests.

This book is about how we can return to a U.S. governance system that is focused on achieving Americans' goal of a better future for our nation, instead of serving special interests. That change depends upon using truth and facts to make decisions. Without agreement on values and some check on elected officials' virtues (i.e., living up to our values), the proposals for system and process changes in this book cannot work, because they rely on the truthful use of agreed-upon credible facts. Time spent debating facts and refuting lies about them is simply another means to ensure nothing gets done to resolve our crises.

Our government officials who live up to a set of values that describes an ethical performance, above the minimum legal requirement, is required to eliminate the legal follies that are destroying America. Having elected officials simply comply with laws (and many have trouble with that) is not sufficient to restore America. Legal follies must be eliminated, and that will require a higher level of ethics than simply not being a criminal; it will require a standard of ethical performance that puts the common good ahead of special interests. Government needs to be able to implement, and enforce, ethical standards based on values that are greater than the minimum legal requirements.

Unfortunately, our government is moving in the opposite direction; the governance system changes that have been made in Washington facilitate more follies. The changes made in Washington have lowered the bar of what is illegal, in order to facilitate more legal follies. For example, allowing more unidentified money in politics from special interests is now legally allowed to enable those with the most money to influence who is elected, which in the past was illegal.

Barbara Tuchman hoped her book on historic follies would encourage citizens to understand and demand the type of government, "rational and clear-sighted," to which we might securely entrust our fates. Unfortunately, her hope for improvement has not materialized; in fact, since her book was published in 1984, U.S. government follies have increased and the governance system in Washington has been changed to increase follies.

We need to learn from past mistakes to avoid choosing paths of folly. Simply "demanding" the use of reason in the face of greed has not worked; however, more can be done. America can do the following:

- Remove the barriers to choosing reason over folly

- Rescind the governance changes that are facilitating a choice of folly

- Choose candidates with established virtues

- Add processes to help choose paths of reason

- Establish and deploy agreed-to values in government that put the common good before special interests.

- Agree to, and use, credible truthful facts in decision making

- Identify and publicly share decisions of folly, and who proposed them. Let sunshine help disinfect Washington.

Thomas Paine's 1776 pamphlet *Common Sense* emphasized the need for a federal government for the early colonies to protect citizen security

(Paine 2019). Barbara Tuchman's book, *The March of Folly*, focused on the need for citizens to protect themselves from government decisions of greed and selfish ambition. If we listen to both authors, we need a strong federal government to protect citizens from the worst in ourselves (e.g., government that provides reasonable regulations on big businesses), and we also need strong citizens (e.g., citizens and non-profits that ensure we have a governance system that prevents follies, makes decisions of reason for the common good, and ensures we take preventive steps needed to reduce our crises) to protect us from the worst in government.

It is sometimes hard to tell if decisions of folly are motivated by incompetence or corruption, because the decision maker usually tries to disguise the decision of folly as a decision of reason. After the harmful results of intentional decisions of folly have been made clear, these decisions are too often excused as just mistakes. For example:

- Saying 100% of scientists are not in agreement that burning fossil fuels causes climate warming is the fossil fuel industries', and some elected officials', attempt to block the country from moving to natural energy (e.g., sun, water, wind, biomass fuels).

- Saying all people should be medicated to have zero pain is Big Pharma's, and some elected officials', disguised attempt to encourage sales of more opioid-addicting drugs.

- Saying the U.S. should initiate an offensive war on Iraq, based on false information on Iraq's nuclear capability, was the oil industries', and some elected officials', disguised attempt to gain control of Iraqi oil fields.

- Saying a wall built on our southern border will be paid for by Mexico

The following table, "Types of Repeated Follies," provides a list of a dozen types of follies that are frequently repeated in government. We should be aware of these types of follies, recognize them when they are presented as a folly, and prevent them from being repeated again and again.

Table 5: Types of Repeated Follies

- Denying that there is a crisis (e.g., climate change and the national debt)

- Taking tax revenues that have been dedicated for a specific issue and spending them on something else (e.g., nuclear waste storage and retirement safety-net funds)

- Allowing a few to harm environmental resources for personal profit, instead of managing our resources in a sustainable way for the common good (e.g., oceans, land, fresh water, and air)

- Continuing government support of a few industries rather than supporting the common good (e.g., coal, oil, Big Pharma, and Wall Street)

- Reacting to disasters rather than setting goals for improvement (e.g., hurricanes, forest fires, mass murders)

- Focusing on short-term rather than long-term planning (e.g., 22 Government shutdowns due to annual budget process problems and no 5-year plan to meet recognized financially responsible debt criteria)

- Focusing on getting more funding for the way we do things now, instead of learning from benchmarks and best practices used throughout the world to be more effective and efficient (e.g., continuous increases in defense spending and health care spending when U.S. expenditures are already much higher than any other countries)

- Focusing on going it alone, rather than partnering with other countries on world crises (e.g., breaking climate control and nuclear weapons control treaties)

- Focusing on reacting to problems rather than preventing them (e.g., continued use of stories and anecdotes in reaction to daily problems instead of using research and trends to understand root causes of these problems to prevent recurrence of them)

- Focusing on one crisis at a time rather than trying to understand the interrelatedness of all crises (e.g., high debt costs are caused by overspending on defense and health care and by the increasing disasters caused by climate warming)

- Believing we *can't* afford to solve a crisis, rather than understanding that solving crises can be done with no-cost or low-cost; solving these crises will save money to help balance the budget

- Continuing to manage broken processes instead of fixing the process (e.g. the same budgeting process has been used for over 20 years and has resulted in 22 government shutdowns)

A Proposal for Adding Values

We need agreed-to values for the benefit of the common good over special interests, in order to use the truth, not lies, when dealing with facts that are the basis for our root cause analyses. In the application for the U.S. Malcolm Baldrige National Quality Award, the criteria ask for organization leadership to articulate their values and how they deploy these values to their workforce. Our government should do what they expect the best organizations in the U.S. to do. We are not talking about America's values right now, but rather the government's organizational values that we want the government workforce, including elected leaders, to live up to. Articulated values define the ethical standards required from government officials; we do need them to do more than simply meet the minimum legal requirements in order for our democracy to function properly.

The first step towards this goal would be for Congress to develop a bipartisan agreement on what the government's values are; the Executive Branch would then need to deploy these values to all government employees, starting with the leadership team.

U.S. State Department Values

The Department of State, an agency of the government, has established the following six core values for their department's employees:

Loyalty – to the United States and its people

Character – maintain the highest ethical standards and integrity

Service – excellence in the formation of policies and programs

Accountability – responsibility for meeting the highest performance

Community – dedicated to teamwork, professionalism, and the customer perspective

Diversity – commitment to having a workforce that represents the diversity of America

These values have been posted in all Department of State offices and are integrated into employees' training (U.S. Department of State 2017).

Another set of values for possible U.S. government consideration is offered by the non-profit Center for Civic Education's National Standards for Civics and Government that government is expected to support:

- Individual rights to life, liberty and the pursuit of happiness

- The public common good

- Justice

- Equality of opportunity

- Diversity

- Truth

- Patriotism

(Center for Civic Education, n.d.)

U.S. government employees should be expected to support these American values, especially when making decisions for the public common good and basing them on truth. These are the values needed in U.S. government in order to address our U.S. crises and the decline of hope in America.

U.S. Allies' perception

A 2016 Pew Research poll showed that 84% of the people in Germany, Great Britain, France, Canada and Sweden (all allies of the U.S.) believed that the American President "would do the right thing regarding world affairs." One year later, in 2017, the percentage that believed our President "would do the right thing regarding world affairs" had fallen to 16% (Bialik 2018). This shows a drastic change in how U.S. allies view how the U.S. is living up to its historical values of doing the right thing under the current administration.

The U.S. government lacks an agreed-to set of values that all government employees, including its leaders, will live by. In order to use a quality approach to improve governance, Congress needs to establish the values they expect all government employees to live by, including being truthful and making decisions for the common good, and deploying those values to all government organizations.

The House of Representatives has an established caucus that could possibly address this need for establishing values in our federal government. That caucus is the Values Action Team: Chairwoman Vicky Hartzler (R), and Co-Chairs, Robert Aderholt (R), Jody Hice (R), and Doug Lamborn (R).

Summary

This chapter identifies a number of barriers to improvement in government that need to be eliminated:

- Too much money in campaigns

- Lack of alignment of the three branches of government

- Lack of alignment of the four levels of government

- Lack of management education and experience in government

- Divisiveness between the two parties

- Increasing financial pressures

- Culture of reaction rather than prevention

- Short-term rather than long-term planning

- Confirmation bias

- Lack of clear values in government

To overcome all these barriers, government leaders must recognize the loss of hope for the future of America and the crises that are collectively causing that loss of hope for most citizens. Our leaders then must align as a team and work together to address the root causes of those crises.

This chapter also identified a number of types of repeated decisions of folly that are contributing to the increase in our crises. Exacerbating our problems are the systematic governance changes that have been made to facilitate more follies that serve special interests instead of the common good. Those governance changes that facilitate folly (the swamp) need to be eliminated. Draining the swamp requires the reversal of the changes to our governance system that created the swamp.

Chapter 4- UNFIXING WASHINGTON

The common meaning of fixed is mended, repaired, or made better, but it has a second meaning of something being rigged (as in a bet) or bought off (as with a politician). Washington, our seat of government, has been fixed in this secondary sense of the word. Changes have been made to "fix" the Washington governance process in favor of special interests, and the changes must be reversed, to unfix Washington so that our government can once again serve the common good. This "fixed" governance system is the Washington Swamp, which needs to be unfixed to drain it. Governance process changes that have been made to create the swamp must be reversed.

The Washington Swamp has allowed our crises to reach a dangerous level. Although many claim we can't afford to do what needs to be done, it is possible to reduce existing U.S. crises while at the same time balancing the U.S. budget. Many businesses use an approach to improvement that can be used successfully in government. Implementing a quality improvement approach to address our crises will also help remove many of those major barriers to improvement in government that were identified in Chapter 3.

Success Examples

Two success stories illustrate how a quality approach can work in government. Both show how government, working with non-profits and research universities, can significantly reduce a major crisis. The first involves a significant reduction in deaths caused by drunk driving, while the second successfully tackles reducing a climate change problem, a hole in the earth's ozone layer.

MADD Success Story:
In the mid-1970s, drunk drivers were responsible for 60% of all traffic fatalities. In response to this statistic, and the deaths of their children, the non-profit Mothers Against Drunk Driving (MADD) was founded in

1980 to address this crisis. They worked with each state's government to implement laws designed to reduce drunk driving deaths. These laws focus on preventing drivers convicted of repeated drunk driving from being able to drive while drunk. Since they began their work, U.S. drunk driving deaths have been cut in half, even though the number of people driving has increased significantly. (Mothers Against Drunk Driving, n.d.)

Overall drunk driving fatalities decreased by 48% between 1982 and 2017. Fatalities decreased by 80% for those under 21 in the same 35-year period (Foundation for Advancing Alcohol Responsibility, n.d.).

Personal story – Drunk Driving Crisis

My brother was killed by a teenage drunk driver in 1971, just a year after he and his wife had adopted a baby boy. The day he died was the worst day for his family, especially his young son who lost his dad. Since then, the age limit for drinking has been raised from 18 to 21, which has substantially cut down on the number of deaths due to teenage drunk driving. My thanks to MADD, and many U.S. states, for taking action to address this crisis.

U.N. Success Story:

The hole in the earth's stratosphere, its ozone layer, was being increased in size in the 1970s. This hole was identified as a crisis by scientists, because the ozone layer is critically important to filter harmful ultraviolet radiation that can harm plants, animals, and cause cancer in humans. The main causes of ozone layer depletion were identified: manufactured chemicals such as halocarbon refrigerants (e.g., Freon), solvents, propellants, and foam-blowing agents [chlorofluorocarbons (CFCs)]. These chemicals caused ozone ($O3$) to break down into oxygen ($O2$). Destruction of the ozone layer was forecast to be an increasing cause of cancer, particularly skin cancer.

In 1987, a global agreement, known as the Montreal Protocol, banned production of CFCs, halons, and other ozone-depleting chemicals. After the ban went into effect in 1989, ozone levels stabilized in the mid-1990s, and the ozone layer began to recover in the 2000s. The earth's ozone layer is now projected to fully recover to the 1980 level by around 2075. Although it will take 100 years to fix this worldwide crisis, we are doing it! This achievement was recognized by United Nations Secretary-General Kofi Annan, who called it "the single most successful international agreement to date" (United Nations, n.d.). All United Nations (UN) member states have ratified this treaty, making it the only universal treaty in UN history (United Nations 2000). This success in regulating CFCs is attributed to collaboration among policy-makers, scientists, and industry leaders worldwide. Acting together on human causes of environmental damage is better than denying that they exist. We should use this example of successful cooperation as a role model for addressing climate change.

It is not too late for our government to recognize the success of MADD and those responsible for the Montreal Protocol, and to learn from them how national and global crises can be reduced successfully. One important aspect of these two important success stories is that both industry and policy makers listened to the scientific research community's facts and the non-profit community's recommendations for solutions; then they acted on those recommendations. Leaders did not focus on how to protect the few manufacturers selling alcohol or making chemicals that were depleting the ozone layer. Elected leaders acted on what was the best for the common good, not what was best for special interests. That type of government collaboration with the university research community and non-profits is a key part of the proposal for use of the approach in this book for dealing with current U.S. crises.

Personal story – Ozone layer depletion

I worked as an engineer in a manufacturing division of AT&T in the 1970s when news of the ozone layer depletion was identified. At the time, we were using a cleaning agent for soldering that was identified as an ozone-depleting chemical. Even though the Montreal Protocol had not yet been established, I was asked to find a replacement chemical, and we implemented a transition to use a new cleaning agent in several factories throughout the U.S. in less than one year.

A Quality Check

The U.S. Commerce Department's National Institute of Standards and Technology (NIST) has developed excellent criteria and approaches for assessing an organization's quality (National Institute of Standards and Technology, n.d.). The National Quality Award exam has been used for years to assess businesses, health organizations, and education. In addition, some U.S. cities, government agencies, and non-profit organizations have applied for this national award. Competing for the award requires completion of a lengthy application, which is then assessed by a team of eight quality, leadership, and performance professionals. While at AT&T, I volunteered to be an examiner for the exam part of the process and was trained by the Department of Commerce as an examiner the first year, and as a senior examiner the second year for the National Quality Award.

The professional examiners visit the business, or organization, to verify that the application reflects what is actually happening. The abbreviated assessment used here is based on public information and my assessment, as a means to provide a quick look at our government through a quality lens. Because the U.S. government is so large, a full Malcolm Baldrige performance evaluation would take a significant effort to develop an application and do the assessment, but it may be well worth that effort someday.

The quality check on the U.S. government system proposed here will use an abbreviated version of the U.S. Baldrige Excellence Framework criteria, to identify strengths and opportunities for improvement in key parts of the U.S. federal government. Feedback to applicants always includes both Strengths and Areas for Improvement.

1. Leadership

Strengths
President Trump campaigned on the slogan, "Make America Great Again." With that slogan, he admitted that America was not as great as it had been in the past, and he promised to make America great again. Admission of the crisis being faced by America, that she is not as great as in the past, is an important first step in improvement.

Opportunities for Improvement
The U.S. lacks clear and measurable goals and plans for achieving a great America.

The U.S. lacks values for leaders and employees that are necessary to achieve a great America.
Our governance system in Washington has been "fixed" to put special interests first and the common good second, thus putting the future of our democracy at risk. It is still being "fixed" to favor special interests.

2. Workforce

Strengths
The U.S. has many departments and agencies that have many well qualified and dedicated individuals, and the resources needed for them to accomplish their responsibilities.

Opportunities for Improvement
There is an inadequate process for the Executive Branch selecting those qualified for senior government leadership positions. There have been a number of criminal convictions associated with the current administration appointees; some have even been found to be collaborating with foreign adversaries.

The number of government shutdowns have caused significant pay delays and other problems, due to the Executive Branch and Congress not having a process to agree on facts and develop the most efficient and effective solutions to crises. This repeatedly punishes innocent federal employees who are trying to do their jobs, and it puts the public and the country in jeopardy when protective agencies are shut down.

3. Operations

Strengths
The U.S. has a checks-and-balances process that gives Congress and the Supreme Court the capability to prevent the Executive Branch from abusing its power. These were included in our democratic government by our founding fathers, who feared the power of a king.

Opportunities for Improvement
The Senate Majority Leader has not allowed a vote on proposed congressional bills in order to transfer decision-making power to the President on several issues. This negates the checks and balances the legislative branch is expected to implement.

The Supreme Court has ruled to allow corporations unlimited amounts of unidentified spending on elections through Super PACs; this ruling has corrupted the U.S. elections process by increasing the power of a few to provide enormous election funding, which is a major cause of many decisions of folly.

Congress lacks a process to develop bipartisan effective and efficient improvements to reduce our multiple crises.

The government system in Washington has been changed to facilitate decisions of follies for the benefit of a few, and these follies are root causes of our U.S. crises. These crises have caused a loss of hope in the future of America, which is a crisis for our democracy.

4. Results

Strengths
The U.S. has generally been good at responding to our repeated disasters.

The U.S. and our allies have significantly reduced the worldwide terrorist crisis.

The U.S. has prevented foreign terrorist attacks on the U.S. since the 9/11/01 terrorist attack disaster.

The U.S. did a good job of recovering jobs lost in the 2008 economic crisis and restoring U.S. GDP economic growth; this success continues in 2019.

Opportunities for Improvement
The U.S. has 23 major unresolved crises that lack goals and plans to reduce them.

These crises are collectively causing the loss of hope in the future of America, and there is no plan to address this.

The U.S. annual budget deficit and the U.S. debt are irresponsible, increasing, and there are no plans to reduce either.

The U.S. annual Gross Crisis Cost (GCC) is enormous and there are no goals or plans to reduce it.

5. Customers

Strengths
Americans generally are proud of America and most still believe it is the greatest country in the world.

Opportunities for Improvement
The majority of Americans believe the lives of our children will be worse than those of their parents. There is a loss of hope in the American Dream and of a better life for each generation.

The majority of Americans are stressed by the unresolved crises in America that are not being effectively addressed.

The vast majority of Americans are very dissatisfied with Washington's performance.

This abbreviated assessment, using national performance excellence criteria, indicates America does have significant strengths, but also has significant opportunities for improvement that need to be addressed. It is the job of leadership to review feedback from assessments like this, and then take the necessary steps to support the Strengths, and to develop plans to address the Opportunities for Improvement. This Quality Check is an important step in the Plan, Do, Check, Act (PDCA) Quality Approach. Later chapters in this book will propose plans for addressing the Opportunities for Improvement identified in this assessment of our federal government.

The Swamp in Washington

The swamp is a metaphor for the system in Washington that has been facilitating decisions of folly to serve special interests, instead of the common good. To drain the swamp in Washington we first need to move from the campaign slogan metaphor about the corruption in Washington to a clear definition of what the swamp actually is, so that we can develop a real plan to drain it. Our founding fathers knew that individuals in Washington would serve themselves and special interests, instead of the common good, if there were not adequate checks and balances in place.

The following Swamp Table lists 27 process changes in Washington governance, which can be considered to be water (or oil) pipes filling up the swamp. This swamp undermines our democratic checks and balances in order to serve special interests. Unfortunately, the faucets for all these pipes are turned on and are helping to fill Washington to overflowing with decisions of folly to benefit special interests. In addition, new pipes are still added to swell the overflowing swamp.

A campaign slogan about the need to drain the swamp is catchy, but insufficient. To drain the swamp, you first need to identify what process pipes are filling the swamp. Of course, the people who installed these pipes to benefit special interests know what they are. Although some politicians talk about draining the swamp in their campaigns, when they get to Washington, they add more process pipes to keep the swamp filled with follies to help their special interests.

To drain the swamp, we need to shut off the faucets on these process pipes that are keeping the swamp filled, and stop adding new pipes.

Collectively, these 27 process changes in Washington have created the swamp, which has shifted our democracy from serving the common good to serving special interests:

Table 6: The Swamp -
Washington Governance Process Changes that Facilitate Follies

Election Rules Process
- Increased gerrymandering of congressional districts after the 2010 census allowed political parties to pick the candidate to be elected, rather than allowing people's votes to do so

- Super Political Action Committees (Super PACs) created in 2010 allow unlimited and unidentified funding of negative attack ads on candidates who do not support their special interests

Election Process
- Accepting, and even encouraging, foreign nations' interference in our elections

- Significant increases in the time spent on divisive campaigning

- News channels allowed to support one particular candidate

Bill/Law Process
- The vast majority, 88%, of house caucuses have been established to serve special interests' objectives, instead of the common good

- Preventing passage of legislation needed to reduce our crises by a political party that opposes it

- Creating huge, complex, multifaceted legislative bills that include follies, which get snuck in and passed as part of a large package of new laws

- Senate Leader blocking votes on proposed judges and bills approved by House and Senate Committees

- Lobbyists' increased ability to influence and shape congressional bills, which then become U.S. laws

Budget Process
- Using government shutdowns by the executive branch to demand funding for specific projects

- Dismissing economic standards for a responsible debt-to-GDP ratio

Agency Head Process
- Appointing agency heads from special interest organizations who put special interests ahead of the common good in their decisions

- Appointing "acting" Cabinet and agency heads to avoid obtaining Congressional confirmation of Executive appointments

- Agency heads deregulating big business to aid special interests over the common good

Executive Branch Process
- Increased use of Executive Orders

- Breaking treaties

- Breaking trade agreements

- Escalating use of sanctions and military threats

- Redirecting use of funds marked for a specific use to a pet project

- Creating a Judicial System that has a partisan political bias

- Fighting between the Executive Branch and Congress over policy in the courts instead of working together to resolve our crises

- Presidential use of leadership position to bully, instead of as a positive 'bully pulpit' (a phrase coined by President Theodore Roosevelt to refer to his office (pulpit) as a terrific position of power from which to advocate for the common good)

- Encouraging divisiveness with daily insults on social media

- Diminishing the value of a free press by attacking it as "fake news," in order to facilitate decisions of folly

- Dismissing scientific evidence about environmental issues and crises in order to facilitate decisions of folly

- Supporting actions of authoritarian governments, while repudiating those of our allies

Politicians who have promised to fix Washington and drain the swamp have actually been "fixing" it to benefit special interests; adding governance changes that help special interests, thereby filling the swamp, not draining it. This fundamental shift in who our democracy serves must be reversed.

Identifying, labeling, and refuting follies is one way to stop them; however, trying to stop follies one at a time will not be effective if we continue to facilitate creation of new ones. The swamp does have to be drained, and the only clear way to do so is by reversing these 27 governance process changes that have created the swamp; reverse what created it. These changes in how Washington governs us have been made intentionally by political masterminds whose goal is to change our governance system in order to serve the special interests that support their funding for political party campaigns.

In January 2019, U2's Bono, Irish singer, venture capitalist and philanthropist, speaking at the World Economic Forum in Davos, Switzerland, offered a definition of capitalism that U.S. political parties and government officials could use as a guide: "Capitalism is not immoral, it is amoral, [that is, lacking a moral sense] and it requires our instruction. It has taken more people out of poverty than any other 'ism' but it is a wild beast and if not tamed it can chew up a lot of people along the way. And in fact, those peoples' lives that it has chewed up are pushing the politics in our homes towards populism" (Robinson 2019). Populism is a political philosophy that supports the rights of the common people in their struggle with the privileged elite; thus, it is a political approach that appeals to people who feel that their concerns are being disregarded by established elite groups. It is ironic that the same political party that supports business special interests over the common good is the political party that is also best at appealing to populism by blaming others (e.g., immigrants, other countries) for the issues and crises being faced by ordinary people.

Leaders should be able to appeal to populism (i.e., people who feel their concerns have been disregarded) by developing goals and plans to address the root causes of the crises most people face every day, which is what this book is about. We need to address the root causes of our crises, not simply blame others and continue with the swamp in Washington that is putting special interests ahead of the common good.

Putting the common good ahead of special interests is not socialism; it is what our democracy was created to do. This attempt to disparage efforts on behalf of the common good is done on purpose, in order to continue business as usual by growing the swamp in Washington and avoid its being drained.

Capitalism isn't bad, Washington is. Washington has gone bad by changing our governance processes to eliminate reasonable and required controls on capitalism, and changing our governance process to serve special interests instead of the common good. Our nation's capital was originally built on a physical swamp that was drained years ago. These recent (past 20 years) changes have created the metaphorical swamp that is Washington today, which we must drain to recover our democracy.

The current administration's key campaign promise was to drain the swamp in Washington; however, this administration has actually done the opposite. This administration has added to the governance process changes that have raised the level of corruption in the swamp, flooding us with follies to favor special interests and ignoring the common good.

A Proposal for Unfixing Washington

Washington has been fixed to benefit special interests. To reverse this, we must reverse governance processes that have created the swamp and reduce our national crises that the swamp has helped to create and fuel.

Governance Process WIN team

The Washington governance process changes that have been made to serve special interests must be reversed. This will require a high-level bipartisan leadership team that could be named the Washington Improvement Now (WIN) Team, consisting of 4 members:

- The President
- The Senate Leader
- The House Leader
- The Supreme Court Chief Justice

This WIN team should be established as the first priority of the President elected in November of 2020. Within the first 100 days of the next President's term, this team should develop a plan for the elimination of the 27 process changes that have created the swamp in Washington. This plan should identify responsibility for elimination of each of these Washington processes, as well as the schedule for completion of each process elimination. This detailed plan, which could be just one page, is needed to drain the swamp and stop creating the follies that are fueling our crises. Only this high-level team, working together with a goal to drain the swamp, can unfix Washington and actually drain the swamp.

The current "fixed" Washington governance process (the swamp) is producing disastrous results that citizen surveys show has caused a loss of hope in the future of America. Our government was intended to be a government of the people, by the people, and for the people; not one of special interests, by special interests, and for special interests.

A Quality Approach to Reduce National Crises

In addition to draining the swamp, by reversing the governance process changes that created it, we also need to reduce the U.S. crises that have been created and fueled by the "fixed" Washington governance process.

Part of our problem is that the urgent always takes priority over everything else, even the important. For example, when government is fighting enormous forest fires, there is no time to discuss the preventive measures needed to reduce the frequency of those fires. When government has to deal with the many individual opioid addiction problems, there is no time to agree on the adequate preventive measures required to reduce the increasing number of opioid addicts. When government has to deal with the mass murderers who are killing school children and people in other public places, there is no time to agree on adequate preventive measures to reduce the gun violence responsible for them. It seems the more disasters we have, the less preventive measures we have; with the poor excuse that we can't afford them.

While many individuals do wonderful work dealing with our many disasters (e.g., extinguishing forest fires, treating addicts, and capturing mass murderers), those fighting the disasters caused by crises would be glad to have a more effective approach used to reduce the crises that are causing the repeated disasters that they have to deal with. First Responders would like to see process changes that reduce the creation of more crises and disasters.

Those who work on prevention can be thought of as our "second responders," developing the preventive actions needed to reduce repeated disasters. We have about 2 million first responders in this country doing an excellent job of responding to our many disasters being produced by our multiple crises. We need a few thousand good second responders to reduce their workload by reducing our crises and disasters.

Political party disagreements on which crises need to be addressed, and what to do about each, have caused divisiveness and inaction. Increased financial pressures from increasing deficits and debt means that there is less money to address our multiple and growing crises. Meanwhile these crises are causing increasingly costly disasters. However, if leaders can agree on *how* to make improvements, that could lead to agreement on *what* to do to reduce the size and costs of our crises. Citizens' support of this approach to addressing our crises is needed to encourage our elected leaders to at least give it a try.

Much of America's divisiveness has resulted from individuals, political parties, groups, cable TV, and the press focusing on arguments about what they each claim to be true. As this argument over different information and even what a fact is becomes more and more divisive over time, it gets harder to change differing entrenched viewpoints and beliefs.

Citizens and government leaders need to step back from what we think we know and believe (which is different for both parties) to objectively identify the facts associated with each of our crises, and from those facts then identify the root causes of each crisis. It is time to stop searching for facts to support preconceived beliefs, and instead begin a meaningful search for the truth.

Once root causes of a crisis have been identified and agreed to, the most appropriate effective and efficient preventive improvements will almost always become apparent. Leaders need to be clear and agree on what the root causes are, before proposing improvements that may or may not be the most effective and efficient.

America needs to come together to establish bipartisan goals to drain the swamp and reduce our national crises. Having agreed on these simple two goals, then we need agreement that we will use a bipartisan quality approach to drain the swamp and address each crisis. We also need to eliminate the barriers to no-cost and low-cost improvements, and begin making real improvements as soon as possible.

Unfortunately, political platforms are frequently based on using the same predetermined solutions to every problem, without fully understanding the facts and the root causes of the many different crises we face. We also need to analyze all the potential improvement options to determine which are the most efficient and effective. There are many no-cost or low-cost effective improvements available.

This common sense "how to" method includes:

- Agreeing on the crises that need to be resolved and setting goals for improvement

- Using verified credible facts to determine the major root causes of each crisis

- Prioritizing the most effective and efficient improvements to address those root causes; the no-cost or low-cost improvements should be implemented first, to begin reducing crises and repeated disaster costs as soon as possible

- Making decisions to pursue the path of reason for the common good

- Developing and managing project implementation plans

- Checking on the crisis results measures to assess progress toward the goal that was set to reduce the crisis

- Taking action, when appropriate, to change and improve the plan to achieve the goal

This approach can be applied to all U.S. crises to provide a common understandable analysis that will lead to a plan to reduce each crisis. Using this approach will help enable both leaders and citizens to understand goals, plans, and results, when dealing with our 23 national crises.

Establishing a common bipartisan approach to deal with all crises will also help gain the necessary citizen understanding and support needed for approval of recommended improvements, based on agreed-to facts and root causes. Furthermore, establishment and implementation of a credible bipartisan approach to deal with the 23 crises will reduce the stress being suffered by Americans today. Credible bipartisan plans can, and will, revive hope, and that hope will reduce the stress that comes with feeling there is no hope for change and no escape from the problems.

The decisions on which improvements are to be made, or not made, should be made by those without a conflict of interest. Those with a conflict of interest should recuse themselves from these decisions. The bipartisan team addressing each crisis should be able to decide whether a team member has a conflict of interest, and if so, the member with a conflict of interest should not be allowed to vote on recommended improvements.

It is time to change from reiterating the same arguments and positions over and over, and start using critical thinking. Repeating an action that hasn't been successful in the past will not become more so through repetition; "The definition of insanity is doing the same thing over and over and expecting a different result" (Quote Investigator, n.d.). We need to unfix the Washington governance process, and we need to reduce the 23 crises that have been fueled by the "fixed" government process.

Proposal for House Crisis Action Teams (House CATs)

Government change could include establishing bipartisan House Crisis Action Teams (House CATs) using critical thinking skills to determine how to reduce each crisis.

This new process for House CATs should include the following steps:

- House Leadership establishes a bipartisan agreed-to list of the current U.S. crises. That list could start with the 23 national crises analyzed in this book.

- Create bipartisan House CATs, drawing on help from non-profits, research universities and others to analyze U.S. crises.

- These House CATs could be established by existing House Caucuses that have already been established to address a national issue/crisis.

- Identify the root causes of each crisis.

- Prioritize the most effective and efficient improvements to address the root causes. That is, prioritize the lowest cost improvements that will produce the best improvement in results (i.e., the most bang for the buck). We have 23 crises to resolve with limited funding; therefore, the improvements must be the most effective and efficient.

- Make choices for improvements based on paths of reason for the common good, not follies to serve special interests.

This change would turn government inside out. It would put the people back inside the "People's House" and put the lobbyists on the outside. That is the opposite of what is happening today, where lobbyists buy a seat at the table that determines how our government is run, through their enormous campaign funding. Unlike credible non-profits that are established by citizens to choose a path of reason for the common good, lobbyists are established by big business to support a path of folly for their own greed. Non-profits today are on the outside, struggling to include a minor change in a bill, while lobbyists are on the inside helping to write the bills. Importantly, IRS rules prevent credible non-profits from making any political campaign donations. However, the businesses that lobbyists represent are free to contribute millions to Super PACs to help candidates' election campaigns, thereby giving lobbyists much more influence than non-profits.

House caucuses that are already formed by House members to address issues could, independently, decide to use a House Crisis Action Team (House CAT) approach to develop recommendations for reduction of our national crises. This would be a bottom-up House member-driven approach. With four House members on each House CAT, an effort to create 23 House CATs would engage 92 House members, or 22% of the 435 House members.

The House CATs would be responsible for setting goals, finding root causes, developing efficient and effective improvements (ranked from best to worst), developing the implementation project plans, and reporting annual results for each crisis. The annual crisis report could become part of a House State of the Union Report on the status of improvement efforts on our U.S. crises. For the many newly elected House members looking for an opportunity to make a difference in America by addressing national issues and crises, this could be a welcome opportunity. The existing House standing committees could still make the final decisions on what recommendations should be given final approval for House legislation; however, we do need some improvements to be approved to address each of our national crises.

All House members with an idea, or proposal, for how to reduce one of our crises could submit their ideas to the appropriate House CAT to be included in their rank ordering of improvements based on effectiveness and efficiency. Each of these House CATs should be maintained until the crisis they are addressing is resolved. Decisions to establish, or close, a House CAT could be a bipartisan House Leadership Team decision.

House CAT Support

Quality coach support could be provided to support the House CATs. The Commerce Department manages the national excellence award process and in doing so recruits, selects, and provides training for volunteer quality professionals who help implement the U.S. national award process. This same department also manages the annual recognition ceremony and a website that shares the best practices of the leading organizations in America. The House CATs' coach support would be best managed by this organization of the Commerce Department that has the experience to provide support, including recognition support, and website sharing of best practices. If support is not done by the Commerce

Department, their standards and processes could be used as a benchmark to learn how to provide the House CAT support necessary. Seeing root causes identified, improvements authorized, and results achieved could rekindle the lost hope for a better future in America.

Information Technology (IT) support is needed for both the crisis teams and for transparent website access for all officials, media, and citizens to the information used in this effort. An accessible organized database should be set up to provide information needed by each team. This website would provide credible facts and data associated with the crisis: improvement goals, measures, results, trend lines, root causes, benchmarks, best practices, proposed improvements, crisis costs, approved improvements, implementation schedules, crisis team members, quality coach, and contributors such as non-profits, research universities, and authors.

House CAT Benefits

One question that might be asked is, why set up a House CAT with four House members to address our national crises? There are several benefits to having a House CAT working on a crisis:

- To develop bipartisan and multi-state proposals for appropriate Federal support actions, increasing the chance of House action

- Use of a common bipartisan agreed-to approach to address all our crises, increasing the chance of support and House action for resulting recommendations

- To develop an agreed-to set of credible facts for improvement recommendations

- Root causes can be identified

- Ranking of potential improvements based on effectiveness and efficiency

- Measurable goals can be set

- Benchmarks of performance can be established

- Clarification of process responsibilities for each organization:
  Cities
  Counties
  States
  Federal
  Business
  Agencies

- Sharing (via website) of:
  Best Practices (worldwide)
  Research University resources
  Non-Profit resources
  Government Agency resources
  Business resources
  Worldwide government resources

- Recognition of success:
  Recognition of successful projects
  Federal recognition of states
  State recognition of counties and cities

- House recognition of CATs that reduce crises

- Recognition of success promotes and encourages continued improvement and replication of successful improvements nationwide. Recognition is an underutilized low-cost tool to promote improvement.

House CAT Costs

A second question is how much effort and cost is a House CAT study going to require? Based on the crisis team work we used to address the Jersey Shore water pollution crisis, the following is an estimate of the time needed for a House CAT:

- CAT team consists of a staff member from four U.S. House members, and a volunteer quality facilitator. Team membership is two from each political party. CAT recommendations should have unanimous bipartisan approval to go forward to the House Caucus and Standing Committees.

- CAT team meeting for 2 hours per month via teleconference for House staff members

- The four House Representatives should review team progress once each quarter in a 2-hour meeting

- The staff team does the study using the quality method and prepares the outputs for the House members' quarterly review and approval

- The approved output of the CAT is forwarded to the appropriate House Caucus or Standing Committee(s) for action

- The staff team calls on available volunteer expert resources to contribute to the CAT study and help prepare for monthly progress reviews. (All resources used should have no conflict of interest)

- An annual report should be issued that shows the number of CAT recommendations and the number acted on by Caucuses, Standing Committees, and by the full House in legislation. This is needed to assess the support for acting on House CAT recommendations.

- Use interested volunteer University, non-profit, and government benchmark resources to help on each crisis analysis.

What can a small House CAT hope to achieve?

Margaret Mead, an American cultural anthropologist of the 1960s and 1970s said: "Never doubt that a small group of thoughtful committed citizens can change the world; indeed, it's the only thing that ever has" (Brainy Quote, n.d.). I am sure that 23 House CATs could change our world.

If the House leadership decides to implement the governance system changes recommended in this chapter, and that work reestablishes citizen hope in the future of America, I believe the House Leadership legacy could be recognized as being on a par with the work of our Founding Fathers and the work of the WW II generation. This work is needed to save America from itself.

This House CAT quality approach to a crisis could also be trialed by any House Representative caucus on the crisis of their choice, by simply forming a team of four interested House members and using the approach outlined in this book.

House Caucuses:

House Caucuses are formed by a group of House members to pursue common legislative objectives. They are formally called Congressional Member Organizations (CMOs) and governed under the rules of the House chamber. The House Administration Committee lists 538 caucuses in the House of Representatives as of June 3, 2019 (Caucuses of the United States Congress).

Most of the House caucuses (about 88% based on my review) on the long list of 538 caucuses, appear to be pursuing objectives to help a particular group, a political party, or other special interest. The multiple crises the U.S. now faces is because Washington has been more focused on helping special interests than the common good. With 473 special interest caucuses (88% of 538 caucuses), House Members are too busy helping special interests to have time to address the 23 national crises facing the country.

There are some caucuses (about 65, or 12% of total caucuses based on my review) that appear to be established to address some of our national crises, or some portion of a national crisis. I have identified a number of caucuses (47) that appear to have an interest in addressing all, or part, of 17 national crises addressed in this book. Those caucuses could establish a House CAT to address our crises. This would use a CAT to help House members address an existing issue/crisis they have already agreed to address. The caucuses that agree to form a House CAT to address their issue/crisis could be trials for this House CAT approach.

The House Rules Committee could establish rules for a Caucus forming a House CAT with four bipartisan members to address a national crisis using the quality approach proposed in this book. This shared approach, if used across all our caucuses, would add credibility and understandability to the output from multiple House CATs and Caucuses on our national crises. Establishing additional House Caucuses to address the remaining six crises in this book should be done by House members interested in reducing those six crises.

Recognizing America has lost hope in the future, and that we have 23 major crises that collectively are causing that loss of hope, House members' focus could be redirected from helping special interests to helping reduce our national crises. The House members on the 473 caucuses serving special interest objectives could suspend, or reduce, their efforts until we have reduced the major 23 crises facing America, revived citizen hope in the future of America, and revived citizen confidence in Washington. Unless we flip the percentage of caucuses supporting special interests (88%) and the common good (12%), it will be very hard to reduce the multiple crises that are affecting the common good and causing loss of hope in the future of America (Congressional Caucuses 2019).

House State of the Union Report

America also needs a House State of the Union Report that shares progress being made in reducing the U.S. crises and in unfixing the Washington governance process (i.e., draining the swamp). Chapter 2 provided my Report Card assessment of progress on our crises (total average grade of F), which could be used as an example of the annual report needed from the House on our crises. This would be complementary to the current Presidential State of the Union address to Congress.

President Trump's 2019 State of the Union address to Congress and to America made me feel good about America and proud of Americans (CNN 2019). That pep talk worked for me, because it shared examples of American heroism in the face of disasters:

- A child surviving brain cancer, who simultaneously raised funds for St. Jude Hospital

- A police officer who responded to the mass shooting in Pittsburgh, although he was shot 12 times, he still pursued the shooters

- Three World War II Vets who served their country in time of war, along with a holocaust survivor

- Two stories about individuals who were addicted to drugs and unfairly locked up in prisons for decades. They were finally released as a result of a Presidential pardon, or the new Congressional First Step Program.

All these heroic stories of Americans responding to disasters made me feel good about Americans, and their capability to respond to disasters. They made me feel proud of them, and proud to be an American.

However, the State of the Union did not provide a report on our progress in reducing the crises that are causing the daily disasters that our American heroes have to deal with. America is like a great city on a hill, and the 23 crises we face every day are the 23 cannons attacking our city. Each cannon can fire a small (e.g., gun violence and health care crises) or large (e.g., wars and financial crises) cannon ball. Each cannon can fire frequently (e.g., gun violence and health care crises) or fire infrequently (e.g., wars and financial crises). These cannons are bombarding America, and Americans, and we have many millions of American heroes who are responding to the disasters these crises create. America has millions of heroic survivors, and we also have the families of those who have not survived these cannon ball attacks.

Like many Presidents before him, the President's State of the Union address was a State of the Union pep talk about the heroes in America who are dealing with the disasters created by our crises. Americans also need to hear what government is doing to disable these cannons that keep firing bigger and more frequent cannon balls at us daily. Americans need a State of the Union crisis status report from the House of Representatives. That status report should include progress made on reducing each crisis and the annual cost of all U.S. crises, our Gross Crisis Cost (GCC).

Summary

Let's take a quick look at Why, What, How, Where, and When this improvement approach could be used:

Why?

An improvement approach is needed because America is facing increasing crises that have not been resolved for many years by either political party. The result is a loss of hope in the future of America. Simply changing leaders, or the political party in control, has not helped reduce our growing list of crises. We don't need to keep changing political parties; we need the political parties to change.

What?

A number of unresolved crises facing America are creating increasing pressure on Americans, and these crises generate repeated costly disasters. A list of 23 crises is collectively contributing to America's decline in hope for the future and is costing America about $9.1 trillion per year. That is our annual Gross Crisis Cost (GCC). These multiple crises are being fueled by a Washington governance process (The Swamp) that has been fixed to serve special interests over the common good.

How?

The use of a quality approach in government, with support from non-profits and cooperation from government leaders, could successfully reduce the crises facing this country. The U.S. also needs agreed-to government values and improved government processes to reduce repeated choices of folly to benefit a few, over choices of reason to benefit many.

Where?

The business quality improvement approach needs to be implemented in the House of Representatives using a House CAT for each U.S. crisis, and a WIN Team to drain the swamp and reverse past follies.

When?

Work should begin now, because these crises are increasing every day, and they will be harder to address as they grow larger.

A change to the approach being used in Washington may sound like a lot of work, particularly in light of the many barriers to improvement in government. It will take some additional learning (e.g., how to use the quality approach/critical thinking approach in Chapter 5 to reduce our crises), but it is very doable if government leaders want to do it. The alternative to reducing crises is to continue to deal with increasing disasters, which continue to be more and more overwhelming. Reducing crises will reduce both the disasters and enormous amount of reactive work requirements in the future. Excellent "second responders" can reduce the need for increasing "first responders." It is our turn, our generation's turn, to do what our parents and grandparents did for us: make America better for the next generation.

Chapter 5 –QUALITY APPROACH

This chapter describes the four improvement steps in a Plan, Do, Check, Act cycle (PDCA) and the appropriate quality methods to be used in each step by a House Crisis Action Team (House CAT). This PDCA improvement cycle can be used to drive continuous improvement. When this cycle is continued year after year, it can create the upward spiral of continuous improvement needed to reach long-term goals. We need to keep improving our government to make it faster, better, and lower cost, year after year; these House CAT teams can help our government do that. This chapter will also show how these methods are very similar to critical thinking skills. All government organizations need to stop using an approach that repeats just doing what they did last year, but with a cost of living increase, and instead begin focusing on improving results at a lower cost every year. That is what competitive businesses must do, and know how to do.

Quality Improvement

To address U.S. crises, the first step is to identify and agree on the crises that we face. In general, Americans have a good understanding of our crises and want them reduced. However, political debate over which of these crises the government should begin to address keeps us from getting started. Elected officials need to stop fighting about which crises to address and just address them all. The House has 538 caucuses with 88% of them working on special interest objectives. We just need 23 House caucuses to adopt a House CAT quality method to reduce our crises for the common good.

Further complicating our current impasse are the individuals who say all our crises cannot be addressed (while they are busy addressing special interest needs), and others who deny that some of our crises even exist. Failure to make the changes we need in America is frequently led by the people who say: it can't be done, we can't afford to change, it is not necessary to change, or it is not worth trying. But, if we don't try to change, we can't succeed.

A great deal of sound research has been done to determine root causes of our crises. However, debate on which research facts to use in determining root causes impedes progress. Credible peer-reviewed research on the root causes of the crises needs to be established as the basis for improvement. We need to stop debating the facts, as a way to do nothing, in order to keep the system we have that is benefiting the few. We can't afford to continue doing what we are doing now.

Although many excellent, citizen-funded non-profits have developed many potential improvements to address the root causes of each of our U.S. crises, debate continues on which, if any, improvements to approve. Improvements should be rank ordered, with the highest priority given to those with the lowest cost and most potential effectiveness. A number of credible no-cost and low-cost improvements exist for each of our crises which should be implemented as soon as possible, in order to begin reducing U.S. crises and the costly disasters they produce. Government needs to recognize that we are facing multiple, interrelated crises that are collectively causing loss of hope in the future of America, and take action to reduce them.

A critical step is the decision of what to do, or not to do, to reduce each crisis. Frequently, this is where our failure occurs, when a path of folly is chosen over a path of reason. We need to identify those decisions that are follies, call them out, and stop making them. The second half of this book will call out the 130 follies that have contributed to our 23 crises.

About 30 years ago, China recognized that communism was not motivating the hard work and innovation needed to improve quality of life in China; therefore, China introduced American-style capitalism into their communist form of government, in order to improve their production capability and the quality of life in China. China made a major governance system change to improve their citizens' quality of life. Since making that change, China has become an economic world leader.

America cannot afford to continue to muddle on as we have done in the past, because muddling on is causing loss of hope in the American Dream. America needs a governance system improvement to reduce our national crises; instead, we have been changing our governance system to serve special interests.

Choosing the best leader is obviously important, but it is typically only about 20% of what needs to be done to address a crisis. Typically, 80%

of the reason for failure is caused by the systemic processes being used in business or government. Broken and out-of-control processes need to be improved to get better results. A great race car driver can't win in a car that is not as good as the other cars in the race. Of course, we need an experienced driver, but we also need a great car. Many aspects of our race car are failing: our debt crisis is like not having enough gas in the tank to finish the race, our health care crisis is like a failing engine, our worker crisis is like worn-out tires, our environmental crisis is like the lack of an aerodynamic body, and our defense crisis is like not having a helmet and seatbelt for the driver. We need good Crisis Action Teams (CATs) (i.e., our race crews) to address each of these crises in order to win the race that America is in with other countries.

One example of our broken government system is the 22 government shutdowns, from 1980 to February 2019, over budget funding issues that were not resolved in a timely manner. Shutting down your own government (the race car) 22 times while in the race is not a good way to win. In addition, our governance decision-making processes have repeatedly enabled a choice of a path of folly to benefit a few, over the path of reason to benefit many, which is like taking your friends for a ride downtown during the race.

America is gambling when it elects inexperienced people to lead the nation (to be our race car driver), in the hope of getting the change needed. Our old rust bucket of a car did not win the race, so let's put in a new inexperienced driver, what have we got to lose? Unfortunately, this is an example of jumping from the frying pan into the fire! We need to improve the car our leaders are being asked to drive. We need crews to fix all aspects of the race car we are driving, and we also need good experienced drivers who have the knowledge and proven successful experience to win the race.

Thomas Paine's pamphlet *Common Sense* was intended to convince citizens to apply common sense to establish the initial federal government for America in the 18th century. This book, *A Path of Reason for America,* attempts to convince citizens, and our government leaders, to use common sense to implement the federal governance changes necessary to restore hope in the American Dream for the 21st century.

Bloom's Taxonomy of Knowledge

Educational psychologist Benjamin Bloom's committee analyzed the courses being taught in our U.S. school system in 1954 and found that the vast majority of our education system was focused on the lower three levels of the knowledge hierarchy: level 1 - Recall, level 2 - Comprehension, and level 3 - Application (Vanderbilt University Center for Teaching, n.d.).

Fifty years after Bloom's work, Maryellen Weimer, Ph.D., found that less than 1% of first-year college courses were focused on the higher-order critical thinking levels: level 4 - Analysis, level 5 - Synthesis, and level 6 - Evaluation (Weimer 2013). Unfortunately, our schools have not incorporated critical thinking skills in classes, as proposed by Bloom's committee; therefore, critical thinking skills are not widespread or commonly used.

Table 7: Comparison of Critical Thinking Levels and Quality Methods

Level	Bloom's Knowledge Hierarchy of Critical Thinking Levels	Quality Methods
4	Analysis	Problem Solving
5	Synthesis	Process and System Improvement
6	Evaluation	U.S. Baldrige Assessment

The three higher-level critical thinking skills enable people to think for themselves instead of simply repeating, referencing, or re-tweeting what others have said, which may be false. These quality methods will be used to analyze each crisis and develop plans to reduce each crisis.

Dr. Chris Frith of the Department of Cognitive Neurology in London discovered that neuron brain connections are created when people do the analysis necessary to make their own decisions, instead of simply doing what they are told to do. According to Frith, "Dead areas of the brain come to life when we make our own decisions." We may not only reduce our crises; we may actually get smarter in the process if we use these critical thinking skills.

Plan, Do, Check, Act (PDCA) Cycle

The descriptions of each of the following improvement methods have been simplified to keep them as usable as possible. Although there are more sophisticated quality tools and methods, using these basic methods in the PDCA cycle is a good place for the U.S. government to start to reduce our crises. To go from great to excellent, there are more sophisticated tools that the best businesses use; however, our government needs to go from poor to good, so these basic tools are more appropriate.

<u>PLAN</u>

Developing a plan is the first step in this four-step improvement cycle. The plan step includes the seven methods, shown below.

<u>Identify and define the U.S. crises</u>

It may sound simplistic, but in order to improve, we need government agreement on what needs to be improved. Congressional leaders need to agree on the major crises America is facing. A government House of Representatives bipartisan leadership team could start with the list of 23 crises in this book, and add or subtract from this list as they see appropriate. The main point here is that the U.S. lacks a bipartisan agreed-to list of crises that need to be addressed, and one is needed.

The list of crises that we can address should not be limited because of fear that America, or the House, cannot address all our crises. America has the resources to address these crises; we are limited only by those who wish to continue to pursue paths of folly for the greed of a few, instead of addressing our crises for the common good. America is only limited by naysayers and those who benefit from the status quo. Today we have 88% of the House caucuses working on special interest objectives, instead of working to reduce the crises affecting the common good.

After agreeing to a list of crises, the next step is forming bipartisan teams to address them. These could be House CATs, formed by House Caucuses that would be responsible for developing the most efficient and effective solutions to reduce each U.S. crisis. The Standing House Committees would retain their responsibility to decide which recommended improvements to implement.

Once these House CATs are formed, they can begin using this approach to developing plans to resolve each crisis. The first step is the definition of each crisis. Chapters 7 through 12 contain definitions of 23 U.S. crises and examples of how to apply this seven-step approach to each crisis, which the House CATs could use as a starting point. It is expected that the House CATs, with help from appropriate government agencies, research universities, and credible non-profits, will make substantial improvements on the example plans in this book, and continue to improve plans annually until all our U.S. crises are eliminated.

In the second half of this book, the existing House caucuses that have been established to address these 23 issues/crises are listed with the co-chairs of each caucus. This includes 47 house caucuses that are addressing one of these national crises, or a part of one.

Research the facts and trends

For each crisis, the bipartisan crisis teams need to agree on facts and trends obtained from credible sources such as: government agencies' reports and data, research universities studies, analysis by credible non-profits, independent surveys, and investigative reports. These facts can then be used to understand the root causes and develop improvements for each crisis. A cautionary note: sources of information from organizations with, or funded by, organizations with a financial conflict of interest, should not be considered credible.

In analyzing these facts, it is important to establish trends for several years to understand the crisis and to avoid the folly of overreacting to normal variation that might occur from one year, or one month, to the next. Trends are also needed to measure the impact of improvements over time. Anecdotal evidence cannot be considered as a basis for improvements, since anecdotes can be found to support any position. Furthermore, anecdotes often appeal to emotion rather than logic. Use of anecdotes, without supporting facts and trends, is a typical tactic of those wishing to pursue a path of folly instead of a path of reason. For example, citing an illegal immigrant murder case as a basis for a particular immigration policy action, when it is a known fact that the overall data show that illegal immigrants have a lower crime rate than U.S. citizens.

Ensuring both public and media open access (e.g., disclosures via website) to the research and data being used to develop solutions to our U.S. crises will help add to the credibility of the data. Those looking for data need to be searching for the truth about the root causes of our crises, not looking for data to support predetermined political positions.

In addition to obtaining information from the above sources, facts and trends from other countries, states, and communities should be obtained to develop benchmarks and to understand best practices. Sharing benchmarks and best practices is essential to encourage replication of best practices throughout the country. For those who claim we can't improve, they just need to look at those who already have improved.

Determine the Goal

Each crisis needs an improvement goal. Developing a goal is critical because it provides guidance for all that follows. Operating without a goal is like not having a destination for a trip; if you have no destination, any direction can be taken. For those who want to take a direction to benefit special interests, not having a goal to reduce crises for the common good is helpful.

This goal needs to be developed in a bipartisan manner because the goal needs to serve as a guide for the long term, not just one or two election cycles. A bipartisan effort will also be required to support the many improvements needed to reach the goal over time, even during periods of shifting government control between different political parties. Once elected leaders realize the impact of our collective crises and multiple follies, which have caused loss of hope in the American Dream, I expect our leaders should be willing to take the necessary bipartisan actions to address these crises.

The goal for each crisis needs to be transparent and simple to understand, in order to enable all of America (states, counties, cities, towns, businesses, non-profits, universities, and individual citizens) to do what they can to help move America toward the goals that are set. Achievable goals can be set using benchmarks of what other countries, states, or communities have already tested and found effective. For example, if the U.S. is doing badly in one area, we could set an initial goal just to get to the world average. Unfortunately, that is the situation we are in on most of our crises. Goals can also be set to attain an annual achievable improvement rate that reduces the crises. Small achievable annual percentage improvements can make substantial improvement over time; as most of us know, that is the substantial benefit of compounded interest over time. As with compounded interest, getting started as early as possible is extremely beneficial. Most of the crises we face have been created over the past 20 years; our plans to reduce them will typically need to be long-term plans. Unfortunately, our government is not very good at long-term planning. By looking at benchmarks of best performances in each crisis area, we can also learn the best practices of how to do better, and we can create a competitive spirit to help motivate improvement to reach the best benchmark of performance.

Establish the results measurements

To be meaningful, goals need to be measurable and have a time frame in which to be achieved. Fear that team members might be blamed later for not achieving the goal often results in a reluctance to create measurement for a goal with a firm time frame. Clearly the House CAT will not have the authority to make all the changes needed to achieve the goal; however, they need to take the leadership responsibility for developing a plan to reach the goal and the leadership to gain support of all those needed for success.

If the results show an improvement trend, but a goal is not achieved by the target year, the target year can be reset. The key is establishing an improvement trend for each crisis and maintaining that trend; with continuous improvement the goal will be reached. Lack of continuous improvement toward the goal indicates a plan change is needed.

It is best to choose an existing single key measure, or indicator, for each crisis goal. That way, a past trend can be used to assess efforts on improvement over time and a widespread understanding and support for the goal to be achieved can be obtained. In addition, it is important to have a credible source for the measure or indicator that is already committed and funded to provide it. The organization chosen for the key measure should be contacted to be sure they plan to continue to provide this information. Having one key measure for each of our 23 crises will enable leaders and citizens to understand and support the 23 goals and measures, rather than being overwhelmed and confused by many bits and pieces of information on each crisis we face. Additional goals and measures may be needed by each crisis team, but the single key crisis goal and measure should be identified to help with the broad effort needed to accomplish the improvement changes needed.

It is also important to have a measure of progress to be able to Act (the A of PDCA), to make changes in the plan if results are not improving. For example, if the overarching goal is to restore hope in the future of America, then citizen surveys about their view of the future of America should be improving over time. If these citizen survey results are not improving over time, perhaps barriers to improvement of crises need to be removed.

Identify root causes

The next step is to identify the crisis root causes based on the facts, trends, and research studies of the crisis. One way to identify root causes is to start by asking "why" questions:

Why is this an unresolved crisis? List those causes.
Then for each cause identified, ask why again, and again, to get to the root causes.

Causes of a crisis need to be identified and agreed to in order to reduce a crisis. It is up to the crisis team to determine which causes are the most significant and addressable, in order to make the largest and fastest reduction in the crisis for the least cost. The next step is to rank order the causes from most significant and addressable in the shortest time frame, to the most difficult and expensive. The goal is to make the most improvement in the key results measure, as fast as possible, to reach the goal at the lowest cost. To use a farm analogy, we need to "pick the low hanging fruit first."

Identify and rank order improvements

After root causes have been determined, the actual improvements that are going to be implemented to address each root cause need to be identified. Although there are many potential improvements for each crisis, given limited funds, the most efficient and effective improvements must be identified. One way to do this was first proposed by Vilfredo Pareto, an Italian economist working in the late 1800s, who developed something called the Pareto principle, which is also referred to as the 80/20 rule. The Pareto principle states that in almost all situations, roughly 80% of the results come from 20% of the improvements (Chappelow 2019). Therefore, the crisis team needs to identify this 20% of possible improvements that can contribute 80% of the results desired, and focus on those each year in their annual improvement plans. Each year that can be repeated, to continue making the most improvement with the least expenditures. For example, we know that 80% of the drug smuggling along our southern border is at Ports of Entry (POE), not in open spaces between them. Therefore, improvements in security at POE should be the priority focus in order to get the most benefit from the expenditures.

<u>Obtain approval for funding and implementation</u>

The next step, and frequently the most difficult, is to obtain approval and funding for the implementation of the recommended improvements from the appropriate responsible organizations. Estimates of the annual crisis cost and the potential savings through crisis reduction need to be made to provide the benefit/cost support for the improvements proposed. We cannot afford high-cost low-effective improvements.

Fortunately, there are many no-cost and low-cost improvements that can be made to reduce our U.S. crises. Chapters 7 through 12 propose 172 possible improvements to reduce our 23 crises, and 74% of those are no-cost or low-cost to the federal government. Unfortunately, it appears these well-known no-cost and low-cost improvements across all our crises have not been implemented, because decision makers are more focused on supporting special interests than the common good. That has to change.

<u>DO</u>

Develop a Project Plan for all approved and funded improvements to manage implementation. All organizations responsible for implementation of this plan should be included in formulating the plan. Key dates and schedules for implementation steps should be set and tracked.

Implementation progress and reports on status should be given to House CATs and interested leaders monthly. The project team will need to resolve barriers, identified by the organizations involved, to implementing the improvements while meeting the cost budgets and the schedule for improvements.

Improved results cannot be obtained until improvements have been successfully implemented. In order to assess the impact of improvements on results trends, a record of implemented improvements and the dates they become effective should be maintained.

Government is known for taking long times to make improvements, with schedule and cost overruns. We need the most improvement we can get as soon as possible, so we need a more business-like approach to getting things done quickly. We are facing multiple crises, and we need to act like the future of our country is at risk because it is.

It took the Executive Branch and Congress only a few days to agree to give $800 billion to Wall Street banks to bail them out, after their speculation caused a financial disaster in 2008. We need that type of speed in approving the many no-cost and low-cost improvements that can reduce all our national crises.

CHECK

Each crisis team should hold an annual review to check and update current facts, studies, and trends pertaining to the crisis. Status of improvements should be tracked. Results on key measures reflecting progress, or lack of progress, toward the goals should be monitored. If successful results are achieved, recognition should be given to those responsible for the success.

Recognition for success encourages continued improvement and replication, and fosters a spirit of competitiveness to improve to be the best. Recognition is a low-cost and underutilized method to encourage improvement. Recognition from the Federal government should be given to state leaders. State leaders should recognize leading counties and cities.

In addition, recognition should be established for the most successful House CATs, to encourage competition in making the most improvement in reduction of our 23 crises. The House CATs, and key supporting organizations, that make the most improvement on their crisis could be awarded CAT trophies; like the Academy Awards, Emmys, and other awards that we have for every category of music. Reducing our U.S. crises should be recognized at the same level of recognition that we have for making a good movie, or singing a good song.

ACT

Update the crisis improvement plan annually as needed, based on the status of improvements, new facts or studies, as well as changes in trend data. Comparing the results to the original objectives is a key to assessing the need for a plan change. Identify barriers that must be removed to achieve success. Best practices should be shared and replication encouraged. This PDCA cycle should be repeated annually to create an upward spiral of continued improvement.

Summary of Quality Approach

This chapter provided a four-step Plan, Do, Check, Act (PDCA) cycle approach, with the methods to be used in each step to address our U.S. crises. Use of these PDCA cycle steps by a bipartisan House CAT, as an agreed-to method of "how" to address U.S. crises, should reduce the partisanship battles that we now see regularly on "what" to do to address U.S. crises. This PDCA cycle approach and these quality methods, used by a bipartisan team, can lead to bipartisan recommendations on what to do, because the team is working together toward a common agreed-to goal, starting from agreed-to facts.

Chapter 6: A PATH OF REASON FOR THE WORLD

In addition to having its own crises, the U.S. is affected by other countries' crises and by world crises. Chapters 1 through 5 of this book show how our crises could be reduced, or eliminated, by improving the U.S. governance system; this chapter shows how to use this approach to improve world governance systems.

Many of the world's crises start as the result of individual countries not addressing their own crises; each country's crises then spread like a cancer into the rest of the world. Some cancers metastasize, or spread, throughout the body, making them more difficult to treat and less likely to be cured. This same process can occur for an individual country's crisis; if it is not treated locally, it metastasizes into a world crisis. Once this happens, there is no clear responsibility to manage it, and there are fewer effective and efficient treatment methods and tools.

From a quality viewpoint, the best approach is for early detection and treatment of each crisis by, and in, the host country, thus preventing one country's crisis from spreading worldwide. It makes sense for the world, and the U.S., to help countries in need to address their crises before they spread to the world; addressing crises early is the most efficient and effective approach. Likewise, we need to take responsibility for keeping our homegrown crises at home and not allowing them to spread.

World Crises and Organizations

Of course, once a country's crisis has metastasized into a world crisis, established world organizations, as well as other countries, need to do their best to help resolve it. The following list includes 20 types of global crises that affect all countries:

- Wars
- Terrorism
- Organized crime and gangs
- Human trafficking
- Homicides, violence, security concerns

- Migration and immigration
- Climate change
- Famine
- Drinking water shortage and pollution
- Poverty
- Nuclear weapons and nuclear waste
- International trade
- Ocean health
- Jobs and job skills
- Disease and epidemics
- Technology transformations
- Cybersecurity weakness
- The need for bad government regime change

Fortunately, there are over 20 existing world organizations that could combine their organizations' efforts to use a quality approach and develop inter-organizational process improvements to address the above long list of world crises:

- United Nations (U.N.)
- U.N. International Children's Emergency Fund (UNICEF)
- U.N. World Tourism Organization (UNWTO)
- U.N. Population Fund (UNFPA)
- World Health Organization (WHO)
- World Bank
- World Bank - International Bank for Reconstruction and Development (IBRD)
- World Trade Organization (WTO)
- World Economic Forum (WEF)
- The Group of Seven (G7) (Russia was dropped for invading Crimea)
- Organization for Economic Co-Operation and Development (OECD)
- International Finance Corporation (IFC)
- World Food Program (WFP)
- International Energy Agency (IEA)
- Organization for Security and Co-operation in Europe (OSCE)
- International Development Association (IDA)

- World Intellectual Property Organization (WIPO)
- League of Nations
- International Federation of Red Cross and Red Crescent Societies
- Amnesty International
- World Court

The U.N. could take the lead with this group of world organizations to use a quality approach to analyze these types of crises and determine how improvements in organizational systems could be made to reduce and prevent world crises. With input from all organizations on the list above (and others not identified here) the U.N. could prioritize a list of world crises that need to be addressed, establish Crisis Action Teams (CATs) similar to those suggested earlier in this book, and develop specific plans for reducing world crises. Perhaps they could also identify countries that need help with their crises to keep them contained and avoid having them spread to the world.

Since most other countries in the world also have crises, we could learn from each other to see how to deal with them. Countries with the best successes can provide benchmarks and best practices for others to learn from. America should be willing to ask for help from each of the best benchmark countries on each of our 23 crisis areas.

Applying a quality approach in government is much more difficult and faces more barriers than it does in business. Likewise, applying it to world crises is even more difficult than applying it in a single country. The cooperation and support of all individual countries is necessary for our world organizations to be able to address the world's crises. The U.S. should be a leader in cooperation with support of U.N. efforts to reduce worldwide crises.

We know from Tuchman's historical analysis, *The March of Folly,* that choosing a path of folly for the benefit of a few over a path of reason for the benefit of many is a worldwide problem. In order to address this problem, each country should develop its own improvements to increase the number of decisions made based on reason, and reduce those based on folly.

Democracy and Autocracy

The Middle-East and North African countries with the highest level of democracy are Israel, Jordan, Kuwait, Turkey, Tunisia, Lebanon, and Morocco (Freedom House, n.d.). But, not a single one of the countries that derive most of their export earnings from oil and gas is a democracy. These countries make so much money from their oil reserves, they do not need to tax their citizens: "No taxation without representation" was a political demand; "no representation without taxation" is a political reality (Diamond 2010). Today oil and gas stand in the way of democracy in the Middle-East; but some day in the future, when we can shake our reliance on fossil fuels, that may change.

Today, America supports autocracies that exist in Mid-East countries that have oil and gas revenues. The U.S. also supports those countries' efforts to suppress democracies from emerging in their countries. That American strategy is in part based on the oil, gas, and financial influence of those autocracies on our leaders; it is also based on a fear that democracies in Muslim majority states may elect radical Muslim leaders.

Can Islam be compatible with democracy? Yes, it can be. Millions of the world's 1.4 billion Muslims live in democracies. However, al Qaeda and radical Islamists in the Muslim world are in conflict with democratic ideals, just like white supremacists in the U.S. are in conflict with democratic ideals. Indonesia, with 260 million people, is the 4th most populous nation in the world, and the world's largest Muslim nation (87% Muslim) with a peaceful democracy and the world's 6th largest Gross Domestic Product (GDP). The Indonesian national motto is "Unity in Diversity." Indonesia could be a role model for the 48 Muslim-majority countries in the world, where the majority of citizens actually do favor democracy.

Another approach to governing is Communism which is intended to serve the common good through a socialist (i.e., government-owned businesses) approach to sharing the wealth. Most of the communist countries have found, however, that without a capitalistic (individually owned businesses) approach to motivate hard work and innovation, insufficient wealth is generated. In China, for example, the Chinese leader Deng Xiaoping adopted capitalist reforms in 1978 to stimulate economic growth in his country, which had previously relied on government-owned businesses. China improved their governance system to allow capitalism, which enabled them to generate more economic growth and thus reduce poverty.

While countries like China are adopting changes that benefit their population, our governance system has done the opposite; it has changed to enable more decisions of folly to benefit special interests. These changes have caused multiple crises and the loss of the American Dream.

Over the past 40 years, many countries have changed. Some, like China, have become more capitalistic, others have become more democratic. A Pew Research Center survey assessed the type of government in 167 countries in the world with a population of at least 500,000 in 1976, and then again 40 years later in 2016 (DeSilver 2019). DeSilver's report shows that countries can and do change their approach to governance. The results of these two surveys show a tremendous increase in democracy in the world, with a concomitant decrease in autocracy:

This major shift to democracy followed the economic failure of the communist Soviet Union in 1991. An economic success in China and an economic failure in the U.S. would likely set back this progress in the world's countries' shift to democracy.

Table 8: Nation Government Type Changes

Type of Government	1976	2016
Democracy	24%	58%
Democracy and Autocracy	14%	29%
Autocracy	62%	13%
Total	100%	100%

World Homicide Crisis

The United Nations Office on Drugs and Crime prepared a report on Global Homicide in 2011 and updated it in 2013 (United Nations Office on Drugs and Crime 2019). This study showed that high homicide rates are fueled by other crises such as wars and terrorism, and that high homicide rates cause fear and migration, which lead to immigration crises. This report on the causes of high homicides in the world and the areas in which they exist is simply the first step in the quality approach, which also requires goals for improvement, root causes, recommended improvements, and results measures.

The following provides an example of how the approach proposed in this book could be applied to this worldwide gun violence homicide crisis:

Crisis Definition

A persistently high homicide rate leads to a fearful population who seek to migrate for asylum elsewhere, which leads to immigration crises worldwide.

Research and Data

All the research data used with this crisis example is from the U.N. Global Study on Homicide. While these data are several years old, we can still learn from the root causes identified in this study. In 2012, worldwide, there were 437,000 intentional homicides; this is more deaths than those killed in all the wars in 2012.

A few specific areas, which account for only 11% of the world's population, have had persistently high homicide rates of greater than 20 per 100,000 population. The global average was 6.2 per 100,000 in 2012.

In this example, we will focus on the area with the highest homicide rate in the world, Central America, with a homicide rate of 27 per 100,000, accounts for 36% of all the world's homicides. This homicide crisis has created a fearful population, which has led to mass migration, itself a cause of the U.S. southern border immigration crisis. Therefore, addressing the root causes of this gun violence crisis in Central America could be beneficial to the U.S. and reduce our southern border immigration crisis.

Central America also has a weak rule of law with a homicide conviction rate of only 22% compared to Europe at 80%. The low conviction rate may be a result of the high homicide rate, which causes an overload on enforcement resources. Weak justice effectiveness is a contributor to high homicide rates, which is a bad loop.

Two countries in Central America have even higher homicide rates than the rest of the area. Not surprisingly, those two countries provide the majority of those seeking asylum in the U.S.:

Central America's Worst Homicide Rate Countries
Honduras   90 homicides per 100,000
El Salvador   41 homicides per 100,000

These persistently high homicide rates combined with a consistently weak justice system and inadequate enforcement has created fear and insecurity in the population, which causes migration of those seeking asylum in safer countries.

To help reduce these high homicide rates, the U.N. developed a small arms weapons treaty that many countries have signed, including the U.S., to control and limit the sale of arms to terrorists, organized crime, and gangs (Weisser 2014). However, our President announced at an NRA meeting in April 2019 that he was withdrawing from that global agreement. The NRA, who spent $30 million to help our President get elected in 2016, supports sales of guns.

The U.N. study found that criminals deported from other countries set up crime organizations or gangs in their home country and contribute to the cycle of high homicides, leading to increased fear and migration of people seeking asylum. When America arrests felons and then deports them, setting them free in their home country, we are supporting the cycle of high homicides: increased fear, leading to migration for asylum, leading to an immigration crisis. Between 1996 and 2015, the U.S. deported 5.4 million illegal immigrants; 2.2 million (40%) of those had committed a felony offense. This is a bad loop. We need to ensure criminals are imprisoned in the country that we return them to.

Benchmarks in the world we could learn from include Western Europe with a homicide rate of only 2 per 100,000, and Singapore at only 0.2 per 100,000 in 2012 (Stranger 2012).

Proposed Goal
Reduce the homicide rates in the high area regions (11% of population) to the world average. This goal would support a goal to reduce migration for asylum and reduce the U.S. immigration crisis caused by that migration.

Measures
- Homicide rates
- Homicide conviction rates

Root Causes
- Countries emerging from a war or civil conflict
- Weapons availability
- Organized crime and gangs
- Drugs
- Weak rule of law (i.e., low conviction rates for homicide)
  (United Nations Office on Drugs and Crime 2019)

Possible Improvements
- Help to end wars, and avoid starting them
- Reduce weapons availability; get all countries to sign small arms treaty; have the U.S. rejoin this treaty
- Crack down on organized crime and gangs with a worldwide effort, like we have done with terrorism
- Reduce drug addiction, which is the incentive for criminal supply of drugs
- Help to improve conviction rates for homicide in the high homicide areas to the world average
- Imprison convicted felon immigrants instead of setting them free in their own country. Establish a World Prison Fund to pay for the imprisonment of illegal immigrant felons in the country they came from.

Potential Savings
Reduce homicides in high crime countries from 200,000 homicides by 80% to the world average, saving 160,000 lives per year.

- Reduce the number of refugees in the world by 50% from 16 million in 2017 to 8 million per year. 53% of the refugees are children (Charlton 2017).

- Assuming a cost of $10,000 per year to care for and house refugees, the worldwide host countries are paying $160 billion per year to host refugees. Cutting that cost in half could save $80 billion per year. This type of savings could encourage host countries to fund a U.N. World Prison Fund to imprison arrested felons. It could also encourage host countries to support other efforts to achieve the goals outlined above, including participation in the U.N. weapons sales treaty.

Summary

This chapter suggests that world organizations, and other countries, could also use the quality approach shared here to address worldwide crises and improve their governance systems. World organizations can also use this approach to review world crises and to improve their organization's capability for improvements; however, that can be only done with the support of all countries that are members of the U.N.

Looking inward, America must be more willing to ask for help from other countries that are the benchmarks of performance in each of our 23 crisis areas; this will help us understand how to apply best practices in America to achieve benchmark performance.

Personal Story – World Crises

In May 2018, I went on an amazing 10-day trip with my fiancée to the Holy Land to visit many sites where major religions had their origin.

Before I went on the trip, I used a number of sources to analyze the water pollution crisis affecting the Gaza Strip. I then created a Power Point proposal on how a quality approach could be used to address the Gaza water pollution crisis, which would be more effective and efficient than past efforts. With help from a friend who had recently retired as the U.S. Ambassador to the Vatican, I arranged an appointment to meet with the Catholic Archbishop of Jerusalem to show him my proposal for addressing the Gaza water pollution crisis. After an hour reviewing the proposal, the Archbishop said to me, "That would take a miracle!" I responded, "I believe in miracles, don't you?" He smiled and agreed to arrange contacts with the local U.N. officials responsible for water quality in the Gaza Strip.

That afternoon, I talked to the U.N. officials from both Israel and Gaza, which included a one-hour review of my proposal with the woman who was the U.N. water quality director for Gaza (interview with Iman Al Husseini, May 24, 2018). She said the proposal was the best review of the Gaza water quality crisis that she had seen, and she felt that the Palestinian and Israeli leaders might be ready for a business quality approach to develop a solution. When I left the meeting, she had agreed to move the proposal forward to government leaders to see if it could be considered.

When I returned to the U.S., I read that the Middle-East peace talks were being refocused to take small steps to improve Israeli-Palestinian relations. I thought that addressing the Gaza water pollution crisis might be one of those small steps. However, after several months, and repeated follow-up emails and calls, I had not heard back about progress in getting this proposal to be considered by leaders in Gaza, Palestine, or Israel. This was a significant disappointment particularly after hearing the initial enthusiasm of the local U.N. directors, and U.S. peace efforts to fund infrastructure improvements in Gaza.

Dr. Shira Efron of the Rand Corp. provided the following information on the Gaza water pollution crisis in 2018 (Efron et al. 2018):

- 97% of drinking water is unfit to consume according to international standards

- 26% of all illness is caused by contaminated water

- 12% of child mortality is linked to intestinal illnesses from contaminated water

- 33% of average income goes toward purchase of water compared to 0.7% in the Western world

The U.N. cannot help solve a crisis in any country without the support of the country (or countries) which created the crisis. On 5/7/19, I emailed my U.N. Director contact in Gaza about my concern that current military tensions between Israel and Gaza might be a cause of increased military tensions between the U.S. and Iran. She responded right away, letting me know that another ceasefire had been established that day between Gaza and Israel, and that Israel was showing concern about all the pollution in Gaza that had also begun to pollute neighboring Israeli territories. She also told me that a new Khan Younis Waste Water Treatment Plant (KY-WWTP) was about to be commissioned; however, there was inadequate electricity to operate it as needed, because the electricity blackouts exceed 50% in Gaza. Given seven years of electricity blackouts in Gaza, controlled by Israel, the U.N. is now looking for a donor for a solar energy plant to provide the needed electricity to the KY-WWTP. In addition, three new waste water treatment plants in Gaza also face the same need for a solar power plant to provide electricity to operate as needed.

I believe that a few humanitarian steps, such as having the U.N., Gaza, and Israel address the water pollution crisis in Gaza, could be a good initial step toward Middle-East peace. Unfortunately, the U.N. can only do what the countries involved are willing to support.

Preface for the Second Half of the Book

The second half of this book will use the quality approach steps from the Plan-Do-Check-Act (PDCA) cycle in Chapter 5 to show how possible solutions can be developed for each of 23 U.S. crises. These are "examples" of how to use this approach to reduce the crises. The proposal here is that government, with House CATs established by interested House caucuses, lead an effort to reduce each of our crises, with subject matter experts' help from credible non-profits and research universities that have no conflicts of interest. The House caucuses that appear to be appropriate to address each of the 23 crises are identified at the end of each crisis analysis.

These 23 crises are grouped into six categories: Finance, Worker, Health Care, Environment, Security, and Democracy, each with its own chapter. These crises are not just the responsibility of government; we all have some responsibility for them, and we all can do something about them.

A personal story of my connection to each of these U.S. crises is provided after the last quality step. These personal stories are included to show how a person can be affected by, or possibly can have a small effect on, each of these crises. Hopefully, these stories will encourage the individual citizen involvement needed to help reduce them. We each can only do a small part, but collectively we can have a big impact.

In sharing examples of how to use a quality approach to reduce each crisis, I am not trying to fix every crisis by myself. I am simply trying to provide examples of how this approach can be used to reduce these unresolved crises. This approach would also provide our government with a process to address other crises, and future U.S. crises, as they develop.

The simultaneous occurrence of multiple unresolved crises has led to the failure of government's ability to meet its responsibilities. For example, government is not meeting its infrastructure maintenance responsibilities, its financial responsibilities to limit debt to a responsible level, its responsibility to address the epidemics of gun violence and drug use, its responsibility to help reduce the working poor, and its responsibility to prevent harm to the environment that we all rely on for our lives. Government needs to reduce our U.S. crises to be able to meet its responsibilities, and a quality approach can be used to reduce our crises.

The PDCA cycle planning step, the P step in PDCA, will be used to analyze each crisis with a common approach:

PDCA Cycle Planning Steps

- Crisis name and definition

- Research facts and trends

- Establish goals

- Establish the results measure

- Identify root causes

- Identify improvements and rank order

- Estimated crisis cost

- Estimated potential U.S. cost reduction in 2024 budget

Analyzing each of the crises using a common approach will help with our ability to understand and manage improvement of multiple crises at the same time. If 23 crises were all analyzed with different approaches, it would become difficult and overwhelming for decision makers, because they would be working with apples and oranges, leading back to the current state of affairs: a lack of decisions needed for the common good.

The following table provides a summary of the estimated annual crisis cost for each of the crises analyzed and the total Gross Crisis Cost (GCC) for all 23 U.S. crises. The GCC estimate of $9.1 trillion per year is equal to 42% of the annual U.S. GDP (Gross Domestic Product). The calculations for these GCC estimates are shown with each crisis analysis in the following chapters. There is an enormous annual cost associated with *not* reducing our crises.

Reducing these crises will require the cooperation and support of government, businesses, and citizens. These 23 crises have been divided into two groups in the following table, based on what I believe is the primary responsibility for reducing these crises. Two thirds of these crises appear to be the primary responsibility of government, and one third the primary responsibility of businesses and citizens. However, when we add up the GCC, it appears that the businesses and citizens third of crises account for 57% of the GCC. This grouping shows that this book is *not* just about a need for the government to fix everything. We also need to have help from businesses and citizens to reduce our crises. Instead of pointing the finger at others, we all need to pull together to address the crises that are threatening the future of America.

Table 9: Gross Crisis Cost (GCC) by Primary Responsibility

Crisis Primary Responsibility	2020 Estimated Crisis Cost/year ($ Billions)	Percent
Government		
National Debt	175	
Wall Street and Corporate Debt	80	
Infrastructure Maintenance	200	
Election Campaign	430	
Use of Drugs	1,000	
Cancer Rate	160	
Gun Violence	300	
Land Air and Fresh Water	535	
Oceans	200	
Climate Change	250	
Nuclear Arms and Waste	40	
Cybersecurity	110	
Border Security	-	
Defense Costs	410	
Total	3,890	43%
Business and Citizens		
Trade Balance	891	
Worker Skills	1,000	
Worker's Fair Pay	482	
College Education Debt	75	
Social Media	1,000	
Diabetes	250	
Health Care Costs	1,500	57%
Total Gross Crisis Cost (GCC)	9,088	100%

Many of our crises are also causes of other crises; as each crisis grows, it provides a snowball effect, causing other crises to grow. Likewise, as we begin to reduce each crisis, it will have the beneficial effect of reducing other crises.

While government is primarily responsible for about two thirds of these crises, and can help to reduce all of these crises, the primary responsibility for about a third of the crises, and about 57% of the Gross Crisis Cost, can be assigned to citizens and business.

Businesses need to help reduce our trade deficit, retrain workers for technology shifts, and pay a fair living wage. Businesses also have to help improve health in America by reducing carcinogens in foods and the environment, and reducing sugar in food. Big business has to stop being the drug dealer most responsible for our drug crisis, stop being the most frequent cause of our economic crises, and stop being the primary source of climate warming.

Government has a necessary role in establishing standards (regulations) for big businesses in order to prevent enormous damage to the country. Without reasonable standards, the worst businesses will elect to maximize profits, forcing others competing in that industry to follow. We cannot expect all businesses to do the right thing for the country, because they are required to do the right thing for their stockholders. Business leaders are required to maximize profits, and to follow the patterns set by those who do whatever it takes to maximize their profits. Government also needs to have a plan to achieve a balanced budget and financially responsible debt levels. Government needs to have a plan to reduce all our crises in order to meet government responsibilities.

The Path of Reason is the path that we need government, businesses and citizens to choose in order to reduce our crises. When Thomas Paine wrote *Common Sense* for 18th-Century America, he advocated replacing the king with a democracy to ensure America would be able to make decisions for the common good, not for the rich and powerful.

My book, *A Path of Reason for America*, is common sense for 21st-century America, with essentially the same message as Thomas Paine's in *Common Sense*, advocating a path of reason to make decisions for the common good, not for rich special interests (Paine 2019).

For each of the following chapters, continuous reduction, or elimination, of the root causes is the key to resolving these crises. Currently we lack goals and plans to reduce our crises.

In order to help understand how the approach proposed in this book can be successful, the following is a brief example, using the quality planning steps, of how I helped the state of New Jersey use this approach to address the worst shore water pollution crisis in the United States. This was described in detail in my first book: *The Dolphins are Back – A Successful Quality Model for Healing the Environment* (Scanlan 1998). This successful crisis reduction effort received recognition from both the New Jersey Governor (Christie Whitman) and Department of Environmental Protection (DEP) Director, as well as receiving the Outstanding Achievement Award from the Renewable Natural Resources Foundation (RNRF), a national non-profit.

Jersey Shore Crisis Definition

The shore tourism sector is the largest economic sector in New Jersey's (NJ) economy and the Jersey Shore is the main attraction in the state of New Jersey. In 1988, Jersey Shore beaches had to be closed to swimming due to pollution that was so severe it killed half the bottle-nosed dolphins in the U.S. Atlantic Ocean (2,500 of 5,000). This shore pollution crisis then caused a Jersey Shore tourism economic crisis.

Jersey Shore Research

The Health Departments of the five counties along the Jersey Shore monitored the water fecal coliform count, which is an indicator of potential bacteria and virus. These data were analyzed to determine the location, by town, of the Jersey shore pollution problems. However, there was no agreed-upon corrective action plan when pollution was found. The response to the pollution problem was simply to put up a "beach closed" sign, not to find and correct the root cause.

A major part of the problem was from Asbury Park, NJ, in Monmouth County, where a sewage treatment plant had broken down, and the bankrupt town could not afford the repairs. The state sued the town for shore water pollution violations, but the town didn't have the money to fix the sewage treatment plant nor the money to pay fines. This was the same Asbury Park that was used as an album title by Bruce Springsteen in 1973 for *Greetings from Asbury Park,* the number one hit from that album was *Blinded by the Light.* It seems from analysis of our crises that we more frequently get blinded by the money.

Pollution sources were also identified from many Jersey towns' sewage pipe systems that were broken and leaking sewage into the storm drain pipes that flow to the ocean. A lack of town sewage infrastructure maintenance, and a lack of identification and repair of leaks after beach pollution, were also root causes of the Jersey Shore pollution crisis.

A number of types of visible sources of beach litter were being washed up on the beaches. This beach litter was more visible than the water pollution, and some initially incorrectly blamed the sources of this litter for the Jersey shore water pollution crisis. A focus on the visible litter, and blame of others for the crisis, interfered with action needed to address the actual root causes of the water pollution. The litter needed to be addressed, but it was not the root cause of the water pollution crisis.

The water pollution was not just a crisis for humans and municipal budgets, dolphins were dying all along the shore. Dolphins are not fish; they are mammals just like we are. Several pathology examinations of dead dolphins revealed a number of possible causes of death.

The first study showed that half the dolphins' livers contained a poisonous toxin from red tide algae. Red tide is caused by algae blooms of millions of toxic dinoflagellates (a parasitic division of algae that eats its prey from the inside) that cause coloration of the water. These red tide blooms can kill massive numbers of marine mammals and fish, leaving a beach covered with foul-smelling fish and marine mammals. It can also poison humans who eat contaminated shellfish. The toxic algae blooms are caused by fertilizer runoff from yards and farms, as well as from sewage leaks into the water. Warmer waters also contribute to the formation of these toxic algae blooms. It was determined the level of red tide poison did not kill the dolphins; however, it could have contributed to a reduced immune system in the dolphins.

A second study found the dolphins had significant doses of tributyl-tin (TBT), a chemical added to marine boat paint to reduce barnacles; later that paint chemical was found to be toxic and suppressed the immune system of the dolphins. Use of this chemical on boats smaller than 82 feet in length was banned in 1988 to reduce marine life exposure to this toxic chemical.

A third study found a virus, which also caused immune system suppression, made the dolphins vulnerable to bacterial infection. The virus and bacteria were contained in sewage allowed into the Jersey Shore from inadequately maintained sewage infrastructure. So, it was the combination of the virus and the bacteria that killed the dolphins. The bacteria gave them pneumonia which their weakened immune systems could not fight.

Jersey Shore Goal

We surveyed Jersey beach-goers to find the goal they wanted for beach pollution closures, and 100% of those surveyed said they wanted zero beach closures due to pollution. There was no measurable goal for improvement, so this was an important citizen-driven goal for the multiple government organizations involved, who all accepted this citizen-driven goal as our team goal.

Results Measure

We decided we needed a specific measure that could be easily understood by all involved. We settled on beach-block-closing days, which counts the number of days that each block of a beach is closed during the summer swimming season of each year. In 1988, there were 803 beach-block-closing days along the 141 miles of the Jersey shore, which encompasses 5 counties and 44 beach towns. We reported, and published, the annual results for the state, each county, and each town.

By 1995, the Jersey Shore ocean beach-block-closings had been reduced from 803 to 4, a 99.5% improvement, thanks to a team of government organizations using a quality improvement approach that was driven by a goal, identified root causes, and implemented effective and efficient improvements as soon as possible.

Root Causes

The visible beach litter included trash from New York City barges used to haul trash to an island landfill. People were quick to blame our northern New York City neighbor for the Jersey Shore pollution problem, based on this visible beach evidence. However, the beaches were closed due to water pollution problems that were not caused by our neighbor.

The virus and bacteria were primarily from sewage being released into the Jersey shore water from inadequately maintained sewage infrastructure along the Jersey shoreline. That infrastructure was primarily the responsibility of the 44 towns along the Jersey shore.

Improvements

The state of NJ dropped the legal suit against Asbury Park and instead moved to help the bankrupt town fund repair of their sewage treatment plant, in order to help restore the Jersey Shore water quality for the common good. Each shore county led an effort to encourage towns to act on the county Health Department water pollution findings. Actions were to have immediate (within 24 hours) identification and repair of the source of sewage leakage causing beach water pollution.

I was able to use the AT&T fiber-optic and switching network as a benchmark model for the Jersey shore sewage pipe and treatment plant network. When AT&T has a failure in our network, we fix it as soon as possible, because service is poor and money is lost with outages. We convinced the Jersey shore counties and towns to use that model of fixing breaks in their sewage network as soon as possible, instead of allowing leaks to continue for months and years.

Each shore town accepted its responsibility to identify the source and repair sewage pipe cracks and leaks within 24 hours following a County Department of Health report of a shore pollution measure.

Sources of beach litter were contacted, and when they were requested to implement improvements to reduce beach litter, they accepted responsibility to do so. All involved accepted their responsibility as part of a team, in order to help meet the team improvement goal.

Cost Savings and Benefits

A significant benefit of improving the Jersey Shore was the recovery of the shore tourism economy, which had dropped by 50% from 1988 to 1989, the year after the beach pollution crisis. The Jersey Shore tourism economy was the largest economic business sector in the state of New Jersey.

A secondary benefit was a savings in city sewage treatment costs. The broken sewage and storm-water pipes, which run side by side, were a cause of sewage flowing into the storm-water pipes and then polluting the shore beaches. In addition, the storm water flowed into the sewage pipes and then to the sewage treatment plants. Unnecessary treatment of this storm water was costing just one Jersey town $1 million per year.

New Jersey moved from having the worst beach water quality, of 30 U.S. states with an ocean, gulf, or Great Lakes shoreline, to among the top two or three states, and has retained that position for the past 25 years.

Recognition and Replication

Recognition awards were given to the county health department directors, town mayors, and the town directors of public works who achieved zero beach closings in the prior year. Replication of successful best practice efforts by leading counties and towns was also encouraged through direct contact with each of the 44 shore towns.

Some of those receiving recognition for their improvement efforts said it was the first time in a 30-year career they had ever received recognition for improvement. Those individuals became our best advocates for replication of best practices. My first book, *The Dolphins are Back,* was written to share this success story, the quality approach used, and the best practices used with the other 29 U.S. states that have an ocean, gulf, or Great Lakes beach shoreline.

I also helped lead a broader NJ effort to help application of quality approaches in Education, Health Care and small businesses through a non-profit, Quality New Jersey. An annual Quality New Jersey (QNJ) conference was held to share and recognize success on this shore project as well as other improvement projects supported by QNJ.

Analysis of current U.S. crises

In analyzing the 23 U.S. crises in the second half of this book, I was surprised at how appalling the U.S. results are compared to benchmarks from other countries. I was equally surprised at how many no-cost or low-cost best practices that could be used to reduce these U.S. crises are being ignored. 74% of the possible 172 improvements shown for the 23 crises in Chapters 7 to 12 are no-cost or low-cost to the federal government; however, they are not being implemented to reduce our very expensive crises. In spite of the severe negative impact of our multiple crises, there is strong resistance to any change in the current system; even going so far as to oppose implementation of no-cost and low-cost improvements. Instead, special interests continue to be supported while the common good is ignored. In my lifetime, America has never faced such a severe combination of crises:

Finance
The U.S. debt-to-GDP ratio has never been so high for such a long period at financially irresponsible levels

Worker
America's number of working poor has more than doubled since 1980

Health
Americans have never had such poor health with such a high cost of health care

Environment
America has never faced such potentially disastrous effects and costs from increasing hurricanes, forest fires, and sea level rise along the coasts

Defense
America has never been more vulnerable as a result of weak cybersecurity, and America has never had such unaffordable defense costs

Democracy
Our democracy has been changed to serve special interests as a priority over Americans' interests. Our election process has been corrupted by money, special interests, political parties, and foreign interests. Our

political parties have become so divisive, they cannot work together to solve our crises.

Each of the above categories of crises could be disastrous for America; collectively they have brought us to the brink of disaster. Yet there is no plan to deal with any of them. There is no plan because some of those in power want to keep the system that serves special interests in place.

President Trump attracted enough citizen support to be elected President in 2016 by simply admitting America had a crisis. By using the slogan "Make America Great Again," he was not only admitting that America was not great now, he was also saying what no other politician had dared to say. Many citizens agreed with his assessment that America had lost its greatness, and they elected a businessman to fix that. Without a specific plan, candidate Trump claimed he could use his business experience to solve America's crises. A lot of people, enough to elect him, hoped that would be the case.

Unfortunately, President Trump's management approach in government has been to blame others for U.S. crises rather than address their root causes. After more than two years in office, our multiple crises have gotten worse, not better; and America is moving closer to bankruptcy, with increasing debt and no plans to address the debt crisis.

Summary

The analyses of the 23 crises in the following chapters provide a number of insights into why these crises have collectively caused a loss of hope in the future of America:

- Multiple crises are collectively causing a disastrous impact on Americans, and the future of America.

- The annual cost of these crises to the U.S. is about 42% of the national GDP, and it is increasing.
- The U.S. lacks goals and plans to address these multiple crises.

- Most of these crises are also causes of other crises, which causes a snowball effect, thus increasing all these crises and their costs.

- One of the reasons we have so many crises is poor performance in most of our crisis areas. This poor performance is clear when we compare it to performance in leading countries. We need to learn from the best to compete effectively.

- 77% of the root causes of our crises are with U.S. government and U.S. businesses, 15% with U.S. citizens, and only 8% with foreign countries. We can't just blame others.

- Blaming others for our crises is a distraction from admitting the real cause of our crises; it is also an excuse to not take the necessary actions to address the root causes of our crises.

- The U.S. needs agreed-to, long-term goals to improve; goals to be equal to the best, with annual improvement objectives to achieve the long-term goals.

- The U.S. needs to be willing to implement proven best practices quickly and encourage continuous improvement.

- Known no-cost and low-cost improvements need to be implemented quickly to make a reduction in our crises.

- Government must work with the research universities and credible non-profits that are working on each of these crisis areas, to enlist their help in determining root causes and suggesting improvement opportunities.

- We must reverse the 130 decisions of folly that have contributed to the creation of our crises, and we need to stop making decisions of folly.

- We need government, business, workers, research universities, non-profits, and citizens to work together to address the root causes of U.S. crises, and to take advantage of all the opportunities for improvement.

- President Trump is not responsible for the creation of our U.S. crises; however, he has not helped to resolve them as promised.

Changing who is in office is insufficient to reduce our crises; we need to implement an improvement approach throughout government.

- Government costs must be reduced while improving results, as is done by excellent companies.

- U.S. business sectors need to help with improvements to reduce our crises.

- Business leaders need to help develop plans to reduce the worker crises in America.

- U.S. citizens need to learn more, work harder, and live healthier lives.

- It is possible to reduce all these crises while moving toward a balanced budget. It will work if leaders decide to use a quality approach to improvement.

- Bipartisan support is needed for all the above.

The following lyrics to the song *I am Willing*, written by Holly Near, are applicable here because many are hurting from our multiple crises, but to be hopeless would dishonor those who came before us. We do need help from our children and from our elders. America can't be hopeless about the change needed to deal with the crises being faced; America needs to be hopeful and *willing to change.*

I Am Willing

I am open and I am willing
To be hopeless would seem so strange
It dishonors those who go before us
So lift me up to the light of change

There is hurting in my family
There is sorrow in my town
There is panic in the nation
There is wailing the whole world round

May the children see more clearly
May the elders be more wise
May the winds of change caress us
Even though it burns our eyes

Give me a mighty oak to hold my confusion
Give me a desert to hold my fears
Give me a sunset to hold my wonder
Give me an ocean to hold my tears
(Near, n.d.)

Chapter 7: FINANCIAL CRISES

We have seen the Soviet Union (now Russia) and Greece fail as a result of financial mismanagement, and Venezuela is currently facing a financial disaster. These failures result from an inability of these countries to make debt payments. If a country defaults on payment of existing debt, it becomes extremely difficult, and much more expensive, to continue borrowing. Defaulting on debt results in a crisis, because it leads to a country's inability to meet the many other responsibilities of government. At one time, big commercial banks assumed countries would always repay their debts; however, after countries in Latin America and Africa defaulted on their loans, that assumption has vanished.

The U.S. has suffered through disasters caused by the 2008 Great Recession and has increased our debt for over a decade to help recover from that economic recession. A focus on military strength while on a path toward financial weakness has been the cause of failure for other countries (e.g., the Soviet Union) and it could be for us unless our financial crises are resolved. Financial failure prevents a country from addressing their remaining crises.

Currently, the U.S. cannot meet the financial standards required to qualify as an EU country member (Schneeweiss 2019). In addition, the U.S. lacks a plan to try to meet this minimum financial responsibility criterion. Today, due to annual deficits and accumulated debt, our financial position is weak, and there is no goal or a plan to attain a financially responsible position.

The Financial Crises include:

Our National Debt is out of control, with no plan to get it under control. This is the crisis that causes a government to be unable to meet its other responsibilities; this is a failure of government. America is already in that position.

Corporate Debt and Wall Street speculation created the 2008 Great Recession, and America appears to be in that position, again. Our trade balance deficit reduces job opportunities and quality of life, and America is already in that position. According to Jared Diamond in his book *Collapse,* continued reduction of quality of life is an indication of a country's collapse (Diamond 2006).

Our infrastructure maintenance backlog is a signal that the U.S. is already unable to meet its government responsibilities to maintain its infrastructure.

Each of these four financial crises will be analyzed using a quality planning approach to develop improvements that will allow us to resolve these crises. These analyses are provided as an *example* for a systemic government improvement approach to resolve U.S. crises.

National Debt Crisis

Definition:
The federal national debt is enormous, financially irresponsible, and increasing without control. In less than 20 years, the federal debt has increased from $5.8 trillion in 2000 to $22.7 trillion in 2019, which is a 290% increase with no plan to reduce it. The financially responsible level of debt-to-GDP ratio, required of all EU countries, is 60% or less. In 2000, the U.S. debt-to-GDP ratio was at a responsible level of 55%. Over this same period, the debt-to-GDP ratio for the U.S. has almost doubled to 108%, with no plans to improve.

We have measured our country's economy by focusing on the Gross Domestic Product (GDP) and unemployment rate. The goal for GDP is set at about 3% growth per year, and the goal for the unemployment rate is not more than 4% of the workforce. When both of those are met, some claim the economy is great. However, GDP is simply a measure of the country's spending, so these two measures at a family level would be like saying, "I still have a job and our spending is up — so our finances are good."

GDP and unemployment are good measures, but they are insufficient. We also need to know if we are spending more than our income. We need to know if we have too much debt and if so, how we are going to reduce it. We need to know how we are going to pay for expected future costs such as maintenance and replacement of our car, maintenance of our home, college costs for children, and retirement savings. When we see the debt-to-GDP ratio for our country is well above 60% and increasing, we should understand that our country's economy is not robust; it is weak. When we understand that the country is not maintaining our infrastructure, we should understand our country's economy is not booming. When we see there is no plan to stop spending more than our income, we should understand our country's economy is not prospering.

Research data and trends:
Based on a number of analyses of our national debt crisis, it is clear the U.S. cannot continue to increase its debt; but continuing to increase the debt is the current plan. We are living on a credit card and just paying the minimum due; that is, we are just paying interest due and nothing on the outstanding balance that we keep increasing. As a result of not paying any of the balance while continuing to borrow, the interest payments are a rapidly growing portion of our total annual budget. As annual debt interest payments grow, there are fewer funds available for other needed areas (Committee for a Responsible Federal Budget 2018).

The government has been ignoring our national debt crisis, but addressing it is central to being able to address our overall U.S. crises situation, and to avoid a national debt default like a few other countries have done.

The national debt has grown so high due to several other U.S. crises:

- 2008 Financial Wall Street crisis and Recession recovery costs

- The military costs crisis

- The health care costs crisis

- The election campaign crisis

To address the national debt crisis, the U.S. needs to address these other crises that are contributing causes of the high national debt. Our high debt inhibits our financial ability to address several other crises, such as:

- College debt

- Infrastructure maintenance

- Worker skills

- Health care coverage

- Environment damage

An important measure of the debt is the debt-to-GDP ratio. Investopedia.com reports that debt-to-GDP ratio is an indicator of a country's ability to pay back its debts. While it is recognized that to fund a war or recession recovery, the debt-to-GDP ratio may have to exceed 60% for a year or two, it is also recognized that maintaining a high debt-to-GDP ratio for an extended period is financially irresponsible. A study by the World Bank found that if the debt-to-GDP ratio of a country exceeds 77% for an extended period of time, it causes a significant slowing of economic (GDP) growth (Caner et al. 2010).

As of 2019, the U.S. has had a debt-to-GDP ratio of higher than 77% for a decade, with no plan to return to a financially responsible level. At a time of "full employment" economy, the 2018 tax cuts were predicted to increase the U.S. GDP growth; however, they were funded by further increasing the debt due to a loss of tax revenue and no substantial reinvestment in capital expansion. In July 2019, many economists were predicting the 2019 U.S. GDP growth to be 2.3%, a decline from 2.9% growth in 2018 (Torry 2019). It appears the World Bank and the EU both know something about economics that the U.S. has yet to learn; excessive debt is detrimental to the economy and GDP.

For a country to be financially responsible, their national debt should be kept to 60%, or less, of the annual GDP. For example, to become a member of the European Union (EU), a country has to have a debt-to-GDP ratio of 60% or less. If one country of the 28 European Union countries has a debt-to-GDP ratio that exceeds 60%, they must have a 5-year plan to reduce their debt ratio to achieve 60%; that reduction plan needs to reduce the debt exceeding the 60% level by at least 5% per year. The U.S. is at 108% and lacks a plan to reduce that debt ratio.

The EU was formed in 1951 by 6 countries as a means to strengthen their collective competitiveness in the world. This change allowed them to deal effectively with an increasingly competitive world. For the past dozen years, the EU has had a positive trade balance, while the U.S. has had a significant **negative** trade balance. The EU country partnership has worked; they did not blame China's improved performance for their problems, instead they took action to save their economies.

Both China (with the introduction of limited capitalism) and Europe (with the creation of the European Union) have made major governance changes to compete more effectively in today's very competitive world; however, the U.S. has made no such change to improve our ability to adapt to this more competitive world. Instead we are borrowing from others to survive, which has led to a diminished quality of life.

America has not yet made the changes needed to deal with an increasingly competitive world. Instead we have been busy making changes to serve special interests; as a result, we have developed multiple crises that collectively have caused a loss of hope for the future of America. Instead of making the changes necessary to help the many affected by an increasingly competitive world, America has increasingly focused on making changes to help a few profit at the expense of many.

The EU debt-to-GDP ratio can provide a benchmark. However, when we look at a benchmark, we are not trying to compare countries to determine whether other countries are better than America. Instead, benchmarks are useful for finding the best results for a particular situation and the best practices to achieve the best results. This is a good way to learn, and possibly improve, in areas where we need to do better. We do not need to get defensive and say, "America is better than all other countries, so we don't need to be like them."

Before we can move forward in addressing our 23 crises, we must admit that our crises exist and are getting worse. Part of that process is to recognize that we are not the gold standard for the world in many areas. We must use the best practices to obtain best results; we need to set our goals for improvement of each crisis using the best practices in our improvement list. One example of a best practice is limiting a country's debt-to-GDP ratio to no more than 60%, in order to be financially responsible and avoid the risks of major financial crises. The U.S. should use that benchmark when setting its financial goals; unfortunately, the U.S. has no financial goals. Requiring a plan to reduce to a 60% debt-to-GDP ratio over time is a best practice of how to achieve a financial goal.

The debt history of our nation shows that we have been financially responsible for most of our history; this unique extended debt mess came about in just the past 20 years. The "U.S. Debt-to-GDP Ratio History," with the causes of changes over time, is shown in the following table (Amadeo 2019).

Table 10: U.S. Debt-to-GDP Ratio History

Year	U.S Debt to GDP Ratio	Cause of Change
1935	39%	
1940	50%	
1945	114%	WWII costs and recession afterwards
1950	89%	
1955	65%	Korean War costs and recession
1960	53%	
1965	43%	
1970	35%	Fed. Reserve raised interest rates
1975	32%	
1980	32%	
1985	42%	Reagan budget increases
1990	54%	Bush Desert Storm military action
1995	65%	
2000	55%	Clinton budget controls
2002	57%	
2004	60%	
2005	60%	**Offensive War on Iraq creating ISIS**
2008	68%	**Wall St. crises and bank bailouts**
2009	83%	**Great Recession & Economic Stimulus**
2010	90%	**Low interest rates War on Terror**
2012	99%	
2015	99%	**Continued War on Terror**
2016	104%	
2017	103%	
2018	99%	
2019 Est.	108%	**2018 Corporate Tax cuts**

The U.S. debt-to-GDP ratio table shows that while there were crisis-driven peaks, the ratio returned to responsible levels until the 2008 Wall St. crisis and Wall St. bailout. Since the 2008 economic crisis, we have drifted up into financially irresponsible levels with no plan to return to responsible levels. This is the first time in America's history that we have had a decade-long debt financial crisis without a plan to address it.

The table above also shows the triggers for this financial crisis:

- The 2003 U.S. offensive invasion of Iraq, in violation of international laws, based on unreliable intelligence information

- Wall St. speculation that caused the 2008 economic crisis

- The costly recovery from the Wall Street-caused Great Recession

- The maintenance of very low interest rates to enable the recovery

- The costly war on terrorism that resulted from the U.S. initiated war on Iraq

- The 2018 tax cuts for Corporate America with no offsetting cost cuts or other tax increases

- Lack of a plan to meet financially responsible debt criteria

This list includes decisions of folly that drove the U.S. into this financial morass. This financial debt crisis, without a plan to address it, is a major reason why surveys of Americans show they have lost hope in the future of America. America can't afford to meet its government responsibilities.

America's current plan seems to be to muddle along by relying on the hope that our past economic strength will provide continued faith in America as a "safe haven" for investment, which then enables us to continue with deficit budgets. However, as we destroy our economic strength, we are eroding faith in America as a "safe haven." The current plan is to move from an irresponsible debt-to-GDP ratio of 108% to a disastrous ratio of 131%, which will lead to loss of faith in America as a "safe haven." We need a plan to return to a responsible debt-to-GDP ratio of 60% to justify our "safe haven" status. Once we lose that "safe haven" status, we will have to face another Great Recession, or worse.

Reuters has reported that all the advanced economies of the world, except for the U.S., have a 5-year plan to reduce their debt-to-GDP ratio. Benchmarks for responsible financial management exist with accompanying best practices. Setting a goal to have a 60% debt-to-GDP ratio and having a plan to reach that goal are two of those best practices.

The U.S. debt is increasing because the U.S. continues to authorize an annual budget deficit. Our national debt hit $22 trillion on 2/11/19 (Chappell 2019), and according to the FY20 Federal Budget, the debt at the end of 2019 is forecast to be $22.7 trillion (Richter 2019). This would put the debt-to-GDP ratio at 108% ($22.7 T/$21.1 T = 108%) for 2019. The current administration has asked for a 2020 budget that included another deficit increase, to over $1 trillion per year.

In the two years from FY 2017 to FY 2019, the U.S. budget deficit increased from $665 billion to $984 billion, a 48% increase. In his election campaign, President Trump promised to reduce both the annual deficit and the national debt. He has not done either; both the deficit and debt have skyrocketed upward, with no plan to reduce either. The Congressional Budget Office has projected the U.S. debt will be over $25 trillion in 2021, and will reach $33 trillion in 2028 (Congressional Budget Office 2019). That will put our debt-to-GDP ratio at 131%. We need a plan to reduce the debt-to-GDP ratio, not a plan to increase it. The processes and results for U.S. financial responsibility are out of control, and there is no plan to get them back under control.

Let's look at a comparison between the U.S. and China using data from Trading Economics, an online platform that provides historical data, economic forecasts, and trading information for 196 countries in the world. China's debt in 2017 was $5.2 trillion, and China's debt-to-GDP ratio was 48%, up from 34% in 2010. China has a 10-year plan to maintain their debt-to-GDP ratio (Trading Economics, n.d.). With the U.S. debt-to-GDP ratio at 108% and China's at 48%, China is in a much stronger financial position. The trade balance is also substantially in China's favor, because China has a huge trade surplus and the U.S. has a huge trade deficit. China's GDP growth rate is also substantially greater than the U.S.

This financial crisis has become the focus of attention for many non-profits who have blown the whistle on our economic disaster. For example, a Keiser Report states, "Trump's economy is not booming; it is blowing up a debt bubble that will burst" (Keiser Report 2018). The Cato Institute sees the U.S. headed for the type of economic crisis Greece currently faces. The Peter G. Peterson Foundation is also working to find fiscal solutions to our financial crisis that will put the U.S. on a sustainable financial path (Peterson, n.d).

Stock market reports also suggest a financial problem. At the end of 2018, both the Dow Jones and S&P 500 indices were down about 6% for the year. 2018 was the worst stock market year since the 2008 Great Recession. 2018 is also the first full year that reflects the results of the current administration's economic policies.

The U.S. GDP growth averaged 1.7% per year over the period 2006 to 2018; it never reached 3% per year during any year in that period (Amadeo 2019). In the second full year of the current administration, GDP growth is projected to decline from the 2.9% growth rate in 2018 to 2.3% in 2019. We cannot rely on GDP growth to reduce our enormous budget deficit and debt; we need to do the hard work of reducing government costs while also improving government performance.

To understand the budget factors that contribute to our deficit and debt, we need to take a look at both expenses and revenues in the U.S. 2019 budget. To eliminate the deficit, we must decrease government costs and increase revenues. The current policy in Washington is to do the opposite: increase costs and decrease revenues.

2019 Budgeted Expenses ($4.407 trillion)

The 2019 U.S. Federal Budget for expenditures is $4.407 trillion, while anticipated revenues are $3.422 trillion, creating a $985 billion deficit (Carter 2018).

Where does our tax money go?

The largest percentage of the 2019 Expense Budget, 24% ($1.06 trillion), is paid to those on Social Security. The Social Security payroll tax was established to ensure citizens would have some money for retirement.

Unfortunately, the government borrowed people's savings and spent the money on other things. This misuse of taxes designated for a special purpose is a type of decision of folly that has been repeatedly made by our U.S. government, contributing to our debt crisis.

As of 1/1/18, the U.S. government had borrowed $2.8 trillion from the Social Security savings account, which is more than 10% of the $22 trillion national debt. The government also borrowed from retirement savings accounts for government and military workers, adding another $1.8 trillion to the U.S. debt. These retirement programs depend on a responsible approach to financial management of the trust funds set up with citizen-funded retirement taxes. Unfortunately, the U.S. does not have a financially responsible approach to dealing with retirement trust funds, leaving citizens unable to count on having the money they paid in specific taxes for their retirement, this money was legally taken from them and their employer, throughout their working life.

The Social Security law requires the fund to buy U.S. Treasury notes, which in effect requires the Social Security fund to loan all employees' and employers' Social Security payroll taxes to the U.S. government at a very low interest rate. Unfortunately, that loan repayment and the interest on it must be repaid by the government, which can only be done through additional taxes, or additional debt, either of which must then be paid for by taxpayers. In other words, the government is borrowing and spending our dedicated Social Security taxes, and the only way to repay them is to tax us again. That is not a good plan.

Obviously, this needs to stop. Social Security needs to stop loaning our retirement funds to the government and start investing them in real investments, like an S&P 500 index fund, which Warren Buffet says is the best investment available. Between 1990 and 2019, the S&P Index has increased from $334 to $2,779, which is an increase of more than 800%. If the Social Security fund had invested $4.6 trillion (the amount they loaned to the government from Social Security and other government retirement funds by buying government bonds) in an S&P index in 1990, that $4.6 trillion would now be a $38.2 trillion government asset (the S&P index growth of over 800%), instead of a $4.6 trillion government debt. Not only would that have been enough to take care of retirement payments without future cuts, it would also have been more than enough to improve health care coverage for all.

Laws prevent the business community from using business retirement fund accounts for their business operations. Business leaders who have done so have been convicted and sent to jail. Those same laws should apply to government officials.

Governmental borrowing from the retirement funds is not the only problem retirees face. Even if the U.S. could repay the trillions owed to the retirement trust funds, the Social Security Trust Funds Board of Trustees estimates that the trust funds will be depleted by 2036 due to the decrease in the worker-to-retiree ratio in the U.S. as America ages. Unfortunately, as Americans continue to live longer, there are fewer workers paying into Social Security, and more retirees are drawing on the fund. Starting in 2036, there will be no funds remaining in the trust funds. At that point, using only payroll taxes will only be able to cover 77% of the benefits promised to retirees.

In order to build up our Social Security system, America needs more workers. This should be a key in our immigration policy. The Trump administration policy is to reduce legal immigration at a time when we need more workers, in order to secure a safe retirement for all.

Not only have Social Security funds been spent, not only do we not have enough workers paying into the system, but the cap set on contributions is unfair to workers at the lower end of the wage scale. Currently, individual Social Security payroll taxes are only taken from the first $132,900 of a worker's salary. Thus, workers earning $132,900 or less per year pay the full 6.2% tax on 100% of their income, which is matched by their employer. However, those earning over $1,000,000 per year pay Social Security taxes on only the first $132,900. Since workers' benefits are determined by the amount they have paid in, those at the lower end of the wage scale, who have paid a high proportion of their salary into the system, receive lower benefits.

The next biggest item in the budget: 15% of the 2019 Expense Budget ($661 billion) goes to the Department of Defense. This is more than twice the amount spent by China, the country with the next largest defense budget. To fund our annual budget deficit by borrowing money from countries like China not only puts us in a weak economic position, but also puts us in a weak defense position, because China could refuse to loan us money at any time. The defense budget consumes almost 20%

of our federal revenues, while China spends less than 5% of their country's revenues on defense.

A close second to the Defense Budget is Medicare, which consumes 14% of the 2019 Expense Budget ($617 billion). Medicare payroll taxes and user insurance payments pay for a significant portion of Medicare costs; however, a portion is paid for from the general funds. Because a large part of Medicare is paid for from Medicare payroll taxes and user insurance payments, Medicare contributes less to our budget deficit than many other programs.

Following Medicare is Medicaid at 9% of the 2019 Budget ($407 billion). Since there is no Medicaid tax, all Medicaid costs are paid from the general fund. Thus, Medicaid is a significant contributor to our budget deficit.

The fifth highest budget category, a significant 8% of the 2019 Budget ($353 billion), goes to the interest payments on the national debt. This is paid from the general tax fund. No services are received from this payment; it is an obligation due from past deficit spending. Interest debt is a major contributor to our budget deficit.

With a $22.7 trillion debt, the $353 billion in interest indicates the U.S. is only paying a 1.6% interest rate on that debt. However, in 2019, the interest payments on the debt are responsible for 36% of the total annual deficit ($353B interest/$985B deficit = 36%). If the debt interest rate increases in the future, the debt interest payments would go up significantly. This is particularly frightening when we are paying interest to China who could raise interest rates at any time. The current administration's escalating confrontational tactics with China could cause an interest rate hike. That is another reason the debt needs to be reduced as soon as possible.

2019 Budget Income ($3.4 trillion)

49% of the 2019 Income ($1.6 trillion) comes from Federal income taxes on individuals.

36% of the 2019 Income ($1.2 trillion) comes from Social Security, Medicare, and other payroll-specific taxes to fund those specific programs.

7% of the 2019 income ($240 billion) comes from corporate taxes. This may appear to be a relatively small contribution from business; however, in countries worldwide, the average corporate taxes have been cut in half to deal with increasing global competition. The U.S. lacks a plan for how to offset this loss of corporate tax revenue.

2% of the 2019 income ($68 billion) comes from excise taxes (e.g., cigarettes and alcohol).

2% of the 2019 income ($68 billion) comes from estate taxes and other miscellaneous taxes.

A nation that has to borrow $1 trillion a year to survive, and has a debt-to-GDP ratio of over 100%, is one of the most economically weak nations in the world. The U.S. is now in the position of needing to rely on other nations, some of which are our adversaries, to fund our annual budget deficits, our debt interest payments, our very high military budgets, and tax cuts for corporations.

Short-term thinking has led to ignoring this long-term debt crisis. The longer we wait to address this crisis, the more onerous the solution will be. If the Federal government operated with a balanced budget, like other levels of government, this crisis would not exist. Balancing our budget will require both cost reductions and revenue increases for a number of years. To get out of this U.S. debt crisis, we need a long-term plan to balance the budget and reduce our debt-to-GDP ratio.

As a reminder, we did have a balanced budget (we even had a surplus, because expenditures were less than revenues) before 2001 under the Clinton administration, and that was done while protecting the environment and growing jobs:

Table 11: Past Surpluses in the Federal Budget

Year	Budget Surplus	Jobs Created
1998	$ 69 billion	3.04 million
1999	$129 billion	3.18 million
2000	$236 billion	1.98 million

We have done better, and we can do better.

Proposal for Balanced Budget and 60% Debt-to-GDP Ratio

A plan to balance the U.S. Federal Budget, achieving a zero deficit by 2025, could be to simply reduce costs by 2% per year. A business in financial trouble would undertake at least a 2% per year cost reduction to return to a position of financial responsibility and sustainability. This could be considered a 2 + 2 budget plan (2% cost reduction and 2% revenue increase per year) to achieve a balanced budget by 2025; if the plan were continued, it could also achieve a debt-to-GDP ratio of 60% by 2035. The 2% revenue increase would come from a 2% GDP growth rate, which is our current rate. I think it may help to see how that can work year by year in the following 2 + 2 Balanced Budget table:
(T = Trillion Dollars and B = Billion Dollars in the following table.)

Table 12: 2 + 2 Balanced Budget Plan

(2% per year reduction in budget costs and 2% per year increase in budget revenues)

Date	Budget Costs	Budget Revenues	Budget Deficit	National Debt	1.6% Rate Debt Interest	GDP	Debt to GDP
	($ T)	($ T)	($ B)	($ B)	($ T)	(%)	($ T)
2017	3.982	3.316	666	20.2	297	19.4	104
2018	4.112	3.333	779	22.0	371	20.7	99
2019	4.407	3.422	985	22.7	363	21.1	108
2020	4.319	3.490	829	23.5	376	21.5	109
2021	4.232	3.560	672	24.2	387	22.0	110
2022	4.148	3.631	517	24.7	395	22.4	110
2023	4.065	3.704	361	25.1	401	22.8	110
2024	3.984	3.778	206	25.3	404	23.3	109
2025	**3.904**	**3.854**	**(50)**	**25.2**	**403**	**23.7**	**106**
2026	3.826	3.931	(105)	25.1	401	24.2	104
2027	3.750	4.010	(260)	24.8	396	24.7	100
2028	3.675	4.090	(415)	24.4	390	25.2	97
2029	3.601	4.172	(571)	23.8	380	25.7	92
2030	3.529	4.255	(726)	23.1	369	26.2	88
2031	3.458	4.350	(892)	22.2	355	26.7	83
2032	3.389	4.427	(1000)	21.2	339	27.3	77
2033	3.321	4.516	(1200)	20.0	320	27.8	72
2034	3.255	4.606	(1400)	18.6	298	28.4	65
2035	**3.190**	**4.698**	**(1500)**	**17.1**	**273**	**28.9**	**59**

This plan would enable our government to obtain a balanced budget by 2025 and return to a responsible debt-to-GDP ratio by 2035.

After 16 years (2020 to 2035) of 2% per year cost reductions and 2% per year revenue increases, the 2035 U.S. budget costs would be reduced by one third from the 2017 budget costs. While that sounds like a big cut, that is what is needed to get back to a financially responsible 60% debt-to-GDP ratio. Many corporations have had to make such cuts over time. To make these cuts, and still maintain an effective government, the U.S. should also reduce our 23 crises that are causing costly disasters that government has to deal with. To reduce these crises and their enormous costs, the follies that caused them must be eliminated and future follies must be prevented or avoided.

The current U.S. budget plan to continue a trillion-dollar deficit each year for the next six years (2019 to 2025), will grow the debt by $6 trillion from $22.7 in 2019 to $28.7 trillion in 2025; the U.S. will have a debt-to-GDP ratio of 121% in 2025. The 2 + 2 budget plan would achieve a debt-to-GDP ratio of 106% in 2025. Although this number is only slightly lower than the current debt-to-GDP ratio of 108%, the ratio would begin to drop significantly after that by simply continuing the 2 + 2 plan.

The best businesses know that continuous improvement can reduce costs, reduce cycle times, reduce defects, and reduce crises. Unfortunately, most government leaders do not seem to know that is also possible in government. Costs can be reduced and effectiveness increased, which is what is required of our government.

The U.S. could reach a balanced budget, that is zero deficit, by 2025, and by 2035 could reach the goal of 60% debt-to-GDP ratio. That is the power of small consistent improvements made over time. For those who think the debt is not a problem, our debt interest payments from 2017 to 2035 will be $5.5 trillion, even with this cost reduction plan.

In order to help the economic recovery after the 2008 Wall Street crisis, the Federal Reserve Bank held the effective federal funds rate, for loans to these same large Wall Street banks that got us into the 2008 economic crisis, to only 0.25% interest, from 2008 through 2015. At the same time, the U.S. was borrowing from other countries at 1.6% interest. No government or business can afford to borrow at 1.6% and loan that money to others at 0.25%. That's what happened, and the banks were free to use this cheap money for speculation. Starting in 2015, the Federal Reserve started increasing the U.S. prime interest rate in 0.25% increments. By the end of 2018 the U.S. prime interest rate had been increased to 2.5%. After seven years of making loans at a lower rate than we were paying for borrowing, that problem was finally corrected.

Here are some guidelines on how to reduce costs while improving effectiveness:

- Identify benchmarks from other governments (country or state) and set goals to achieve the best of the benchmarks

- Identify best practices of the best benchmarks and incorporate them

- Set goals to get to benchmark performance

- Define the goal of the cost reductions needed and enlist employee help in reaching the goal (e.g., achieve a balanced budget and a 60% debt-to-GDP ratio)

- Define a timeline to reach the goals

- Do not simply cut all organizations' budgets equally

- Do not cut budgets with little notice

- Reduce or eliminate reliance on consultants, and use employees as your consultants for how to improve effectiveness and efficiency

- Maintain cost of living and pay raises to retain the best people, increase morale, and maintain commitments to the organizational goals

- Ask employees for input on how to cut waste or errors. Focus on eliminating waste and errors to improve effectiveness and efficiency.

- Ask employees what rework is being done in their departments due to errors in other departments. Focus on eliminating rework by eliminating those errors; reduce defect rates.

- Identify what work could be automated, or have automation improvements, to reduce manual work. Prioritize those IT changes with the IT department.

- Fund IT and other improvements necessary to reduce costs and improve effectiveness

- Identify possible duplication of efforts, and consider consolidation if that will reduce duplication

- Reverse past decisions of folly that caused crises and disasters

- Prevent future decisions of folly that will create crises and disasters

- Avoid starting new organizations, or projects, that are not essential and affordable, until the financial goals have been met: balanced budget and 60% debt-to-GDP ratio.

- Reduce debt and debt interest payments by reducing deficit budgets

- Require suppliers to improve their effectiveness and efficiency every year, and reduce the number of suppliers to those that are the most effective and efficient

- Open up competition from qualified suppliers to allow international competition (e.g., prescription drugs)

- Increase funding to organizations where needed to be effective (e.g., cybersecurity), and cut more where an organization's costs are worse than benchmarks

- Where appropriate, outsource some functions to more efficient and effective organizations

- Increase utilization of public-private partnerships

- Celebrate and recognize organizations and individuals that help meet the cost-reduction goals

National Debt Crisis Follies
[(C) denotes citizen follies, (G) denotes government follies]

- Continuing to increase our budget, deficit, and debt without concern for the burden to future generations (G)

- Supporting short-term profits for businesses, without regard to the much larger cost to all (G)

- Borrowing $1 trillion per year while having a debt-to-GDP ratio over 100% (G)

- Taking $4.8 trillion in funds from Social Security and Government employee retirement funds, without a plan to repay those retirement funds (G)

- Treating all government trust funds as a piggy bank to borrow from, instead of using normal trust fund management to save and invest the funds (G)

- Cutting the 2018 corporate tax rate, without making cost reductions to offset the revenue loss (G)

- Increasing the expense budget in 2019, without the revenue to support the expense increase (G)

- Continuing to live with significant waste in government (G)

- Living without a long-term financial plan to reduce the annual budget, reduce the deficit, reduce the national debt, get to a balanced budget, and get to a financially responsible debt-to-GDP ratio (G)

Possible Goals
Eliminate our financial weakness
Develop and maintain responsible financial criteria like those established for the EU countries

Attain a Federal annual balanced budget by 2025, and agree to avoid deficit budgets in 2025 and beyond

Attain a debt-to-GDP ratio of 60% by 2035, and maintain 60% or less from 2035 and beyond

Possible Results Measures
Debt-to-GDP ratio reduction (Goal of 60% debt-to-GDP ratio by 2035)

Annual Federal budget reduction (Goal of 2% per year reduction through 2035)

Likely root causes
Tax cuts provided for businesses that were not offset by cost reductions

Cost increases in budgets

Budgets that include an annual deficit

Borrowing from funds dedicated for retirement safety nets

Waste and payment mistakes

Possible Improvements
(* Asterisk indicates no- or low-cost to the federal government)

*Change Social Security and other retirement required fund investments to S&P 500 index to provide a return on investments rather than funding U.S. debt. (That is managing a trust fund as a trust fund, instead of a piggy bank to borrow from.)

*Eliminate mistakes that are causing waste

*Establish a plan for a 2% per year reduction of our budget costs

*Use the 2% cost reduction and an annual 2% revenue increase to reduce the budget deficit and obtain a balanced budget by 2025

*Use the budget surplus to reduce debt between 2025 and 2035

*Continue using cost reductions and revenue increases to obtain a debt-to-GDP ratio of 60% by 2035

*Collect Social Security payroll taxes on 100% of all income, not just on earnings up to $132,900 per year

Develop a plan for U.S. government repayment of the $4.8 trillion borrowed retirement funds. It will take over 40 years and require $115 billion per year as a budget item to repay these borrowed retirement funds. As these funds are repaid, they should be invested in an S&P 500 index fund to begin earning a return on investments. Budget cost cuts elsewhere will be needed to cover this $115 billion budget item, which is needed to eliminate this liability.

Crisis annual cost
The annual crisis costs result from our being above the world average in our debt. If the U.S. were at a financially responsible level of debt, which is about half the amount of debt we currently have, we would be paying half the amount of interest. The cost of this debt crisis is about $175 billion each year.

Federal Budget cost reduction opportunities for 2024
The Congressional Budget Office has forecast that as a result of the 2018 corporate tax cuts, increasing annual deficits, and rising interest rates, the annual debt interest payments are expected to be driven up from $353 billion to $818 billion per year by 2027, a $465 billion per year increase in interest payments. This is more than double what we are currently paying. If we continue with business as usual, interest on our debt will soon be the single largest budget item. With implementation of a 2 + 2 budget plan, the interest on the debt will still go up, but by only $40 billion from 2019 to 2024. That is less than 10% of the increase currently planned.

Potential House Caucuses to implement House CAT Improvements:
Pension Protection for Working Americans Caucus: Chair Rick Nolan (D)

Waste-Cutting Caucus: Co-Chairs Ralph Norman (R), Dave Brat (R)

Government Efficiency Caucus: Co-Chairs Jackie Walorski (R), Gerry Connolly (D)

Personal Story – National Debt Crisis

While in college in the 1960s, one of my courses was Economics. I recall the professor telling us (over 50 years ago) that the U.S. could continue to increase its debt without incurring any problems at all. I disagreed with the professor and refused to accept that Economics principle. I knew from my math classes that the interest on the debt would become a burden to future generations. In addition, I had read Ben Franklin, who advised that debts obligate you to the lender. I got a grade of "D" in that class, in part for refusing to accept the principle that debt could be increased forever with no problem.

My parents grew up during the depression so they learned to budget and save, and to avoid debt and interest payments. That education from depression-era economics of saving and avoiding debt was passed on to me and enabled me to retire at 55, when job circumstances indicated that was the right choice for me.

Wall Street and Corporate Debt Crisis

Definition:
Risky Wall Street speculation and high corporate debt continues to be a crisis.

According to The Balance, a financial website, "Wall Street is the center of American capitalism ... [and] refers to all the banks, hedge funds, and securities traders that drive the American financial system. The original purpose of the securities market was to raise funds for companies to grow, be profitable, and create jobs" (Amadeo, January 2019). However, that changed with the abolition of the Glass-Steagall Act in 1999, which allowed banks to speculate rather than invest. This deregulation, allowing speculation, was the major cause of the 2008 financial crisis.

Speculation is the purchase of an asset with the hope that it will become more valuable in the near future. In the world of finance, speculation is the practice of engaging in risky financial transactions in an attempt to profit from short-term fluctuations, rather than investing in the production of goods and services for a long-term return on capital.

Many speculators pay little attention to the fundamental value of a security and instead focus purely on projected price movements. Speculation is a high-risk form of investment, indeed some view speculation as nothing more than gambling. Derivatives are a form of speculation, which require regulation.

Individuals who gamble do so with their own money. Speculators use other people's money to gamble; they are using America's money, and when they win, they make a lot of money for themselves, but when they lose, the government takes money from citizens to bail them out.

Total U.S. corporate debt, financial and non-financial, in August 2018 was at an all-time high, over 45% of GDP, or about $10 trillion. When corporate debt hit 45% of GDP in the past, it was followed by the Tech Bubble crash or the Housing bubble crash (Roberts 2018). Too much debt is a dangerous thing, which usually leads to disaster.

Wall Street Speculation (Financial)
To understand the Wall Street crisis risk, we need to review the causes of the 2008 financial crisis that put the whole country in the Great Recession and led to the creation of our debt crisis. Countrywide Financial, a private mortgage loan business, began providing mortgages to lower-income home buyers who did not qualify financially for big home loans. Countrywide took bonuses at home loan closings for the mortgage loans, and then worked with Wall Street firms who packaged these bad loans into bond packages, which were falsely rated AAA by the Credit Agencies being paid by the Wall St. banks. Everyone made money selling what were known to be bad loans, all of which was allowed by the 1999 U.S. deregulation of the banks.

Countrywide was providing so many mortgages that the government loan agencies, Fannie Mae and Freddie Mac, felt compelled to follow the Countywide lead; they also lowered their loan standards and issued bonds with bad loans.

Follies on the part of Countrywide, Wall St., credit-rating agencies, and the government loan agencies, allowed them to make money for themselves and put the common good at risk. The root cause of this folly was deregulation of the banks. The Obama administration pushed for and reestablished bank regulation; however, the current administration is working to deregulate banks again.

The Dodd-Frank Wall Street Reform Act was passed in 2010 under the Obama administration to provide the oversight of derivatives, which would be regulated by the Securities and Exchange Commission (SEC), in order to prevent a repeat of the 2008 Wall Street economic disaster that caused the Great Recession. However, in May 2018, after pledging to repeal the Dodd-Frank bank regulations, President Trump signed a bill (now law) exempting dozens of banks from the Dodd-Frank Act's banking regulations; this risks a reduction in the financial stability of the U.S. once again, while benefiting a very few (Investopedia, n.d.).

The 2008 crash occurred when some people who were given big home loans could not make the payments and had to default; many lost their investments and their homes. The country's housing market also tanked when all these repossessed houses were put on the market by the banks at reduced prices. The other losers in this were the buyers of the Wall Street bonds of packaged mortgage loans that had been falsely rated AAA.

Luigi Zingales, Finance Professor at the University of Chicago, and Oliver Hart, Economist at Harvard University, argues that the easiest way to make money on Wall Street is to borrow low-interest money and take extreme risks for high returns, because there is a sense that government will step in if required (Zingales et al. 2019). Wall Street speculation executives can get lucky and make a bundle, or they can get unlucky and walk away while Uncle Sam picks up the loss. That temptation is hard for many to refuse.

Government deregulation of banks tempts banks to gamble. Government bailouts of banks when they lose increases that temptation for high rollers to gamble. The Office of the Special Inspector General for the Troubled Asset Relief Program said the banks that were "too big to fail" in 2008 have gotten even bigger. Prior to 2008, there was an implicit guarantee that the government would step in to prevent failure; that guarantee is now explicit (Office of the Special Inspector General for the Troubled Asset Relief Program 2014). Eighteen banks now each have more than $100 billion in assets, and the current administration is trying to deregulate them in order to allow them to take increased risks.

The U.S. needs to assess, and contain, the speculation risks being taken by these 18 big banks. A few possible ways of managing this risk are:

- The financial institution must have adequate capital (i.e., collateral) to deal with the potential loss on the speculation risk being taken.

- Set higher interest rates for banks borrowing government money, based on the speculation risk levels they are taking with our money.

- If the banks buy insurance on their speculation bets, the insurance company must have adequate assets to pay off the insurance claims. This is required to avoid another bailout.

In 2008, Congress received only three days' notice that the U.S. was in a financial crisis, due to speculation that risked the collapse of the entire U.S. financial system. This crisis, they were told, would require an $800 billion bailout for Wall Street. Financial disasters can happen suddenly; however, when the financial crisis that created them is in plain sight for a long time, it should be reduced with reasonable regulations.

Research Data for Corporate Debt

A primary driver behind the current Stock Market price bubble is low interest rates for an extended period. To recover from the 2008 Great Recession, the Federal Reserve pumped trillions of low-interest dollars into the financial system, which they call "quantitative easing." The Federal Reserve does not print money; they simply create it out of thin air, in digital form. Between 2008 and 2015, the Federal Reserve created $3.5 trillion to loan at very low interest rates to financial institutions.

These ultra-low interest rate loans encouraged corporations to borrow heavily; as a result, non-financial corporate debt has increased 40% since the 2008 high (Colombo 2019).

This dramatic increase in corporate debt has been caused by long-term, very low interest rates set to help corporations recover from the recession. However, some large corporations have borrowed to pay dividends and buy back stock simply to pump up the stock market bubble in the short term instead of making long-term investments to produce goods competitive in the world market. In 2018, U.S. corporations spent $1 trillion on stock buybacks (Egan 2019). This inflates stock prices but does not provide investment in production needed to deal with our trade deficit or produce new jobs.

Inflating stock prices by increasing debt is not a viable long-term strategy, and it increases risks when interest rates begin to return to normal. In 2018, as interest rates began to increase a bit, stocks on the Dow Jones and S&P 500 indices both fell 6% for the year. The root cause is not the interest rate increase; it is too much debt that was created by too long a period of very low interest rates.

As companies increase their debt, they risk having their credit rating drop to junk grade, which could cause a drop in the stock market. If interest rates rise and if the economy slows, some companies may not be able to make their required debt payments, which would result in defaults and possible bankruptcies. If a company receives a junk rating, its interest rates for new debt go up, thus creating a potential crisis for that company. If enough companies face this crisis, it becomes a crisis for the country. So how do we know when there is too much debt?

One measure to assess whether there is too much debt uses a cash-to-debt ratio which essentially provides a picture of a company's overall financial health. The ratio is calculated by taking the amount of a business's cash flow from operations and dividing that by the business' debt. A high cash flow-to debt ratio is good, and a low ratio is bad. The cash flow-to-debt ratio fell to 12% in 2017, the lowest level ever for corporate America (Turak 2018) (Corporate Finance Institute, n.d.).

Wall Street and Corporate Debt Crisis Follies
[(G) denotes government follies (B) denotes business follies]

- Deregulating banks to allow the unregulated sale of derivatives in 1999. (This is Glass-Steagall Act dilution) (G)

- Pushing for deregulation of banks again in 2018 (G)

- Supporting speculation (gambling) with the government's and citizens' money (G)

- Allowing loans without adequate loan standards (G)

- Allowing banks to pay the credit-rating agencies that rate their bond offerings, resulting in misleading credit ratings from those agencies (G)

- Allowing financial institutions to speculate without adequate capital reserves (G)

- Allowing insurance companies for Wall Street speculation risks without adequate rates and adequate assets (G)

- Providing very-low interest loans to banks, that then use that money for high-risk speculation to get much higher returns (G)

- Business Boards allowing CEOs to borrow and increase corporate debt, in order to buy back stock and pay dividends to inflate stock prices, to get big annual bonuses (B)

Possible Goals
Prevent another economic crisis as a result of irresponsible borrowing and speculation

Reduce speculative risks by improving corporate median credit rating from "BBB" to "A," and reduce the amount of corporate debt

Improve percentage of corporate loans with adequate loan standards

Improve U.S. corporate cash flow-to-debt ratio

Possible Results Measures

Median credit rating for corporate debt

Corporate debt as a percentage of the U.S. GDP
Percentage of corporate loans that meet loan standards

U.S. Corporate cash flow-to-debt ratio_

Likely Root Causes

The root causes are similar to the follies above, because decisions of folly for the few often become the root causes of crises for the many

Very low interest rates for a long time

Low-interest loans given to high-risk borrowers

Lack of reasonable loan requirements for borrowers

High-risk speculation by companies without adequate capital assets to handle a loss

Insurance on speculative bets that has inadequate insurance rates and inadequate insurance assets

Credit rating agencies that are paid by banks cannot be relied on for trustworthy credit ratings

Banks that are too big to fail allowed to get even bigger

Possible Improvements
(* Asterisk indicates no- or low-cost to the federal government)

*Raise federal interest rates to banks to discourage borrowing for speculation

*Ensure there are adequate standards for borrowers to avoid or minimize defaults

*Reduce total corporate debt and the percentage of this debt that is made with low-credit companies

*Ensure that the 18 large financial Institutions (each with greater than $100 billion in assets) have adequate capital reserves for their level of speculation

*Ensure that insurance companies for speculative investments have adequate rates and adequate assets for the insurance they are offering

*Ensure that the three national credit rating agencies are impartial by paying them by the federal government (instead of financial institutions) for their rating services, which could be funded by a small transaction tax on the bond offerings

Crisis annual cost
The government does not have a reserve fund to bail out the next Wall Street financial disaster, but we probably should have one because we seem to have assumed that liability. It cost us $800 billion to bail out Wall Street after the 2008 crisis; we probably should have put their repayment of those bailout funds into a Wall St. liability fund for the next crisis. Since we did not do that, we should probably put $80 billion per year into a Wall Street liability fund to be able to handle the next crisis.

Federal Budget cost reduction opportunities
This is a crisis that needs to be avoided. This is a cost-avoidance area, not a cost-savings area.

Potential House Caucus to implement House CAT improvements
No existing caucus identified.

Personal Story – Wall Street and Corporate Debt Crisis

On Monday September 29, 2008, the day of the 2008 Wall St. crash, the Dow Jones average experienced the largest drop in its history. At that time, my wife and I had investments with Lehman Brothers investments. This was the largest bankruptcy in the history of the United States. This was the one bank that was not bailed out. The bank had become so involved in speculative subprime (high-risk) mortgages that it effectively had become a real estate hedge fund, so when the market crashed, they lost it all. My wife and I lost $100,000, which put an unhealthy dent in our retirement savings. No one offered to bail us out. I now have a better financial advisor, and I am in a fund that avoids high-risk investments. The crash taught many people to assess the debt and credit risk associated with their investments.

Trade Balance Crisis

Definition of Trade Balance Crisis
A country's trade balance is the difference between the total amount of the country's imports and the total amount they export. A healthy and positive trade balance occurs when a country exports more than they import.

Our trade balance is currently a deficit, in the red, and growing worse; this trade deficit contributes to other financial crises. Between 2000 and 2019, our trade deficit increased by almost 70%. The European Union countries, by contrast, have had a trade surplus for the same period.

Research data and trends
Between 2017 and 2018, our trade deficit increased 12.5%. According to the N.Y. Times, this was exacerbated by the current administration's $1.5 trillion tax cut, financed by increased government borrowing, and by the tariff increases initiated (Tankersley et al. 2019).

The Council on Foreign Relations reported that the U.S. trade deficit in 2018 was $700 billion in goods and services, the result of importing $3.2 trillion and only exporting $2.5 trillion. Our primary exports are aircraft, medical equipment, petroleum, and agricultural commodities, mostly purchased by governments and businesses. Our primary imports are computers, telecom equipment, consumer goods, and automobiles.

According to Harvard University of Economics Professor Martin Feldstein, the trade deficit arises because the United States as a whole – including government, business, and consumers – spends more money than it makes. To finance this trade deficit, funds are then borrowed from foreign lenders, which only adds to our already enormous debt.

The U.S. is buying more goods and services from other countries than they buy from the U.S.; the other countries are getting more of our money. This enables these other countries to:

- Pay their workers more to increase their standard of living

- Invest in business assets to be more competitive

- Invest in government infrastructure to improve public services

- Maintain a higher GDP growth rate – due to business investments and increased worker wages

- Maintain a lower debt-to-GDP ratio

- Fund their military defense expenditures, without borrowing to do so

Thus, while other countries are improving their future through their positive trade balance, ours is declining. Our trade balance deficit contributes to other U.S. crises, resulting in a decreasing quality of life and a loss of hope in the future.

To reduce trade deficits, we need to produce more to sell to other countries, and buy less from them. Raising tariffs, a tariff war, simply makes people in both countries pay more for products and services, which is essentially a government tax on goods and services. Further, faced with high U.S. tariffs on their exports to us, some of our trading partners may switch from the U.S. to other countries for their imports.

<u>Our negative trade balance is due to a number of factors, including:</u>

- Extended very low interest rates discourage savings while encouraging consumer borrowing and spending; we are now buying more and saving less than historically

- Increased U.S. business investments in other countries, helping other countries' trade balance

- Declining U.S. workforce-to-retiree ratio

- U.S. workforce participation rate is at a 48-year low

The U.S. has developed this negative trade balance over a long time, and it cannot be reduced with short-term fixes. The U.S. lacks a long-term government and business partnership strategy to improve our trade deficit. That strategy, for example, could include:

- A goal to be the leader in new technologies

- Businesses' plans to be the leader in new technologies

- Reskilling our workforce to be ready for new technology shifts

- Government support and incentives for shifts to new technologies with production in the U.S.

- Increasing our workforce participation rate by having workers trained in the skills needed for jobs in new technologies

- Increasing our cybersecurity capabilities to protect intellectual property

Our U.S. trade strategy cannot be to return to the past; it must be to go forward into the future.

As of May 2019, the U.S. strategy to improve our trade deficit was a tariff war started with China, which is in a much stronger economic position to fight this war:

- China has a much lower debt-to-GDP ratio (58% versus our 108%)

- China has a much higher GDP growth rate (6% versus our 3%)

- China has a higher workforce participation rate (69% over our 63%)

- China has control of the rare earth minerals required for high-tech equipment

- China is developing worldwide trading partners, supporting their trade agreements with other countries with loans to those countries

- China is our banker, loaning money to the U.S. that we need to finance our annual deficits; they could decide to stop those loans at any time

- The U.S. farm exports to China can be provided by other countries, and China is already trading with them

- China's leaders have long-term, 10- and 20-year plans, while U.S. leaders are primarily focused on trying to achieve a quick fix for next year's election

After more than a year of the current administration's tariff wars, U.S. exports fell 5.2% in the second quarter of 2019, while imports rose slightly compared to a year earlier (Torrey 2019). This is the wrong direction for both imports and exports.

As a result of the negative impact of the tariff trade war on our economy, the Federal Reserve cut interest rates by a quarter point on 7/31/19, an indication we have a weaker economy as a result of the tariff wars. In addition, cutting interest rates increases our financial risks, as discussed earlier.

While our enormous trade deficit may seem complex, we simply buy too many goods and services from other countries and produce too few goods and services to sell abroad. We need to reverse this by producing more for other countries to buy, and reduce our own consumption of goods from other countries. We can do that, but it is hard long-term work, not a quick fix.

Adding tariffs that increase the cost we pay for others' goods may provide an incentive to reduce purchasing others' goods, but retaliatory tariffs also reduce other countries' incentives to buy from us. Ultimately, we may all pay more for what we buy and end up with the same trade deficit. A further downside for us is that our trading partners could find other more reliable trading partners, resulting in a long-term reduction in our exports.

Trade Balance Crisis Follies
[(G) denotes government follies; (C) denotes citizen follies; (B) denotes business follies]

- Increasing our trade deficits over many years, which was supported by government, business, and the Cato Institute (G)

- Breaking trade agreements with countries (G)

- Starting a trade tariff war (G)

- Developing a consumer buying-driven economy, instead of a business investment-driven economy (C) and (B)

- A low U.S. workforce participation rate (C)

Possible Goals
Eliminate the U.S. Trade deficit

Reduce the U.S. trade deficit by 5% per year until eliminated

Possible Results Measures
U.S. Balance of Trade deficit (with a goal to reduce it by 5% per year until balanced)

Likely Root Causes
Extended very low interest rates that encouraged borrowing

Workforce-to-retiree ratio declining

Workforce participation rate at a 48-year low

U.S. businesses investing in other countries instead of the U.S., which enables others to produce more than we do

U.S. citizens buying more and saving less than in the past

Certain governments have trade tariffs, or subsidies, that create an unfair market. For example, some countries provide financial support for new technology growing industries (e.g., solar power, artificial intelligence) in the early years to capture a world market share for the future

Lower labor costs in other countries

Possible Improvements
(* Asterisk indicates no- or low-cost to the federal government)

*Increase interest rates to encourage savings over spending

*Increase the U.S. workforce, perhaps through increased legal immigration

*Encourage more U.S. (and international) business investments in America by changing U.S. tax codes

*Encourage individual savings (e.g., having employers match employees' 401k contributions)

*Nudge people to use 401k saving programs by making the default option for 401K employee savings 5% instead of 0% (Thaler and Sunstein 2008).

*Encourage other countries, our trading partners, to increase their minimum wage.

*Quit spending billions of U.S. dollars to dredge U.S. rivers to access U.S. ports for super-sized foreign container ships in order to make international shipping costs even cheaper. (River dredging also contributes to flooding of coastal cities.)

Set a goal for the U.S. to be the technology leader in the world, and support that goal with specific plans.

Crisis annual cost
I am defining the annual crisis cost as the cost resulting from our having a higher trade deficit than the world average. The annual cost of this crisis is equal to the annual U.S. trade deficit, which was $891 billion for goods in 2018. Getting to a balance in our trade would get us to the average in the world.

Federal Budget cost reduction opportunities for 2024
Decreasing our trade balance deficit has no direct U.S. budget line item savings.

Potential House Caucuses to implement House CAT Improvements
Buy American Caucus: Co-Chairs David Joyce (R), Dan Lipinski (D)

Rare Earth Caucus: Chair Hank Johnson (D)

Personal Story – Trade Balance Crisis

On October 1, 2015, the cargo-container ship El Faro was lost at sea when poor weather forecasting sent the ship directly into Hurricane Joaquin. All 33 crew and maintenance workers aboard died (El Faro means The Lighthouse in Portuguese).

On the evening of September 29, 2015, El Faro left Jacksonville, Florida, and headed down the St. John's River. My fiancée and I were having dinner on the riverside deck of the Sandollar Restaurant when the cargo-container ship sailed by. I noticed the name El Faro and made a mental connection with it: a friend named Faro had written a book about his life growing up in Iran and immigrating to America, where he became a physician. His stories of life growing up in Iran were very similar to many stories of a young boy growing up in the U.S., involving family and friends.

The Coast Guard investigation into the cause of the ship's sinking involved public hearings in Jacksonville. These hearings were reported in detail by the Jacksonville newspaper, *The Times Union*. My Coast Guard friends told me to expect that the ship's captain would be blamed for the ship's sinking, because a captain shoulders all responsibility for a ship at sea. However, in reading the public hearing reports, I identified over 50 defects in the ship itself, in the ship's communications, and the ship owner's support processes for a ship sailing into a hurricane.

When I shared my quality analysis with the Coast Guard investigation team, the Coast Guard agreed with my conclusion that it was the simultaneous occurrence of over 50 defects that caused the disaster. Their final report included many recommendations for widespread improvements in marine cargo shipping safety. Florida's U.S. Senator, Bill Nelson, also agreed, and sponsored a bill that later became law to require some important changes in marine cargo safety. The ship 's owner, TOTE Marine, was planning to send a sister ship of El Faro's (also 40 years old) to Alaska for service there, but after hearing the Coast Guard findings, TOTE agreed to junk the sister ship.

Very cheap cargo-container shipping costs are being enabled by a lack of adequate marine ship maintenance and adequate safety support capabilities from shore. Changes made following the El Faro disaster will help reduce that crisis, and hopefully prevent a similar disaster.

Infrastructure Maintenance Crisis

Definition
U.S. infrastructure has not been maintained adequately and is deteriorating. According to the American Society of Civil Engineers (ASCE), we will need $2 trillion to meet the nation's infrastructure requirements over the next 10 years, which is about $200 billion per year (American Society of Civil Engineers 2017).

Throughout America at every level of government, infrastructure, which includes transportation, roads and bridges, sewage systems, storm drainage systems, and electrical power systems, has not been adequately maintained and improved. In addition, to avoid repeated costly infrastructure damage, coastlines need to be made more resilient to increasingly strong storms.

Research data and trends
In their 2016 Infrastructure Report Card, the ASCE reported that 40% of our bridges were 50 years old, and that 9% of our 614,387 bridges were structurally deficient. These 55,300 structurally deficient bridges saw 188 million trips a year. The most recent backlog of bridge rehabilitation costs was $123 billion (Brady 2018).

Other countries maintain and protect their infrastructure. Europeans pay more for gas in order to maintain their transportation infrastructure. Our generation has been less willing than previous generations to pay the cost of maintaining and improving our infrastructure. Furthermore, our transportation system focuses almost exclusively on private transportation (roads for cars) rather than public transportation (busses, trains, trolleys, etc.). Public transportation is better for the environment (fewer emissions), requires fewer roads, is a necessity for those who can't afford a car, and is more efficient at moving people from place to place.

The last time the federal gas tax was raised was 1993, when it was set at 18.3 cents per gallon. If that gas tax had simply been adjusted for inflation, in 2019 it would be 31 cents per gallon. If it had been adjusted to keep the tax at the same percentage of the gas price it would be 41 cents per gallon. Adjusted for inflation, the federal gas tax in 2019 could be providing 70% more funding for transportation infrastructure. Had it kept pace with gas prices, it would provide 128% more funding for transportation infrastructure.

The ASCE estimated the nation needs at least $271 billion to meet current and future needs of our wastewater system. ASCE gave America's infrastructure maintenance a D+ grade.

Infrastructure Maintenance Crisis Follies
[(G) denotes government follies]

- Inadequate maintenance of infrastructure throughout America at every level of government (G)

- Insufficient gas taxes to pay for the cost of maintaining our road and bridge infrastructure (G)

- Choosing to promote private transportation (cars) over public transportation, which benefits the gas and oil industry as well as the wealthy, hurts those in need of public transportation, and damages the environment (G)

Possible Goal
Reduce the U.S. 2017 infrastructure gap of $2 trillion by providing sufficient funding for maintenance and improvements (ASCE's U.S. infrastructure gap)

Possible Results Measure
ASCE Infrastructure gap

Likely Root Cause
Chronic, insufficient funding to address maintenance, improvements, and growth needs of the country's infrastructure

Possible Improvements
(* Asterisk indicates no- or low-cost to the federal government)

*Increase federal gas tax to adequately fund transportation infrastructure, and dedicate gas tax fees to these improvements

*Increase water and sewer usage fees to fund adequate water, drainage, and sewage systems

Increase use of alternative transportation, such as trains between cities and bicycle trails in cities (benchmarks are in Europe)

Crisis annual cost
The ASCE estimates the nation needs a $2 trillion funding for infrastructure repair and improvements in 11 infrastructure categories over the next decade, which is a $200 billion per year crisis cost.

Federal Budget cost reduction opportunities
America needs to increase the amount budgeted for our infrastructure costs by increasing the infrastructure usage fees (e.g., sewage and water fees) and taxes (e.g., gas tax).

Potential House Caucuses to implement House CAT Improvements
Infrastructure Caucus: Co-Chairs Elizabeth Esty (D), Garret Graves (R), Sean Maloney (D)

Public Works and Infrastructure Caucus: Co-Chairs Dina Titus (D), Brian Fitzpatrick (R)

Public Transportation Caucus: Chair Dan Lipinski (D)

High-Speed and Intercity Passenger Rail Caucus: Co-Chairs David Price (D), Zoe Lofgren (D), Seth Moulton (D), Earl Blumenauer (D)

Trails Caucus: Co-Chairs Jeff Fortenberry (R), Earl Blumenauer (D)

Personal Story – Infrastructure Maintenance Crisis

Bridge Maintenance
On June 28, 1983, at 1:30 a.m., the Connecticut Turnpike/I95 Bridge collapsed over the Mianus River in Greenwich, Connecticut, killing three and injuring three more when two cars and two tractor-trailers fell 70 feet into the Mianus River. The bridge carried three lanes of traffic in each direction. About one hour before that bridge collapsed, I drove over it on a trip from my home in New Jersey to my parents' summer cottage on Lake Whittemore in Greenfield, New Hampshire. All four of my children were in the car with me: Scott 14, Maury 13, Michelle 9, and John 6. The cause of the bridge collapse was rust and metal fatigue. If the bridge had collapsed one hour earlier, I would not be writing this book, and my four children, ten grandchildren, and one great-grandchild would not be alive today.

Bike Trails
Amelia Island trails are a small segment of the planned 2,000-mile national East Coast Greenway (ECG) multi-use paved off-road trail (i.e., walking, running and bicycling) that will run from Maine to the Florida Keys. Although Amelia Island's population is still growing, there are no plans to increase road capacity on the island. Therefore, a safe island-wide trail network could help to minimize the impact of increased vehicle traffic, and reduce parking problems on this small island that has 25,000 residents and 600,000 tourists per year.

As a volunteer, I have worked with the ECG national trail non-profit for the past 14 years to help plan Amelia Island trails, obtain grants, and encourage local support to enable safe bicycle trips and exercise on our small island. My primary volunteer community project is as the CEO of Friends of Amelia Island Trail, Inc., a small non-profit. The island is only 3 miles wide, but our Atlantic Ocean Beach is 13 miles long. A safe walking and bicycling path to our beach could reduce reliance on cars and help to reduce beach parking problems.

Financial Crises Summary

As of May 2019, our country could not meet the European Union (EU) financial criteria to be an EU member, and we have no plans to meet any financially responsible debt criteria. Our national debt is higher than it has ever been, and it continues to rise.

Corporate debt is also at an all-time high, inviting the sort of crisis that led to the disastrous 2008 financial crisis. Our negative trade balances weaken our economy both nationally and internationally. Borrowing from other countries to pay the interest on our debt further weakens our position in the world. Today, our financial position is dangerously weak, and we have no goals or plans to strengthen it. We also have no plans to provide funding to reduce our infrastructure maintenance crisis.

Chapter 8 – WORKER CRISES

The Worker Crises include four key areas that affect workers' ability to earn a living wage, as well as America's ability to compete in the world: Worker Skills, Worker's Fair Pay, College Education Debt, and Social Media. Each of these crises will be analyzed using the quality planning approach.

Worker Skills Crisis

<u>Definition</u>
America is facing rapid technology shifts and increasing world competition, resulting in a need for new skills. While U.S. unemployment has dropped to an all-time low (about 4% in 2018), the 4% of the population who want to work but are unemployed apparently do not have the skills that match the jobs available. In 2018, there were 6 million people looking for work, and during the same time there were 6 million jobs available.

The Federal Reserve Chairman, Jay Powell, noted that about 500,000 working-age citizens are out of the workforce. They are neither employed nor looking for work, bringing America's workforce participation rate to a new low. This is a sharp reversal of our country's history of being hard-working and industrious people (Pelley 2019).

In mid-2016, the percentage of our population over 15 that was working, or looking for work, was only 63% (Gorman 2016). This figure puts us 96th on the list for workforce participation (Index Mundi, n.d.). That same year, China had a 69% workforce participation rate, giving them about a 10% workforce participation advantage for production of goods and services. This advantage China has contributes to our trade deficit with them, since they have a higher percentage of citizens working to produce goods and services.

Research facts and trends

Lauren Dixon, a Senior Editor for the magazine *Talent Economy*, interviewed a number of people who had researched U.S. workforce participation and found that the major causes of the low U.S. workforce participation rate were:

- The 2008 Great Recession put a lot of people out of work. Baby boomers, over 55, had trouble getting reemployed after the recession.

- More people, ages 20 to 24, have chosen to continue their education before starting work, in part because of the poor job market following the 2008 recession.

- Many people on disability due to pain have become addicted to opioids and are unable to return to work.

- More young people are addicted to video games and social media.

- Released prisoners have trouble getting a job, and the U.S. has a very high imprisonment rate: 2.27 million people were incarcerated in jails and prisons across the country in 2017, a 500% increase over the last 40 years. The U.S. incarceration rate is now 5 to 10 times higher than other industrialized countries (Equal Justice Initiative 2016).

- A significant percentage of Americans (16%) are not counted as working because they work for cash to avoid paying taxes.

- The minimum wage is not sufficient for many to reenter the workforce at the entry level. (Dixon 2018)

In addition, major technology shifts require many workers to acquire new skills in order to participate in the workforce. Examples of technology shifts include:

- Shift from coal and oil to natural gas, solar, and wind energy

- Use of robots displaces manufacturing workers

- Shift from retail shopping at brick-and-mortar stores, which provide retail jobs, to online retailers who require fewer employees

- Planned use of Artificial Intelligence (A.I.) to replace many current jobs, including truck drivers

Trying to keep jobs in sectors that are becoming obsolete doesn't work. Coal is one such sector. One of President Trump's campaign promises was to bring back the coal industry; this promise helped him win the state of Pennsylvania and the Presidency. However, after the first two years of his presidency, more coal mines were shut down than during the last four years of the Obama administration. This statistic has nothing to do with either Obama or Trump. Natural gas, solar, and wind power are more competitive energy sources than coal. In addition, scientists have told us that unless users switch to non-fossil fuels by 2030, we will not be able to continue life as we know it on Earth; therefore, many consumers and businesses are trying to reduce their use of fossil fuels.

Coal miners can reskill for new energy source technologies if given the opportunity to do so. The U.S. should have been working on plans for reskilling and bringing new energy industries to states where many coal mines are closing. Putting plans like this in place for technology shifts takes advance planning and some incentives from government. Trying to hold on to the past will not make our country great. Instead, we must go forward with the future technologies or get left behind. We must have plans to help workers transition into the occupations technology changes require.

Artificial Intelligence (A.I.) presents a real threat to our current job market. Kai-Fu Lee, the CEO and owner of Face++ Cognitive Services and the A.I. leader in China, claimed that 40% of the jobs in the world could be replaced with A.I. by 2035 (Pelley 2019). A.I. may soon replace truck drivers, which provides the highest number of jobs for men in America.

The U.S. should develop a reskilling process to help truck drivers develop the new skills needed during this A.I. technology shift, and we need to begin planning for that now. Our existing college system is able to undertake the necessary reskilling of America, but that reskilling needs to be funded. Perhaps a type of G.I. bill could fund this required reskilling education.

A.I. takeover of jobs is not the only threat to workers. Many companies are moving operations overseas where labor is cheaper and taxes are lower, which is causing plant closings in our country. A reskilling tax assessed on those corporations, based on the number of employees laid off, could be used to help workers transition to a new field. Reskilling is a necessary survival technique for today's workers to keep them in the workforce.

Isabel Sawhill, an economist at the Brookings Institute, wrote *The Forgotten Americans: An Economic Agenda for a Divided Nation*, which studies this reskilling issue and provided a number of useful facts:

- 38% of the working population does not have a 4-year college degree

- A lack of well-paying jobs has made this group more pessimistic about the future

- The current level of income inequality is higher than it has been since the 1920s

- College is unaffordable for many because college costs have increased 300% between 1982 and 2017

- Low-income wages have remained relatively flat during this same 35-year period

- Only cheap labor can compete with today's machines

Sawhill offers the following recommendations:

- Both individual and government need to do better to deal with this crisis

- Increased vocational education and assistance is needed to retrain and relocate workers

- More training and retraining of workers by business

- A minimum wage of $12 per hour, with increases indexed to inflation

- An expanded child care credit to help working parents

- A tax credit for low-income wage earners

- Subsidized lifelong learning
                    (Sawhill 2018)

All these recommendations are focused on helping low-income workers survive recessions and technology shifts. Most people do not want handouts; instead, they want jobs that pay a living wage and help during technology transitions that affect their industry.

The U.S. needs to support improvements that advocate for workers in this new age of rapid technology shifts and increasing world competition. While engineers are planning new technology like A.I., planning for reskilling workers that will be affected must be undertaken simultaneously. Developing both the technology and the workforce necessary to use it will ensure a smoother transition for workers and businesses.

Robert Half, a global firm that studies staffing, has conducted recent surveys that show how business can help this need for reskilling. In March, 2019 the surveys found:

- While 42% of job applicants do not meet job requirements, 84% of companies are willing to provide up-skilling training

- 9 out of 10 employers offer financial support for professional certifications
                    (Robert Half 2019)

Amazon is one business that has committed to invest in reskilling their employees. In July 2019, they authorized spending $700 million to retrain about a third of its 300,000 U.S. workforce by 2025. Other big companies, like Walmart and AT&T, have also announced training programs in recent years (Casselman and Satariano, 2019).

Retraining and reskilling is not a problem that needs to be dealt with solely at the national or corporate level. Birmingham, Alabama, for example, has made a successful transition to deal with a technological shift. In the first half of the 20th century, Birmingham was known as the "Pittsburgh of the South" because it was an industrial center for mining, as well as iron and steel production. In addition, Birmingham, along with Atlanta, was one of two primary southern railroad hubs. In the latter half of the 20th century, Birmingham diversified to include college education, medical care, telecommunications, insurance, and banking as their major economic industries. Today Birmingham is one of the most important business centers in the Southeast and is the location for the University of Alabama School of Medicine, the School of Dentistry, and the University of Alabama at Birmingham. Transitions from one technology to another can be done at the city level, with university, state, and federal support.

Worker Skills Crisis Follies
[(G) denotes government follies]

- False promises to bring back old outdated technologies (G)

- Lack of plans to reskill displaced workers in an era of high technology shifts (G)

- Lack of plans to bring new technology jobs (e.g., solar power) to areas with workers in old technology jobs (G)

- Fighting against technological shifts instead of preparing workers for them (G)

Possible Goal
Improve U.S. workforce participation rate to be equal to China at 69%

The actual U.S. workforce participation rate was 63% in April 2019. An increase of 1% point per year for 7 years would help reduce the trade deficit by increasing production of American goods and services

Possible Results Measure
U.S. workforce participation rate

Likely Root Causes
Technology shifts

Lack of a plan for needed reskilling

World competition

A decline in workforce industriousness and an increase in addictions

Minimum wage inadequate to attract entry-level workers

Possible Improvements
(* Asterisk indicates no- or low-cost to the federal government)

*Worker use of online training opportunities

*Worker use of employer training opportunities

*Worker use of employer tuition assistance programs

*Increase the federal minimum wage, and index it to inflation

Improve low-income worker tax credits

Provide job reskilling in our vocational and college systems, funded by a tax on employers who outsource jobs to other countries

Reduce addictions and improve industriousness

Crisis annual cost
Having a 10% lower worker participation rate than China costs the U.S. about 10% of our GDP. The GDP is expected to be about $21.5 trillion in 2020; therefore, the 10% low worker participation rate is a cost of about

$2 trillion per year in GDP. If we assume about half of that is from the lack of reskilling, the Worker Skills crisis cost is about $1 trillion per year in GDP loss.

Federal budget cost reduction opportunities for 2024
A $1 trillion per year increase in GDP with 5% of that going to the Federal Government could provide $50 billion per year in increased revenue. When our Federal government has a trillion dollar per year deficit, it may be hard for them to care about saving $50 billion; however, you can't save a trillion without saving billions.

Potential House Caucuses to implement House CAT Improvements
21st Century Skills Caucus: Co-Chairs Ryan Costello (R), Dave Loebsack (D)

Future of Work Caucus: Chair Lisa Blunt Rochester (D)

Skilled American Workforce Caucus: Brenda Lawrence (D), French Hill (R)

Career and Technical Education Caucus: Co-Chairs Glenn Thompson (R), Jim Langevin (D)

Innovation and Entrepreneurship Caucus: Co-Chairs Jared Polis (D), Darrell Issa (R)

Middle Class Jobs Caucus: Chair Raja Krishnamoorthi (D)

Full Employment Caucus: Co-Chairs Marcy Kaptur (D), Frederica Wilson (D)

Personal Story – Worker Skills Crisis

I was fortunate enough to get a college education with a degree in Electrical Engineering (1966) when that was a very sought-after skill. After joining AT&T, I went back to college at night, earning a Master's degree in management to be eligible for promotion. For two years I had Mackenzie Consultants helping develop my Product Management skills on the job, and I also attended Executive Education programs at universities to develop international business knowledge. My working career included learning on the job and taking quality education classes (including the National Quality Award training classes), to learn quality improvement methods and tools. I have had to repeatedly reskill during my 33-year career, which really involved three 11-year careers: Electrical Engineer, Product Manager, and Quality Vice President.

I see my children reskilling at an even faster rate than I did. My three children in IT all regularly update their IT Certificates, and my daughter in Education is now completing her Ph.D. program. Reskilling is a requirement in the 21st Century.

Worker's Fair Pay Crisis

Definition

Salaries below a living wage create the working poor; these are people who are working full time but not making enough to support themselves and their family. From 1995 to 2017, there has been a 193% increase in the CEO-to-worker pay ratio; that is, corporate Chief Executive Officer pay is rising much faster than the ordinary corporate worker's pay. The money fueling this increase in wages at the top could be used instead to pay a living wage to those at the bottom of the wage scale.

Research data and trends

Over the past 50 years, the pay gap between the top corporate leaders and the rank-and-file workers has increased continuously. During this period, low-income wages have remained stagnant, resulting in more working poor. The CEO-to-average worker pay ratio was 20 to 1 in the

1950s; between 1978 and 2017, it increased tenfold. In 2017, it had risen to 361 to 1 (Hembree 2018).

The worldwide availability of low-cost labor, with increasingly lower costs for international container transport, has contributed to this problem. The U.S. lacks a plan to address this increasing problem which will affect the next generation, a generation that will also be left with government financial and environmental bills to pay.

Regularly scheduled increases in the minimum wage are required to lift all workers out of the ranks of the working poor. These workers are not in a position to negotiate a living wage themselves, and individual businesses cannot offer a fair wage on their own because they must compete with others who will not offer a fair wage unless required to do so. If low-wage workers are not paid a living wage for their work, the government is burdened with social programs to support the working poor *or leave citizens hungry and homeless*. However, our government which is deep in debt, cannot afford to subsidize the working poor, so the needed social programs are inadequate to lift workers out of the working poor category.

Why is fair pay a crisis? In 2017, 39.7 million Americans lived in poverty (U.S. Census Bureau 2018). If you add to that the number living close to the poverty line, the number increases to about 20% of the U.S. population. This includes 16 million children who live at or below the federal poverty line, and children living in poverty are at risk for serious problems in both the short and long term.

The Brown School at Washington University in St. Louis studied the cost of childhood poverty in America and estimated a yearly cost of $1.03 trillion (Schoenherr 2018). Children in poverty are more likely to experience serious health problems, both physical and mental, and more likely to engage in crime to deal with their economic situation. Not only do the children suffer, our country loses the economic productivity from these individuals who could have been achievers. "Estimating the Economic Cost of Childhood Poverty in the United States" shows that not paying a living wage to workers has a very high cost to America (McLaughlin and Rank 2018).

The fair pay crisis hits women disproportionately. Women are the primary breadwinners in 40% of households; in homes where the woman is the primary breadwinner, 63% of them are headed by single mothers who are the only breadwinner (R29 Brand Experiences 2018). In an era where low-wage jobs are insufficient for a single person, low wages certainly cannot support a woman and her child. The problem women face as primary, or only, breadwinner is further exacerbated because women take home just 80 cents for every dollar earned by men (Van Pelt 2019). In many low-income families, headed by a single mother, or a couple both of whom work outside the home, much of the income has to be used to pay child care.

A good understanding of the struggle of working people in America can be found in the United Way's study of the Asset Limited, Income Constrained, Employed (ALICE). The United Way's ALICE income level is the income needed to meet basic needs for housing, child care, food, transportation, health care, communications, and taxes. The 2016 ALICE report for Florida found that 45% of Florida's families had insufficient income to meet basic needs. In Florida, half of the jobs paid less than $15 per hour, and two thirds of jobs paid less than $20 per hour (United Way ALICE, n.d., 1-4). Unfortunately, the hourly wage necessary for one parent to support a family is $27.58. So, in Florida, 66% of the jobs do not pay enough for a single parent to support a family.

The United Way study also found that from 2010 to 2016, while the overall number of households in Florida increased by 8%, those earning less than the basic needs income increased by 10%. This study shows that not only do we have an enormous working poor problem, it is getting worse.

The problems faced by the working poor are due in large measure to the dramatic increase in salaries at the opposite end of the salary spectrum. In the 1950s, CEO compensation was 20 times the average worker pay; less than 70 years later, it was 361 times the average worker pay. The average compensation for a CEO in 2017 was $13.9 million per year, while the average production worker earned only $38,613 per year (Hembree 2018). That translates to an hourly rate of $6,950 per hour for a CEO, while the average production worker earns a little over $19 per hour (assuming 40 hours work per week for 50 weeks a year).

One mid-sized company, CareCentrix, with 500 workers in the healthcare services industry, decided to put workers and executives in the same boat. When John Driscoll became CEO in 2015, the company revenue growth had stalled, profit margins had declined, and they were losing 30% to 40% of their workforce every year. Entry level jobs, where turnover was the highest, were being paid the federal minimum wage of $7.25 per hour. Driscoll talked with his first-line employees and found they could not live on a minimum wage. Their family life crises overwhelmed their ability to perform their job. He had his finance chief analyze what it would take to double the entry level pay to a more reasonable $15 per hour. He found that he could dramatically increase the pay of all 500 employees for the same amount that was allocated to increase compensation for the top 18 executives. He proposed the executive team freeze their own compensation in order to significantly increase the pay of the 500 workers; all of them agreed. The business tripled in 5 years, and in 2018, the company broadened profit sharing to include every employee. In 2019, the entry level wage at CareCentrix was $16.50 per hour (Driscoll 2019). Increasing the minimum wage can result in both improved productivity and success for businesses.

The idea of a minimum wage is a relatively new one. The first U.S. minimum wage was established about 80 years ago when the Fair Labor Standards Act was passed in 1938. This act set the minimum wage at 25 cents an hour. The goal was to set a minimum wage that would keep workers out of poverty, but it has not done so because it has not kept up with inflation. Today, the federal minimum wage is $7.25 per hour, which is $15,080 per year (Bureau of Labor Statistics 2017). In most parts of America, that is not sufficient to provide basic necessities: food, shelter, health care, transportation, etc. for a single individual. The U.N. defines poverty as "…a denial of choices and opportunities, a violation of human dignity. It means lack of basic capacity to participate effectively in society." If the initial federal minimum wage had been indexed to the consumer price index, it would be $10.41 today. If it had kept pace with executive pay increases, it would be $23 per hour.

The Massachusetts Institute of Technology (MIT) has a living wage calculator for U.S. states and cities. In 2018, the city with the lowest cost of living in the country was McAllen, Texas. A single person must earn $10.32 per hour to be able to afford to live there. If the U.S. minimum wage had been indexed to inflation, a minimum wage worker would receive $10.41 per hour, or just enough to provide a living wage to a single individual in the lowest cost city in America. Today, the national minimum wage of $7.25 is not a living wage anywhere in America. In New York, for example, the MIT calculator estimates a living wage for a single adult is $16.14 per hour. The numbers go up sharply when there are children involved. In New York City, the living wage for a single parent with 2 children is $40.89 per hour (Massachusetts Institute of Technology 2019).

In 2018, the Federal Poverty Level (FPL) was set at $12,140 per year for a single person. Some government subsidy, to help with health insurance costs, is provided for those with incomes up to four times the $12,140 FPL. $48,560 per year is the income level at which just basic needs for housing, food, transportation, and health care can be met. By underpaying workers and overpaying executives, the business world is pushing support for the working poor onto the government, which is neither just nor affordable. Given the current administration's attempts to cut funding for these programs, the working poor will suffer even more in the future.

A few baby steps have been taken to address this problem. Starting in 2019, U.S. publicly traded companies must calculate how CEOs' compensation compares with the median pay of all employees and disclose the rationale in regular filings. This is a requirement of the 2010 Dodd-Frank Act aimed at achieving increased financial responsibility in business after the 2008 economic crash and recession. The Dodd-Frank Act also requires publicly traded companies to let stock holders have a non-binding vote on whether they approve of the CEO compensation. One way to provide a message from stockholders to Boards of Directors is to vote no on CEO compensation increases when CEO-to-worker compensation ratio is greater than 100 to 1.

There are several reasons why the CEO-to-worker pay ratio has increased so dramatically. The primary reason is a shift in CEO compensation from just cash salaries, to salaries and very large company stock bonuses that are connected to company stock price performance. When Boards of Directors approve stock compensation for stock price improvements, it is not the same as approving cash payments for a salary; very big stock bonus compensation numbers seem to be approved easily. CEOs then focus on the quickest way to improve the stock price, which is not necessarily the same as improving the business by investing to grow the business. Stock prices are always increased when CEOs announce closing of plants and layoffs that will reduce expenses and increase short-term profits. Stock prices are increased when CEOs use available money to buy back stock from the market, instead of investing in growing the business. Some CEOs even borrow money to buy back stock to increase stock prices and executive bonuses, resulting in an increase in the company debt.

The focus on stock price for CEO compensation has also contributed to our negative trade balance, because moving manufacturing offshore to lower-wage countries cuts costs and increases stock prices in the short term. However, many companies that have moved manufacturing offshore for short-run gains have gone out of business over the long run. The U.S. has lost whole industries that have followed a policy of maximizing short-term profits, while paying CEOs a large bonus to do just that. Many CEOs and Boards of Directors are not planning for the business's long-term good, but are focusing instead on their individual short-term gain. Their decision to maximize individual short-term financial gain instead of the long-term health of the company is a business decision of folly.

The average wage in U.S. company-owned factories in our neighboring country Mexico is only $1.50 per hour, which is a poverty-level wage there. The U.S. needs to encourage our friends in Mexico to establish a reasonable minimum wage for their people. This could be part of U.S. trade agreements set up to help the working poor worldwide, help level the worldwide wage competition, and help reduce U.S. companies moving jobs to other countries.

Another possible approach would be to cancel CEO stock compensation for any year in which there has been short-term stock price financial manipulation, through such things as stock buybacks and borrowing funds to pay dividends. These short-term financial manipulations drive up stock prices in the short term at the expense of the long term; these methods add debt and reduce financial investments in the business operations that could improve productivity, and competitiveness, in the long term.

Since businesses and the federal government have not addressed this CEO-to-worker pay ratio problem, some cities and states in America are taking the lead. In 2019, many states are leading the way to a more reasonable minimum wage per hour as shown in the following "Minimum Wage by State" table:

Table 13: Minimum Wage by State
(2019)

State	$ Hourly Min. Wage
Washington	12.00
Massachusetts	12.00
California	12.00 (greater than 25 employees)
California	11.00 (less than 25 employees
Arizona	11.50
New York	11.40
Colorado	11.10
Maine	11.00
Vermont	10.78
Oregon	10.75
Rhode Island	10.50
Hawaii	10.10
Connecticut	10.10
Maryland	10.10
Alaska	9.89
Minnesota	9.86
Michigan	9.45
Arkansas	9.25
South Dakota	9.10
Nebraska	9.00
New Jersey	8.85
West Virginia	8.75
Missouri	8.60
Ohio	8.55
Montana	8.50
Florida	8.46
Nevada	8.25
U.S. Federal	7.25

(Jacksonville Times Union 2019)

The state of Washington leads with a minimum wage of $12 an hour. Seattle, Washington is the fastest growing city in America and in 2019 Seattle's largest employers (those having more than 25 employees) will offer a minimum wage of $16 an hour. The Seattle area is headquarters to large tech firms, so perhaps other tech firms will follow this lead. Seattle, with Amazon, Microsoft, and other high-tech firms, shows us that being a technology leader can help to be able to pay a higher minimum wage, and that paying a higher minimum wage can help business growth rates.

Worker's Fair Pay Crisis Follies
[(B) denotes business follies; (G) denotes government follies]

- Over the past several decades, the pay gap between the top corporate leaders and workers has continued to increase (B)

- By underpaying workers and overpaying executives, business is pushing support for the working poor onto the government, which cannot afford it (B)

- Neither business nor government have plans to address the increasing problem of an inadequate living wage, and the pay gap which will affect future generations, and this is putting an unaffordable burden on government (G)

Possible Goal
CEO-to-average worker pay ratio of 100 to 1. (The actual ratio was 361 to 1 in 2017, up from 30 to 1 in 1978.)

Possible Results Measure
CEO-to-average worker pay ratio

Likely Root Causes
- Greed at the top of corporations

- Financial manipulations of stock prices to increase CEO bonuses

- Reduced ability of unions to negotiate

- Lack of a living minimum wage indexed to inflation

- Lack of a fair tax code: earnings on investments are taxed less than worker earnings

- Increase in service industry jobs, which are typically lower-wage jobs

Potential Improvements
(* Asterisk indicates no- or low-cost to the federal government)

* Cancel annual stock compensation for CEOs and other executives if financial manipulations were used in that year

*Establish capital gains tax rates and estate tax rates that are equal to the income tax rate schedules that apply to working people

*Establish a living minimum wage that escalates with inflation

*Provide for a corporate tax rate increase if the gap between CEO pay and average worker pay is above a set level (e.g., 100 to 1)

*Ask corporations to provide a 5-year plan to get to a CEO-to-average worker pay ratio of not more than 100 to 1 and recognize those that participate

Annual crisis cost
The Medicaid Health Care Insurance Federal Budget to help the working poor in 2019 is $412 billion. The budget for the Supplemental Nutrition Assistance Program (SNAP) (formerly Food Stamps) to help the working poor is $70 billion. Thus, the cost of having working poor is at least $482 billion each year in assistance and subsidies. This does not count the estimated annual cost of over $1 trillion per year for childhood poverty (Center on Budget and Policy Priorities 2019).

Federal Budget cost reduction opportunities
If the number of working poor was cut in half by a combination of reskilling and higher minimum wages, the cost of these government assistance programs could be cut in half; perhaps this could occur over a

10-year period. A 25% reduction in poverty by 2024, through reskilling and a fair minimum wage, could save $120 billion per year in Medicaid and SNAP. The U.S. shouldn't reduce or eliminate benefits to those in need (the current administration's approach); it should work to reduce the number of people in need of benefits. Helping those in need with a hand up, not a handout, takes 5-year planning, not one-year budget slashing.

Potential House Caucuses to implement House CAT Improvements
Labor & Working Families Caucus: Co-Chairs Linda Sanchez (D), Stephen Lynch (D)

Out of Poverty Caucus: Co-Chairs Barbara Lee (D), G.K. Butterfield (D)

Homelessness Caucus: Co-Chairs Alcee Hastings (D), Eddie Bernice Johnson (D)

Personal Story – Worker's Fair Pay Crisis

From the age of 12 when I started as a newspaper boy, to 55 when I retired from AT&T, I always had a job. As a paperboy, I earned a few cents per paper. At 15, I got a job in a gas station and earned approximately $1 per hour; more importantly, I began to develop work skills and learned how to repair cars in order to keep my used car running. At 16, I was old enough to get a job in a grocery store, where I worked throughout all my years in high school and college, earning about $1.50 to $2 per hour; in addition, I benefitted from being a member of the union. I went to a co-op university, so I worked in my engineering career field for 6 months and attended classes for 6 months each year. The pay from my co-op job was just enough to pay for all my college tuition costs, with my second job in the grocery store covering my car and weekend dating costs.

I worked hard during those years, probably harder than I did after graduation when I started with AT&T with an Electrical Engineering (EE) degree that catapulted my hourly pay to about $5 per hour. I came to recognize that workers with lower skills work just as hard, or harder, than more educated workers, and they deserve a fair salary that is sufficient to avoid living in poverty or requiring government subsidies.

Fair pay is a way to respect the inherent worth and dignity of every person. Help with a hand up enables people to become financially independent.

College Education Debt Crisis

Definition

College students are graduating with a debt burden that can take a lifetime to pay off. These same students will also be faced with bills to pay for the U.S. national debt and environment damage.

In 2018, 69% of college students graduated with an average debt of $29,800. Average college loan debt has risen 62% in the last 10 years (Student Loan Hero, n.d.). Between 1999 and 2019, total U.S. student loans increased from $90 billion (Indiviglio 2011) to $1.57 trillion (CNBC 2019). In 2019, student loan debt is 17 times higher than it was 10 years earlier.

The Worker Skills, Worker's Fair Pay, and College Education Debt crises are all related. They are all putting an enormous burden on Americans who want to work hard and achieve a reasonable standard of living.

Research data and trends
In 2019, the $1.57 trillion in student loans was the 2nd largest consumer debt category behind mortgage debt. Student loan debt is greater than both auto loan and credit card debt combined.

Since 1985, higher education costs have surged more than 500%; thus, a 4-year education that cost $10,000 in 1985 now costs $50,000. That cost makes college out of financial reach for many young people and is affecting our world standing in percentage of the population with college degrees. World leaders are now South Korea, Japan, Canada, and Russia at about 55% of their population with college degrees, while the U.S., at 40%, is just slightly above the world average of 38% (Value Colleges, n.d.).

Some individual colleges and universities are trying to tackle the problem. Indiana University, for example, put a number of programs in place to help students avoid graduating with a crippling loan debt. Their most significant program is a simple annual letter to the students that clearly informs them of the debt they are incurring and the cost of that debt. This simple report includes:

- Total education loan debt incurred to date
- Interest rate that will be charged on the debt

- Monthly payments that will be required

- Cumulative payments that will be required; loans plus interest

- Projected interest to be paid

(Nykiel 2019)

Due to the interest on the debt over time, students will pay about 40% more for the part of their education costs that they borrow. This annual loan letter to students, plus some other programs, have resulted in 2017-2018 graduates having 19% less student debt than the students who graduated 6 years earlier. Based on their success, more states, Nebraska and Florida, will now require similar loan information be disclosed to students annually.

Higher education is, increasingly, not optional. The Georgetown Center on Education and the Workforce predicts that by 2020, 65% of all jobs in America will require an education beyond high school (Carnevale et al. 2013). During the first quarter of 2018, college graduates earned weekly wages that were 80% higher than those of high school graduates. More education is one way to reduce the working poor; however, college has been getting more expensive and paying down college loans reduces the wage benefit of college.

Prices at private non-profit 4-year colleges doubled, and prices at public 4-year schools tripled over a 30-year period (College Board 2018). Comparing our 2018 college costs to other countries, we find college costs are substantially lower in other countries:

Table 14: Least Expensive College Costs by Country
(2018)

Country	College Cost per Year $
Germany	0
Switzerland	1,168
China	3,300
Canada	4,939
Japan	5,228
U.S.	8,202

Reference: (Safier 2018)

There are a few hopeful signs on the horizon. For example, New York University (NYU) medical school announced a tuition-free program starting in 2019. Chairman of the Board Ken Langone donated $100 million to this fund, and he helped raise another $350 million. This scholarship fund will enable free-tuition scholarships to the medical school in perpetuity. Ken Langone, who made his fortune from investing in Home Depot, is an example of what a successful business leader, with strong connections to our universities, can do to help reduce college debt for students (Stahl 2019).

Another example of innovative approaches to financing higher education comes from Morehouse College. At the 2019 graduating class ceremony, the commencement speaker Robert F. Smith, a graduate of Morehouse and the richest African-American in America with an estimated worth of $5 billion, announced he would provide scholarships to the entire 396-member graduating class that would enable them to pay off all their student debt. This is estimated to be a $40 million scholarship gift. Smith then asked the graduating class to pay it forward with their own scholarship donations in the future (Erb 2019).

The U.S. accepts the largest number of foreign college students of any country in the world, at 1.1 million in 2018. The next largest country was the U.K. at about 0.5 million. From 1995 to 2015, the percentage of foreign students in U.S. graduate computer science and electrical engineering programs increased from 48% to 79% (National Foundation on American Policy 2018); only 21% of those in these programs were U.S. citizens in 2015. The top foreign country sending students to the U.S. is China. However, when we look at all students who travel to other countries to be educated worldwide, the U.S. is not even in the top ten: China, India, Saudi Arabia, South Korea, Canada, Vietnam, Taiwan, Brazil, Japan, and Mexico. Foreign college education is an option for U.S. students, who may be interested in finding the best worldwide education available at the lowest cost. If America wants to be a technology leader in the world, we need more students in our own advanced computer science and engineering programs, and more students in the best programs in the world.

If a student is willing to travel, 40 countries in the world offer free, government-funded college education, including Germany, Denmark, and Scotland. In order to help fill their country's shortage of skilled workers, Germany offers 900 tuition-free programs in English. Brazil has a registration fee, but no tuition. In Finland there are no tuition fees, but living costs must be covered by the student. France has no tuition and a small registration fee of about $200 per year at public universities (Value Colleges, n.d.). Many of these countries offer these free-tuition, or low-tuition, rates to students from other countries. Guidance counselors in U.S. high schools could include more international options in the information provided to their students.

Reducing college debt can take other tacks. Helping find the lowest cost loans is one example. Fifteen percent of the college loan debt was borrowed from private loan companies at interest rates that ran as high as 14% per year. Even though federal loans are available at 2.5% per year, more than half of undergraduates do not take full advantage of federal low-interest loans before borrowing from high-interest private loan companies.

Students also need to be aware that the type of college is likely to have an effect on college loan debt:

- At public colleges 66% of students graduated with debt averaging $25,550

- At private non-profit colleges 75% of students graduated with debt averaging $32,300

- At private for-profit colleges 88% of students graduated with debt averaging $38,950

(Student Loan Hero 2019)

Guidance counselors can use these statistics to help high school students decide which college they can afford.

While many young Americans choose to earn an advanced degree in order to compete in today's economy, the costs and debt burden are often prohibitively expensive. An MBA degree carried the lowest average debt ($42,000), a Law degree ($140,616) was next, and a Medicine degree ($161,772) was the highest. Graduate school debt accounted for about 40% of all college debt.

Preventing debt is better than planning to help pay it off later. More needs to be done to help future students avoid creating college debt.

College Education Debt Crisis Follies
[(C) denotes citizen folly; (G) denotes government folly]

- Encouraging students to go to schools they cannot afford (C)

- Encouraging students to borrow money to finance their education (C)

- Not providing more vocational or technical training and lower public college tuition rates to meet the technology shift skill requirements (G)

- For-profit schools charging higher tuition for inferior education (B)

Possible Goal
Stop the increase in the average new student's college debt, and begin an annual decrease

Possible Results Measure
Average student loan debt

Likely Root Causes
Students choosing a school they cannot afford
(Public college students graduate with less debt.)

Students not fully aware of debt costs
(Private loans are much more expensive than federal loans, and many young people do not understand the impact of interest compounded over time.)

High cost of college tuitions
(Costs have doubled or tripled in the past 30 years, while wages lagged.)

Few colleges offer co-op work, for pay-as-you-go opportunities

Insufficient scholarships

Insufficient family savings for college; savings are impossible for the working poor

Possible Improvements
(* Asterisk indicates no- or low-cost to the federal government)

*High School counselors, parents and colleges helping students choose schools they can afford (Establish guidelines for college debt limits.)

*Utilizing non-profit community organizations to help advise students on college selection (e.g., Take Stock in Children)

*Colleges helping students minimize the debt they acquire; as well as establishing goals to reduce the average student debt of graduating seniors

*Send students an annual letter providing all their loan information

*Share and utilize best practices from the states and colleges with the lowest student debt

*Reduce the number of high-interest private loans

Increase the number of scholarships available, making that a higher priority of alumni funding campaigns (NYU Medical School is a best practice example.)

Minimize tuition increases at state public colleges; provide sufficient state funds

Improve High School preparation for college to reduce remedial college course requirements that increase college costs with no college credits

Crisis annual cost
With student loan debt of $1.5 trillion, if we assume it is possible for students to pay that off in 20 years, the cost of this crisis is $75 billion per year.

Federal Budget cost reduction opportunities for 2024
In September 2017, the U.S. Department of Education reported that the default rate of student loan borrowers was approximately 11.5% (U.S. Department of Education 2018). That percentage may sound low, but it means that about 580,000 students are defaulting on their loan payments. A default is defined as no payments for at least 9 months. 11.5% of $1.5 trillion would be a $172 billion loss on federal government student loans.

A total of $1.5 trillion in loans have already been issued, primarily federal loans at low interest rates. By reducing new student debt, future defaults could be reduced by 10% in 2024, from $144 billion to $130 billion, for a savings of $14 billion a year in 2024. While $14 billion per year is not much at the Federal level, every billion counts.

Potential House Caucus to implement House CAT Improvements
Higher Education Caucus: Chair Andre Carson (D)

Personal Story – College Debt Crisis

I was able to attend a co-op school (Northeastern University) in Boston, Mass., which alternates six months of school with six months of work in a five-year program to earn a BS degree. The co-op approach enabled me to graduate debt free with a BS degree in Electrical Engineering (EE). While this took an extra year (with no summer vacation breaks), I graduated with a degree and two years of engineering work experience.

While this took an extra year (with no summer vacation breaks), I graduated with a degree and two years of engineering work experience.

Many students will continue their education beyond an undergraduate degree and need to avoid debt accumulation there as well. My daughter, for example, currently has a scholarship that covers 100% of the tuition in her Ph.D. program, which she is enrolled in while also continuing her full-time work. Many employers will pay for higher education degrees obtained for their employees.

Make sure your children and grandchildren have good information and advice for their college choice that will minimize their debt burden.

Social Media Crisis

Definition

Today, American citizens are spending less time studying and working, because more time is being spent on social media. In 2018, the average person in the U.S. spent 11 hours per day in front of devices: smart phones, computers, video games, tablets, radios and TVs (Nielsen 2018). Ten years earlier, in 2008, that average was about 8 hours. This 3-hour, 38%, increase is mostly spent on smart phones.

Research data and trends

In his writings, Ben Franklin's major focus was on personal industry (i.e., work ethic) which he believed to be the most critical virtue needed in America. In his list of 13 virtues, Franklin stated: "Lose no time; be always employed in something useful." That concept of personal industry embraces both work and study. Time, according to Franklin, is the most important asset we all have, and it is limited; once lost, it can never be recovered, and replacements can't be purchased. Essentially, time is life. Franklin's advice for a successful life was to encourage everyone to value their time, using it to work, save, and study in order to do better. Ben Franklin's advice is still very relevant today, and it is a key to reducing our worker crises (Franklin 1726).

According to the Pew Research Center, the percentage of Americans who are active on Facebook increased from 5% in 2005 to 69% in 2019 (Pew Research 2019). The average time spent on screens by teenagers on entertainment and social activities in 2016 was:

Table 15: Teenage Average Screen Time
(2016)

Entertainment and Social Media	Teenagers' Time
TV/Cable/Streaming	2 hours/day
Social Media	9 hours/day
Total	11 hours/day

(Sun 2017)

If we assume we sleep 8 hours per day, that leaves 16 hours we are awake. Eleven of those 16 hours, or 69% of our awake time, are spent viewing or listening to a device. That leaves 5 hours to do everything else, which is not enough time to create a healthy, happy, and productive life.

In 2017, children under the age of two watched various types of screens an average of 42 minutes per day; children between 2 and 4 were watching various screens an average of two hours and 39 minutes per day; and kids 5 to 8 spent nearly 3 hours per day on screens. Those national averages are well above the recommended limits for healthy children. Children need time reading, playing with others, and engaging in physical activities. Children who get too much screen time early in life are likely to spend even more time in front of a screen later.

Multiple studies have linked too much screen time with physical and mental health issues. In 2018, the American Heart Association issued a warning that too much screen time can increase the odds that children will become overweight and obese (Molina 2018). Furthermore, not only is social media addictive, it is taking time from our youth that they need to exercise and develop skills to assure a successful and healthy future.

Early childhood is a period of rapid development and a time when family lifestyle patterns can boost health gains. Infants and toddlers under the age of 2 should not spend any time in front of a screen; instead, they should be read to, for up to an hour at a time. For children ages 2 to 5, screen time should be limited to no more than one hour per day (American Academy of Pediatrics 2016). Toddlers who spend two hours or more per day in front of a screen are more likely to behave badly or have ADHD. At least three hours of physical activity per day is recommended for infants and younger children (World Health Organization 2019).

Although the internet can provide access to useful information, it can also provide misinformation and outright lies. Many websites encourage hate, violence, and increased political divisiveness. Furthermore, especially for children, the internet can be a forum for bullying, shaming, and exclusion. The U.S. Federal Communications Commission has set standards for TV broadcasts but lacks standards for internet information. Since the internet seems to be replacing print media and TV time, standards are needed here as well.

Social Media Crisis Follies
[(C) denotes citizen follies; (G) denotes government follies]

- A culture that is not spending sufficient time to reskill in order to keep up with rapidly changing technology (C)

- Not teaching critical thinking skills in our schools or homes (G)

- Not using critical thinking skills in our government (G)

- A cultural shift away from our value on work ethic towards increasing time on social media and TV (C)

- Allowing very young children too much screen time (C)_

Possible Goal
Decrease time spent on TV and social media by 2% per year for adults and teenagers in order to increase time spent on work and learning by 2% per year.

Possible Results Measures
Average daily time spent on TV and social media by children, teenagers, and adults.

Likely Root Causes
Addictive social media, video games, and TV (cable and streaming)

Too much screen time allowed for very young children (infants to 8 years)

Possible Improvements
(* Asterisk indicates no- or low-cost to the federal government)

*Parents reduce screen time for toddlers and children to the recommended healthy limits

*Adults and teenagers agreeing to reduce TV and social media use

*Implement broadcast standards for the internet to reduce or eliminate sites encouraging divisiveness, hatred, and violence

Crisis annual cost
We assumed half the 10% GDP loss from our low workforce participation rate was from lack of worker skills. If we assume the other half is from lack of U.S. worker industriousness, that is also $1 trillion per year of GDP loss, the estimated cost of this crisis.

Federal Budget cost reduction opportunities
The GDP will benefit if citizens spend less time on social media and more time studying, reskilling, and working. Again, if we assume just 5% of that

$1 trillion GDP ends up in taxes for the federal government, that would provide $50 billion per year additional federal revenue.

<u>Potential House Caucuses to implement House CAT Improvements</u>
No existing caucus identified.

Personal Story – Social Media Crisis

One of my assignments during my AT&T career was as the first Cell Phone Product Manager. Bell Labs had just invented Cellular Service to replace the prior very limited, and very expensive, mobile phone service. The first several years of cellular service were terrible, because it took years to build the cell site network coverage required to provide uninterrupted service. In addition, before we had sufficient volume to develop cell phone chips, the first cell phones had to use printed wiring boards for the transmitter and receiver which were put in the trunk of a car and wired to the driver's console. I recall being interviewed on a late-night TV show and asked about the future of what was initially very expensive and poor cellular service; I boldly projected that more than half of American adults would have a cell phone someday as both the service and technology improved over time. I was laughed at for being too optimistic for what was, at the time, an expensive and poor-quality service. My kids now laugh at the videotape of that interview, because I was too pessimistic in my forecast.

Chapter 9 - HEALTH CARE CRISES

The Health Care Crisis category includes five crises that directly affect the health and life of U.S. citizens: Use of Drugs, Diabetes, Cancer Rate, Gun Violence, and Health Care Costs.

The U.S. is spending about 18% percent of GDP on Health Care, while other advanced countries are only spending an average of 11% of GDP. Many of these other countries have universal health care, and they are still paying significantly less of their GDP for health care. We would need to reduce our U.S. Health Care costs by 40% just to get to the average that other advanced nations spend on their health care.

Major reasons why our health care costs are higher than other advanced countries include:

- A population that has become less healthy over the past few decades

- An aging population

- A major drug usage crisis, including both legal and illegal drugs

- Prescription drugs cost much more than in other countries

- Medical system costs are higher than in other countries

- Our health care system focuses on repair rather than prevention; other countries focus on prevention

- Economic incentives for doctors to overprescribe medicines, over test patients, and undertake unnecessary surgeries

Our health care system is essentially a repair business; when a person is sick, hurt, or wounded, the medical community tries to fix the problem. While medical repair is a good thing, our health care system needs to focus on prevention in order to improve our health and to reduce our health care costs.

The following is a quality analysis of each of the five Health Care Crises listed above.

Use of Drugs Crisis

Definition
In 2000, there were 17,000 U.S. drug overdose deaths; by 2017, that number increased to 72,000. This is a 320% increase in 17 years (Mukherjee 2018). Drug overdose deaths are now higher than those from car crashes or gun violence.

This horrendous number of drug overdose deaths is explained in part because the average number of drugs used per person in the U.S. far exceeds the number used per person in other countries. The use of addictive opioids for pain management is so far out of control that the Centers for Disease Control and Prevention has recognized it as an epidemic, which they define as more than 100 deaths per day.

A major cause of excessive drug use has been the overprescription of addictive legal pain medication. Once a person becomes addicted to these drugs, and the doctor is no longer willing to continue to write prescriptions, the new addict turns to the readily available, but illegal, suppliers who have even more potent addictive drugs for sale. According to the National Institute on Drug Abuse, opioids are a class of drugs that include heroin, synthetic opioids such as fentanyl, and pain relievers available legally by prescription, such as oxycodone (OxyContin®), hydrocodone (Vicodin®), codeine, morphine and many others.

Research data and trends
3.8 million people in the U.S. were using prescription opioids in 2018. Opioid overdoses killed 33,000 people in 2015. This number increased by more than 50% to 50,000, in 2017. The U.S. has the highest percentage of people who are addicted to prescription pain medications than any other country in the world. Although the U.S. has only 5% of the world's population, we consumed approximately 80% of the world's prescribed opioids (Gusovsky 2016).

This crisis began with the drug OxyContin, a semi-synthetic opioid manufactured by Purdue Pharma. Their initial business filing for approval with the Food and Drug Administration (FDA) in 1995 falsely claimed it was not addictive. After getting FDA approval, Purdue hired the FDA doctor who had approved OxyContin for an executive position at Purdue Pharma. Purdue continued to reassure doctors in brochures and videos that concerns related to OxyContin addiction were exaggerated. Furthermore, Purdue's sales representatives were trained to tell physicians that OxyContin was less addictive than other opioids, a claim that had not been recognized by the FDA. The Sackler family (owners of Purdue Pharma) made more than $4 billion between 2008 and 2016 on opioid sales.

Over 20 years after FDA approval of OxyContin, several states have sued the pharmaceutical companies for approximately $200 billion in state treatment costs associated with the opioid epidemic. The treatment and deaths of those addicted have created enormous costs, more than 50 times the amount of Purdue Pharma's profits (CBS News 2018).

In March 2019, Purdue agreed to pay $270 million to the state of Oklahoma in an opioid treatment settlement of a suit by the state. That is the first of more than 1,600 lawsuits pending against Purdue Pharma. On August 27, 2019, Purdue Pharma offered to set up an opioid trust fund with $10 to $12 billion, as part of bankruptcy filing, to settle all the lawsuits against them (Spector and DiNapoli 2019).

The costs of the opioid crisis include health care, criminal justice, and lost productivity. In 2015, this epidemic cost our country $504 billion (White House 2017). From 2015 to 2017, the opioid deaths increased by 50%; so, the 2017 annual treatment costs of this crisis probably also increased by 50%. We can estimate that the total cost of the U.S. drug crisis will be closer to $1 trillion per year by 2020.

The White House asked for $17 billion in the 2019 federal budget to help with treatment of the opioid crisis. While $17 billion may sound like a lot of money, it is only 8% of the states' treatment costs which are $200 billion.

The problem of opioid addiction is not a new one. When David Courtwright, a history professor at the University of North Florida, studied opioid epidemics in Europe, he found that in the 1870s and 1880s, the per capita use of opioids tripled when physicians increased the use of morphine for pain. The epidemic died out when physicians quit prescribing morphine for pain and began prescribing safer drugs, such as aspirin. Addicts aged out of their addiction; that is, they either died of disease, or overdose. In his book, *Dark Paradise: A History of Opioid Addiction in America,* Courtwright argues that the only viable resolution to past opioid epidemics was to stop prescribing opioids to patients who have not been given them before. In articles for the *New England Journal of Medicine* and briefings before Congress, he argues that this approach should be used to combat opioids in the U.S. (Courtwright 2001).

A computer model which could be used for developing an opioid policy was created by the Massachusetts General Hospital Institute for Technology Assessment. Their model predicted opioid (both legal and illegal) overdose deaths would increase from 33,100 in 2015 to 81,700 in 2025, a 147% increase. Their model also projected that by 2025, 50% of new addicts would be created from legal prescription opioids and 50% from illegal drugs (e.g., heroin and fentanyl). Of those new addicts, however, 80% of the 2025 overdose deaths would be from the more potent illegal opioids (Massachusetts General Hospital 2019).

These predictions have been born out in 2017 data. Drugabuse.gov reported a total of 70,237 drug overdose deaths in 2017, an increase of more than 400% in less than 20 years. Of the 2017 drug overdose deaths, about two thirds (68%) were from opioids (Centers for Disease Control and Prevention 2018).

Unfortunately, the opioid addiction crisis is fueled by money. The higher the opioid addiction rate, the higher the demand for illegal drugs and the more profitable it becomes for drug smugglers. The sale of illegal drugs has become a source of funding for criminal activity both in this country as well as in other countries that supply our addicts. The growth of this profitable drug market has led to drug cartels, primarily in Central America where drug lords rule. People trying to escape the violence in these countries has led to increased asylum immigration seekers, fueling our southern border crisis.

Use of Drugs Crisis Follies
[(G) denotes government follies; (B) denotes business follies; (C) denotes citizen follies]

- The initial, false business filing by Purdue Pharma for OxyContin was approved by the FDA (G)

- The American Medical Association giving guidelines to doctors to prescribe pain medication in order to achieve zero pain for patients (B)

- Overprescription of addictive legal pain medication (B)

- Excessive per person drug use in the U.S. (B) (C)_

Possible goal
Reduce the number of those who die annually from a drug overdose.
(Goal 5% reduction per year to return to the 2000 level of 17,000 deaths per year, a 75% reduction from the 70,000 deaths in 2017.)

Possible Results Measure
The number of drug overdose deaths

Likely root causes
OxyContin is FDA approved and legally available, even though it was falsely claimed to be non-addictive.

Significant overprescription of legal pain medications.

Increased illegal drug use stemming from addiction to legally prescribed drugs.

The response time of emergency aid reaching overdose victims is too slow (e.g., accessibility to naloxone for reversal of opioid overdose effects).

Insufficient treatment opportunities for those addicted to opioids.

Possible Improvements
(* Asterisk indicates no- or low-cost to the federal government)
_*Withdraw, or severely limit, FDA approval of opioids for patients who have never used opioids.

*More responsible behavior by drug prescribers to reduce opioid overprescription.

*Use Drug Enforcement Agency's licensing power to aggressively restrict the number of physicians able to prescribe selected opioids.

*Create a federally approved guideline for the use of opioids that will serve as a basis for malpractice claims when violated by doctors.

*Prescribe more non-drug treatment options for those in pain.

*Stop China's shipments of fentanyl to the U.S. via the U.S. Postal Service. (Laws need to be changed to enable the U.S. Postal Service to use the same processes used by Federal Express, which can deny suspicious drug shipments.)

Additional Customs Border Protection (CBP) agents in U.S. Postal Service and Federal Express international hubs.

Reduce smuggling of drugs into the U.S.

Increase enforcement crackdown on drug-dealers.

Faster response time for treating overdose cases.

Make naloxone available for all first responders.

Improved treatment opportunities for those addicted.

State Medicare Expansion to enable better drug treatment for lower income addicts. (For example, Florida has not accepted Medicare Expansion, yet it was the state that had the most "pill mill" clinics that distributed huge quantities of opioids.)

Crisis annual cost
The annual cost estimate for the opioid drug crisis was about $756 billion per year in 2017. With the opioid crisis still growing, and adding in other

drug crisis costs, a reasonable estimate of the annual drug crisis cost in the U.S. will be about $1 trillion per year for 2020.

Federal budget cost reduction opportunities
The Federal budget plans to spend only $17 billion in 2019 to deal with this enormous epidemic. In the next 5 years, it is unlikely that the need, and therefore this cost, can be reduced. However, in the long run, this epidemic can be slowly eliminated if the U.S. does not allow opioid prescriptions to new patients, thereby avoiding creation of new addicts.

This is an enormously costly crisis, and the costs are mostly at the individual family, community, and state levels. The Federal government enabled this crisis with the approval of opioids, and it should take steps to reverse the approval of opioids for new patients. This is a preventive, no-cost way to eliminate this crisis.

Potential House Caucuses to implement House CAT Improvements
Prescription Drug Abuse Caucus: Co-Chairs Hal Rogers (R), Stephen Lynch (D)

Addiction Treatment & Recovery Caucus: Co-Chairs Tim Ryan (D), Jim Sensenbrenner (R)

Personal Story – Use of Drugs Crisis

After my surgery for stage IV colon cancer in 2017, I was offered opioids for the pain. I refused this offer and took only Tylenol to avoid possible addiction. I had a week or two of significant pain, which is now long forgotten. The driving reason for my refusal of opioids is that I had seen one of my adult children's close friends, a brilliant young man who was very religious, become addicted to opioids and this addiction destroyed their friendship.

My grandchildren also have friends who have become addicted to opioids, and they cry when telling me about the loss of these friends. Their families have spent thousands of dollars on multiple unsuccessful rehab treatments.

Diabetes Crisis

Definition

The incidence of diabetes has increased from 4.4% of the population in 2000 to 9.4% in 2015, which is a 113% increase (Centers for Disease Control and Prevention 2017). During this same 15-year period, another 27% of our population became pre-diabetic. Without a change in lifestyle habits, these people are at risk for developing diabetes. Nearly half the adult U.S. population has prediabetes or diabetes.

Obesity, a major factor determining the chances of developing diabetes, increased from 30.5% of the population in 2000 to 40% in 2015 (Hales 2017). Obesity is responsible for more than an increase in diabetes; it has also been cited as a contributing factor to between 100,000 and 400,000 deaths per year in the U.S. Obesity is causing more deaths per year than our drug epidemic.

Research and Data

Diabetes is a group of diseases that affect how your body uses blood sugar (glucose). Glucose is vital to your health because it's an important source of energy for the cells that make up your muscles and tissues. It is also your brain's main source of fuel. Diabetes can lead to excess sugar in your blood which can lead to serious health issues. Being overweight and inactive is strongly correlated with diabetes (Mayo Clinic 2019).

The terms "overweight" and "obese" are medical terms that are defined by a person's Body Mass Index (BMI), a calculation based on a person's height and weight to measure body fat. You can enter your height and weight on various websites to have your Body Mass Index (BMI) calculated. The following table lists the BMI for people who are normal weight, overweight, obese, and extremely obese (National Heart, Lung, and Blood Institute, n.d.).

Table 16: Body Mass Index Categories

BMI Category	BMI
Normal weight	18.5 to 24.9
Overweight	25.0 to 29.9
Obesity	30.0 to 39.9
Extreme Obesity	40.0 and above

Although many of us fight to maintain a healthy weight, we are simultaneously being tempted to spend time in sedentary activities like watching television or movies, and using social media. In addition, massive advertising campaigns, many running on the media we are watching, tempt us to eat items that contribute to increased weight. These items include fast foods, high-sugar drinks, processed foods, breads, and sweets. Our country's businesses seem to have an effective campaign going to increase obesity and diabetes; we need an effective campaign to decrease both.

The problem caused by ultra-processed food is not limited to our country. Health researchers in France studied the effects of ultra-processed foods on health. Ultra-processed foods are manufactured industrially from ingredients that include additives used for preservation and cosmetic purposes. These ultra-processed foods include snacks, desserts, and ready-to-eat meals such as frozen dinners. The number of calories in these ultra-processed foods was double that for the same weight of other foods. People who eat ultra-processed foods tend to be younger and lower income, with a higher BMI and lower level of physical activity. Furthermore, individuals who consume these ultra-processed foods have an increased risk of early death. These findings were published in the Journal of the American Medical Association (JAMA) (Schnabel et al. 2019).

Our weight crisis, much of it due to processed food and inactivity, is alarming. In 2015 and 2016, the percentage of adults, aged 20 and over, who were overweight was 72%, and the percentage who were obese was 40%, according to the Centers for Disease Control and Prevention (CDC). The CDC reported that the 93 million people in the U.S. (40% of our population) who were obese resulted in an annual Health Care Cost increase of $150 billion per year (Centers for Disease Control and Prevention 2018).

Unfortunately, the U.S. leads the world with our obesity rate. A 2015 study of countries in the Organization for Economic Co-operation and Development (OECD), ranked countries on obesity (Organization for Economic Co-operation and Development, 2017, 5), as shown in the following table:

Table 17: Obesity by Country

Country	Obesity % of Population
U.S.	38.2%
Germany	23.6%
Spain	16.7%
Italy	9.8%
Japan	3.7%

The average obesity rate worldwide was 13% in 2016. Our obesity rate of 38.2% of the population puts us at three times the world average (World Health Organization 2018).

Being overweight causes an increased risk of cancer, heart disease, and diabetes. It is therefore a major cause of the increase in the cost of U.S. health care. The health care costs resulting from being overweight exceed even the costs associated with smoking.

The rise in obesity is particularly alarming in children who will face the cumulative effects of this health hazard for their entire lives. The prevalence of obesity in high school students increased from 10% to 15% from 2000 to 2017 (Centers for Disease Control and Prevention 2017) (Infogram, n.d.).

This alarming increase in obesity is not limited to the United States. According to the World Health Organization (WHO), China's overall rate of obesity in 2009 was less than 5%; however, in some major cities where fast foods and sugar-filled drinks are available, the obesity rate has climbed to 20% (World Health Organization, n.d.). The combination of a "western diet" and more sedentary life style (i.e., office work rather than farm work) is beginning to cause major health problems and economic costs in China. Less exercise combined with more fast food and sugary drinks leads to significant increases in obesity rates.

Linked to the obesity epidemic is the increase in the incidence of diabetes in the U.S., as documented by the Centers for Disease Control and Prevention (Centers for Disease Control and Prevention, n.d.):

Table 18: U.S. Obesity and Diabetes Increases

Year	% Obese	% of People with Diabetes	# of People with Diabetes
1958	10%	1.0%	1.6 million
2000	30.5%	4.4%	12.1 million
2015	40%	9.4%	30.3 million

90% of those with diabetes were overweight or obese.

In addition to the 30.3 million people with diabetes, 84.1 million are pre-diabetics.

Poor diet is the leading cause of death in the U.S., according to a study by the Tufts University Friedman School of Nutrition Science and Policy. They have estimated the cost of obesity is $1.7 trillion per year (Mozaffarian and Glickman 2019).

Researchers now know that the major cause of diabetes is a combination of genetics and lifestyle, which leads to the development of insulin resistance. Insulin resistance occurs when the body does not use its own insulin as well as it should. Being overweight is a risk factor for diabetes, as are sedentary lifestyle, family history, ethnicity, and consuming too much sugar. The increase in sugar in so many processed foods and drinks is also a major cause of increased obesity and increased diabetes.

While genetics is not a factor that can be changed, lifestyle is. The auto industry changed to develop cars that were safer and had improved gas mileage. The food industry could reduce the amount of sugar in processed foods, which will probably require some regulation to do so. One positive example is the American Beverage Association's (ABA) recent announcement of a goal and plan to help reduce sugary drink consumption in America by 20% (American Beverage Association, n.d.).

For this crisis in particular, prevention is the key to reduction. Because it is so hard to lose weight once it is gained, focusing on the next generation is a crucial approach to this crisis. However, children generally follow the lifestyle of their parents; therefore, to have a healthy next generation, parents need to set the example by eating healthier and exercising more. A place to start is in the grocery store, because we eat what we buy. Healthy eating starts with healthy shopping.

Family meals at the dinner table, without TV and cell phone distractions, are important to encourage healthy eating habits. Family meals also provide needed family time. Several studies have shown that more frequent family meals decrease the risk of childhood obesity, probably because a planned family meal is usually healthier than a fast food dinner. It also has the added advantage of being less expensive.

Another key to preventing obesity is to get more exercise and avoid a sedentary life. Unfortunately, in the past 10 years, the average American has gone from sitting about 5 ½ hours per day to 6 ½. That is the wrong direction. The time spent watching TV has remained stable, but the time sitting at a computer or cell phone has increased. Inactivity is unhealthy; it contributes to obesity, diabetes, and heart disease (Yang et al. 2019).

The increase in overweight and obesity, which contribute to diabetes, has many causes. Ultimately, however, we each need to consume less and exercise more. Net calories consumed each day need to be equal to net calories burned in order to maintain weight. Calories consumed need to be less than those burned to lose weight. For those with cell phones, which seems to be most of us, there are free apps to help track calories consumed and calories burned on a daily basis.

Diabetes Crisis Follies
[(B) denotes business follies; (C) denotes citizen follies; (G) denotes government follies]

- The increase in the amount of sugar and fat in so many processed foods and foods served in fast-food restaurants (B)

- Insufficient education on the importance of a healthy diet and guidelines on how to avoid becoming overweight or obese (G)

- Insufficient multi-use paths for walking, running, and bicycling that can be used for short trips instead of driving (G)

- Increase in a sedentary lifestyle brought about by spending more time on social media and in front of TV screens (C)

Possible Goal
Reduction of the percentage of the U.S. population with diabetes

Possible Results Measure
Annual percentage of U.S. population with diabetes

Likely Root Causes
Increased intake of sugar in many processed foods

Increased intake of sugar-filled drinks

Increased reliance on high-calorie fast foods

Lack of exercise (i.e., a more sedentary lifestyle)

Lack of education and incentives for our youth and adults

Possible Improvements
(* Asterisk indicates no- or low-cost to the federal government)

*Reduce sugar in processed foods

*Reduce the amount of sugar-filled drinks consumed

*Reduce the calories in fast-food meals
(All the above improvements may require some regulations)

*Develop healthy exercise and meal plans for individuals and families

Educate children about the importance of diet and exercise

Provide trail networks for walking, running, and bicycling

Incorporate salad bars and reduced-sugar foods in school lunches

Crisis annual cost
An August 2019 estimate by the Tufts University Friedman School of Nutrition Science and Policy on the cost of diabetes was $327 billion per year, with the total cost of obesity at $1.7 trillion per year.

Federal Budget cost reduction opportunities
If we assume the Federal government is paying half the cost of this crisis, and individuals are paying the other half, a reduction of 2% per year should result in about a 10% reduction in the government's cost by the year 2024, which is a $170 billion savings.

Potential House Caucuses to implement House CAT Improvements
Diabetes Caucus: Co-Chairs Tom Reed (R), Diana DeGette (D)

Food Safety Caucus: Chair Rosa DeLauro (D)

Personal Story – Diabetes Crisis

Like most people, I have had to struggle to stay at a healthy weight. At the age of 75, I am 6 feet tall and weigh 183 pounds. Based on my height and weight my BMI is 24.8, which falls just within the limits of normal. A BMI of 25 and above is considered overweight. My physician, and I, would like for me to be 10 pounds lighter. For the majority of my adult life, I weighed over 183 pounds, and my BMI calculation showed me overweight.

I am very fortunate now because my fiancée is a great cook who makes healthy and delicious meals. While I was working on this book, she wrote a cook book to share her recipes with family and friends.

Exercise is a key part of maintaining a healthy weight. For the first 19 years of retirement, I was able to play doubles tennis three days a week for two hours. Unfortunately, a fall on the tennis court in May 2018 tore my rotator cuff, ending my tennis days. Many people experience irreparable injury as they age, which can affect their exercise routine. My fiancée and I both live on the beach in Florida, so we can walk on the beach many days. I also lead the bicycle trail effort on the island and have access to an off-road bicycle path that goes two miles north and four miles south from my home; I can bicycle for lunch or to get a few things at the store.

The key is to find exercise you enjoy because that is what helps you stick with it. This is one reason I miss my tennis and my tennis friends. Bicycle, run, walk, play, or work out at the YMCA; just move, and have fun doing it every day.

Cancer Rate Crisis

Definition
The U.S. has a high incidence of cancer, a high death rate from cancer, and a high cost of cancer care. 38% of men and women in the U.S. will

be diagnosed with cancer at some point in their lives, based on 2013-2015 data (National Cancer Institute 2018).

Between 1999 and 2017, new cancer diagnoses increased by 34%, from 1,291,000 to 1,735,000 (National Institutes of Health 2018). During this same 18-year period, our population increased by only 19% (NIH 2018). Thus, the new cancer diagnosis rate has been increasing at almost double the rate of our population increase.

Research data and trends

In 2017, the U.S. saw 1,735,000 new cases of cancer diagnosed and 609,000 deaths from cancer (NIH 2018). That is more deaths per year than from the drug, diabetes, and gun crises combined. The estimate for new cancer cases for 2019 is 1,762,450, about a 2% increase.

Cancer can strike at any age. Cancer is the second leading cause of death among children from age 1 to 14. Cancer incidence rates increased by more than 22% for children and adolescents between 1975 and 2012 (American Cancer Society 2016).

Beyond the toll in human suffering, the cost of this disease is staggering. In 2017, the national annual expenditure for cancer care was $147 billion (NIH 2018). The following year, the U.S. was ranked as the fifth worst country in the world for cancer rates (World Cancer Research Fund, n.d.).

Here again, as with other health-related crises, prevention makes sense; however, little is being done in the field of prevention. Carcinogens (cancer-causing substances) continue to permeate our environment, the food we eat, and the air we breathe. Instead of developing plans to reduce carcinogens, the current administration changed the U.S. Environmental Protection Agency (EPA) rules in 2018 to enable release of more carcinogens into the air by coal-burning plants.

Cancer types and rates do vary across the country. A study of cancer rates by Ohio State University showed nearly double the liver cancer rates in areas with blue-green algae during the period of 1999 to 2010. Microcystins released from blue-green algae (cyanobacteria) have been found to be correlated with increased liver cancer. The only cluster of increased liver cancer rates in Florida was found to be near Lake

Okeechobee, where microcystins have been found to be 300 times the U.S. recommended safe level (Simon 2019).

There is no antidote for this toxin, and pets exposed to toxic algae can die in days. According to the Environmental Protection Agency website, harmful algae blooms can have a severe impact on human health and are a major environmental problem in all 50 states (U.S. Environmental Protection Agency, n.d.). Algae blooms are caused by a combination of sunlight, slow moving water, and too much nutrient pollution from human activities, especially from excess fertilizer which leads to polluted storm water runoff. Exacerbating these problems are inadequately maintained septic and sewage systems that leak human sewage into our waterways. This is another example of how our crises are interconnected: in this case, infrastructure, environment, and health crises.

Another form of cancer is caused by the Human Papillomavirus (HPV). This term refers to over 150 viruses that can cause warts or cancer. Nearly 80 million people, 25% of our population, are currently infected with HPV. Fortunately, there is a vaccine to prevent the HPV virus. The CDC recommends that 11- and 12-year-olds receive the vaccine, at the time children receive other vaccines, to avoid becoming infected. The Centers for Disease Control and Prevention (CDC) recommends use of the HPV vaccine; however, only about 50% of our children are fully vaccinated, which requires two shots (Centers for Disease Control and Prevention 2018).

There are some solutions to reduce cancer rates that do use prevention. This approach seems to be working with smoking, for example. NIH reports that reduction in smoking has been the most significant factor in reducing cancer deaths; however, cigarette smoking in 2018 still accounts for 3 of every 10 cancer deaths and is still the most significant cause of cancer deaths.

Thanks to improved medical treatments, cancer death rates have been decreasing. The American Cancer Society has reported that from 2006 to 2016, the death rate from cancer has decreased by 1.8% per year for men and 1.4% per year for women. This lower cancer death rate is a step in the right direction, but our increased incidence of cancer is not. While we are doing a good job on repairing those with cancer to reduce death rates, we are not doing such a good job on prevention (National Institutes of Health 2019).

New studies have found that when our immune system is strong, it can kill early cancer cells. To increase prevention, individuals should eat healthy foods and exercise regularly, which seems like a common solution to many of our health crises. In the analysis of the diabetes crisis and social media crisis, we found that children were eating a less healthy diet and getting less exercise than they had in the past. This could cause a weaker immune system and an increase in the cancer rate for children. Again, the crises we face are interrelated; some of them are causing other crises, creating a negative crisis spiral. One low-cost solution to our health crises is to eat healthier and exercise more.

Another factor in the increase in cancer rates is an increase in chronic stress. According to Anil Sood, M.D., professor of Gynecologic Oncology and Reproductive Medicine at MD Anderson Cancer Center, "Chronic stress can also help cancer grow and spread in a number of ways." Chronic stress can inhibit an immune system process that kills diseased cells and prevents them from spreading. Chronic stress can also increase the blood supply that can speed the development of cancerous tumors (Heid 2014). Unfortunately, 55% of Americans are suffering from daily stress, a much higher percentage than the world average of 35%. Reducing our 23 national crises will help reduce the chronic stress in the U.S., and thus help reduce our high cancer rate. Again, we see that these multiple crises are interrelated and create a bad spiral when the crises are increasing, but create a good spiral when they are decreasing.

Cancer Rate Crisis Follies
[(C) denotes citizen follies; (G) denotes government follies]

- Carcinogens that cause cancer are allowed in our food (G)

- Carcinogens that cause cancer continue to be released into our environment (G)

- Not getting available vaccines for cancer (C)

- Continuing to smoke, not eating healthy foods, and not exercising sufficiently (C)

Possible Goal
Reduce the annual cancer rate incidence

Possible Results Measure
Annual U.S. new cancer diagnoses

New U.S. cancer rate compared to the world average

Likely Root Causes
Carcinogens in many processed foods

Release of carcinogens into the air and water by industry

Exposure to the sun without sun protection

Blue-green algae caused by water pollution

Insufficient use of available HPV vaccine

High chronic stress in the U.S.

Possible Improvements
(* Asterisk indicates no- or low-cost to the federal government)

*Food suppliers agree to reduce carcinogens in processed foods (regulations may be needed)

*Industry agrees to reduce the release of carcinogens into the air and water (regulations may be needed)

*Individuals use sun protection products for themselves and their children to prevent skin cancer

*Individuals taught more about foods that contain carcinogens (i.e., processed foods and deli meats)

*Increase HPV vaccination rate

Reduce pollution of fresh waters

Crisis annual cost
The direct medical care cost of cancer in 2017 was $147 billion, and it is expected to rise to around $200 billion per year by 2020. The U.S. new cancer incidence rate is 40% higher than the rest of the world; therefore, 40% of U.S. medical cancer care costs is the cost of our crisis, or $80 billion per year. Lost productivity would probably double that cost to about $160 billion per year.

Federal Budget cost reduction opportunities
Assuming the federal government pays half of the $147 billion direct medical costs of cancer through Medicare and other health programs, their share is $73 billion per year. If we reduce the cancer rate by 1% per year, from 38% in 2019 to 33% in 2024, that 5% reduction could save a total of $10 billion per year in Federal government medical costs for cancer in 2024. This is not proposing a reduction in care for those in need; it is proposing we reduce the number of people who are in need of care.

Potential House Caucuses to implement House CAT Improvements
Cancer Prevention Caucus: Co-Chairs Debbie Dingell (D), Barbara Comstock (R)

Cancer Caucus: Co-Chairs Derek Kilmer (D), Brian Higgins (R)

Deadliest Cancers Caucus: Co-Chairs Anna Eshoo (D), Joe Kennedy (D)

Childhood Cancer Caucus: Co-Chairs Mike McCaul (R), Jackie Speier (D), G.K. Butterfield (D), Mike Kelly (R)

Lung Cancer Caucus: Co-Chairs Brendan Boyle (D), John Rutherford (R)

Personal Story – Cancer Rate Crisis

My wife died fifteen months after being diagnosed with stage IV colon cancer that had metastasized, or spread. Five years later, I was also diagnosed with stage IV colon cancer. Currently (2019), I am very lucky to be one of the 14% with stage IV colon cancer for whom chemo is effective; I am now in remission. However, I have to continue chemo treatments every other week to stay in remission. I feel very lucky to be alive, but I would like to see more preventive efforts to reduce new cancer rates in the next generation.

After my very healthy wife, Jane Redfern Scanlan, died from a very sudden stage IV colon cancer, I researched the subject. It appears that Europe and the U.S. have different protocols for cancer detection. The U.S. recommends screening colonoscopies for everyone based on the following parameters:

- Age
- Family history of colon cancer
- Polyps found in prior colonoscopies

Both my wife and I faithfully followed the recommended U.S. protocol for our colonoscopies; however, at the time of our cancer diagnosis, both of us had colon cancer that had already progressed to stage IV. Stage IV means the cancer has already spread from the colon to other parts of the body; therefore, surgery alone cannot cure it, and the likelihood of 5-year survival drops to 14% (American Cancer Society, n.d.).

Since 4% of the population gets colon cancer, Europe tries to identify who is in that 4% group *prior* to their getting cancer. For those individuals in the 4% group, more frequent colonoscopies are recommended; less frequent colonoscopies are recommended for those not in the 4% group. Two additional parameters are used in the Europe protocol to identify this 4% group early enough for preventive treatment:

- The presence of a long colon (the length of the colon is

- significantly longer than average for 10% of men and 20% of women)

- Weight (Overweight or underweight)

My wife Jane had a long colon, which we found out at her first colonoscopy. The significance of a long colon is that it makes the colonoscopy technically more difficult and there is more colon available to develop cancer. In addition, my wife was thin, in the underweight category. Furthermore, polyps were found on her first colonoscopy. We were never told that a combination of these three risk factors put Jane into the 4% high-risk group, placing her at higher risk of developing colon cancer. Because the U.S. does not use the European protocol of identifying those most likely to get colon cancer, her colon cancer was not detected until it was too late.

I asked the American Cancer Society to consider adopting the European protocol and was told that the U.S. would have to do years of study with patients in this country, which would be too expensive. Adopting a best medical practice from other countries should be possible based on credible studies and experience.

Gun Violence Crisis

Definition
The U.S. death rate from guns is three times higher than the world average. In 2000, there were 30,000 gun deaths in the U.S. Seventeen years later, in 2017, that number had increased to 39,773, a 33% increase (Centers for Disease Control and Prevention 2019, 12). Just in one year, from 2016 to 2017, there was an additional 7% increase.

Research data and trends
Fifty percent of the entire world's 251,000 gun deaths in 2016 happened in only six countries that make up only 10% of the world's population. The other five countries on this list generally have a weaker law enforcement and justice system than the United States.

Table 19: Highest Gun Deaths by Country (2016)

Countries	Gun Deaths
Brazil	43,200
United States	37,200
Mexico	15,400
Colombia	13,300
Venezuela	12,800
Guatemala	5,100

(Vox 2018)

A comparison of gun death rates with other countries shows the U.S. gun death rate is more than three times the world average and more than 50 times that of Japan, the country with the fewest gun deaths. Most developed nations have much lower gun death rates than we do, as shown in the table below:

Table 20: Lowest Gun Death Rates by Country (2016)

Developed Countries	Gun death rate/100,000 population
Japan	0.2
United Kingdom	0.3
Canada	2.1
World average	3.4
United States	10.6

Unfortunately, it is not just adults who are being killed. In 2018, an average of eight children were killed each day by firearms (Gander 2018). 2019 is on track to continue the horrible rate of mass shootings we had in 2018.

Gun deaths among children in the United States is 36.5 times the average rate observed in other high-income countries according to the University of Michigan Injury Prevention Center (NBC News 2018). That is perhaps the saddest statistic in this whole book. There has been no federal action to reduce this awful statistic in the seven years since the mass shooting in 2012 at Sandy Hook elementary school in Newtown, Connecticut that killed 20 children who were only six or seven years old, and six adult staff members.

Although the U.S. makes up less than 5% of the world's population, it accounts for 31% of all mass shootings (Centers for Disease Control and Prevention, 2019, 12). In 2018, the U.S. had 340 mass shootings, a rate of almost one a day. The Gun Violence Archive defines a mass shooting as one in which four or more individuals are wounded or killed. In these 2018 shootings, 1,579 people were killed or injured (Gun Violence Archive, n.d.). A white supremacy network is behind a number of mass shootings in Jewish and minority places of worship; however, the U.S. has continued to treat these mass shootings as isolated individual cases, and has not worked to break up the white supremacy network or the intentional stirring up of hatred that fuels these mass shootings.

Overwhelmingly, the home-grown terrorists who perpetrate these mass shootings are young, white, American-born men who are upset, or riled up, by an alt-right group. They seem to believe they do not have the life they are entitled to have. Typically, they buy an assault weapon, and other guns, within a year of committing a mass murder. In July 2019, a mass shooting occurred in California after an angry 19-year-old man drove to Nevada, bought an assault rifle and multiple 30-round high-capacity magazines. Less than 30 days later, he killed three people, two of whom were young children.

Similar mass murders could be eliminated by implementing a Federal law that requires buyers to be 21 to buy a gun (the same age required to buy a beer) and eliminates the sale of assault weapons and high- capacity magazines. Hunting and self-defense do not require assault weapons and high-capacity magazines. Assault weapons were specifically designed for the military to enable soldiers to kill the maximum number of people in the fastest time. These weapons were designed for use in war, not a shopping mall or a school.

On Sunday, August 4, 2019, the 216th day of the year, the U.S. reached our 250th mass shooting following the mass shootings in El Paso, Texas and Dayton, Ohio, on the same weekend. In the Dayton mass shooting, the magazines used contained 100 rounds of ammunition. The El Paso mass murderer had posted hate documents on the internet stating he was targeting Hispanics. Hate is not a mental illness; it is a learned choice: hate or love. When internet sites and political leaders encourage people to choose hatred of minorities over love, it affects the decisions young men, and others, make.

While the NRA and some politicians claim the major cause of gun violence is mental illness, less than 4% of all violent crime and less than 1% of gun homicides are committed by those who have mental illness. These percentages are higher in the case of mass shootings, but even there only 15% to 25% of mass shootings involved someone with a serious mental health issue (Kiesel 2018).

More than one mass shooting per day should be more than sufficient for congress to pass a law to eliminate sales of military-type assault weapons and high-capacity magazines to civilians. Congress needs to put the common good ahead of the special interests of the NRA.

One reason we are seeing so many acts of domestic terrorism, so many mass murders, is that America has weak gun laws in comparison with other developed nations. Although we claim to be focused on law and order, our weak gun laws allow gun purchases without any background checks and military assault weapons can be bought for personal use. Further exacerbating the problem, there is no penalty for allowing known mentally ill individuals to have access to assault weapons, which was the case in both the Sandy Hook mass shooting at an elementary school in 2012 and the Parkland, Florida, mass shooting at a high school in 2018. Between the Sandy Hook school shooting in 2012 and May 2019, over 600,000 Americans have been killed or injured by guns (Newtown Action Alliance 2018). Almost 100,000 have been killed or injured with guns each year, and our federal government has not acted to reduce this crisis.

A few states have instituted strong gun laws, but with neighboring states having weak gun laws, the mass shootings continue. We need federal action to deal with our gun violence and mass shooting crisis. A federal law could follow the lead of states that have banned the sale of assault weapons, which include: California, Connecticut, Hawaii, Maryland, Massachusetts, New Jersey and New York. These states have paved the way for us, but seven states are not enough stem the shooting. As a nation, we should be outraged at this wanton murder. We can't afford to continue to see our children die in mass shootings, while the majority of the nation lives in fear of the next one.

Other countries do not live in fear of gun violence. A review of gun laws in 10 countries published in the journal *Epidemiologic Reviews* found that new legal restrictions on purchasing guns, such as background checks on all purchasers, reduced gun deaths and injuries. Restricting the purchase of weapons (i.e., by enforcing background checks) can reduce partner homicides, and requiring safer gun storage can lower the number of unintentional deaths caused by, or inflicted on, children (Santaella-Tenorio et al. 2016, 152-153).

The U.S. also needs to recognize that there is a clear relationship between guns and drugs, and between drugs and poverty. Young men in poorer communities, without a perceived legal economic job path to success, feel their only option is to choose an illegal career path like dealing drugs or other contraband, requiring them to have guns to protect themselves. Addressing the crisis of providing job skills and providing adequate living wages for low-income jobs would help to address a major root cause of both the drug crisis and the gun crisis.

Gun violence has many, often visible, costs to our country. Washington Post reporter Michelle Singletary listed some of these gun violence costs, which include:

- Lost wages
- Medical bills
- Increased law enforcement costs
- Increased building security costs
- Lower property values
- Long-term prison costs

(Singletary 2018)

Other costs include treating the psychological damage to those who witness a mass shooting, especially students who often have problems in school following a shooting. These problems may include lowered test scores. Taken all together, these costs are huge: the Giffords Law Center to Prevent Gun Violence has estimated that the annual cost of gun violence in the U.S is $229 billion per year, based on studies in 2015 (Giffords Law Center 2019).

Gun advocates often use the tired argument that blaming guns for mass murders is like blaming cars for drunk driving deaths. Well, let's take a quick look at how Mothers Against Drunk Driving (MADD, n.d.) cut drunk driving deaths in half, and compare it to how we deal with guns:

Table 21: How We Deal with Cars and Guns Differently

How We deal with Cars	How We deal with Guns
Raised drinking age from 18 to 21	You can buy an assault weapon at 18
Server is liable for over serving alcohol that results in a DUI crash	No liability for supplying an arsenal of weapons and ammunition which results in a mass murder
Driver's license loss for drunk driving	No license for a gun and no loss of guns for threatening to kill
Drunk driving deaths have been reduced in half	Gun deaths continue to rise

Guns are different than cars; guns are built to kill. However, I am willing to begin treating guns like we treat cars, in order to cut gun deaths in half like we have done with drunk driving. Those of us who are mad about continued mass murders in our schools, churches, theaters, and public places should follow the lead of MADD. The people in Dayton, Ohio, shouted after the mass murder there in August, 2019, "Let's DO SOMETHING!" Actually, just doing "something" is not enough. We need to do enough to reduce mass shootings to zero and significantly reduce annual gun deaths.

We not only need to eliminate assault weapons sales here in the U.S., we need to stop being the arms supplier to Central American countries overrun by drug lords. The U.N. prepared an arms treaty to reduce the supply of arms to terrorists and criminals throughout the world. In April 2013, the U.N. Arms Trade Treaty was overwhelmingly approved by the 193-member U.N., including the U.S., to regulate international trade in arms. However, the National Rifle Association (NRA) opposed this treaty and as a result, in April 2019 at an NRA annual meeting, President Trump announced he was revoking the U.S.'s status as a signatory to this U.N. Arms Trade Treaty. So, we are now the only country in the world selling arms to terrorists and drug dealers.

Gun Violence Crisis Follies
[(G) denotes government follies]

- Weak gun laws (G)

- Military assault weapons available for civilian use (G)

- Background check loopholes let criminals and the mentally ill buy guns (G)

- No penalty for allowing known mentally ill people access to assault weapons (G)

- Continuing the propaganda that more guns can lower gun violence, when the opposite is true (G)

- Not consulting best practices of other countries and implementing them (G)

Possible Goals
An annual reduction of gun violence deaths, with a goal to be at the world average by 2029

Annual reduction in the number of mass shootings, with a goal of zero

Possible Results Measures
Annual gun violence deaths

Annual mass shooting deaths

Likely Root Causes
Lack of background checks on all gun purchasers

Allowing purchase of military assault weapons for personal use

Poor communities with inadequate paths for legal success

No penalties for allowing known mentally-ill people to have access to assault weapons

Allowing white nationalist networks to encourage and support mass murders of Jewish, Muslim, and other minority groups

Possible Improvements
(* Asterisk indicates no- or low-cost to the federal government)

*Restrict the sale of military assault weapons to military and police

*Ensure background checks are implemented for all gun purchasers

*Institute penalties for allowing known mentally-ill people or criminals to have access to assault weapons

*Authorize police to confiscate weapons from people where a risk to life is assessed to be present; enable the weapon's owner to appeal the confiscation in court (i.e., Red Flag Laws)

Provide skills training needed for successful jobs and adequate pay for those in lower-income jobs

Crisis Annual Cost
Studies have shown the cost of gun violence in the U.S. was $229 billion in 2015 (Giffords Law Center, n.d.). Since both gun sales and mass shootings have continued to increase, we can assume that cost will be closer to $300 billion in 2020.

Federal Budget cost reduction opportunities for 2024
If we assume the U.S. takes the necessary steps to reach the world average for gun violence (3.4 deaths per 100,000) in the next 10 years, we could cut the annual estimated cost of U.S. gun violence ($229 billion) by two thirds. In 5 years, by 2024, the U.S. could save half that, which is one third of $229 billion ($75 billion per year). Of that amount, the actual Federal government cost might be only 20%; hence, there could be a possible $15 billion federal budget savings by 2024.

Potential House Caucus to implement House CAT Improvements
No existing caucus identified.

A Gun Violence Prevention Task Force does exist:
Chair Mike Thompson (D); Vice Chairs Jason Crow (D), Lucy McBath (D)

Personal Story – Gun Violence Crisis

When my daughter was working as a high-school English teacher in Florida, she had to deal with students who arrived at school with handguns. Thankfully, she had a trained security officer on campus to call upon for help.

On October 27, 2018, my granddaughter, attending the University of Pittsburgh, was living only one block away from the Jewish Tree of Life Congregation where a mass shooting occurred. Eleven people were killed and seven injured just one block away from my granddaughter. The shooter used an AR-15 assault rifle and three Glock handguns. Today, Americans cannot worship or go to school without fear of being murdered. These terrorists are not foreigners, but native-born Americans who chose to kill their fellow citizens.

While I was in Vietnam as an Army 1st Lieutenant, I was told that I would only be issued a .45 caliber pistol and not an M-16 assault rifle, because I was an officer. I knew I needed an M-16 to deal with snipers; I had been qualified as a marksman with the M-16 but could not hit a barn door 25 feet away with a .45 pistol, so I insisted I be issued an M-16 rifle; I got my assault weapon. The M-16 assault weapon is a weapon specifically designed for combat and enables the user to kill the maximum number of people in the shortest possible time. Assault weapons were not designed for civilian use and they should not be sold to civilians.

Health Care Costs

Definition
Health Care costs are higher in the U.S. than in any other country in the world, and they are increasing. In 2000, U.S. health care costs were about $1.5 trillion; by 2017, they had ballooned to $3.5 trillion (Peterson-Kaiser Health System Tracker 2018).

Research data and trends

The U.S. is an aging nation with increasing numbers of people who require increasingly expensive medical care. U.S. health care costs were 18% of the GDP in 2016, while the average for 11 other high-income nations was only 11% of their GDP (CNBC 2018). U.S. Health Care costs would have to be reduced by 40% to move from 18% to the advanced country average of 11%.

Instead of decreasing, our costs are increasing. The per capita spending by Medicare grew by 7.3% per year between 2000 and 2010. The Affordable Health Care Act's reductions in payments to providers and plans helped slow Medicare per capita spending to 1.5% growth per year between 2010 and 2017. However, the Medicare Part D (prescription drug benefits) per capita spending is projected to grow at an average annual rate of 4.6% over the next 10 years (KFF Henry J. Kaiser Family Foundation 2018).

Part of the problem with health care costs in this country is inflated prices. Harvard University's T.H. Chan School of Public Health found that prices across the board for health care services are inflated. Drugs, in particular, are much more expensive in the U.S. than in other countries. In spite of all the money spent on health care, the U.S. has worse outcomes from our medical care system than other developed countries (Harvard T.H. Chan School of Public Health 2018).

Overall health is determined more by social services than by medical intervention. Our relative lack of social services (i.e., assistance for housing, food, and child support) in the U.S., as compared to other countries, contributes to higher health care costs. For example, the member countries of the Organization for Economic Co-operation and Development spend an average of $1.70 for social services for every $1 spent on medical care. The U.S. spends just $0.56 on social services for every $1 spent on medical care, less than one third of what other countries are spending. The European Union, with a higher ratio of social services to health care expenditures, has better health outcomes, including lower rates of obesity, diabetes, cancer, and heart disease (Brookings Institution 2016). Social services are preventive, while our health care system is reactive.

Taking a preventive approach is one way to decrease Health Care costs. By reducing the need for medical treatment for drug addiction, diabetes, cancer, and gun violence, we can cut costs and have a healthier, more productive population.

The U.S. population consumes more prescription drugs per capita than any other country in the world. Pain medications are particularly overused, and led to the opioid crisis. In addition to pain medications, Attention Deficit/Hyperactivity Disorder (ADHD) medications are also overused. In France, for example, only a hospital can prescribe an ADHD medication for a patient.

Further exacerbating the health care costs problem are the financial incentives offered to doctors. In the U.S., about half of all doctors are receiving economic incentives from drug companies for prescribing their drugs (Van Groningen 2017). Our drug companies have become greedier. Over the past two decades, U.S. manufacturers have systematically raised the cost for insulin products needed by diabetics by more than tenfold. For NovoLog FlexPens, a popular brand of insulin, uninsured patients in the U.S. pay $630 a month; just across the border in Canada, patients requiring FlexPens pay $47 a month. That cost drops to $42 a month in the United Kingdom, and $28 a month in Australia (U.S. Congresswoman Judy Chu 2019).

Some doctors and surgeons have also moved towards recommending treatments that are more profitable for them as opposed to better for the patient. Unnecessary surgeries are high on this list, among them cesarean (C-section) surgery. In 2017, 32% of all U.S. births were by C-Section (Centers for Disease Control and Prevention 2018). But the World Health Organization (WHO) has reported that the C-section rate for births should be about 15%, based on health factors. Although it is more convenient and economically beneficial for doctors to perform a C-section than allowing a natural birth, a natural birth is lower cost to the patient and a better health practice for both baby and mother than surgery (WHO 2016).

While many countries have a nationalized health care system which enables them to pay 40% less for better health care than the U.S., our country seems opposed to a national health care system. This is in part because we do not trust our federal government to manage our health care properly; there is good reason for that distrust, because they have spent our taxes for Social Security and Medicare on other things.

In general, U.S. citizens do not trust our federal government to manage anything. Surveys show that confidence in our federal government has fallen; currently only 17% of the population have confidence in our federal government. Even though we can't trust our federal government to implement a nationalized health care system, we can learn from some of the best practices in nationalized health care systems and implement them here. Those best practices include:

- Agreed-to goal of achieving the best possible health care at the lowest possible cost with coverage for all citizens

- Identification of best practices for medical protocols

- Protection of doctors from legal suits if they have followed approved best practices and protocols

- Setting reasonable prices for prescriptions

- Setting a reasonable time limit on prescription patents – less than the current 20 years

- Laws to prohibit Big Pharma from incentivizing doctors to overprescribe medications, or prescribe more expensive medications

- Laws to prohibit Big Pharma from paying other drug companies *not* to produce lower cost generic drugs when patents run out

- Government regulation to ensure lower costs of generic drugs are available, and to ensure adequate care for lower income patients whose insurance is subsidized

- Eliminate economic incentives for doctors to overprescribe medications, over test, and implement unnecessary surgeries

Health Care Cost Crisis Follies
[(G) denotes government follies]

- A government approach that treats medical care and drugs as the solution to good health, rather than supporting healthy living (G)
- Government support of pharmaceutical companies, rather than patients (G)

- Ignoring benchmarks and best practices from other countries(G)

- Spending Medicare trust funds on other things, instead of investing them to pay for future liabilities (G)

Possible Goal
Reduce the percentage of U.S. health care costs to the average of other high-income nations, from 18% to 11% of GDP by reducing 1% per year from 2021 to 2028

Possible Results Measure
Annual percentage of U.S. GDP spent on health care

Likely Root Causes
Higher prices for prescriptions and medical services

Overprescription of legal drugs

Lack of a healthy diet and exercise for individuals

Lack of adequate funds and programs spent for social service support

Doctors economically incented to overprescribe, over test, and over implement unnecessary surgeries

Possible Improvements
(* Asterisk indicates no- or low-cost to the federal government)

*Allow international pharmaceutical companies to compete for prescription drug sales, allowing competition to obtain market-based prices

*Reduce the 20-year time for a drug patent

*Government approval for reasonable prescription drug prices while under a monopoly patent

*Make it illegal for drug companies to pay other companies to *not* produce lower-priced generic drugs

*Establish an industry and government team to identify best practices that, if followed, will protect doctors from malpractice actions. Doctors will be at risk for malpractice actions if they substantially violate best practice guidelines.

*Provide reimbursement incentives to doctors who follow best practices

*Eliminate economic incentives for doctors to overprescribe, over test, and over implement unnecessary surgeries

*Allow individuals to shop for the best prices for prescriptions

*Encourage families to implement healthy diets and exercise programs

*Recognize and use best practices from other leading health care countries

*Manage the Medicare trust fund as a trust fund, not as a piggy bank to borrow from

Increase social service support funding

Provide community trail networks for walking, running, and bicycling so people can make shorter trips without a car

<u>Crisis annual costs</u>
I am defining this annual crisis cost as the cost resulting from our being above the world average: America spends 18% of its GDP on health care, while other high-income countries average 11%. The 7% percentage point difference between our health care costs and those of other high-income countries costs us $1.5 trillion per year. This is the estimated cost of this crisis in 2020.

The approximately one million deaths per year that will occur in the U.S. from our Drugs, Diabetes, Cancer, and Gun violence crises have not been included in this cost estimate.

Federal Budget cost reduction for 2024
The Federal government's general budget for Medicare and Medicaid is approximately $600 billion per year. If we could reduce that annual cost by 40% in a decade, and by 20% in 5 years to get to the world average, then in 2024, the U.S. could save 20% of $600 billion per year which is a $120 billion reduction in the 2024 federal budget.

This would not cut health care funding for current services. Instead it would cut the costs of providing future health care services by using best practices and reducing greed in the system to provide lower-cost services. It also would require citizens to adopt a healthier diet and exercise regimen to reduce our illness rate. This approach takes long-term planning, not one-year budgeting.

Potential House Caucus to implement House CAT Improvements
Public Health Caucus: Co-Chairs Rob Wittman (R), Gene Green (D), Kay Granger (R), Lucille Roybal-Allard (D), Jim McGovern (D)

Personal Story – Health Care Cost Crisis
While I was in the oncology clinic to receive my second chemotherapy treatment for stage IV colon cancer, I was told my white blood cell count was too low to receive the chemotherapy. Because the chemo attacks all your cells, not just the cancerous ones, your white blood cell count has to be high enough to fight the infections that can occur following chemotherapy. I was told to go home, without getting my chemo treatment, and come back the following week to give it another try.

I went to see a dietician and asked what I could do to raise my white blood cell count. She recommended that during chemotherapy, I adjust my protein requirements using the following calculation: my weight (in pounds) divided by 2 is equal to the number of grams of protein I needed to consume daily. Based on my weight (180 pounds), I needed 90 grams of protein per day to keep my white blood cell count up during chemotherapy. At the time, my protein intake was only 20 to 30 grams per day. So, I increased my protein intake to 90 grams per day and never had another low white blood cell count. I also never missed another chemotherapy treatment, and those treatments put my cancer into remission. This saved my life.

I shared with my oncologist this valuable information from my dietitian about protein requirements needed by patients undergoing chemotherapy, providing him with an additional credible reference from the University of Pennsylvania (Penn Medicine OncoLink 2018) that recommended the same protein requirements. I asked my oncologist to share this dietary protein information with other patients: he notified me that he would start incorporating the protein requirements for his patients right away. I was grateful not only that my oncologist had saved my life, but that he also would be passing on to other patients the valuable information I had learned, which was supported by a credible reference. From my own experience, I know this will improve treatment effectiveness for patients (i.e., by not missing chemotherapy due to a low white blood cell count) and decrease treatment costs (i.e., by not needing to obtain additional lab tests when a white blood cell count is low).

My wife takes heart medications that cost $250 for 30 pills when her prescriptions are filled through any of the pharmacies in our area; almost $10 per pill. The same prescription can be obtained from a Canadian pharmacy for $16 per 30 pills, or about $0.50 per pill. This is about 5% of the U.S. prescription price. Her heart doctor gave her information on how to order her prescriptions directly from Canada for about 5% of the cost.

Congress passed a bill that prevents Medicare from negotiating prescription drug prices, which enables U.S. pharmaceutical companies to maintain high prices and keep their profits up. These artificially high prices hit low-income people the hardest and increase our government medical health care costs. Some states are taking action to help reduce prescription costs. For example, in 2018, Vermont became the first state to pass a law allowing prescription-drug importation; however, a year later, Vermont had not yet gotten the required federal health agency approval. In 2019, the state of Florida also proposed a state bill to enable prescription-drug importation.

Summary of Health Care Costs crisis

The Health Care category includes five crises that directly affect the health and lives of U.S. citizens. We are spending 18% percent of our GDP on health care, while other advanced countries spend only 11% of GDP for theirs. To improve, we each need to live a healthier lifestyle, and the medical system has to incentivize the use of best practices from other countries

Chapter 10 – ENVIRONMENT CRISES

Our environment provides the land we grow food on, the waters we obtain fish from, and the air we breathe, to provide life as we know it on this planet. Our environment is essential to our life, the life of all creatures, and the life of future generations. The three environment crises discussed in this category include: Land, Air, and Fresh Water; Oceans; and Climate Change.

Land, Air, and Fresh Water Crisis

Definition

One indicator of health in our society, used by the Centers for Disease Control and Prevention (CDC) is the infant mortality rate. In 2017, the U.S. had 5.8 infant deaths per 1,000 live births, which was a 13% improvement over the 2000 infant death rate of 6.7 per 1,000 births. In 2015, 4 million babies were born in the U.S., and infant deaths were about 23,600, or about 6 deaths per 1,000 births (Centers for Disease Control and Prevention, n.d.).

The five countries in the world with the fewest infant deaths have an infant mortality rate of 2, or fewer, deaths per 1,000 live births; this means the U.S. is almost 3 times more lethal for infants than these leading countries. Two of the leading countries in the world are Finland and Japan, which should be looked to for best practices. Babies are like the proverbial canary in the coal mine; they are an early, more sensitive detector of pollution. Pregnant women need to be extra careful about what they eat, the water they drink, and the air they breathe.

Research data and trends

The U.N. estimated that in 2016, 12.6 million deaths worldwide were attributable to an unhealthy environment. The World Health Organization (WHO) reports that air pollution accounts for 8.2 million, about 65%, of those deaths (WHO, 2016). Overuse and harm of environmental resources is causing both health issues and billions of dollars per year in government cleanup costs. According to Dr. Margaret Chan, WHO Director-General until 2017, "A healthy environment underpins a healthy population" (WHO 2016).

Air, water, and land pollution; chemical exposures; climate change; and ultraviolet radiation contribute to more than 100 types of diseases and injuries.

Diseases strongly linked to environmental issues include:

- Diseases related to reproductive health
- Cancer
- Parkinson's disease
- Autism
- Asthma

(The National Institute of Environmental Health Sciences [NIEHS] 2019)

NIEHS also identified over 40 chemicals that cause these illnesses. For example, documented air pollution contributes to asthma and lung diseases (NIEHS 2019).

The costs associated with trying to clean up these environmental pollutants are astronomical. The EPA estimated that between $335 million to $681 million per year is required just for superfund site cleanups. This estimate was made in 2011, and the costs have gone up since then. They also reported that 1 in 4 Americans lives within three miles of a contaminated site, posing a serious risk to human health and the environment (Center for Public Integrity 2011). According to the Center for Public Integrity, the EPA has allocated about $250 million per year for superfund cleanup of toxic sites, only a fraction of the amount needed (Center for Public Integrity 2011).

There are more than 1,300 federally designated hazardous "Superfund Sites" in America that were created by factories and landfills. Superfund sites, the nation's most contaminated land, are often concentrated in highly populated areas. The current administration's proposed cut in the EPA budget also cuts the Superfund clean-up budget by 25%.

Part of the problem is that we have so many pollutants that have gone unchecked over many years. Coal pollution alone, of our air and water, was costing the U.S. over $345 billion per year in 2010 (Reuters 2011). It is reasonable to assume those annual costs have increased to closer to $500 billion per year in 2020.

The problems of pollutants do not just affect our country. In October 2017, The Lancet Commission on pollution and health issued a report on the global impact of environmental pollution, and their findings are alarming. In 2015, 16% of all global premature deaths were caused by pollution of the environment – more deaths than all who died in wars that year. The global cost of pollution was $4.6 trillion per year, which was 6.2% of global GDP for 2015 (Green Car Congress 2017). Mother Nature does not recognize country borders, so air pollution spreads quickly throughout the world, making it a global problem that we need to work with the U.N. and other countries to solve.

While part of our environmental pollution is due to known factors such as coal burning, new manmade chemicals are being added to our environment at an alarming rate. Many, if not most, of these chemicals have not been tested for their effects on people or the environment. Since 1950, more than 140,000 new chemicals have been introduced, with 5,000 produced in high volume. Less than half of these 5,000 high-volume new chemicals have been tested for safety. Thus, we have no idea what the long-term effects of these chemicals will be. Not introducing harmful chemicals into our environment is less costly than cleaning up widespread disasters after pollution has occurred.

In 2017, the EPA had four goals for environmental improvement:

- Address climate change and improve air quality
- Protect U.S. waters
- Ensure safety of chemicals and prevent pollution
- Protect human health

Between 1990 and 2017, our air quality improved as introduction of air pollutants dropped significantly. Over that 27-year period, nine different air pollutants (among them lead, carbon monoxide, sulfur dioxide, and nitrogen dioxide) were reduced. The combined reduction of these nine key air pollutants was 74% during a period when the economy tripled in size (U.S. Environmental Protection Agency, n.d.). This significant reduction in air pollution while the economy grew reflects the cooperative efforts of environmental non-profits with local, state and federal governments, to encourage and plan business emission reduction plans. These data show we can improve our environment and grow the economy; we do not have to pollute to grow. Carbon dioxide, the main cause of climate warming, was not included in this EPA analysis (BBC 2019).

Although significant improvements have been made, this trend is unlikely to continue. In 2018, the current administration eliminated EPA goals and replaced them with three philosophies:

- Refocus the agency
- Restore power to the states
- Improve processes and adhere to the law

A quarter century of good progress in improving air quality, which affects our national health, was due to the EPA goals and plans for improvement. Now those goals have been eliminated. Without goals to get better, there can be no improvement.

It is not just air quality that needs to be improved. The U.S. spends about $35 billion per year on trying to decrease our water pollution (Keiser, Kling, and Shapiro 2018). Pollution of land and water from agriculture fertilizer runoff is a huge component of the problem. Florida, for example, has been facing continued shore water pollution from agriculture runoff that has had devastating effects on Florida shore communities and the Everglades. The newly elected (November 2018) Republican Florida Governor, Ron DeSantis, has made this his number one priority. Two days after DeSantis took office, he unveiled sweeping measures to clean up Florida's troubled waters. This included spending $2.5 billion in funding for environmental improvements and launching more aggressive policies to address the algae-choking Lake Okeechobee (the largest lake in Florida and the second largest natural freshwater lake in the contiguous U.S.) and red tide polluting the state's coasts (Gross, 2019). The new governor also committed to appoint a Chief Science Officer to ensure Florida is enacting legislation and regulation based on sound science.

Land, Air and Fresh Water Crisis Follies
[(G) denotes government follies; (B) denotes business follies]

- Authorizing pollution of the environment (G)

- Authorizing non-sustainable overuse of the environment (G)

- Lack of a sustainable plan for our natural resources (G)

- Treating the cost for polluting and overusing the environment as zero for those authorized to pollute and overuse (G)

- No testing of chemicals for harm to people and the environment before release (G)

- Deregulation that increases pollution of the environment (G)

- Not adequately funding plans to enforce the Clean Water Act and the Clean Air Act (G)

- Businesses not acknowledging that less pollution is in their best interest (B)

Possible Goals
Return to the EPA goals that existed prior to the current administration – goals which led to many years of environment improvement

Address climate change and improve air quality

Protect U.S. waters

Ensure safety of chemicals and prevent pollution

Protect human health

Possible Results Measure
Return to the EPA results measures prior to the current administration.

Likely Root Causes
Industry overuse or harm of the environment for short-term profits

Agricultural fertilizer runoff

Lack of testing of new chemicals for environmental harm

Energy companies' use of fossil fuels

Individual pollution and overuse of water

Individual overuse of fossil fuel energy

Allowing pollution of common resources with no charge to the polluter

Possible Improvements
(* Asterisk indicates no- or low-cost to the federal government)

*Test new chemicals for environmental harm, before introduction

*Develop sustainable plans that stop subsidizing the overuse

*Plan reduction of pollution allowed into environmental resources

*Encourage individuals to prevent water pollution, perhaps by charging for water pollution (e.g., the carbon tax for air pollution)

*Reduce water waste (e.g., leaking infrastructure water systems)

*Encourage individuals to use renewable energy (e.g., solar power by home owners and small businesses)

*Encourage businesses to use renewable energy

*Encourage alternative crops that have a smaller environment footprint

*Encourage urban farming to lower transportation costs and pollution

*Change the culture of a throwaway society (e.g., plastic water bottles)

*Reduce unnecessary packaging and use of plastics

*Restore environmental protections and regulations

Crisis annual costs

The crisis cost resulting from our air pollution was estimated at $324 billion per year in 2010. It is reasonable to assume those costs have increased to about $500 billion in 2020. Water pollution cleanup costs have been $35 billion per year, and superfund site cleanup costs are about $0.5 billion per year. Therefore, this annual crisis cost in 2020 is about $535 billion per year.

Federal Budget cost reduction opportunities

The costs of environmental pollution show up as increased health care costs and environmental cleanup costs. Reducing air, land, and fresh water pollution can save billions of dollars per year. By taking preventive steps to continue to reduce the amount of pollution allowed in the U.S. year after year, we can improve health and reduce costs. However, due to unfunded cleanup of past pollution problems, no 2024 budget savings can be projected. We need money in the budget to clean up past pollution problems.

Potential House Caucus to implement House CAT Improvements

No existing caucus identified.

Personal Story – Land, Air, and Fresh Water Crisis

Shortly after retiring to Amelia Island, Florida, in 2000, I was recruited by a true environmental hero and neighbor of mine, MaVynee Betsch, known as the Beach Lady, to be the Conservation Chairperson of the Nassau County Sierra Club. I found that the Florida Forever conservation program had never been used to preserve land in Nassau County, and I helped get the state of Florida to buy two small islands on the north side of the Amelia River for preservation; they are now part of the local Fort Clinch State Park, which dates back to before the Civil War. Support from the state of Florida made that acquisition of these islands possible, and the community is grateful for that support.

I also helped led the efforts to establish the first two Nassau County Tree ordinances:

- A Canopy Road Tree Ordinance that can be applied to protect all canopy trees, along canopy tree-covered roads, which are in the public right-of-way on roads in Nassau County. A canopy tree is one whose branches extend across the road, providing shade. A canopy tree- road is one lined with canopy trees, thus providing a tunnel of shade for the motorists, bicyclists, and pedestrians. About a dozen canopy tree-covered roads have been protected, including the one that I live on, Amelia Island Parkway.

- A Tree Ordinance for the unincorporated south half of Amelia Island provides requirements to save some trees when building new developments on the island.

The creation of these two tree ordinances was accomplished thanks to Nassau County government support.

I participated with my neighbors at American Beach to help convince the neighboring Amelia Island Plantation (AIP) to donate the largest sand dune in Florida, the Nana Dune on American Beach, for conservation. That sand dune is now part of the Timucuan Ecological and Historic Preserve and part of the U.S. National Park system. This is the only land in Nassau County that belongs to a National Park.

We need to have respect for the interdependent web of which we are a part. We all can make a difference in our local communities, and many local efforts can help make things better nationally and globally. Think globally, act locally.

Oceans Crisis

Definition
Our U.S. oceans are being polluted while our ocean resources (e.g., fish supply) are being overused. U.S. oceans are a separate environmental crisis, because the oceans have different problems and thus need different solutions. For example, only states and the federal government own the U.S. oceans. It would seem that should make it easier to do a better job than we do on our land mass in protecting this environmental resource, but we have been doing worse.

International laws provide that all countries have an Exclusive Economic Zone (EEZ) that extends 200 nautical miles from the territorial seas, which are 12 nautical miles from the shoreline. Shipping lanes for foreign countries are allowed in the 200 nautical mile EEZ, but not in the first 12 nautical miles of territorial waters from the shoreline. Each country has the following sovereign rights and responsibilities for their EEZ (United Nations Convention on the Law of the Sea, 1982, 45-46):

- Conserving and managing natural resources

- Exploring and use of resources

The United States, like all other countries with an ocean border, lays claim to territory stretching out into the ocean. While the U.S. had made good progress in improving some protections for our oceans from 2000 to 2016, unfortunately in 2017 and 2018, the current administration has moved to roll back those ocean protections significantly. Proposed roll-back changes include expansion of off-shore oil drilling and revoking protections to Marine Protected Areas (MPA).

The National Oceanic and Atmospheric Administration (NOAA) had established the National Marine Protected Areas (MPA) Center in 2000 to protect MPA for future generations. Our oceans need MPA, which are established to protect ecosystems, preserve resources, and sustain fisheries. These MPA include both fully protected areas and multi-use areas; the multi-use areas are used for boating, diving, recreational fishing, and other recreational activities (Marine Protected Areas, n.d.).

As of 2017, the U.S. has 23% of its EEZ in strongly protected MPA. However, the Secretary of the Interior in the current administration has recommended that protections be removed for about half of the U.S. MPA. The two areas recommended for removal of MPA protections would reduce the U.S. MPA protection of EEZ waters from 23.2% to 12.5%. The areas recommended to have protection removed include:

- Pacific Remote Islands, a U.S. island territories area which is the most widespread collection of marine life protected areas on the planet under a single country's jurisdiction. It was created in 2009.

- Rose Atoll, a protected wildlife area within the U.S. territory of American Samoa, which is the southernmost point belonging to the U.S. It was created in 1973.

(Marine Conservation Institute and Atlas of Marine Protection 2017)

Reduction of these protected areas is being planned to serve the oil and gas industry special interests while sacrificing areas established to sustain a source of fish for everyone. Mother Nature provided us with a source of fish to feed the multitudes, and our government is planning to destroy that miracle Mother Nature has provided for us.

Research data and trends

The oceans surrounding our country have an enormous value, especially for the East and West coast states, the Southern Gulf states, Alaska, and

Hawaii. For far too long, our oceans have been overfished, over drilled, used as a garbage dump, and generally treated as an unlimited resource.

The Ocean Conservancy (OC) is the largest ocean non-profit organization creating science-based solutions for a healthy ocean. One of the OC's findings is that creating a protected space in the ocean that could be used as a nursery for fish, could result in producing sufficient fish to enable a sustainable fishing area. This solution shows how to prevent overfishing, but these types of preventive solutions require more Marine Protected Areas, not fewer (Ocean Conservancy, n.d.).

Protecting the ocean from overfishing is not the only problem we face. Plastics have been found in the bodies of 60% of all sea birds and 100% of all sea turtles, according to the OC. They report that there are 250 million metric tons of plastic in the oceans and another 8 million metric tons entering our oceans every year. (A metric ton is equal to 1.1 U.S. tons.) Solutions to reducing this problem include:

- Producing less plastic

- Better recycling and waste management

- Increase producer responsibility for damage caused by their products

A team of researchers from the U.K. and Norway has estimated the global cost of ocean plastic pollution to be $2.5 trillion per year (Tree Hugger 2019).

It is not just plastics that are polluting our oceans; raw sewage is being discharged into the oceans in disgusting amounts. U.S. municipalities have not updated our very old sewage infrastructure systems in a number of areas that still have combined storm water and sewage pipes instead of having separate pipes for each. This means that during rainstorms, these cities often release raw, untreated sewage into our rivers. This sewage overflow then flows from our rivers into our oceans, because the sewage treatment plants do not have the capacity to treat both sewage and storm water simultaneously during a heavy rainstorm. Storm water and sewage should not have been put in the same pipe, and old systems using only one pipe need to be updated to a two-pipe system; alternatively, the treatment plant capacity needs to be increased to handle both sewage and storm water.

The EPA reported that our U.S. ocean and Great Lakes beaches were open and safe for swimming 95% of the time in 2018, about the same as 2017. At the same time the Environment American Research and Policy Center (EARPC) found that 58% of U.S. beaches had pollution exceeding the EPA beach action value at least one day in 2018 (Bryant 2019). Both the EPA and EARPC reports are correct. The U.S. has had a continuous widespread ocean and Great Lakes beach pollution problem, with 5% of all U.S. beaches closed due to pollution on an average day, and over 50% of U.S. beaches having a pollution problem at least once each year.

The U.S. has been focused on measuring beach pollution and posting signs that advise beachgoers about pollution in the beach water. The U.S. lacks needed goals and plans to eliminate the root causes of pollution, not just warn about it. According to Baba Dioum, a Senegalese forestry engineer and conservationist:

"In the end, we will conserve only what we love,
we will love only what we understand, and
we will understand only what we are taught."
(Microcosm Aquarium Explorer, n.d.)

Because we have not understood our oceans and their limited resources, we have polluted and overused this valuable asset.

Oceans Crisis Follies
[(G) denotes government follies]

- Treating our oceans as an unlimited resource (G)

- Allowing our oceans to be used as a dump for sewage, toxic plant runoff, and plastics (G)

- Allowing our oceans to be overfished (G)

- Allowing our oceans to be drilled for fossil fuels, causing a great risk to valuable coastal tourism, local residents, natural resources, and marine mammals (G)

- Allowing harmful noise pollution in our oceans from seismic testing for fossil fuels, and military sonic testing. (This is harmful to marine creatures that use sound for life-sustaining communications) (G)

- Ignoring the need for a sustainable plan for U.S. oceans (G)

- Proposing to cut the U.S. Marine Protected Areas by half (G)

Possible Goals

Maintain the percentage of our oceans that are MPA protected and increase the number of MPA that are fully protected (Currently 23.2% of EEZ has some level of MPA protection)

Reduce the number of overfished ocean areas, and continue to improve fisheries management by using best practices

Reduce the amount of toxic materials (including plastics) allowed to flow into our oceans

Reduce the number of sewage overflow releases from combined sewage pipe systems by enforcing the existing Clean Water Act

Do not expand fossil fuel drilling rigs in U.S. oceans and the Gulf

Reduce U.S. ocean beach pollution

Possible Results Measures

Percentage of our oceans that are in Marine Protected Areas

Number of overfished U.S. fisheries (which are regional ocean areas)

Number of marine mammal and fish species managed for sustainability

Estimated tons of toxic materials allowed to flow into our oceans

Number of raw sewage overflow releases from combined sewage pipe systems

Area of the coasts protected from oil drilling

Percentage of U.S. ocean and Great Lakes beach days closed to pollution, and the percentage that has to be closed at least once a year due to pollution

The Ocean Conservancy and Oceana are two leading ocean non-profits that can help by providing facts about the condition of the oceans, as well as proposals for effective and efficient improvements.

Likely Root Causes
Special interests (e.g., Big Oil, agriculture industry) influencing decisions of folly for their own benefit

Inadequate maintenance of sewage and storm drain infrastructure maintenance in older cities

Lack of enforcement of the existing Clean Water Act (CWA)
Lack of a process to prevent plastics, and other toxic materials, from flowing into our oceans

Lack of goals and plans for improvement

Possible Improvements
(* Asterisk indicates no- or low-cost to the federal government)

*Maintain our Marine Protected Areas to ensure protection of our ocean resources

*Prevent new fossil fuel drilling in our oceans

*Use of cellulose, or other alternatives, in place of plastics in new products

Improved waste management and recycling to prevent, or stop, plastics and other toxic materials from flowing into our oceans.

Fund an infrastructure improvement plan to replace the antiquated combined sewage/storm drain systems that still exist in older cities (5% per year replacement)

Repair broken storm drain and sewage systems when they are found to be a cause of pollution

Crisis annual cost
Ocean pollution includes plastics, sewage, fertilizer runoff, and many other items. Since the U.S. has 5% of the world's population, we could assume the U.S. is responsible for about 5% of the plastics in the ocean. That cost would be about $125 billion per year. Sewage and fertilizer runoff cause algae blooms, which are causing states to spend billions per year to reduce the resultant killing of fish and tourism-killing blooms. Overfishing and pollution cause great losses to the fishing industry, the tourism industry, and the coastal building industry. U.S. ocean pollution costs will probably be close to $200 billion per year in 2020.

Federal Budget cost reduction opportunities
The potential cost reductions are primarily associated with states bordering our oceans and the Gulf of Mexico. Tourism and fishing industry revenues rely on keeping our oceans healthy and open for beach swimming and fishing. The states and ocean-side communities are responsible for preventing beach pollution. No federal budget cost reduction is seen as possible.

Potential House Caucus to implement House CAT Improvements
Oceans Caucus: Co-Chairs Don Young (R), Suzanne Bonamici (D)

Personal Story – Oceans Crisis

My parents had a wonderful cottage on a lake in New Hampshire (NH) where my kids loved to go for vacations to see their grandparents and enjoy the lake. In 1989, when we lived in New Jersey, I decided to take my four children (ages 11 to 19) to the Jersey Shore for vacation instead of to NH. They all wanted to go to the lake, but I insisted we should try the ocean one year to see what it was like. On Saturday morning, we arrived at our rental house; on Monday, the beach was closed due to pollution and stayed closed the whole week. My kids were, understandably, upset about my decision to vacation at the Jersey Shore. The newspapers reported that the beach closure we faced was part of a massive closure of Jersey shore beaches, which I found out later was due to sewage pollution.

The following Monday, I called Dave Rosenblatt, manager for the Jersey shore water quality at the NJ Department of Environmental Protection (DEP). I asked Dave if he could use some help to tackle this pollution problem. I offered to help by using the AT&T quality approach to identify root causes and develop solutions. He accepted my offer to help, and I assisted Dave as part of my AT&T community projects. Together, we worked with the 5 shore counties and 44 shore towns to make a 99.5% reduction in Jersey Shore beach pollution, which helped NJ to move from being the worst state for shore pollution (of the 30 states bordering an ocean, the Gulf, or a Great Lake) to one of the best.

After helping with the NJ shore improvement project, and receiving recognition from environmental groups and the state of NJ; the Ocean Conservancy (OC), the largest non-profit focused on oceans, asked me to join their Board of Directors, where I served for 10 years. I helped the OC set ocean goals for specific areas such as marine mammals, fish, and an increase in Marine Protected Areas.

While I was on the OC board, I was asked to do a quality check on the government's Manatee Recovery Plan. Manatees, who are slow-moving marine mammals, had been an endangered species for 30 government's Manatee Recovery Plan. Manatees, who are slow-moving marine mammals, had been an endangered species for 30 years, and none of the federal Manatee Recovery plans (updated every 5 years) had helped improve their population recovery. By analyzing university studies, I found that manatees had the lowest successful birth rate of all marine mammals. We also knew that almost all injured manatees had been hit by motor boats or jet skis; those being tracked were even identified by their scars from these boat hits. When the low birth rate statistics were combined with the boat hits, it seemed to me that boat hits were a major cause of pregnant manatees losing their calves. I recommended that "slow speed zone" signs be established in waters frequented by manatees to reduce the number of manatee casualties caused by boat hits, analogous to posting "slow speed zone" signs on roads near schools to protect children. When the Manatee Recovery Plan was revised to include this change, boaters objected to having to slow down. However, when they did so, the manatee population more than doubled and manatees have now been taken off the endangered list. Boaters now seem happy to slow down and enjoy seeing a manatee as they enjoy the river and the life in it.

Climate Change Crisis

Definition

Climate change, the accelerated warming of the earth's average temperature, is already causing an increase in disasters, and a significant increase in global warming is forecast. Some government leaders refuse to admit this is a crisis, because they do not want to deal with it.

Due to this country's continued reliance on petroleum and coal products, the U.S. has contributed to increasing the rate of global warming. We have only 5% of the world's population but produce 15% of the world's carbon emissions that contribute to climate warming.

Although the U.S. reduced carbon emissions from 2015 to 2017, carbon emissions increased by 3.4% after the current administration withdrew from the Global Climate Treaty in 2018 (Earth 2019).

Research data and trends

A U.S. National Climate Assessment report issued in November 2018, by the current administration, provides the following information on global warming (National Climate Assessment 2018):

- Extreme weather has become more frequent, intense, and of longer duration, as a result of climate and ocean warming.

- The last few years have broken records for weather-related damage (e.g., forest fires, hurricanes, and flooding) and have cost the U.S. nearly $400 billion since 2015.

- This damage is not just costly but affects other crises as well. For example, air pollution from forest fires is creating a major health risk. Air quality in California has hit hazardous levels due to forest fires.

- The lower 48 states have warmed 1.8 degrees Fahrenheit since 1900, with more than half of that (1.2 degrees) in just the last few decades. Small temperature changes can contribute to the creation of major storms; for example, small changes in the ocean temperatures enable a hurricane category 2 storm to quickly change to a category 4 storm, causing massive destruction of coastal communities.

- The forecast is for the country to be 3 to 12 degrees Fahrenheit hotter by the end of this century, depending on how much greenhouse gases are released into the atmosphere.

- Holding to the lower rate of climate warming (i.e., 3 degrees Fahrenheit) would cut the estimated disaster costs in half from $500 billion per year to $250 billion per year.

Global warming is caused by several factors; chief among them is carbon emissions. The U.S. is the 2nd largest source of carbon emissions in the world, with China being the largest. The Global Climate Treaty goal is to limit future temperature increases to no more than 1.8 degrees Celsius (equal to 3.24 degrees Fahrenheit).

Carbon dioxide emissions accumulate in the atmosphere and create a blanket effect that warms the planet. Between 1960 and 2019, the carbon dioxide in the atmosphere increased by 30%. A 30% increase in just two generations is alarming when we realize that the Earth's atmosphere has been protecting human, and other, life on earth for almost 2,000 generations. Carbon pollution is damaging to our atmosphere, which in turn causes severe damage to our planet. As we did with the damage we caused to the ozone layer of our atmosphere, we need to take action to stop the source of this damage. The atmosphere is our planet's roof; if we had a hole in the roof of our house, we would not ignore it and keep allowing rain and wind to make it worse.

Global warming feeds on itself: as temperatures rise, there is an increase in energy use for air-conditioning, which means power companies are releasing more carbon into the atmosphere, causing more climate warming. This creates a vicious cycle. Worldwide, demands for energy are still being filled by burning fossil fuels, rather than from non-polluting sources like solar. In 2018, for example, 80% of all energy worldwide was provided from fossil fuels like coal, oil, and gas, while only about 20% was provided by renewable energy sources such as water, solar, and wind turbines (Institute for Energy Research 2019).

Beyond the technical problems associated with climate change, scientists also have to contend with those who refuse to admit that climate change constitutes a crisis. Katharine Hayhoe, Ph.D., Director of the Climate Science Center at Texas Tech. University, and lead author of the Fourth National Climate Assessment, has addressed some of the falsehoods being used to avoid dealing with the climate crisis. The following information refutes these falsehoods:

- <u>Climate scientists are split on climate warming</u>
  Untrue. 97% of all scientists agree that our climate is warming and humans are causing it.

- <u>Climate change will not affect me</u>
  Untrue. Climate change is causing hurricanes to be more intense, forest fires to be more frequent, and rising ocean levels that threaten coastal communities. These events are happening now.

- The weather still gets cold, it still snows
  This shows the confusion between weather and climate change. Just because the winters are still cold does not mean climate change isn't occurring. Climate change is the long-term average of temperature which is increasing. In 2017, across the U.S., we had three times more record high-temperature days than we had record low-temperature days.

- Climate change is just a natural cycle
  Untrue. Over the past few decades, energy from the sun has been decreasing, so we should be getting cooler, but we are not. The next natural cycle on the geologic calendar should be another ice age, not more warming. We are not in a natural cycle.

  (Hayhoe 2018)

Lies about climate change are initiated and circulated by those who want to do nothing about it because they are profiting from the status quo. Doing nothing serves the greed of a few and ignores the needs of the rest of us.

Climate change is not only real; it is costing us billions of dollars. In 2017, the U.S. spent over $230 billion in disaster relief (National Geographic 2017). The following year, the Defense Department reported that nearly half of the 292 defense sites near coast lines have been affected by floods in recent years (U.S. Department of Defense 2018).

These costs are being felt at the local level as well. Florida is facing a $2.7 billion price tag for infrastructure and public building recovery costs in the panhandle of Florida from the destruction caused by hurricane Michael in October 2018 (Kennedy 2019). This was a category 2 storm that quickly changed to a category 4 storm due to warmer than usual Gulf waters.

Recent studies have identified two natural barriers we have on Florida's east coast to protect us from hurricanes: lofty cross winds and cooler oceans along the coast, which help to reduce the intensity of hurricanes as they approach shore. However, climate warming is degrading both of these natural protective barriers and lessening their ability to protect us (Kossin 2018). In spite of this, the Trump administration has withdrawn from the global climate treaty and deregulated coal plants to release more carbon dioxide, fueling this crisis rather than ameliorating it.

The current administration has targeted 11 major regulations for repeal or relaxation in order to save fossil fuel companies $11.6 billion. These rule changes would result in up to 1,400 premature deaths per year, an increase in greenhouse gases of about 1 billion tons over the next decade, increased risk of water pollution from fracking, and fewer safety checks to prevent offshore oil spills. The Associated Press (AP) also reported that the current administration was underreporting the costs to society in order to justify rollbacks of environmental protections (Brown 2019).

In February of 2019, Michael Mann, a Climate Scientist at Penn State University, said that the world needs a 5% to 10% reduction in carbon emissions each year for the next ten years to contain the global warming to the 3-degree Fahrenheit warming limit goal (Mann 2019).

So how do we reduce our carbon emissions? Mark Jacobson, a Stanford University Professor, has proposed a transition to clean energy that could satisfy 100% of the U.S. energy needs by 2050, at 20% of the current annual U.S. energy costs. That is a reduction from the current $5.9 trillion per year for energy costs to $1 trillion per year in 2050. Such a transition, from fossil fuels to clean energy, would take an investment of $5.8 trillion, which could be spread out over 30 years. An investment of $6 trillion that will provide a savings of almost $6 trillion per year is a great investment (Jacobson 2017). This change would also produce many new jobs to get this new form of energy source in place.

Can this really be done? Yes, it can, and it has already been done by some. Two companies, Apple and Google, have already made the transition to 100% clean energy. Two states, Hawaii and California, have already established a plan to transition to 100% clean energy. These examples show it can be done, and it can be done with a reduction of energy costs and a reduction in the enormous disaster costs of global warming. The fossil fuel companies will lobby to prevent such plans; some politicians will stand in the way of limiting carbon emissions because their election campaigns are supported by the fossil fuel industry. However, we must ignore the fossil fuel company myths and replace nay-saying politicians. Then we must work to minimize further carbon emission damage to our planet; this is the only planet we have.

At the same time, we are working to reduce carbon emissions to slow climate warming, we need to also prepare for the effects of the damage already done to the atmosphere. Carbon emissions of the past, and those being spewed out today, have caused climate warming and sea level rise. The climate will continue to warm, and the sea level will continue to rise based on the damage already done, and the damage we are continuing to do. Therefore, we also need to prepare for future (hopefully minimized) climate warming and sea level rise. For shoreline property owners, towns, cities, counties, and states, that means resiliency planning is needed to deal with sea level rise, stronger and higher storm surges, and heavier rainfall.

Again, we should be looking for benchmarks and best practices. The Netherlands is mostly below sea level, so they have learned how to deal with this problem. We can and should learn from their best practices. After hurricane Sandy wiped out the Jersey shore, the state of NJ established a Resiliency Planning Director who has been working to learn from the best and develop a resiliency plan for the 140 miles of Jersey shore. The current NJ Resiliency Planning Director is Dave Rosenblatt, the young NJ Department of Environmental Protection (DEP) manager who I had coached 20 years earlier on how to use a quality approach to prevent shore pollution.

On the west coast, residents of the San Francisco Bay area consider themselves to be at ground zero for sea level rise in the U.S.; they have had an 8-inch sea level rise over the past century. The San Francisco Bay area has 400 miles of shoreline, and leaders have developed resiliency strategies for each separate segment of that shoreline.

A blueprint resiliency plan for the bay area was released on May 2, 2019, by urban planners and ecosystem planners who envision a ring of man-made reefs, rocky beaches, and graded marshlands around the shoreline. The 225-page San Francisco Bay Shoreline Adaptation Atlas is a plan that others could use as a resource for their own plan. This plan calls for using nature, rather than trying to fight nature, by using eco-friendly features that support wildlife and absorb, rather than repel rising tides. The approach was developed by the San Francisco Estuary Institute, an urban planning research center. Warner Chabot, the Executive Director of the Estuary Institute, believes the San Francisco resiliency plan will become a national model. Chabot was a Vice President at the Ocean Conservancy about 15 years ago when I was on the Board of Directors, so I have also had the chance to share this quality approach with him, which we used to help set goals and help make improvement for our U.S. oceans (San Francisco Estuary Institute 2019).

The U.S. coastline communities need to learn from the best plans and practices to develop their own resiliency plans. The federal government needs to help share resiliency benchmarks and best practices, encourage and support replication, and recognize leaders.

Climate Change Crisis Follies
[(G) denotes government follies]

- Claiming global warming is a falsehood to be denied (G)

- Withdrawing from global climate treaties and refusing to help address this crisis (G)

- Relaxing previously agreed-to carbon reduction agreements and plans (G)

Possible Goal
Reduce U.S. carbon emissions as a percentage of the world's emissions to be equal to the U.S. percentage of the world's population. In 2018, we had 5% of the world's population but 15% of the world's carbon emissions. Reach this goal by 2040 with a steady reduction in U.S. carbon emissions.

Possible Results Measure
U.S. percentage of the world's carbon emissions

Likely Root Causes
Fossil fuel use

Methane gas release

Rejection of scientific facts supporting climate change and the need to take action

Withdrawal from the world climate change treaty, which included this country's voluntary commitments to address this crisis

Possible Improvements
(* Asterisk indicates no- or low-cost to the federal government)

*Government policies should support the scientific facts explaining climate change

*The U.S. should rejoin, with all other countries, the world's *voluntary* plans to limit global warming increases

*Pass and implement a carbon tax (a bipartisan bill for this has already been proposed in Congress)

*Plan and support a transition from fossil fuels to renewable energy (states could follow the Hawaii and California plans)

States and businesses develop plans to transition to clean energy
Increase individuals' use of, and access to, renewable energy (e.g., solar power, wind, and use of cellulose as a fuel)

Crisis annual costs
Climate change disaster costs have been estimated at $250 billion per year; these costs could double to $500 billion per year if climate change causes more than a 3-degree Fahrenheit temperature increase. This does not include the needed expenditures to make our shoreline cities resilient.

Federal budget cost reduction opportunities for 2024
The U.S. will have to work hard to limit the increase in global climate change in order to just hold U.S. disaster relief to $250 billion per year. By stringently limiting carbon emissions, we can potentially avoid an increase in the $250 billion per year currently being spent on disaster relief costs. Unfortunately, the U.S. is not working on this crisis. It will be very costly to continue to ignore or deny this problem, probably adding another $250 billion per year to U.S. disaster relief costs, in order to allow fossil fuel companies to make a few more billion dollars in profits.

<u>Potential House Caucus to implement House CAT Improvements</u>
Climate Solutions Caucus: Co-Chairs Carlos Curbelo (R), Ted Deutch (D)

Coastal Communities Caucus: Co-Chairs Frank Pallone (D), Bradley Byrne (R), Denny Heck (D), Lois Frankel (D), Charlie Crist (D)

Natural Disaster Caucus: Chair Mike Thompson (D)

Green Schools Caucus: Chair Alan Lowenthal (D)

Grid Innovation Caucus: Co-Chairs Jerry McNerney (D), Bob Latta (R)

Personal Story – Climate Change Crisis

Since I live in Florida, the Sunshine State, I decided to put solar panels on the roof of my house in 2010. My Home Owner Association (HOA) initially objected, saying that solar panels would impair the beauty of the area. But Florida has a law that allows individuals to install solar panels on houses in HOAs as long as there is an effort to make them as unobtrusive as possible. The HOA agreed that the solar panels could be added to the rear roofs on my house. These solar panels paid for themselves by 2016 (just 6 years after installation), through reduced electric fees. They have been helping reduce carbon emissions, and my electric bill, for almost 10 years. I was the first homeowner to install solar panels in my HOA.

I live just 60 miles north of St. Augustine, Florida, where former Mayor Nancy Shaver had a vulnerability study done to determine what affects climate change and sea level rise will have on that coastal city. That study found that by 2030, 30% of St. Augustine roads will be flooded 90 days per year – flooding that will include pollution from buried septic tanks, gasoline tanks, and landfill debris. I have two granddaughters living in St. Augustine and I would not want them to have to wade through water contaminated with sewage, gasoline, and chemicals to get to school.

It can help a lot if we all do our part to reduce our own carbon

Summary

Three environment crises were discussed in this category: Land, Air, and Fresh Water; Oceans; and Climate Change.

We have been both overusing and abusing our environmental resources, and we lack sustainable plans for our fisheries and our planet. A recent book by Jared Diamond, *Upheaval*, addresses these crises on a world scale, and he has three simple recommendations for improvement:

- Acknowledge the crisis

- Acknowledge that you can do something about it

- Don't blame someone else

We should also stop taking actions that make these crises worse, and start taking actions to improve our situation.

Chapter 11 – SECURITY CRISES

This chapter will use the quality approach described earlier to analyze four Security Crises: Nuclear Arms and Waste, Cybersecurity, Border Security, and Defense Costs.

Nuclear arms are the cause of most of our major confrontations in the world, which include those with North Korea, Iran, and Russia. Nuclear arms use is also the major threat to the world. While we had many years of nuclear arms reduction under U.N. treaties, that has been reversed in the past few years, and we are now in an arms race again.

Cybersecurity is the weakest part of our security system, and it has been getting weaker, not stronger, over the past few years. Because of our weak cybersecurity system, our entire economy and democracy are at risk and under attack daily.

Over the past 20 years our Border Security problems improved continuously; however, U.S. government actions over the past few years have created a southern border immigration crisis.

Our defense costs are significantly higher than any other country. We can't afford these high defense costs, which have been getting higher over the last few years.

Nuclear Arms and Waste Crisis

Definition
Insufficiently controlled nuclear weapons and nuclear waste, anywhere in the world, are a serious threat to the future of our planet. Nuclear arms treaties had helped reduce this threat over the past years; however, recently the U.S. has withdrawn from those treaties and is returning to a nuclear arms race.

Nuclear weapons are a relatively new world threat. Their first use was in 1945 when America dropped two nuclear bombs on the Japanese cities of Hiroshima and Nagasaki, killing about 220,000 civilians. The result was devastating and caused Japan to surrender and ended World War II. Forty years later, in 1986, at the Chernobyl nuclear power plant in the Ukrainian Soviet Socialist Republic, the most disastrous nuclear power accident to date occurred, with estimates of around 10,000 fatalities. Nuclear material is radioactive, and it can kill cells directly or cause mutations to cells, causing cancer. The U.S. has increasing quantities of nuclear waste that must be safely contained for thousands of years. Nuclear arms control and nuclear waste control have been a top security crisis for decades; a crisis that needs constant vigilance.

With the discovery of nuclear weapons and the creation of nuclear energy, we opened a modern-day Pandora's Box – one that can destroy the world. Now that the nuclear box has been opened, and its evil released in the world, we have to try to contain it. While there are international treaties trying to do just that, these treaties can only work if they are honored and implemented by all countries in the world, with United Nations verifications.

The current administration chose to withdraw from nuclear arms control treaties, rather than maintain and enforce them. In just 2 years, the President has withdrawn from about half our nuclear treaties, including ones with Iran and Russia. As a result of these treaty withdrawals, Iran announced they would reestablish programs to enrich uranium to higher levels; this moves the world from having been in control of Iran's nuclear weapons development, to being out of control.

Research facts and trends
The Treaty on the Non-Proliferation of Nuclear Weapons (NPT) is an international treaty whose objective is to prevent the spread of nuclear weapons and technology, with a goal of nuclear disarmament. That treaty is aimed at containing the threats posed by nuclear material, putting it back into the box we opened. Sixty-eight countries, including the U.S., signed this initial treaty in July 1968 (United Nations Office for Disarmament Affairs, n.d.).

Fifty years later, in December 2018, 190 of the world's countries had signed this treaty. Countries that sign the treaty agree never to acquire nuclear weapons, but they may pursue the peaceful use of nuclear power. The "Nuclear-weapons States," that is, countries that already have nuclear weapons, agreed to share benefits of peaceful nuclear technology (e.g., energy) and to pursue disarmament aimed at the ultimate elimination of their nuclear arsenals. The treaty is reviewed every five years. Over the years, rules have been implemented to strengthen it, such as controls on the nuclear supplier's group and enhanced verification measures and protocols of the International Atomic Energy Agency (International Atomic Energy Agency 2017).

The Non-Proliferation Treaty (NPT) defines nuclear weapons states as those countries that had built and tested a nuclear explosive device before January 1, 1967.

Table 22: Nuclear Weapons States
(Pre-1967)

Country	Nuclear test date
United States	1945
Soviet Union (later Russia)	1949
United Kingdom	1952
France	1960
China	1964

While the NPT has helped to limit the spread of nuclear weapons throughout the world, there are countries that have not signed this nuclear treaty and have developed nuclear weapons since 1967.

Table 23: Nuclear Countries Who Have Not Signed the NPT
(post 1967)

India
Pakistan
North Korea (joined in 1985 and withdrew in 2003)
South Sudan (founded in 2011)
Israel (also believed to possess nuclear weapons)

The U.S. and the world should be working to get all five of these countries to sign the NPT, agree to the UN verifications in the treaty, and join other countries' efforts to eliminate the nuclear threat to the world.

The countries that have not signed the NPT pose a serious threat to their enemies and to the rest of the world. For example, Iran signed the treaty but fears Israel, who has not signed. This fear of an enemy with nuclear weapons is causing Iran to pursue nuclear weapons. During President Obama's administration, after many years of international sanctions, Iran agreed to stop all efforts to create nuclear weapons and agreed to U.N. ground inspections. Trust but verify. In 2018, the current administration withdrew from the international treaty with Iran. That was a step in the wrong direction for the world's efforts to control and reduce nuclear weapons. The following year, in 2019, the current administration suspended the treaty with Russia on the control of intermediate missiles, the Intermediate Missile Force (IMF) agreement. These treaties, and their enforcement, are essential if we want to try to save the world from nuclear annihilation.

We should be creating more treaties, not cancelling the ones that have been put in place by hard work over many years. Treaties need enforcement with on-the-ground inspections, and country sanctions if necessary. However, a single country cannot implement effective sanctions if other countries don't support the sanctions, which usually involves restricting trade. For sanctions to be effective the U.S. needs to partner with our allies; our current strategy of withdrawing from treaties risks returning to an arms race and escalation to military actions.

Some other countries also seem to be moving in the wrong direction. Russia announced in December 2018, that they now have a new hypersonic rocket that can carry a nuclear warhead and travel at approximately 20 times the speed of sound. The speed of sound is 760 mph, which means this new rocket travels at 15,200 mph, a speed so fast that our existing defense system cannot detect it and therefore cannot respond in time to intercept it. In response to this new technology, acting Secretary of Defense Patrick Shanahan asked for $1 billion to upgrade our defense system to deal with this threat. Subsequent reports indicate this Russian nuclear-powered rocket may be an unreliable technology.

On a more positive note, headway has been made to reduce stockpiles of nuclear weapons. The United States has eliminated over 13,000 nuclear weapons, which constitutes 80% of its deployed strategic warheads, and 90% of its nonstrategic warheads, thereby reducing our reliance on nuclear weapons. After the economic collapse of the Soviet Union, the

U.S. also purchased thousands of nuclear weapons from the Soviet Union to convert into reactor fuel. However, the original five authorized nuclear weapons countries (U.S., Russia, UK, France and China) still have 22,000 warheads in their combined nuclear weapons stockpile, and recently have shown a reluctance to further disarm.

If we think about the major threats to world peace in the world today, they are all associated with nuclear weapons threats:

- Iraq - The U.S. attacked Iraq, under President Bush, out of fear that Iraq was developing nuclear weapons. We were wrong about that, and our war on Iraq spawned ISIS and years of war and chaos in the Middle-East. The Middle-East and the world are still suffering with the consequences of that U.S. decision to start a war in the Middle-East.

- Iran – The current administration withdrew from the world-negotiated treaty with Iran; a treaty that had stopped Iran's nuclear weapons development programs. One year after our withdrawal from that treaty, Iran has announced they plan to restart manufacture of nuclear materials. This announcement has led to escalating military actions to enforce sanctions. International sanctions were used to get Iran to agree to the NPT treaty. A U.N. verifiable treaty was much better than reverting to U.S. sanctions that require military escalation for enforcement, while Iran is developing nuclear materials.

- Russia – The current administration suspended the treaty with Russia on the control of intermediate missiles, the Intermediate Missile Force (IMF) agreement.

- North Korea – North Korea has withdrawn from the NPT. Their continued development of nuclear weapons and missiles is causing increased tensions in the world.

The world had developed a strategy to work together to reduce and prevent the spread of nuclear weapons. It appears that strategy is being demolished by the U.S. for a go-it-alone, country-by-country confrontational approach, using our power to try to bully other countries to drop their nuclear plans. A worldwide NPT alliance, with U.N. verifications, is a better strategy than U.S. one-on-one confrontations, because a U.S. go-it-alone bully strategy can escalate into disastrous military actions.

Unfortunately, it appears that our current President is focused on being the big deal negotiator for one-on-one deals, while withdrawing from the world's long-time successful alliance efforts for nuclear containment. The NPT and the U.N. strategy for nuclear containment is a long-term preventive strategy of working with all countries to move forward together to put the nuclear monster back in the box. The U.S. is playing with dynamite here, with its go-it-alone confrontation strategy; actually, the nuclear threat makes dynamite look like a sparkler. Choosing to use a bully approach for negotiations, with nuclear weapons as our big stick, has already led to U.S. Presidential threats of using nuclear weapons.

Instead of helping to enforce the United Nations' right to oversee nuclear verification in Iraq, the U.S. pushed for and led a preemptive (offensive) war on Iraq that spawned the Islamic State of Iraq and Syria (ISIS) terrorist groups. Beyond creating global terrorist actions, this war also resulted in Iraq aligning with our adversary, Iran. Ultimately, this war was based on very weak and incorrect intelligence information about weapons of mass destruction that did not exist. The people who pushed for this decision claimed Iraqi oil would pay for the war and believed U.S. corporations would get the rights to Iraqi oil. One of the most vocal in the call for war was Vice President Dick Cheney, who had been CEO of Halliburton and was allied with the oil industry. This was clearly a choice of folly over reason, not a mistake.

Instead of continuing U.S. support of the Iran nuclear disarmament treaty, our current administration withdrew from this treaty in 2018. This withdrawal was supposedly based on Iran's support of terrorism; however, withdrawal from this nuclear arms treaty does not help to reduce terrorism. Unfortunately, this treaty withdrawal seems to have been based more on a political campaign promise, rather than critical thinking.

There has been little effort to persuade our allies (Israel and India) to join the nuclear NPT treaty to reduce fears in the Middle-East. We could use their support to further isolate the few remaining countries that have not signed the NPT.

<u>Radioactive Waste</u>
Nuclear technology is used for more than weapons. Ten countries currently use nuclear energy to generate power.

Table 24: Nuclear Power Countries

United States
Russia
Germany
France
United Kingdom
Japan
South Korea
Switzerland
Belgium
Netherlands

Radioactive waste, which is hazardous to all forms of life and takes thousands of years to decay, is a by-product of nuclear power generation. Governments who have signed the Non-Proliferation Treaty (NPT), including the U.S., have accepted responsibility for managing and storing their nuclear waste as safely as possible. The International Atomic Energy Agency (IAEA) joint convention on safety reviews all countries' waste management and storage processes against the IAEA safety standards (International Atomic Energy Agency 2017).

Several types of nuclear waste have an extremely long half-life for decay (i.e., the natural process of disintegration) of thousands, or millions, of years. This toxic nuclear waste has to be treated and stored safely for extremely long times, increasing the risk of safety problems. In the past, several countries stored nuclear waste in the ocean (1954 – 1993); fortunately, that is no longer permitted by international agreements.

The U.S. currently has 75 nuclear power plants in 35 different states, and spent nuclear fuel is stored at each of these sites. In addition, nuclear weapons' waste is stored at four more sites (Stanford Earth 2018).

In order to fund long-term safe storage of all nuclear waste deep in mines and encased in steel, the U.S. levied a tax on the nuclear power companies to fund safe storage of nuclear waste. But instead of finding a storage site, the government spent the $40 billion collected for this purpose on other things. Spending taxes dedicated for specific purposes on other things is a repeated folly of our government in a number of areas (e.g., Social Security and Medicare payroll tax funds).

Nuclear Arms and Nuclear Waste Crisis Follies
[(G) denotes government follies; (B) denotes business follies; (C) denotes citizen follies]

- Not getting all countries to sign the nuclear treaty agreement, which creates a fear of nuclear weapons' attacks from enemies with this capability (G)

- Instead of supporting the U.N.'s right to perform nuclear verification in Iraq, the U.S. pushed for and led a preemptive (offensive) war on Iraq (G)

- Instead of supporting the Iran nuclear disarmament treaty, the U.S. withdrew from this international treaty that included U.N. inspections for verification (G)

- The five authorized nuclear weapons countries still have 22,000 warheads in their combined nuclear weapons war chest, and have shown a reluctance to continue with the agreed-to disarmament plans (G)

- The U.S. has continued to increase quantities of hazardous nuclear waste that must be contained and stored as carefully as possible for thousands of years, or longer (G)

- Instead of using the $40 billion collected from private nuclear power companies for safe storage of nuclear waste, the money was spent on other things (G)

Possible Goal

Reestablish, maintain, and implement international nuclear treaties that include U.N. verifications to reduce the risk of nuclear disaster

Possible Results Measures

Reestablish, maintain, and enforce all nuclear treaties

Reduction of nuclear arms warheads

Number of countries not signed on to the arms treaty

Reduction in production of the worst types (i.e., those with very long decay life) of nuclear toxic waste (goal of zero)

Likely Root Causes

Nuclear technology availability

Mismanagement of nuclear toxic waste storage funds

Selfish ambition and attempt to bully other nations

U.S. go-it-alone approach

Fear of other countries' nuclear arms capability

Possible Improvements

(* Asterisk indicates no- or low-cost to the federal government)

*Reestablish and enforce nuclear international treaties

*Encourage the few countries that have not yet signed the NPT to sign it

*Use newer nuclear technologies with shorter half-lives to reduce production of the most dangerous older types of nuclear wastes

Research safer methods of storing nuclear wastes

Fund needed improvements to maintain a viable nuclear defense system, including the ability to intercept Russia's new high-speed rockets

Establish a single safe site for nuclear waste storage

Crisis annual costs
Defense News reports that the Congressional Budget report of 10/31/17 estimated that the total cost to modernize and maintain our nuclear weapons over the next 30 years would be $1.2 trillion. That is $800 billion to operate and sustain existing weapons, and $400 billion to modernize them. Divided by 30 years, that is about $40 billion per year. That $40 billion per year is the estimated 2020 annual cost for the nuclear weapons. That is the cost if they are not used; of course, if they are used, the cost will be much greater. We also have to pay about $500 million per year to nuclear power companies to store nuclear waste on their sites.

Federal Budget cost reduction opportunities for 2024
If the U.S. were to comply with the existing nuclear treaty and continue to reduce our weapons, along with other nuclear countries, we could reduce the nuclear threat in the world and cut our nuclear weapons costs in half over the next 5 years, saving about $20 billion per year by 2024.

The U.S. Department of Energy has a budget of about $6 billion per year to deal with nuclear waste. The Nuclear Waste Act of 1982 established a tax on the nuclear power industry to pay for waste management of nuclear energy waste. This fund should now have $40 billion in it, dedicated to build a deep mine facility to safely store that nuclear waste. Unfortunately, the government took this money and spent it for other things; so today, the nuclear power companies are storing this nuclear waste on their own power plant sites. Because the government spent the power company storage taxes on other things, we are faced with paying the power companies $500 million per year to store their own waste on their own sites. The cost of that government decision is the $40 billion that the U.S. government spent on other things, plus $500 million per year to store waste on 75 less-secure nuclear waste sites.

Potential House Caucus to implement House CAT Improvements
Nuclear Security Group: Co-Chairs Jeff Fortenberry (R), Pete Visclosky (D)

Personal Story – Nuclear Power Crisis

On March 28, 1979, the Unit 2 reactor at Three Mile Island near Middletown, PA suffered a partial meltdown. This was the most serious nuclear accident in our nuclear power plant history. Although no one was killed, the accident produced concerns about the possibility of future radioactive-induced health effects, particularly cancer. My family (wife and four young children) lived about 150 miles northeast of Three Mile Island in Chester, New Jersey. We were told that the winds were blowing our way and we should all stay indoors for the weekend with windows and doors shut while the radiation release blew over our homes.

My wife died of cancer and I was also diagnosed with cancer. No direct cause and effect can be proven between the Three Mile Island disaster and these cancer cases. However, I would feel better about the health of all my family had we not been exposed to the release of radiation from a partial meltdown of a nuclear power plant reactor.

If the goal is survival, then we need to support continued reduction of nuclear weapons and safe storage of nuclear waste.

Cybersecurity Crisis

Definition
The increasing number of intrusions into our cyberspace indicates a major security weakness. Our government, our business economy, our financial transactions, our essential services, and our news all depend on having a secure information technology infrastructure. A single intrusion can have a disastrous impact on our country.

Our country, with three times more cyber intrusions than any other country, has the weakest cybersecurity in the world. The number of U.S. cyber incursions is not only very high, but it has increased tenfold from 2006 to 2015 (Department of Homeland Security 2018, 2). This crisis is by far the fastest growing of all the 23 crises analyzed in this book.

Research and Data

According to the Department of Homeland Security (DHS) website, the U.S. faces major cybersecurity threats and risks from a wide range of organizations, including nation-states, terrorists, and criminals. The services under attack are equally wide ranging. These services include: electricity, water, transportation, finances, health care, news, and global supply chains for businesses (Department of Homeland Security, 2018, 2).

Virtually everything necessary for our economy, our lives, and our safety is at risk from this combination of nation-state, terrorist, and criminal cyber attacks. An important system not shown on this DHS list above is our election system, which was affected by foreign state cybersecurity attacks in the 2016 presidential election. This intrusion affects the fundamental credibility of our democracy.

The Justice Department investigated the U.S. 2016 Presidential election and found that Russia repeatedly penetrated our IT infrastructure to steal political information, and set up phony websites with false political information. Russian penetration of the U.S. IT infrastructure continues to undermine elections in the U.S. When a foreign nation can penetrate and use our information technology (IT) infrastructure to inflame political divisions with false information, to help the candidate of their choice become our President, it is clearly a crisis.

Research facts and trends

According to the U.S. Department of Commerce's National Institute of Standards and Technology (NIST) website:

- To protect America, we need to protect, defend, and secure our IT infrastructure and digital networks

- Our IT infrastructure relies on collaboration between industry and government, and it uses voluntary framework standards and practices to promote the protection of our critical IT infrastructure

- A National Vulnerability Database has been established to identify IT infrastructure weaknesses, and those weaknesses need to be addressed
(National Institute of Standards and Technology, n.d.)

If we use number of intrusions as the measure, our country is now three times worse than any other country. We need to establish goals and measures for secure cybersystems, with plans to support those goals, in order to protect our IT infrastructure.

The Department of Homeland Security (DHS), not the Defense Department, is responsible for our cybersecurity. According to the DHS website, their security strategies include:

- Voluntary protection by each organization of their own network by minimizing vulnerabilities

- Preventing or disrupting cybercrimes

- Building security and resilience into our IT infrastructure
(Department of Homeland Security, 2018, 1)

Their short list of fairly nebulous "strategies" appears insufficient to deal with this crisis. The size and scope of our cybersecurity crisis includes the following facts:

- More than 20 billion devices are expected to be connected to the internet by 2020

- The number of cyber incidents increased tenfold from 2006 to 2015

- The threats to U.S. IT infrastructure from those pursuing political influence and financial gain are growing

- Threats from nation-states are growing, and some are continuing with ongoing attacks

- Attempted intrusions on government networks occur daily

- In 2015, one intrusion resulted in compromise of the records of 4 million government employees and affected 22 million people

- IT tools required to commit cybercrimes are increasingly powerful, while costs to implement them continue to drop

Ransomware now attacks both frontline systems and back-up drives. The city of Baltimore's computers were shut down for a week in 2019 by a ransomware attack. Baltimore was the seventh U.S. city to be attacked by a ransomware attack in just the first five months of 2019. This is more than double the number of cities attacked in all of 2018.

Attacks from outside are not the only danger facing the internet. The dark web facilitates the easy sale of illicit goods and services, such as firearms, forged passports, and malware. The dark web is a part of the internet that isn't visible to search engines, and requires the use of a special browser that hides your identity by routing page requests through a series of proxy servers; it is a hotbed for criminal and illicit activity. The dark web sites sell stolen identity credentials, credit card numbers, drugs, guns, and software tools to hack into people's computers. It is also a major hub for human trafficking crimes. Dark web site addresses end with .onion, instead of .com or .org.

DHS has established seven goals:

- Assess cybersecurity risks
- Protect government information systems
- Protect critical infrastructure
- Prevent and disrupt criminal use of cyberspace
- Respond effectively to cyber incidents
- Strengthen the security and reliability of a cyber ecosystem
- Improve the management of DHS cybersecurity activities

While the items on this list are an important beginning, they lack quantifiable, long-term goals and annual objectives that can be used to determine annual progress, and to assess the adequacy of the improvement plans. Goals must be linked to measures and timeframes to achieve objectives. For example, a goal could be to reduce the number of daily cyber intrusion incidents by 25% per year. The U.S. has had a tenfold increase in cyber attacks from 2006 to 2015, so an aggressive goal and plan are needed to start a decrease in cyber intrusions.

<u>Below are a few examples of how to add a quantifiable measure to the DHS goals:</u>

- Increase the number of critical networks that meet security standards each year

- Increase the percentage of all networks meeting DHS security standards

- Decrease the number of cybersecurity intrusions on critical infrastructure networks each year

- Decrease the total number of cybersecurity intrusions each year

The DHS Office of Strategy, Policy, and Plans has committed to perform an annual check on the DHS strategy, and provide feedback on strengths and areas for improvement. Without quantifiable goals and measurable results, it will be very hard to assess the effectiveness of the DHS strategy. The DHS plan is to update their strategy only every 5 years. DHS should update their strategy (plan) based on the annual check, and implement recommendations for improvements in their strategy. That is simply using the Plan-Do-Check-Act (PDCA) cycle on an annual basis.

One goal of the DHS is to ensure all government agencies maintain an adequate level of cybersecurity. However, an "adequate level" of security needs to be defined and measurable. In addition, there should be a report on the government agencies that are not meeting the "adequate" level, and their plans to meet it by a certain date.

One strategy of DHS is to deploy best practices and use the most effective and efficient improvements. Although that is a good practice, it lacks a specific prioritized improvement plan that includes which best practices will be used, and when and where they will be implemented to achieve measurable goals.

DHS has identified 16 critical infrastructure sectors that are at risk, and DHS is working with all of them to understand cyber risks and maintain cybersecurity; unfortunately, they lack specific improvements and specific results measures for cybersecurity. All 16 sectors should be evaluated to assess the "adequate" level of security required, and they should be required to have plans to achieve the adequate security level by a certain date.

Although DHS has plans to address crime and drug cyber activities, as with the critical infrastructure sectors, specific results measures and specific improvement plans are lacking.

A major cybersecurity intrusion came from Russia in 2016 to influence the election of our current president. Russian President Vladimir Putin announced that he supported candidate Donald Trump, probably because Trump's campaign supported elimination of U.S. sanctions on Russia, including economic sanctions on Russian leaders. Two years later, this Russian cyber-intrusion continues, but it is not mentioned in the DHS cybersecurity strategy. The Russian intrusion into U.S. elections undermines free and credible elections, the key to our democracy. DHS has not prioritized the cyber threats to be addressed and the improvements to be made (Vox 2017).

Other countries have also made cyber intrusions into our IT networks. A Chinese group captured the code for U.S. cybersecurity tools during a National Security Agency (NSA) attack on a group of Chinese state-sponsored hackers. In April 2017, these U.S. cyber-weapon tools were then dumped into the dark web for others to use. Since then, these U.S. cyber tools have been used to cripple the U.K. health system, shutdown shipping operations to the Ukraine, and paralyze other services in the Ukraine such as the airport, postal service, gas stations, and ATMs. This same Chinese hacking group has made numerous attacks on U.S. space, satellite, and nuclear propulsion technology companies (Perlroth, Sanger, and Shane 2019).

Cybersecurity experts warn that the next major war will likely be initiated by a major cyber attack. Russia, China, Iran and North Korea are the major countries using cyber warfare against the U.S. (U.S. Council of Economic Advisers 2018). These continued cyber attacks show that we are actually in a cybersecurity war now, but we are not acting as if we were. One of the major reasons for the trade war with China is to try to get them to stop hacking into U.S. companies and stealing trade secrets. A more reliable strategy would be to actually secure our IT infrastructure systems, our finance systems, and our computer files that contain trade secrets. Asking criminals to not steal is not as effective a strategy as improving the locks and the security system on your home.

Although the U.S. Government cybersecurity budget was supposed to be $15 billion per year, the current administration cut the National Institute of Standards and Technology (NIST) budget for cybersecurity by 18% (Statista 2019). NIST is responsible for planning improvements to our cybersecurity and for setting the cybersecurity standards that our government agencies need to meet. Planning to improve our cybersecurity should be at least on a par with planning for our physical defense, which has a much larger and increasing budget.

The Department of Defense (DOD) budget is $661 billion in 2019, but the most likely point of attack in any coming war will be our IT systems, which the Department of Defense is not responsible for. The Department of Homeland Security (DHS) is responsible for our border security and cybersecurity, but its whole budget is less than 10% of what the DOD has to spend. Furthermore, DHS' focus and priority are on physical border security, not cybersecurity. Cybersecurity is our greatest security weakness, but what the DHS had to address it is only about 2% of what the DOD budget has.

Cybersecurity Crisis Follies
[(G) denotes government follies]

- Russian intrusion into the U.S. 2016 election campaign is not mentioned in the Department of Homeland Security (DHS) cybersecurity strategy (G)

- U.S. cybersecurity goals lack quantifiable measures and objectives, that could be used to determine annual progress and assess U.S. cybersecurity improvement plans (G)

- The U.S. continues to allow the dark web to operate and provide cyber tools for criminal activities (G)

- The U.S. is cutting the small cybersecurity budget, while increasing physical defense spending, in spite of the fact that cybersecurity is our greatest security weakness (G)

Possible Goals
Reduce total daily cyber intrusion

Eliminate major, ongoing, nation-state political intrusions within 1 year

Eliminate the dark web

Possible Results Measures
The number of daily cyber intrusions

The number of annual nation-state attacks

The size of the dark web

Likely Root Causes
The rapid growth and dependence on the internet

The internet is an open-to-all system for business, individuals, and government, with voluntary security

No built-in security capability for end-devices and network computers

The increase in nation-state cyber attack forces

The lack of an adequate cybersecurity capability in the U.S.

Significant cuts to the budget of the organization that is responsible for developing all government cybersecurity standards

This crisis is not a top priority of our Executive Branch

Possible Improvements
(* Asterisk indicates no- or low-cost improvements to the federal government)

*Those connected to the internet update their devices to include software for cybersecurity protection

*Those connected to the internet implement cybersecurity tips to prevent users allowing hackers into their systems

Disable the dark web

Prevent foreign nation-state cybersecurity attacks

Eliminate the availability of tools for cybersecurity attacks

Pursue and capture more cybersecurity criminals

Restore NIST cyber budget cuts, to ensure adequate funding

Develop future devices and computers with built-in security capabilities to reduce cybersecurity crime and nation-state attacks

Fund research into areas that could improve cybersecurity (e.g., China is pursuing development of a new quantum computing internet to eliminate all cyber intrusions)

Crisis annual cost
The White House Council of Economic Advisers reported in February 2018 that the estimated cost of malicious cyber activity in the U.S. was between $57 billion and $109 billion in 2016. That number will probably be closer to $110 billion in 2020.

Federal Budget cost reduction opportunities for 2024
Yearly losses from cyber-attacks are $50 billion to $100 billion. The goal should be to cut that cost in half through our cybersecurity efforts, which could save the U.S. as much as $50 billion per year. While the current dollar costs may not seem high, we must recognize that the potential costs are inestimable. Our entire economy could be shut down through a cyber attack; or we could elect a president with help from our adversaries, again.

Our government is currently spending about $15 billion per year on cybersecurity. Given the tremendous economic risks this threat poses to the economy, the amount dedicated to our defense's weakest point is clearly insufficient. That budget should be increased, perhaps doubling its current amount to $30 billion per year; therefore, the 2024 budget would see an increase of $15 billion on this line item.

Potential House Caucus to implement House CAT Improvements
Cybersecurity Caucus: Co-Chairs Mike McCaul (R), Jim Langevin (D)

Personal Story – Cybersecurity Crisis

One of my best friends in college at Northeastern University was Steve Walker. We both were in the same Electrical Engineering classes and the same ROTC classes. He was near the top of our class of about 20 students and went to work for the National Security Agency (NSA) when he graduated. While he was there, Steve created the first firewall for IT security. NSA let Steve have the property rights to this first firewall system, which allowed him to set up a business to sell the software to businesses to help them secure their own IT infrastructure.

Of my four children, three are working in the IT industry, all with some portion of their work focused on securing their companies' IT systems or helping their business customers secure their IT systems.

Security breaches for IT systems are an escalating threat. Zak Doffman reported in Forbes magazine that millions of Chinese security cameras can be used by hackers to spy on users (Doffman 2019). One of the references Doffman cites was from a study that had been published just one day earlier by John Honovich and John Scanlan (my youngest son), both of whom work at Internet Protocol Video Marketing (IPVM), the leading source of video surveillance information and online training (Internet Protocol Video Marketing, n.d.). Surveillance equipment is commonly the target of cyber attacks, because the equipment often designed without adequate security, which is compounded by the fact that it is also installed in an insecure manner.

An Internet Protocol (IP) camera can receive and send video and audio control information via the internet; hence, it is very important to have adequate cybersecurity to protect who can control the use of "security" cameras.

There is no police force established to provide security in the area of cybersecurity, so we each must ensure our own computers and financial accounts are secure. Estimates have been made that as much as 80% of all cyber intrusions occur because computer users have not followed cybersecurity basics. To find a list of user cybersecurity tips, simply search the internet for cybersecurity user tips.

Border Security Crisis

Definition
We had actually seen significant improvement in the southern border illegal immigrant crisis from 2000 to 2017. Total arrests of illegal immigrants on the southern border decreased from $1,600,000 in 2000 to $300,000 million in 2017, an 81% reduction. However, FY 2018 saw 404,000 arrests (an increase of over 100,000), and the number in the first seven months of FY 2019 increased to 464,000. If this rate of increase continues, we could see 800,000 arrests for FY 2019 (U.S. Customs and Border Protection 2019).

The U.S. Border Security crisis has four components:

- Illegal Immigrants: The illegal immigration crisis at the southern border has gotten significantly worse in 2018 and 2019 after many years of improvement. U.S. policy changes have contributed to this reversal.

- Legal immigration process capability: We have an inadequate processing capability for those seeking asylum; processing in the past took months, but now it takes years, raising the cost in both dollars and human suffering.
- Illegal Drugs: Unwanted illegal drug smuggling occurs by air, sea, and through tunnels as deep as 70 feet. More than 85% of Mexican border drug smuggling is said to go undetected through Ports of Entry (POE).

- Terrorism: The 9/11 terrorist attacks were performed by 19 airplane hijackers who came to the U.S. on commercial flights using legal visas to gain entry.

Illegal Immigration

Our combined U.S. border with Canada and Mexico is 7,000 miles long; however, the Department of Homeland Security's (DHS) top priority is securing just the southwest land border against illegal immigration, smuggling of drugs and other contraband, and terrorists' activities. Their plan uses apprehensions along the Mexican border as their primary indicator of border security.

DHS Southern Border illegal immigrant improvement results:

- Total arrests of illegal immigrants on the southwest border decreased 81% between 2000 and 2017. Recently, however, there have been significant increases.

- Only 1.5% of those arrested in 2019 for illegal crossing have a criminal record; most are simply seeking asylum.

- The Total Interdiction Rate (TIR), the percentage of illegal crossings stopped, had improved from about 50% in 2006 to about 75% in 2016.

- The Recidivism Rate, the percentage of illegal immigrants who, after being deported, tried for a second time to enter this country, dropped from 31% in 2005 to 12% in 2016.

- The estimate of "got-aways" (i.e., illegal immigrants not caught) on the southwest border dropped from 600,000 in 2006 to 100,000 in 2016, an 83% reduction.

All these measures show very good results to prevent or reduce illegal immigration through 2016. The issue was on its way to becoming a non-crisis. No other crisis covered in this book had such great improvement results prior to the 2016 Presidential election; yet this crisis was chosen as the number one crisis to address by President Trump when he won the election. Instead of continuing to improve, as it had been doing, illegal immigration on the southern border has gotten worse in 2018 and 2019.

One major reason for the reduction in illegal border crossings in the past may have been the North American Free Trade Agreement (NAFTA), implemented in 1994, which provided many new jobs in Mexico along the border, and thus reduced the need to come to America for work.

After years of reduced illegal border crossings, we saw a surge in February 2019, when 76,000 migrants crossed the border without authorization. This was nearly double the number in February 2018, and an 11-year high (Dickerson 2019). The current administration's actions to reduce *legal* immigration have contributed to this sudden sharp increase in *illegal* immigration. Those actions include:

- Significantly poorer performance in processing asylum cases, where the time to wait for a court case for an asylum request has shifted from months to years

- Significantly reduced limits on legal acceptance of refugees seeking asylum. The U.S. legal refugee limit ranged between 70,000 and 85,000 per year for 17 years between 2000 and 2016. Under the current administration, the legal refugee limit has been reduced each year as follows:

   FY 2017: 50,000
   FY 2018: 45,000
   FY 2019: 30,000
   FY 2020: 18,000
   (Sanchez 2019)

- Significantly harsher treatment of those seeking asylum at Ports of Entry (POE), where children have been separated from families. This causes some to pursue illegal entry.

There is also an increase in families seeking asylum from gang-controlled countries in Central America. The current U.S. administration has cut assistance to countries plagued with gun violence, continued to deport criminals back to their home country rather than have them imprisoned, and dropped out of the U.N. treaty to stop selling weapons to gangs in these countries. Increased gun violence and the decreased rule of law in these countries are causing an increase in asylum seekers. The current administration's policies have contributed to this increase in asylum seekers, while simultaneously reducing the number we will accept. This combination has increased U.S. illegal immigration on the Southern Border and created a crisis after years of continuous improvement.

A complete border plan is needed, one that uses appropriate technology, POE security improvements, legal immigration processing improvements, and possibly a wall in appropriate sections of the border. In early 2019, in response to the border crisis created by the current administration, Congress, with a Democrat-controlled House of Representatives, passed a bill for improvements in Southern Border security that addressed needed POE security improvements and needed legal immigration processing improvements. That new 2019 Congressional Border Security law and funding should enable continued improvement on reducing *illegal* immigration and improvements in processing *legal* immigration. However, businesses' use of E-Verify to reduce attracting and hiring illegal immigrants still has not been made a legal requirement. Business access to low-cost illegal labor is apparently considered more important than stopping this incentive that attracts illegal immigration.

The estimates of the cost of undocumented immigrants to the U.S. have a wide range. Meg Wiehe, Deputy Director of the non-partisan Institute of Taxation and Economic Policy non-profit, suggests it is worth looking at whether or not these undocumented low-wage workers are paying their fair share. She explains that on the tax side, they pay income taxes and Social Security taxes like others; however, they have to use fake Social Security numbers. Therefore, undocumented workers end up paying into Social Security but will never get credit for those payments. They are also not eligible for the earned income tax credit, for which low-income citizens are eligible. In addition, they are not eligible for other low-income welfare benefits that citizens get, such as the Supplemental Nutrition Assistance Program (formerly the Food Stamp program). Therefore, these undocumented, low-income immigrants pay a higher tax rate and get lower benefits than similar low-income citizens. They are filling hard labor low-income jobs to produce the food we all enjoy in the grocery store, and they are doing it at a lower cost for America. Economically, America is benefiting from the use of illegal immigrants (Institute on Economic Taxation and Policy 2017).
Furthermore, both legal and illegal immigrants have a lower crime rate than U.S. citizens, so they actually help to reduce the crime rate and the cost associated with dealing with crimes.

One area where undocumented immigrants benefit equally with low-income citizens is public education for their children. America provides free public education in order to prepare future generations to be eligible for higher-paying jobs, who will pay higher taxes resulting from increased earnings. Public education is an investment in the future that has paid off for America.

Drug smuggling
Drug smuggling into the U.S. is driven by our drug addiction epidemic; demand drives supply. Based on the National Survey on Drug Use and Health in 2014, the American Addiction Centers arrived at the following conclusions:

- 7 million American adults have a drug abuse disorder

- Drug abuse and addiction costs America $200 billion annually in healthcare, criminal justice, and lost workplace production

- An estimated 900,000 adolescents suffered from an illegal drug addiction in 2014

- Heroin addiction in young adults (ages 18-25) doubled from 2004 to 2014 (Substance Abuse and Mental Health Services Administration 2015, 2)

Unlike the immigration crisis, which had been significantly reduced over the past decade, the drug crisis and drug smuggling crisis has been on the rise. Unity Behavioral Health, which operates rehabilitation centers specializing in addiction treatment, reports:

- The number of heroin users tripled from 2003 to 2014

- U.S. teens are twice as likely to use illegal drugs as their European counterparts

- The number of deaths due to opioids has increased by a factor of four since 1999
  (Unity Rehab, n.d.)

According to the U.S. Centers for Disease Control and Prevention (CDC), in 2017:

- 11% of U.S. citizens, 12 years of age and over, have used illegal drugs

- Between 2002 and 2014, the rate of heroin deaths increased by a factor of five
    (NIH National Institute on Drug Abuse, n.d.)

The Commissioner of DHS's Customs and Border Protection (CBP) provided the following information to the Senate during a hearing:

- There is a heroin epidemic at our southwest border

- The Heroin Response Strategy is a collaborative partnership between public health and law enforcement

- The CBP has a responsibility to stop drugs at and between Ports of Entry (POE)

- Heroin and fentanyl are smuggled across all our borders: land, sea, and air (U.S. Drug Enforcement Agency, n.d.). Drugs are smuggled on commercial airplanes, boats, and mail service.

- CBP requires a broad capability that can address all the avenues of drug smuggling.

This report from the CBP Commissioner lacked measurable goals for improvement.

Between 1991 and 2016, prescriptions for pain medications in the U.S. increased by 380%, from 76 million to 289 million per year. At the same time, drug companies increased the strength of some of their opioids to make them more powerful than morphine. In 2002, 1 in 6 opioid prescription drugs were stronger than morphine; only ten years later in 2012, 1 in 3 opioid prescriptions was for a drug stronger than morphine. Thus, from 1991 to 2016, pain medication prescriptions increased by almost a factor of four, while pain medication strength doubled. This combination created our current drug epidemic. Many of those who had become addicted found that illegal opioids were cheaper than prescription drugs; they moved on to illegal opioids like heroin and fentanyl. Because fentanyl is a much stronger synthetic opioid, it carries a much higher risk of death by overdose.

This opioid crisis is a uniquely American problem, supported by our private insurance companies that favor the use of drugs over alternative medical treatments, such as acupuncture, massage, biofeedback or rehabilitation exercises. U.S. prescription rates for opioids are 40% higher than any other developed country.

Our current administration's actions on the southern border to mistreat those who want to apply for *legal* immigration have created increased *illegal* immigration. Likewise, our government's approval of an addictive pain drug, coupled with our medical system's overprescription of that addictive drug, has created our opioid epidemic.

Cartoonist Walt Kelly's character Pogo said: "We have met the enemy and he is us" (Humor in America 2014).

Border Security Crisis Follies
[(B) denotes business follies; (G) denotes government follies]

- Lack of a comprehensive border security plan to include requiring E-Verify technology, adequate Ports of Entry security, and needed legal immigrant processing cycle time improvements. (The February 2019 Border Security Congressional bill, which was enacted into law, will help with rectifying this folly.) (G)

- Penalizing government workers who are helping to secure America, with multiple government shutdowns and delay of pay, as a means to demand that Congress fund more money for a huge border wall. (G)

- The current opioid crisis began with the FDA approval of oxycodone which was based on false information about its addictive qualities; this was the match that lit the drug fire. (G)

- Pharmaceutical companies and our medical system have fueled the opioid crisis by introducing and overprescribing legal opioid pain medications such as oxycodone. (B)

- The drug companies increased the strength of some of their opioids to be more powerful than morphine, essentially pouring more gas on the fire. (B)

- The U.S. private insurance system favors use of drugs over alternative medical treatments, such as exercises to reduce pain. (B)

Possible Goals
Reduction in illegal immigration

Reduction in annual drug overdose deaths

Possible Results Measures
Annual illegal immigration arrests on the Southern border

Annual drug overdose deaths

Likely Root Causes
Illegal immigration is being encouraged when businesses are not required to use the E-Verify system to hire legal workers

Illegal immigration is being increased by intentionally harsh treatment at U.S. POE and by poor performance on processing asylum requests

Illegal drug smuggling is driven by addicts' high demand; a demand created by U.S. pharmaceutical corporations and our medical system

U.S. POE system needs improved drug detection capabilities

Possible Improvements
(* Asterisk indicates no- or low-cost to the federal government)

*Stop creating incentives for illegal immigration; require businesses to use E-Verify

*Provide a less punitive and more supportive approach at the U.S. POE for those seeking asylum from gun violence-ridden countries

*Stop the medical community from creating drug addicts, who then create the demand for drug smuggling

*Rescind the FDA approval of oxycodone and similar drugs for new patients who are not already addicted or reliant on opioids

*Rescind the medical guidelines to prescribe pain medications to achieve zero pain; living with a bit of pain is better than being a drug addict

Follow up on immigrants with approved visas, to eliminate over-stays

Improve the drug detection capability (The February 2019 Border Security law may have addressed this)

Eliminate the legal immigration processing backlogs and reduce the asylum immigration processing cycle time from years to days

Help reduce the gun violence in Central American Countries by rejoining the U.N. weapons sales treaty, restoring some funding to help reduce gun violence, and imprisoning criminal immigrants in the country they came from, rather than releasing them in these gun violent countries that are the source of asylum seekers.

Crisis annual cost

Immigrants, legal or not, make a positive contribution to the U.S. economy. Because drug costs were covered in the Use of Drugs Crisis section under the Health Care crises in Chapter 9, no additional crisis annual costs are assigned to this border security crisis.

Federal Budget opportunities for cost reduction in 2024

The Department of Homeland Security's 2019 budget is $47.5 billion, which includes securing all our physical borders and providing cybersecurity. The bulk of this DHS budget is for physical security (not cybersecurity) to reduce illegal immigration and illegal smuggling, as well as to prevent terrorism. Increased use of technology could help improve this physical effort and reduce costs; for example, requiring businesses to use the existing E-Verify system to reduce illegal immigration. With increased use of technology, this budget could be reduced about 5% per year for the next 5 years. This would attain about a 25% reduction in 5 years, about $2 billion per year, to achieve a total reduction of about $10 billion per year in 2024.

Potential House Caucus to implement House CAT Improvements
Border Security Caucus: Co-Chairs Brian Babin (R), Andy Biggs (R)

Border Caucus: Co-Chairs Raul Grijalva (D), Filemon Vela (D)

Refugee Caucus: Co-Chairs Mario Diaz-Balart (R), Zoe Lofgren (D), Chris Smith (R), Joe Neguse (D)

Personal Story – Immigration Crisis

Unless we are Native Americans, we are all immigrants or descendants of immigrants; so, we all have a personal story that relates to this issue.

I am Irish. In the 1840s there was a Great Famine in Ireland. The resulting mass starvation caused the death of about 1.5 million people. As a result of the famine, another 1.5 million left Ireland. This mass migration included my paternal grandparents. I visited the Famine Museum when I was in Ireland in 2005, and I learned that the famine was caused by a potato crop disease that had lasted two years. The Irish could not grow other crops because of the poor soil, which was the result of deforestation. Over time, the Irish had cut down the trees for heat or construction, and had not planted new ones. With all the trees cut down, wind and rain washed away the topsoil. Thus, we see an example of an environmental crisis, leading to a health crisis, leading to an immigration crisis – interconnected just as our U.S. crises are today.

I am lucky to be in the U.S. today because in the past, this country welcomed most immigrants seeking a better life. Today, we hear President Trump telling the world that "Our country is full." He seems not to understand that this country was built by immigrants, and that we still need them for our future; particularly now, with a reducing worker-to-retiree ratio in our country.

Hopefully, America will return to our long tradition of treating immigrants with justice, equity, and compassion, valuing their contributions to our country.

Defense Costs Crisis

Definition
Although the U.S. spends more on our military than any other country in the world, our cybersecurity defenses are inadequate to protect our IT infrastructure and our elections. In 2000, the U.S. defense budget was $302 billion; it has increased 138% to $718 billion for 2020. A 3% per year increase for 10 years would have resulted in only a 38% increase.

Research and trends
The U.S. annual defense expenditures have consistently been significantly higher than any other country. Perhaps such high spending on defense has also contributed to bad political decisions to use our military in an offensive way, rather than simply for defense. Those decisions to make our Department of Defense (DOD) also a Department of Offense have been a further cause of increased military costs.

Other countries (e.g., particularly Russia in the 2016 Presidential election) have used very low-cost cyberwarfare to penetrate our country's internet and social media in order to disrupt our society and our elections, thus working to support regime change in the U.S. Improved cybersecurity is needed to defend America from foreign attacks; we need this more than we need an increase in our already superior position in nuclear weapons, ships, planes, and tanks. We also need an effective cyberforce more than we need a new space force.

One of the reasons for our cybersecurity weakness, and our continued increased expenditures on tanks, planes, and ships, may be that the DOD is not responsible for cybersecurity. Instead, cybersecurity has been assigned to the Department of Homeland Security (DHS) which has as its highest priority to build a 4th century wall on our southern border, instead of providing the cybersecurity we need in the 21st century.

Our use of the DOD for offense is one of the major causes of the multiple crises that we are still in today. President George W. Bush led our country in the invasion of Iraq as a preemptive (offensive) military strategy. This preemptive military action has paved the way for more overseas action since then.

U.S. military spending is now 260% higher than China, the next closest country in military expenditures. While we spend almost 20% of our country's budget revenues on defense, China is only spending about 5% of their revenues on defense.

Of the 15 countries with the highest military expenditures, 13 of them are U.S. allies; only China and Russia are our foes (Business Insider 2018). The U.S. and our allies are spending about 5 times as much as our two foes, as shown in the following table, "Military Expenditures by Country." We need to remember that the Soviet Union failed because they were spending too much on their military. The U.S. is ignoring or not adequately addressing many domestic crises, while overspending on defense; we have a financially irresponsible debt with no plans to address it.

The U.S. is a lot more likely to fail from continued internal financial mismanagement than an attack from a foreign foe.

Table 25: Military Expenditures by Country

Country	2017 Military Budgets (in $ billions)	Percent
U.S.	610	44%
China	228	
Saudi Arabia	69	
Russia	66	
India	64	
France	58	
United Kingdom	47	
Japan	45	
Germany	44	
South Korea	39	
Brazil	29	
Italy	29	
Australia	27	
Canada	21	
Turkey	18	
U.S. and Allies	1,100	79%
China and Russia	294	21%
Total	1,394	100%

The current administration sent Congress a proposed fiscal year 2020 budget request of $750 billion for national security, $718 billion of which was for the DOD (U.S. Department of Defense 2019). That leaves only $32 billion for all other security issues, the most pressing of which is cyber security, the area in which our country is most vulnerable.

Jim Pillsbury, author of *The Hundred Year Marathon,* says that China's strategic approach to their military expenditures focuses on using the most effective and efficient weapons. For example, China has a $2 million missile that can destroy a $5 billion aircraft carrier. China is also focused on using 21st century low-cost cyber capabilities and has a balanced budget that is focused on being the world economic leader (Pillsbury

2015). China knows that financial power, not military might, will determine the world leader of the future.

While the U.S. needs to control our military budget, the current administration has proposed significant defense budget increases, including a new Space Force as a completely independent military branch. This is in direct conflict with the global treaty we have signed to not use armaments in outer space. In light of the U.S. debt crisis, and our treaty agreements, the U.S. needs to focus on reducing military expenses and improving inadequate cybersecurity forces, rather than forming a new Space Force.

A Defense Strategy for the 21st Century

America needs a defense strategy for the 21st Century that addresses what is needed to prevent our country and our democracy from failing. To defend our democracy, we need to avoid an economic crisis while simultaneously addressing our 23 crises, which will require reducing defense spending to a reasonable percent of our GDP. To reduce our defense costs, we need to return to having a DOD instead of a Department of Defense which is also taking a preemptive stance. This change is what got us into the mistaken and expensive Iraq war; preemptive wars are a mistake for any country.

We also need to stop supporting regime change efforts in other countries by supplying weapons and other military aid. Those foreign civil conflicts lead to violence and suffering, which cause migration and immigration crises. Furthermore, these U.S. efforts for regime change have resulted in creating more enemies than friends, as was the case with the regime change we supported in Iran in the 1970s, and more recently in Iraq. The best way to have other countries become democracies, and allies of America, is for us to be a role model of democracy, and provide a bit of help to them occasionally, to deal with their crises.

Cybersecurity is the key to the defense of America in the 21st Century. Given the current performance of the Department of Homeland Security (DHS), we need a change. Our cybersecurity responsibility should be moved to the DOD, because the U.S. is currently under constant successful cyber attacks from foreign nations, including Russia, China, and North Korea. Such a change would allow DHS to focus on improving their immigration processing capability, and the DOD to shift their enormous resources to address our cybersecurity crisis.

Defense Cost Crisis Follies
[(G) denotes government follies]

- Annual U.S. defense expenditures have consistently been highest in the world (G)

- Creation of a preemptive (offensive) military policy (G)

- Proposing the addition of a new military branch, the Space Force (G)

- Approval of a huge defense budget increase for 2019 and 2020 (G)

- Spending more than we can afford on military, while not adequately addressing our multiple unresolved domestic crises (G)

- Cutting the cybersecurity budget when that is our major security weakness (G)

- DHS not having cybersecurity as their top priority (G)

Possible Goals
Reduce our total defense expenditures as a percentage of GDP

Set a goal to reduce defense spending from 3.5% of GDP to 2.5%

Possible Results Measure
Defense budget as a percentage of GDP

Likely Root Causes
The Military Industrial Complex is always pushing for increased expenditures on conventional military arms

Politicians usually push for an even bigger defense budget than asked for by the Defense Department, in order to serve special interests in their home state

Political decisions to use our Department of Defense for offensive attacks on other countries

A civilian force that duplicates the U.S. officer force at U.S. bases

Lack of a long-term strategic plan to retain our financial strength in the world and address all our crises

Possible Improvements
(* Asterisk indicates no- or low-cost to the federal government)

*Eliminate the use of preemptive force by our DOD

*Eliminate all U.S. efforts at regime change in other countries

*Reduce the military budget

Improve our cyber defense capability

Develop a long-term strategic plan for retaining America's financial and defense leadership, while resolving the multiple U.S. crises

Crisis annual cost
Our $750 billion 2020 defense budget is one of the largest categories in our nation's budget. China, the country with the next largest defense budget, spends 2.1% of GDP while we are spending 3.5% of GDP on defense (Forbes 2015). If we spent 2.1% of our GDP, we could save $410 billion per year. This $410 billion per year is the cost of our defense crisis.

Federal budget cost reduction opportunities for 2024 budget
Given the need to eliminate our deficit spending, our defense budget needs to be reduced.

An increase in GDP growth of 2% per year, compounded, would provide 11% growth in 5 years. To reduce the Department of Defense costs to 2.5% of GDP in 2024, the budget for 2024 would be about $582 billion.

That is only a 5% reduction from the military budget that we had in the 2017 budget, but it would enable a $170 billion reduction in the 2024 budget from the 2019 budget.

<u>Potential House Caucus to implement House CAT Improvements</u>
No existing caucus identified.

Personal Story – Defense Costs Crisis

Like a lot of patriotic young men at the time, I volunteered to serve in the Army during the Vietnam War. I remember noticing that there were two offices for every senior officer position at the U.S. base where I was working. One office was for the military officer who was rotating between home and combat assignments, and the other office was for a civilian manager who did not serve in combat; two men shared one job. I thought at the time that this was an unnecessary duplication of effort and salaries.

Today, a significant part of defense costs is still being used to pay civilians for duplicate jobs, rather than paying our troops and supporting them after serving. Recognizing a 5% budget cut is needed from the 2017 to the 2024 defense budget, this is where that 5% budget cut should be focused – not on cuts to troop compensation or veterans' benefits.

When I arrived in Nha Trang, South Vietnam, in January 1968, as a junior officer, the secure officers' compound was reserved for senior officers; therefore, I was assigned to quarters in a small hotel down the street guarded by a 65-year-old South Vietnamese soldier. My initial assignment was as the night duty officer for the Strategic Communications Company, so I was alone in my hotel room asleep on the morning that two North Vietnamese companies attacked the senior officers' secure compound on the same street as my hotel. All those in the officers' compound were killed. Alone in my room, I was trapped while a counterattack fought the enemy that had taken the area as part of the Vietcong and North Vietnamese Army Tet Offensive (named after the Tet holiday, Vietnam's New Year). On their own initiative, Private Koenig, a draftee from New York who had worked on Wall Street, and a career sergeant from my communications company, drove through enemy-held area in an open jeep to rescue me. We raced back to the base under sniper fire, driving around dead bodies in the street. I wish that I had recommended these two for a medal for rescuing me; however, at the time it just seemed as if this was a normal part of daily life in a combat zone.

was a normal part of daily life in a combat zone.

The enemy's Tet Offensive attack on 100 cities, and our ensuing counterattacks, resulted in the largest battle of the war, in which we lost about 10,000 U.S. troops, almost 20% of all those U.S. killed in that 10-year war. It took several months before the U.S. won that extended battle; however, it caused us to lose the war. Just prior to the Tet offensive, General Westmoreland and President Johnson had announced that our country had won the war. When the Tet offensive followed that announcement, the country lost trust in our leaders and did not want any more deaths in this war being fought halfway around the world.

Johnson decided not to run for reelection in 1968; however, it took President Nixon five more years before we finally pulled out of Vietnam. Our country is slow to recognize, admit, and correct mistakes; this carries a high cost in both human lives and dollars. Historian Barbara Tuchman includes the slowness of the U.S. getting out of Vietnam, after it was obvious we should have, as one of the historic follies in her book, *The March of Folly.* I was lucky to have survived one of her historic follies.

Over the years since our war in Viet Nam, we have entered into other overseas wars and found that it is easy to get into a war, but difficult to end it. Often, we have found that the only way out is to abandon our allies on foreign soil, which has led to their slaughter without our troops there and a diminishment of our world reputation as a reliable ally. Hopefully, in the future America will resist jumping into wars, and better understand how difficult it is to get out of them, without abandoning our allies.

Summary – Security Crises

This chapter provided an overview of four Security Crises, with examples of how the Plan step of the PDCA cycle could be applied to address these four crises. The analysis of these four crises includes 23 decisions of folly that have contributed to the creation of these four security crises. A few of those follies include decisions to:

- Break nuclear arms treaties

- Spend funds dedicated to nuclear waste management on other things

- Continue to increase military spending on conventional weapons, and to continue spending more than twice the amount of the next largest country on military

- Increase harsh treatment of immigrants seeking asylum, instead of helping to address the causes of increased asylum seekers

- Not requiring businesses to use the existing E-Verify system to reduce the incentive for immigrants to come illegally to the U.S.

- Not addressing the root causes of the drug crisis, which is driving increases in drug smuggling

- Not making cybersecurity a top priority or establish measurable goals for improvement of this critically weak link in the U.S. security system

Chapter 12 –DEMOCRACY CRISES

This chapter covers three Democracy crises: Election Campaign, Government, and Political Party.

Our election campaign crisis has destroyed the "One person - One vote" principle on which our democracy is base. Today, money is determining the winners in our elections. These winners then make decisions of folly to favor those who financed their election. Those decisions benefit the greed of a few, over the well-being of many.

Our government crisis is the loss of hope in the future of American; a loss of hope in the American Dream. As the analyses were being done of our 23 crises, I began to recognize that our crises have many common root causes; these common root causes taken together have created a democracy crisis.

Our political party crisis is a result of the increased divide between our parties. As each move further to the left, or right, we find increased divisiveness. The increasing inability of the parties, both elected officials and citizens, to work together to address America's crises is itself a crisis. While the far right has become more anti-government and pro-special interest, the far left has begun proposing more free services for working people to compensate for the damage done by the special interests. Both of these extreme positions increase the severity of our crises.

Election Campaign Crisis

Definition
The results of the recent campaign funding law changes are dramatic: presidential campaign expenditures have increased from $1.4 billion in 2000 to $2.4 billion in 2016, which is a 71% increase (Open Secrets, n.d. [Money]). Fueling this increase are the huge sums of money given to candidates by special interests. Currently, money controls election outcomes so many political candidates find themselves in a catch-22 position: take the special interest money and get elected, or refuse the money and lose the election. If politicians take the special interest

money, they then feel obligated to repay these special interests. By making governance decisions that favor the special interests, they will continue to receive financial help in the next election. This quid pro quo is a major cause of too many decisions of folly (i.e., legal corruption); these decisions of folly are root causes of our U.S. crises.

America has always been proud of the principle "One person - One vote," which should result in a fair and representative government that is the cornerstone of democracy. The enormous amounts of special interest money now being spent on election campaigns, particularly at the federal level, have compromised that principle. Further eroding the "One person - One vote" principle is the process known as gerrymandering, in which district boundaries are redrawn to favor a particular political party. Since the party in power gets to redraw these boundaries, they can essentially pick the voters, instead of the voters picking the elected officials. In addition, we now have foreign interests hacking into our political party systems and election systems, using phony social media sites to influence our election outcomes.

Research Data

The Center for Responsive Politics is a non-profit, nonpartisan research group that tracks the effects of money and lobbying on elections and public policy. They offer a history of election law changes that have contributed to our election campaign crisis (Open Secrets, n.d. [2016]).

The Federal Election Campaign Act of 1974, following President Nixon's Watergate scandal, set contribution limits for all federal campaigns and established the Federal Election Commission (FEC) made up of six voting members to enforce election laws.

The 2010 Supreme Court "Citizens United" decision, in a close 5 to 4 vote, ruled that corporations are people, which lifted limits on corporate campaign expenditures. Corporations, which remain anonymous, can now spend unlimited amounts on messages, encouraging votes for or against specific candidates, as long as they do not coordinate directly with a candidate. This decision, reversing corporate donation restrictions that had stood for over a century, ushered in the era of the Super Political Action Committee (Super PAC); the court's decision eliminated transparency in election campaign expenditures.

The Presidential election expenditure table below shows how campaign funding has increased:

Table 26: Presidential Election Expenditures

Year	$ Billion Spent	Candidates
2000	1.4	Bush versus Gore
2004	1.9	Bush versus Kerry
2008	2.8	Obama versus McCain
2012	2.6	Obama versus Romney
2016	2.4	Trump versus H. Clinton

(Metrocosm 2016)

In addition to the above expenditures for 2016, both candidates received free media time; Trump received about $5 billion worth of free media time, while H. Clinton received about $3.2 billion (Confessore and Yourish 2016). Each television network, or radio station, could choose the candidate they wanted to support, which had a substantial impact on the election. Historically, news media were required to offer candidates equal time.

At the same time, Congressional election expenditures have increased by more than 300% from 1998 to 2018.

Table 27: Congressional Election Expenditures

Year	$ Billion Spent
1998	1.6
2002	2.1
2006	2.8
2010	3.4
2014	3.6
2018	5.7

(Open Secrets 2018)

For 2020 federal elections, individual donations directly to candidate campaigns cannot exceed $2,800 per candidate. These individual contribution limits are linked to inflation and increase each year.

On top of these donations, individuals can donate up to $5,000 to each regular PAC for it to represent their interests. Only individuals can donate to PACs, not corporations. PACs can then donate this PAC money, up to $5,000 per candidate, for each election.

The Supreme Court created Super PACs, which are different from PACs, allowing corporations to donate unlimited amounts in campaign election funds to push their special interests. Special interest Super PAC campaigns can launch negative attack campaigns on candidates who are supporting the common good over special interests. Super PAC attack ads can be run, and funded, by unidentified corporations.

In the 2016 election, 2,393 registered Super PACs spent $1.1 billion on election campaigns, but 94% of those Super PAC expenditures were made by only 3% of the Super PACs; that is, only 78 Super PACs were responsible for $997 million of the $1.1 billion total election expenditures. Two thirds of those 78 Super PACs are classified as conservative (Open Secrets, n.d. [2016]). This special interest money is controlling elections and leading to decisions of folly, which leads to our crises, which leads straight to a loss of hope in the American Dream.

This influx of massive amounts of money is crucial in determining election outcomes. From 2000 to 2018, Congressional candidates spending the most money won House races about 90% of the time, and Senate races about 80% of the time (FiveThirtyEight 2018). More campaign money wins most of the time, and politicians know that.

Since these Super PACs were created by a 2010 Supreme Court decision protecting free speech by unidentified corporations, it is important to understand that the Supreme Court can limit free speech when it violates the rights of others, *or violates a compelling government interest.* It seems clear now, in 2019, that the 2010 Supreme Court decision enabled unidentified special interest money to increase substantially in election campaigns, and that special interest money has resulted election outcomes that have led to many decisions of folly by those elected officials, which have contributed to our many growing crises.

The 105 government decisions of folly have created 23 U.S. crises, which are causing about $9.1 trillion per year in annual crises' costs and the loss of hope in the American Dream. The combination of these crises and this loss of hope results in a compelling government interest being violated as a result of the 2010 Supreme Court decision. The Supreme Court could reverse its 2010 decision, now that we know that decision has helped to cause *a violation of a compelling interest of the government*; a loss of hope in the American Dream.

Foreign Interference in Elections

America now has a new type of special interests involved in our elections: foreign countries, notably Russia, are influencing U.S. elections. When the Soviet Union collapsed, about 50% of the Soviet Union assets were legally stolen from the Russian government and Russian people by Russian oligarchs, members of a small group of business executives who run the country. These oligarchs accumulated much of their wealth when the Soviet Union assets were privatized. They were allowed to legally buy valuable assets, including oil fields, at about 10% of their fair market price. To protect their illicit assets, these oligarchs have invested in other countries, in case an honest Russian government should take control from President Putin and order the people's money be returned.

A good book to read to understand the Russian oligarchs' motivation is *Red Notice* by Bill Browder, which is about the creation of the Magnitsky Act passed by Congress in 2012 (Browder 2015). The Magnitsky Act, named for Browder's accountant who was killed in a Russian prison, allows the U.S. to freeze the ill-gotten Russian oligarch assets that are invested in the U.S. The Russian oligarchs, including Putin, would like to have the Magnitsky Act eliminated, in order to unfreeze billions of their illicit assets that were invested in the U.S.

Candidate Donald Trump encouraged Russian interference during the 2016 U.S. presidential election, which was much like accepting the gift of the Trojan horse. Historian Barbara Tuchman identifies the Trojan decision to accept the enemy gift as a path of folly that we should learn from. Donald Trump encouraging, and accepting, Russian help to win the 2016 election was a folly similar to the Trojan horse gift.

There are concerns about other such gifts that President Trump may have accepted in the past. He defaulted on six businesses in the past, during which time he did not pay workers on his projects or repay the banks that loaned him the money to pay his workers. However, he was always able to find a new bank to give him more loans for his next project. One such bank, Deutsche Bank, has given President Trump $2 billion in loans. Even after defaulting on a $45 million loan repayment to Deutsche Bank in 2008, he was able to receive another $300 million loan from them. In April 2019, Deutsche Bank was facing action by both U.S. and U.K. regulators over $20 billion to $80 billion in Russian money laundering. Deutsche Bank has been dubbed the Global Laundromat for Russian oligarchs with links to the Kremlin.

Gerrymandering

Gerrymandering is a practice intended to provide one political party a political advantage by manipulating voting district boundaries. The resulting district is known as a gerrymander, named after the first politician creating such a district that looked like a salamander on the map; his last name was Gerry. The system is rigged to facilitate this, since the political party in charge of each State Legislature gets to draw the boundaries of the districts in their states at redistricting time, which enables partisan district creation. Every ten years, the states get to redraw the congressional district lines based on population changes found in the census. The next census will occur in 2020. While the boundaries are intended to enable representative votes of the population, gerrymandering of boundaries enables a political advantage for one party. This is clearly another folly decision for selfish ambition. Unfortunately, pursuing decisions of folly for selfish ambition is now considered smart politics by many political party leaders.

After the last census in 2010, the Republicans had control of most of the state legislatures and used that power to their advantage in drawing legislative district boundaries (Chinni and Bronston 2018). In 2016, North Carolina and Pennsylvania were two of the most gerrymandered states. That year, North Carolina Democrats won 47% of the popular vote, but ended up with only 23% of the elected Congressional representatives. That same year, Pennsylvania Democrats won 48% of the popular vote but ended up with only 27% of the elected Congressional representatives.

Courts ruled the districts were gerrymandered and ordered a remedy, but no change was made in time for the 2018 Congressional election.

Illegal gerrymandering results in an unrepresentativegovernment. While most gerrymandering has been done by Republicans in the past decade, Democrats also have a history of gerrymandering.

Gerrymandering can also lead to single-party control of a number of districts, which results in an increased political divisiveness in Congress. Unfortunately, there is no political need to compromise on the part of the increasing number of House Representatives who, due to gerrymandering, have no competition from the other party in their district.

Seven states are so small, they have only one congressional district; therefore, they do not have to do a redistricting plan. Four states employ independent commissions, which do not employ politicians, to draw district maps. Two states appoint political commissions, which have only politicians on the redistricting commission. In the remaining 37 states, the state legislatures are primarily responsible for drawingcongressional district lines. To avoid continued political gerrymandering of districts, all U.S. states should change to an independent commission process, similar to the one used by the four states that have already done so (Ballotpedia, n.d.).

Electoral College

In spite of our favorite motto, "One person - One vote," our presidential election is not determined by the vote of the people. Instead, the constitution allocates each state a number of Electoral College electors; the number is equal to the total number of each state's representatives in the House and Senate. It is these electors who choose the president, not the vote of ordinary citizens. The Presidential candidate who gets the majority of electoral votes wins the U.S. Presidential election.

In general, the candidate who wins the popular vote in a state gets all the state's electors, although a handful of states use different rules. Each state decides how to allocate their electors in the presidential race. A problem with the system arises because each state gets two Senators, no matter how large or small the state; therefore, the Electoral College does not fairly represent the citizen population.

Our forefathers decided to have the President elected by state-elected politicians, rather than citizens, because they felt that there was inadequate national communication in 1787 to enable citizens to adequately determine the best national candidate.

Two of the past three U.S. Presidents, George W. Bush and Donald Trump, were elected by these state-appointed political representatives to the Electoral College, *not* by the majority of the citizens' vote. That 1787 national communications problem has been addressed over the past 240 years. It is time to let citizens, rather than politicians, decide our president. It is time to reclaim the "One person - One vote" principle that we claim our democracy is based on, and ensure that the election of the President of the U.S. is the candidate the majority of citizens have voted for.

Election rules enforcement

In addition to helping special interests have more control of our elections, Washington has also managed to strip the power of the Federal Election Commission (FEC). The FEC was to have been the six-member bipartisan enforcer of election campaign rules, but today it is not fully staffed and has a huge backlog of election complaints. The result is that the FEC now tends to perpetuate the system for special interests to support more decisions of folly. The FEC has become another part of the swamp in Washington today.

Campaign Time

One final problem with our election system today moves beyond campaign funding and explains, in part, why our campaign expenses have gotten so out of hand. We elect representatives for relatively short times, and competition is intense, so campaigning for reelection begins almost as soon as a person has been sworn in. Obviously, if a person has to campaign continuously, the campaign will require a huge war chest. Several other countries have tackled this problem.

A benchmark for campaigning, which the U.S. could use as a model, is the Corrupt and Illegal Practices Prevention Act passed by the United

Kingdom (UK) in 1883, limiting election campaign funding and campaign time.

This act focuses on limiting total election spending, rather than limiting election donations. For example, in the 2005 U.K. election, each political party was limited to expenditures equivalent to $42,000 for each candidate running for office. The maximum individual donation to a political party was limited to $280 per donor, regardless of where the donation came from: a citizen, a union, or a business. No foreigners are allowed to donate money or in-kind services.

U.K. candidate expenditures are also limited; in 2005, the limit was $10,000 for the entire election. These limits increase each year with the inflation rate. Paid TV advertisements are strictly forbidden; instead, all TV channels are required by law to give the main parties and their leaders carefully measured free time at peak viewing hours to state their cases.

Another best practice in the U.K. is their limit of the campaign period to about 6 weeks. For a substantial part of that time, Parliament closes to allow candidates to focus on election campaigns. By contrast, our U.S. Presidential election campaigns last 2 years, or more. Compared to the U.K., we are spending about 17 times as much time on elections and 28 times as much money on campaigns (MacLeod 1997).

Closer to home, other countries are also limiting the length of campaigns: Mexico limits their election campaigning to 5 months, while Canada limits election campaigning to 2½ months (Kurtzleben 2015).

These three countries could provide us with benchmarks for improving our election process. It's important to note when considering benchmarks from other countries, the goal is not to judge if the benchmark country is better than the U.S.; the goal is to identify the best results possible in a particular area, like campaign funding, and try to see if we can get better results by using best practices.

If other countries can have elections for 4% of our costs (adjusted for population), we should consider reducing our campaign time and funding. When our elected officials are busy raising campaign funds and campaigning, they are not doing the job they were elected (i.e., hired) to do for the people. In any other field, if a person hired to do a specific job spent their time using social media, traveling, and looking for another job, they would be fired. We seem to have accepted the fact that our elected representatives will spend a significant portion of their time raising campaign funds, traveling, and campaigning for their next job. This comment applies to both parties: our campaign election system needs to be fixed.

Our elected officials need less time spent on fund raising and campaigning, and more time on doing the job they've been elected to do: working on the people's business and working on reducing our 23 crises.

Finally, constant campaigning leads to infighting among candidates, which reduces their ability to work well with those same individuals, to do the work of the people. Attacking an individual publicly in the morning makes it impossible to work with them in the afternoon. More time campaigning is more time spent creating divisiveness.

Election Campaign Crisis Follies
[(G) denotes government follies]

- Allowing Super PACs unlimited funding to influence campaign outcomes (G)

- Encouraging, and accepting, foreign nations' interference in our elections (G)

- Continuing to rely on politicians (i.e., the Electoral College) to elect the President, instead of the vote of the citizens (G)

- Gerrymandering voting districts to benefit one political party (G)

- Spending too much time and money on divisive campaigning, and too little time working together on reducing our crises (G)

Possible Goals
Restore "One person - One vote" as the cornerstone of our democracy

Eliminate campaign funding by special interests

Reduce expenditures and time spent on election campaigns

Possible Results Measure
Campaign donation limit: reduce allowable campaign donations to a level that the average person can afford, such as $100 per candidate per election, so that "One person - One vote" has meaning again. (This $100 donation per candidate is comparable to the U.K. benchmark.)

Likely Root Causes
Political party gerrymandering of congressional districts

Business Super PAC money used in campaigns to run negative ads

Business lobbyists' influence through campaign donations

Foreign countries' influence on our elections through hacking and social media

Too much time spent by incumbents on election campaigns instead of governing

Possible Improvements
(* Asterisk indicates no- or low-cost to the federal government)

*Eliminate gerrymandering of house district boundaries by political parties; all states establish independent redistricting commissions

*Eliminate special interest PACs and Super PACs, thus reducing their influence on U.S. elections

*Eliminate negative attack ads

*Limit individual candidate campaign donations to $100 per individual and $100 per business, indexed to inflation

*Require income tax disclosure and all foreign relationship disclosures by all Presidential candidates, as a means to improve the vetting process and reduce foreign government influence in our elections

*Candidates for elections should not encourage or tolerate foreign interference in our elections and not encourage in-kind services, such as

hacking and false social media posts (e.g., Wikileaks release of private campaign emails stolen by Russians)
*Limit campaigning to 30 days prior to Election Day

*Establish a system based on the principle of "One person-One vote" for the U.S. President (e.g., replace the Electoral College with citizen votes).

Crisis annual cost
The annual cost of this crisis is the annual cost of all the other crises, which is about $9.1 trillion per year. However, we can't count each crisis cost twice. If we assume that just one more crisis is created each year by continuing with this Election Campaign crisis, then we can assume that will add a crisis cost of about $430 billion per year for each new crisis created.

Federal Budget cost reduction opportunities for 2024
Our election campaign crisis is a root cause of over a hundred follies, and the creation of all our U.S. crises. The federal government costs associated with just one additional crisis created by continuing on this path of folly could be estimated at about 25% of a single crisis cost, or an average of about $100 billion per year.

Potential House Caucus to implement House CAT Improvements
NO PAC Caucus: Chair Ro Khanna (D)

Voting Rights Caucus: Co-Chairs Marc Veasey (D), Bobby Scott (D), Terri Sewell (D)

Task Force on Election Security: Chair Bennie Thompson (D)

Government Crisis

<u>Definition</u>
Our government is facing a crisis: Americans have lost hope in the American Dream. The cumulative effect of our multiple crises is onerous and exhausting in our day-to-day lives, and our elected leaders lack goals and effective plans to address these crises.

<u>Research and Data</u>
The research and data on our Government Crisis are contained throughout this book, as well as in the surveys of citizens' frustration with Washington. When I started this book, I did not have a government crisis on my list of crises; however, after doing an analysis of our crises, I discovered:

- Our multiple crises are enormous and growing

- For each crisis, we average 5 follies, 4 of which are made by government

- The system in Washington has been fixed to facilitate more follies

- Simple no-cost and low-cost improvements to reduce our crises are not being implemented

- The national debt is twice the financially responsible level, with no plans to reduce it

- Washington has put special interests first and America's interests last

- We lack goals and plans to reduce our multiple and growing crises

The corrupt swamp in Washington, which has been created over the past 20 years, needs to be drained and cleansed. That will require reversing the 27 governance changes that created the swamp. Every day that goes by without establishing goals, creating a plan, and formulating actions to reduce our growing crises, allows our crises to become more disastrous, more overwhelming and harder to resolve. Given the magnitude of the problem facing us, there is a danger that our political parties could make the mistake of moving toward extremes of right-wing fascism or left-wing socialism. Adding fascism or socialism to our current crises would only further the decline of our democracy, and ultimately create chaos in the world.

We need to change the following behavior at the individual and government level:

- Empowering an autocratic leader

- Blaming racial and religious minorities for our problems

- Blaming other countries for our problems

- Blaming the free press by calling truthful reporting fake news

- Putting nationalism ahead of individual rights

- Withdrawing from world trade and treaty agreements

- Relying on military strength rather than negotiations

- Utilizing force with increasing brutality as our approach to problems

- Mocking and suppressing any opposition rather than having civil debate

- Referring to white nationalists or racists as 'good people'

The above behaviors are the behaviors of a fascist government, not a democratic one.

Handing control to an autocrat who will tell us who to blame for our problems has a certain appeal; it absolves us from the need to act to address the root causes of our crises. But act we must, to address the root causes of our democracy crisis, if we want our country to survive.

There are no goals or plans to address our crises, our irresponsible debt, or the increasing deficit. Our government has never been in such a dire situation. Our politicians are either unwilling to admit we have most of these crises, or they do not understand how to address them.

Government Crisis Follies
[(G) denotes government follies; (B) denotes business follies]

- Washington put special interests first and America second (G)

- Allowing 23 huge national crises to continue growing; crises that collectively have caused America to lose hope in the future and our American Dream (G)

- For each crisis, we average 5 follies, 4 of which are caused by government (G)

- Rigging the system in Washington to facilitate more follies (G)

- Simple no-cost and low-cost improvements to reduce our crises are not being implemented (G)

- Tolerating a lack of goals and plans to reduce our multiple and growing crises (G)

- Political divisiveness and leaders putting party before country have prevented the teamwork needed to make improvements (G)

- Denial of the existence of our Government Crisis and denial of several of the other huge crises we are facing (G)

- A complete lack of a responsible financial plan for the future (G)

- The national debt is about twice the financially responsible level with no plans to reduce it (G)

- A lack of agreed-to values for the common good in Washington leaders (G)

- Business focus on short-term stock prices and executives' annual compensation bonuses (B)

- Businesses engaged in risky speculation and debt increases (B)

Possible Goal
Restore hope in the future of America and the American Dream.

Possible Results Measure
An annual Pew Research Center survey of citizens on their view of the future of America and their confidence in our government leaders.

Possible Improvements
(* Asterisk indicates no- or low-cost to the federal government)

Improvements can be made by addressing the follies and root causes of this government crisis:

*Put citizens first and special interests a distant second

*Establish House Crisis Action Teams (House CATs) to use a quality approach to address each of our 23 huge and growing crises

*Reverse the follies that have caused the U.S. crises

*Reverse the system in Washington that has been rigged to facilitate more follies, changing it to facilitate decisions for America

*Implement simple no-cost and low-cost improvements to reduce our crises

*Establish goals and plans to reduce our multiple and growing crises

*Agree to work together with bipartisan teams, putting country before party, starting with House Crisis Action Teams (House CATs)

*Admit we have a government crisis, and recognize all the other crises we are facing

*Develop a financially responsible plan to reduce the national debt, which is about twice a responsible debt level

*Establish and deploy a set of values in government, this is needed to implement a quality approach

*Eliminate the business model that focuses on short-term stock prices and compensation of executives, based on annual stock price changes

*Reduce business speculation and debt

Government Crisis Costs
America is not assured of a better future just because we are America. Each generation has had to work hard to make the future of America better for the next generation. Unfortunately, in the last 20 years we have not worked to make the future better for future generations; instead, we have some who have worked to make special interests richer, and America poorer. That shows up in the following ways:

- The CEO-to-average worker pay ratio increasing from 50 to 1 to 361 to 1 (Worker's Fair Pay crisis in Chapter 9)

  - The U.S. annual budget with a 30% shortfall in revenues to pay for expenditures (National Debt crisis in Chapter 7)

  - The U.S. debt-to-GDP ratio now being almost twice the financially responsible level (National Debt crisis in Chapter 7)

  - U.S. trade deficit being the worst in the world (Trade Balance crisis in Chapter 7)

  - Insufficient action to stop mass shootings of our children in our schools (Gun Violence crisis in Chapter 9)

  - Insufficient action to limit opioid distribution, the primary cause of our opioid epidemic (Use of Drugs crisis in Chapter 9)

Our country cannot survive with this approach of putting special interests first and ordinary citizens a distant second. Unless we do something to address this crisis now, the next book on this subject may be by an historian such as Barbara Tuchman, to explain why all our follies have led to the failure and demise of America, a once bright and promising country. Unfortunately, power corrupts, and the power in Washington has been used to facilitate legal corruption.

Our problems are fixable; we citizens, and our leaders, must agree that we want to fix them, and then just do it.

Potential House Caucus to implement House CAT Improvements
No existing caucus identified.

Personal Story – Our Government Crisis

Americans have lost hope in the American Dream, of a better future for each generation of Americans, because of all the simultaneous crises we face.

Like many other people, I have children, grandchildren, and now my first great-grandchild. Their future is being compromised, because we have let this government crisis happen, and we have done nothing to address it. My generation has not taken the steps necessary to protect and improve our government; instead, we have chosen to allow special interests to be served, instead of America's interests. The result is the loss of hope in the American Dream for the current generation, and for America's future generations.

When my generation was young, it was easy to see the American Dream and believe it was achievable. For example, I earned a relatively low-cost co-op college education for my BS degree, and graduated debt free.

I had a 33-year career with AT&T, who paid for my Master's degree, which I earned by taking evening courses after work. AT&T provided matching contributions to my retirement savings plan for many years, and provided me with a pension that is paying approximately half what my salary was at retirement. AT&T consistently provided the employer match for my Social Security payroll taxes over the course of my career. I have had a lot of help in achieving my American Dream.

Today in retirement, I receive full Social Security payments, my pension, and monthly withdrawals from my IRA savings plan. Combined, these enable me to have a good retirement life, with a bit left over to help fund college costs for my grandchildren. I also have the Medicare Program, a health care supplemental insurance, Dental Insurance, and a Long-Term Care insurance plan to keep my health care costs in check.

My children's situations are different: they do not expect our

Political Party Crisis

Definition

Our political parties have become so divided, they cannot work together to solve our crises. They are also responsible for the follies that serve special interests, and have contributed to the creation, and fueling the growth, of our crises. They have put party before country, contributing to the loss of hope for the future of America.

Research and data

George Washington warned the country about the danger of political parties in his farewell address to the country: "However [political parties] may now and then answer popular ends, they are likely in the course of time and things, to become potent engines, by which cunning, ambitious, and unprincipled men will be enabled to subvert the power of the people and to usurp for themselves the reins of government, destroying afterwards the very engines which have lifted them to unjust dominion" (Mount Vernon, n.d.).

The research and data for the political party crisis unfortunately confirm the prediction of George Washington. Most people probably feel like yelling, "Lock 'em up!" when they read about the people who have intentionally implemented 105 government decisions of folly that have contributed to the creation of our 23 crises. However, we can't lock them up, because they have been clever and cunning enough to make all these follies legal. They have fixed Washington to support legal corruption. If we can't lock them up, we should at least be able to vote them out. However, to vote them out, we need to know who created these follies, and which political parties they represent. Appendix A includes a list of the 23 crises with the 105 government follies that created them. Each reader can review this appendix to make an assessment of which political party was primarily responsible for the majority of these follies. These follies are helping special interests instead of the common good.

Types of Follies Repeated Throughout Multiple Crises:
[(G) denotes government follies]

- Denying crises (e.g., climate change and the national debt) (G)

- Dedicating tax revenues collected for a specific purpose, and then using them for other purposes (e.g., nuclear waste storage and retirement safety-net funds) (G)

- Using common environmental resources by and for the benefit of a few (e.g., oceans, land, fresh water, air) (G)

- Continuing government support of a few large businesses (e.g., coal, oil, Big Pharma, Wall Street) rather than the common good (G)

- Focusing on reacting to disasters rather than setting goals to avoid repeat occurrence of them (e.g., hurricanes, forest fires, mass murders) (G)

- Focusing on short-term rather than long-term planning (e.g., 22 government shutdowns due to annual budget process problems, no 5-year plan to meet recognized financial responsibility criteria) (G)

- Focusing on more funding for the same old approaches to a problem, instead of learning from benchmarks and best practices used throughout the world in order to be more effective and efficient (G)

- Focusing on a going-it-alone approach, rather than partnering with other countries on world crises (e.g., breaking climate control and nuclear weapons control treaties) (G)

- Focusing on reacting to problems, rather than preventing them by using a quality (critical thinking) approach (e.g., continued use of stories and anecdotes to react to daily problems, instead of using research and trends to understand root causes of crises, and prevent recurrence of problems) (G)

- Focusing on one crisis at a time, rather than trying to understand the interrelatedness of all U.S. crises (e.g., high debt costs caused by overspending on defense and health care, increasing disasters caused by climate warming) (G)

- Accepting the belief that we can't *afford* to solve a crisis, rather than understanding that solving crises can often be done at no cost or low cost; and solving these crises will save money to help balance the budget (e.g., 74% of the improvement recommendations in Chapters 7 through 12 are no-cost or low-cost to the U.S. government) (G)

- Continuing to try to manage broken processes, instead of fixing the process (e.g., the same budget process has been used for over 20 years, and it has resulted in 22 government shutdowns) (G)

Repeated follies that support special interests over the common good are created as a result of applying broad predetermined political party solutions, rather than determining the root causes of our crises and the appropriate solutions to eliminate the root causes of each individual crisis.

Today unfortunately, political parties have put political party before country, and their divisiveness is preventing the cooperation needed to work as a team to address our crises. Without common agreed-to goals for the good of the country, the political parties cannot work together.

The following table provides examples of how broad political party policies can conflict with the appropriate solutions needed to address the root causes of our crises:

Table 28:
Party Political Policies   versus   Solutions to Root Causes of Crises

Party Political Policies	Solutions to Root Causes of Crises
Believing government is bad and business is good	Responsible management of both government and business
Supporting special interests	Supporting America's interests
Promoting widespread deregulation	Implementing regulations where appropriate to prevent repeated crises
Promoting broad tax cuts	Implementing taxes as needed to balance the budget, fund infrastructure, etc.
Promoting military force and negative sanctions	Using State Department negotiations, positive economic incentives, and when needed, a hand-up for struggling countries
Adopting anti-immigration policies	Implementing immigration reform
Promoting a go-it-alone against the world approach	Developing treaties with allies and working with the U.N.

Each political party has its own priorities. For example, a Republican National Committee Trump Agenda Survey, in June, 2019, listed these:

- Build a border wall
- Fully enforce immigration laws
- Cut job-killing regulations to keep the economy growing
- Make the Republican-passed tax cuts permanent
- Confirm more federal judges who pledge to follow the original Constitution

- Encourage domestic exploration and production of domestic energy sources
- Renegotiate trade deals
- Continue to reequip and rebuild our military
- Stand up for veterans' benefits
- Develop a plan to rebuild infrastructure
- Fix our broken health care system

Of this list of 11 priority improvements, only two or three address reducing one of the 23 U.S. crises in this book.

The 2016 Democratic Party Platform Priorities included the following (Democrats 2016):

- Raise incomes and restore economic security for the middle class
- Create good paying jobs
- Fight for economic fairness and against inequality
- Bring Americans together and remove barriers to opportunities
- Protect voting rights, fix our campaign finance system, and restore our democracy
- Combat climate change, build a clean energy economy, and secure environmental justice
- Provide quality and affordable education
- Ensure the health and safety of all Americans
- Principled leadership
- Support our troops and keep faith with our veterans
- Confront global threats
- Protect our values
- Be a leader in the world

The Democratic Party political platform list of priorities aligns more closely with the list of 23 crises that we need to reduce.

While it is unreasonable to expect the two parties to agree on a common political party platform, they can, and must, recognize our common crises and work together to reduce both our crises and the follies that created them.

Both parties also need to put their political party wish lists on the back burner, in order to work together to reduce the crises that we face. If we want to survive as a country, they must also work together to unfix Washington to prevent the continued creation and fueling of more crises by more follies.

To reduce our crises and follies, both parties need to agree to use a common quality approach on *how* we will address each crisis: identify the root causes, develop the most efficient and effective plans, and approve low-cost and no-cost improvements as soon as possible.

In order to get political party leaders to come together to address our crises, we as voters need to vote for candidates who are willing to work together on reducing the crises affecting America, as well as unfixing our Washington governance system. We need candidates from both parties who are willing to use a factual analysis of root causes, together in a bipartisan way, to address our crises and to develop and approve solutions. We also need both political parties to realize that as a result of the follies they have supported, or allowed to happen, our democracy is now on thin ice. It is time to put our country first, our political parties second, and special interests third. If we want to reduce the divisiveness, we need to vote for candidates who are willing to work together to reduce our U.S. crises.

Political Party Crisis Follies
[(G) denotes government follies; (C) denotes citizen follies]

- Following broad, predetermined political policies on every crisis, rather than analyzing root causes and identifying the most efficient and effective solutions (G)

- Prioritizing political parties and party priorities, rather than addressing our country's crises (G)

- Protracted length of election campaigns (G)

- Using social media for personal insults and lies (G)

- Being unwilling to work together on a common list of crises, to develop and use the same facts in order to identify the root causes (G)

- Voting for candidates who will not work in a bipartisan way to address our crises (C)

- Putting special interests ahead of the country's interest and the common good (G)

Possible Goal
Political parties agree to work together to solve our crises, eliminate our follies, and unfix the corrupt system in Washington that facilitates follies.

Possible Results Measures
Establishment of bipartisan House Crisis Action Teams (House CATs) to address each of our crises. The appropriate House Caucus could be the team that establishes the House CATs, to develop the solutions to our crises and to lead the implementation of those solutions.
An annual House State of the Union Report on the status of our crises.

Possible Improvements
(* Asterisk indicates no- or low-cost to the federal government)

*Citizens vote for candidates who will work on bipartisan solutions to our crises

*Establish bipartisan House CATs by appropriate House Caucuses

*Elimination of past follies
*Put country interests before special interests

*Put country before political party

*Unfixing the Washington governance system that favors special interests over American interests by facilitating follies

Crisis Cost

The political parties own a significant responsibility for the $9 trillion per year in our annual U.S. Gross Crisis Cost (GCC).

Potential House Caucus to implement House CAT Improvements

Honor and Civility Caucus: Co-Chairs Mike Johnson (R), Charlie Crist (D)
Civility Caucus: Co-Chairs Emanuel Cleaver (D), Kevin Yoder (R)
Civility and Respect Caucus: Co-Chairs Steve Stivers (R), Joyce Beatty (D)

Personal Story – Political Party Crisis

We have had great leaders, from both parties, who should be role models for today's elected officials. Teddy Roosevelt, a Republican, fought special interests and established the National Park System to protect unique areas of our country. About 50 years later, my personal hero, John F. Kennedy, a Democrat, appealed to us all by saying: "Ask not what your country can do for you, ask what you can do for your country." Both of these leaders had volunteered to serve in their country's military in wartime, risking their lives for America. Their military service in combat gave them a good understanding of the military troops they were commanding, and the consequences of military conflict when they became Commander in Chief. Both of these leaders put their country before their political party; they should still serve as role models for leaders of both political parties.

On May 27, 2019, I participated with my Vietnam Veterans' group, Vietnam Veterans of America Chapter 1088, in the color guard at our Fernandina Beach Memorial Day ceremony on Amelia Island in Florida. I remembered, as I do every year, the U.S. service members in Nha Trang, Vietnam, who lost their lives in a compound down the street from me when we were hit with the surprise Tet Offensive attack in January 1968. I also remembered that in a combat area, we had no partisan divisiveness, because we had a common goal: to serve our country. If we truly want to honor those who lost their lives in service of our country, we need to agree on establishing common goals to serve our country, and pull together as a team to get it done.

Many have lost their lives for our country and our democracy. This ultimate sacrifice should not be squandered on millionaires trying to become billionaires, and special interests pursuing greed.

Summary of Our Democracy Crises

Our Democracy Crises included three crises: Election Campaign, Government, and Political Party.

Our Election Campaign Crisis has destroyed the "One person - One vote" principle on which our democracy is based. We need major reform of our election campaign process to eliminate the causes of corruption in our election process. Our Election Campaign Crisis is a critical one to address, since it is a cause of many other crises.

Our Government Crisis is the result of Washington putting special interests first, and America's interests a distant second. Washington has enriched special interests, and in doing so, has made the rest of America a lot poorer. The follies and causes of this crisis have been identified; now we have to reverse the decisions of folly and eliminate the root causes. The only thing standing in the way of doing that is citizens and elected leaders deciding to do it.

Loyalty to political party has unfortunately become more important than loyalty to the country; elected officials are voting with their party instead of with their constituents, or their conscience. Political parties are controlling our elected officials' votes to serve the political parties' interests, not the interests of the country. A common focus to eliminate our U.S. crises is needed as a way to come together, reduce divisiveness, and restore hope in the future of America.

SUMMARY of – A PATH OF REASON FOR AMERICA

The governance process in Washington has been changed to facilitate follies that help special interests instead of the common good. More than a hundred government follies have created and fueled multiple national crises. The collective burden of these crises has caused Americans to lose hope in the future of America. The annual cost of these crises, the Gross Crisis Cost (GCC), is more than $9 trillion each year. Washington lacks the goals and plans needed to reduce our growing crises. Instead, our politicians continue to change the Washington governance processes that facilitate more follies to help special interests, not the common good.

Americans have voted for change of *individuals* in Washington, but those elected have not made the changes needed to unfix Washington; they have done nothing to reduce the decisions of folly that help special interests. Instead, Washington persists in making things worse for the American people; the swamp is not draining – it is growing.

Washington governance process changes have "fixed," or rigged, Washington to fill the swamp in order to facilitate decisions of folly to serve special interests. The current administration is still fixing Washington to produce more follies to fill the swamp. Those governance process changes must be reduced, or eliminated, to drain the swamp; the swamp is a product of decisions of folly, these follies are producing and fueling our crises, and the crises are producing millions of personal disasters daily.

A Path of Reason for America proposes a solution:

- Reverse the past decisions of folly (105 government follies) that have been made to serve special interests instead of the common good.

- Drain the Washington swamp that is producing the follies that fuel our crises, by reversing the 27 process changes that have been made to "fix" Washington in order to serve special interests instead of the common good.

- Eliminate our national crises (23 and additional ones to be identified) by using a quality approach to set goals, develop plans, and implement values to support decisions for the common good.

- Form House Crisis Action Teams (House CATs) and use the quality approach described in this book to continuously reduce all our U.S. crises; House CATS will provide annual improvement reports on progress.

- Reduce the enormous cumulative cost of all our crises, the Gross Crisis Cost, and begin to restore our country to its former place of prominence in the world.

- Reduce federal government costs slowly until we reach a responsible debt-to-GDP ratio of 60% or less.

- Restore our democracy to serve the common good it was intended to serve, rather than special interests.

- Through all of the above, restore trust in government (Washington, D.C.) and hope in the American Dream.

- Use *A Path of Reason for America* as a GPS for restoring our Democracy and hope in the American Dream.

The first half of this book explains the quality approach and what is required to use it in government. The second half of the book provides examples of how this quality approach could be used to reduce 23 national crises, including proposals for 128 no-cost or low-cost improvements.

Most of these no-cost or low-cost improvements to reduce our crises do, however, have some cost for one or more special interest groups. Unfortunately, Washington has been putting special interests first, which is why these no-cost and low-cost improvements have not been implemented. The fact that Washington is taking care of special interests, instead of America's interests, is our Democracy Crisis.

President Trump was elected to make a change; however, in spite of what he promised, and what he continues to say, our crises have actually become worse. He promised to drain the swamp in Washington, but the current administration has continued to make changes in the Washington governance process that help to fill the swamp, not drain it.

The parents and grandparents of my generation did what they needed to do to make America strong for us. It is now our turn to do the same: make America strong for the next generation.

President John F. Kennedy popularized the words, possibly spoken first by 18th century statesman Edmund Burke: "The only thing necessary for the triumph of evil is for good men to do nothing." It is time for good men and women to do something; drain the swamp by changing our "fixed" government process to eliminate follies, crises, and the loss of hope in the American Dream.

In the 1960s, our President challenged the country to land a man on the moon, and we did it! The next President who takes office in January 2021 should challenge the country to return hope in the American Dream before the end of the decade.

When we work together, great things can happen. Having to figure out how to get to the moon in the 1960s was quite a challenge, since the technology to do so did not yet exist; but we faced the challenge, invented the technology, and put a man on the moon. Today, the solutions to our crises already exist; we just need to implement them. To do that, we must agree, as a country, that the common good is more important than special interests.

Attachment A is a one-page proposal for Washington Improvements that need to occur in the first 100 days of the President who takes office in January 2021.

Attachment B is a two-page proposal for Crisis Improvements that need to be implemented within the second 100 days.

Attachment C is a 10-page list of the Government Follies that need to be reversed within the third 100 days.

However, we should not look to government to fix all aspects of our American crises. Each citizen has a role to play, including:

- Living a healthy lifestyle that incorporates proper nutrition and exercise

- Obtaining the education necessary to support a satisfactory quality of life

- Including adequate savings as part of individual personal budgets

- For those with families, provide the values and financial support children need

- Volunteering to help in the community, utilizing personal skills to follow individual passions

- Voting in elections for candidates who are committed to follow a path of reason for America

Appendix A – First 100 Days – Of President elected in Nov. 2020

Jan. 20, 2021 – April 30, 2021: Washington Improvements Now (WIN):

1. Ask government leaders to read *A Path of Reason for America,* and develop a one page plan for what they can, and will, do to help America get back on a path of reason.

2. Ask large businesses to develop goals and a one page plan to improve the U.S. trade balance, reskill workers for technology shifts, and reduce the CEO-to-average worker pay ratio, along with support needed from the government.

3. Ask all citizens to develop their own one page plan to achieve a healthy weight, reskill to deal with career technology changes, and create a financial plan that includes saving for investments.

4. Develop a one page plan for draining the Swamp in Washington, by eliminating the 27 process changes that co-opted our democracy to facilitate follies that serve special interests. This plan should include assigning responsibility for eliminating each of the 27 Swamp processes by a specified date.

5. Establish 23 House Crisis Action Teams (CATs) in the House of Representatives to lead the development and management of the improvements required to eliminate the 23 national crises covered in this book.

6. Suspend all House of Representatives caucuses that are focused on helping special interests until the 23 national crises are eliminated and trust in government is restored.

7. Establish and deploy a one page list of values that all government employees, including leaders, are expected to live by. Those

values should include being truthful, and to put the common good ahead of special interests. Violation of values should be justification for dismissal.

8. Establish a plan for an annual House State of the Crises report to the nation. Schedule a report for the second Wednesday of every January, beginning in 2022 for the year 2021. (A state of the Nation Crises Report for 2019 is provided in Chapter 2 -Crises.)

Appendix B – Second 100 Days –of President elected in Nov. 2020

May 1, 2021 – August 8, 2021: National Crises Improvements:

These key improvements are to be recommended by House CATS, and approved by the appropriate sponsoring organizations, in the second 100 days of the President taking office on January 20, 2021:

Financial Crises: (Chapter 7)
1. Approve a long-term financial plan to achieve a balanced budget and a debt-to-GDP ratio of 60% or less. (e.g., the 2 + 2 Budget Plan)
2. Approve adequate regulations to ensure we do not repeat the 2008 economic crisis that caused the 2008 Great Recession.
3. Approve a gas tax increase to fund the infrastructure maintenance backlog.
4. Stop the trade tariff war.

Worker Crises: (Chapter 8)
1. Approve a plan to support and encourage worker reskilling training.
2. Approve a plan to improve the minimum wage and have it increase with inflation.
3. Approve support funding for programs that help students minimize their college loan debt.
4. Approve support funding for programs that teach critical thinking skills in our schools, along with personal health, career, and financial planning.

Health Care Crises: (Chapter 9)
1. Stop allowing prescription of addictive opioids to patients who have never been given them.

2. Approve a plan with the food industry to reduce carcinogens and sugar in our foods.
3. Stop sales of assault weapons and high-capacity magazines to civilians, and implement universal background checks for all gun sales.
4. Allow Medicare and Medicaid to let international suppliers compete for prescription drug sales, to obtain market-based pricing.

Environment Crises: (Chapter 10)
1. Develop a plan to fund the cleanup of superfund sites that pollute our land, and eliminate sewage overflow systems that pollute our waterways.
2. Reestablish the Clean Air and Clean Water regulations that were eliminated by the current administration.
3. Eliminate the current administration's plan to cut our ocean Marine Protected Areas in half.
4. Rejoin the international treaty on reducing climate change; restore the regulations to reduce carbon emissions that have been cut by the current administration.
5. Restore the EPA goals and plans that were eliminated by the current administration.

Security Crises: (Chapter 11)
1. Reestablish U.S. membership in Nuclear International Treaties that the current administration has withdrawn from.
2. Establish goals, plans, and funding to reduce cybersecurity intrusions.
3. Require all businesses to use E-Verify to ensure that their employees are not illegal immigrants.
4. Eliminate the reduction in annual legal immigrants imposed by the current administration and reduce the processing time from years to days.
5. Develop a plan to improve our defense while reducing defense costs.

Democracy Crises: (Chapter 12)
1. Eliminate gerrymandering by establishing independent redistricting commissions
2. Eliminate Super PACs

3. Dramatically reduce allowed campaign funding and time.
4. Secure both political parties' agreement to work together to establish goals and plans to reduce our 23 national crises.
5. Secure both political parties' agreement to suspend efforts aimed at helping special interests until we eliminate our national crises and restore trust in government.
6. Secure agreement from all elected officials and candidates for office to agree to avoid personal attacks and focus on resolving our crises.

Appendix C – Third 100 Days of President elected Nov. 2020

Aug. 9, 2021 – Nov. 16, 2021: Government Folly Reversals:

The following is the list of 105 government follies that have helped to create and fuel our 23 national crises. By the end of the 1st year of the President taking office in January 2021, we should have a plan to reverse the follies that can be reversed, and develop a schedule for doing that. I have added an asterisk (*) to those follies that I believe can be reversed, and there are only 8 of these 105 follies that I believe cannot be reversed. Therefore, our government should develop a plan and a schedule to reverse the other 97 follies. This should also be the responsibility of the leadership of the Washington Improvement Now (WIN) team that develops the plan to remove the 27 processes that created the Swamp in Washington.

It may help you decide how to vote in future elections if you have an idea of which political party was primarily responsible for each of these 105 government follies. To do your own assessment of political party responsibility for these follies, note R if Republicans are responsible, D if Democrats are responsible, and R & D if both are responsible; then tally your results in the table appearing at the end of this list.

[R = Republican, D = Democrat, R & D = both parties responsible]

National Debt Crisis Follies
1. *Continuing to increase our budget, deficit, and debt without regard to the burden being placed on future generations

2. *Living without a long-term financial plan to: reduce the annual budget, reduce the deficit, reduce the national debt, get to a balanced budget, and get to a financially responsible debt-to-GDP ratio

3. *Borrowing $1 trillion per year, while having a debt-to-GDP ratio over 100%

4. *Continuing to accept significant waste in government

5. *Taking $4.8 trillion in funds from Social Security and government employee retirement funds, without a plan to repay those funds

6. *Treating all government trust funds as a piggy bank to borrow from, instead of using normal trust fund management to save and invest the funds

7. Cutting the 2018 corporate tax rate, without making cost reductions to offset the revenue loss

8. Increasing the expense budget in 2019, without the revenue to support the expense increase

9. *Supporting short-term profits for businesses, without regard to the much larger cost to all

Wall Street and Corporate Debt Crisis Follies

10. *Allowing financial institutions to speculate without adequate capital reserves

11. *Allowing banks to pay the credit-rating agencies that rate their bond offerings, resulting in misleading credit ratings from those agencies

12. *Allowing companies insuring Wall Street speculation risks to have rates and assets inadequate to cover losses

13. *Supporting bank speculation (i.e., gambling) with the government's and citizens' money

14. *Allowing business loans without adequate loan standards

15. *Providing very-low interest loans to banks, which then use the money for high-risk speculation, to get much higher returns, while having the government bail-out their losses

16. Deregulating banks in 1999 to allow the unregulated sale of derivatives

17. *Pushing for deregulation of banks again in 2018_

Trade Balance Crisis Follies

18. *Increasing our trade deficits over many years, which was supported by government, business, and the Cato Institute

19. *Breaking trade agreements with other countries

20. *Starting a trade tariff war_

Infrastructure Maintenance Crisis Follies

21. *Inadequately maintaining infrastructure throughout America and at every level of government

22. *Insufficient gas taxes collected to pay for the cost of maintaining our road and bridge infrastructure

23. *Choosing to promote private transportation (cars) over public transportation, which benefits the gas and oil industry as well as the wealthy, and hurts those in need of public transportation, as well as damaging the environment

Worker Skills Crisis Follies

24. *Lack of plans to reskill displaced workers in an era of high technology shifts

25. *Lack of plans to bring new technology jobs (e.g., solar power) to areas where older technology jobs are decreasing

26. *Fighting against technological shifts instead of preparing workers for them

27. *False promises to bring back old, outdated technologies (e.g., coal)

Worker's Fair Pay Crisis Follies

28. *Failure on the part of both business and government to address the problem of an inadequate living wage, and the pay gap which will affect the next generations, thus putting an unaffordable burden on government to support the working poor

College Education Debt Crisis Follies

29. *Not providing more vocational technical training and lower public college tuition rates to meet the technology shift skill requirements

Social Media Crisis Follies

30. *Not teaching critical thinking skills in our schools

31. *Not using critical thinking skills in our government_

Use of Drugs Crisis Follies

32. *The initial false business filing by Purdue Pharma for OxyContin was approved by the Food and Drug Administration (FDA)

Diabetes Crisis Follies

33. *Insufficient education, and facilities, for our youth to enable them to develop a healthy body and avoid becoming overweight

34. *Insufficient facilities in many communities for walking, running, and bicycle paths that can be used instead of driving for short trips

Cancer Rate Crisis Follies

35. *Carcinogens that cause cancer continue to be put in our food

36. *Carcinogens that cause cancer continue to be released into our environment

Gun Violence Crisis Follies

37. *Not looking at best practices of other countries and implementing them

38. *Weak U.S. gun laws

39. *Military assault weapons available for civilians' use

40. *Background check loopholes let criminals and mentally ill individuals buy guns

41. *No penalty for allowing known mentally ill people access to assault weapons

42. *Perpetrating the myth that more guns lead to less gun violence

Health Care Costs Crisis Follies

43. *A government approach that treats reactive medical care and drugs as the solution to health problems, rather than supporting healthy living

44. *Ignoring benchmarks and best practices from other countries

45. *Spending Medicare trust funds on other things, instead of investing them

46. *Government support of pharmaceutical companies, rather than patients

Land, Air, and Fresh Water Crisis Follies

47. *Lack of a sustainable plan for our natural resources

48. *Treating the cost for polluting and overusing the environment as zero, thus rewarding those who pollute and overuse environmental resources

49. *Lack of testing new chemicals before release for potential harm to people and the environment

50. *Authorizing pollution of the environment

51. *Authorizing overuse of our natural resources, which is not sustainable

52. *Deregulation that increases pollution of the environment

53. *Not adequately funding plans to enforce the Clean Water Act and the Clean Air Act

Oceans Crisis Follies

54. *Treating our oceans as an unlimited resource

55. *Lack of a sustainable plan for our oceans

56. *Allowing our oceans to be used as a dumping ground for sewage, toxic plant waste, agriculture runoff, and plastics

57. *Allowing our oceans to be overfished

58. *Allowing our oceans to be drilled for fossil fuels, causing great risk to valuable coastal tourism, local residents, and natural resources including marine mammals

59. *Allowing harmful noise pollution in our oceans from seismic testing for fossil fuels, and military sonic testing

60. *Proposals to cut the U.S. Marine Protected Areas (MPAs) by half

Climate Change Crisis Follies

61. *Claiming climate warming is a falsehood; denying that it is not causing more frequent and stronger hurricanes, tornadoes, and more frequent forest fires

62. *Withdrawing from global climate treaties and refusing to help address this crisis

63. *Relaxing previously agreed-to carbon reduction agreements and plans

Nuclear Arms and Waste Crisis Follies

64. *Not getting all countries to sign the nuclear treaty agreement creates a fear of nuclear weapons' attack from enemies, and thus encourages escalation of weapons' stockpiles

65. *The five authorized nuclear weapons countries still have 22,000 warheads in their combined nuclear weapons war chest, and have shown a reluctance to continue with the agreed-to disarmament plan

66. *The U.S. continues to increase the amount of hazardous nuclear waste that must be contained and stored as carefully as possible for thousands of years, or longer

67. The $40 billion collected from private nuclear power companies for safe storage of nuclear waste was spent on other things

68. Instead of supporting the U.N.'s right to perform nuclear verification in Iraq, the U.S. pushed for and led a preemptive (offensive) war on Iraq

69. *Instead of supporting the Iran nuclear disarmament treaty, the U.S. withdrew from this international treaty that included inspections for verification

Cybersecurity Crisis Follies

70. *U.S. cybersecurity goals lack quantifiable measures and objectives that can be used to determine annual progress and assessment of the adequacy of U.S. cybersecurity improvement plans

71. *The U.S. continues to allow the dark web to sell cyber tools for criminal activities

72. *The Russian intrusion into the U.S. 2016 election campaign still continues two years later, and is not mentioned in the Department of Homeland Security (DHS) Cybersecurity Strategy

73. *The U.S. is cutting a small cybersecurity budget, while increasing defense spending, even though cybersecurity is our greatest security weakness

Border Security Crisis Follies

74. The current opioid crisis began with the FDA approval of oxycodone based on false information; this led ultimately to an increased demand for illegal drugs in the U.S.

75. *Lack of a comprehensive border security plan to include requiring E-Verify technology, adequate Ports of Entry security, and improvements in legal immigrant processing cycle time

76. *Penalizing government workers who are helping to secure America, by causing multiple government shutdowns and the concomitant delay of pay, as a means of blackmailing Congress into funding more money for a huge border wall

Defense Costs Crisis Follies

77. Annual defense expenditures have consistently been significantly higher than any other country in the world

78. *Spending more than we can afford on military, while not funding our multiple unresolved domestic crises

79. *A preemptive (offensive) military policy

80. *Proposing the addition of a new military branch, the Space Force

81. Approval of a significant Defense budget increase for 2019 and 2020

82. *Cutting the cybersecurity budget when that is our major security weakness

83. *DHS, the agency responsible for cybersecurity, does not have cybersecurity as their top priority

Election Campaign Crisis Follies

84. *Allowing Super PACs unlimited funding to influence campaign outcomes

85. *Gerrymandering voting districts to benefit a political party

86. *Spending too much time and money on divisive campaigning, and too little time working together on reducing our crises

87. *Continuing to rely on politicians (i.e., the Electoral College) to elect the president, instead of relying on the vote of the people

88. *Encouraging foreign countries to interfere in our elections

Government Crisis Follies

89. *Allowing the existence of 23 huge and growing crises that collectively have caused America to lose hope in the future, resulting in the loss of the American Dream

90. *Tolerating a lack of goals and plans to reduce our multiple and growing crises

91. *Accepting political divisiveness and leaders who are putting party before country, thus preventing the teamwork needed to make improvements

92. *A complete lack of a responsible financial plan for the future of the country

93. *Continuing to accept a national debt that is double the financially responsible level, with no plans to reduce it

94. *Denying the existence of our Government Crisis and several of the other huge crises we are facing

95. *4 of 5 follies per crisis being made by the government

96. *Rigging the system in Washington to facilitate more follies

97. *Refusing to implement simple no-cost and low-cost improvements to reduce our crises

98. *Washington has special interests first and America a distant second

99. *A lack of values shared by Washington leaders, the values that are necessary to serve the common good

Political Party Crises Follies

100. *Using broad political policies on every crisis, rather than analyzing root causes and identifying the most efficient and effective solutions

101. *Putting political party before country

102. *Protracted length of election campaigning

103. *Being unwilling to work together to develop and use the same facts on our crises, in order to identify the root causes

104. *Continuous personal insults broadcast on social media

105. *Putting special interests before country

Worksheet to Tally Primary Responsibility for

Government Follies:

Republican		Democrat		Both R & D		Other		Total	
#	%	#	%	#	%	#	%	#	%
								105	100%

Swamp – Follies - Crises

We need to eliminate our swamp, in order to eliminate our follies, in order to eliminate our crises, in order to eliminate our repeated disasters.

To Eliminate our Swamp

Both parties have allowed the 27 process changes in Washington to be implemented that have created the Swamp which facilitated the 105 government follies; the swamp will continue to facilitate more follies to serve special interests over the common good. That Swamp must be drained by eliminating those 27 process changes that shifted our democracy to serve special interests instead of the common good. All three branches of our government must work together to drain the Swamp.

To Eliminate our Follies

The results of your own assessment of which political party is primarily responsibility for the 105 government follies indicates which political party is more focused on serving special interests than the common good. No matter which party is responsible for these past follies, we need both parties to work together to reverse them and to prevent more follies.

To Eliminate our Crises

I have identified and analyzed 23 national crises; the House of Representatives can add to this list as they see fit. The House of Representatives currently has over 500 caucuses formed to serve a particular common interest of house members; my assessment is that 88% of these caucuses are focused on serving special interests. House caucuses should establish House Crisis Action Teams (House CATs) using the quality approach described in this book, to reduce our 23 national crises and to serve the public interest, not special interests.

To eliminate our crises, we also need to refocus our House caucuses. With over 500 House caucuses I could only identify 47 that addressed one, or a part, of our 23 national crises. That is about 12% of the House caucuses. From the analyses in this book, those caucuses have been ineffective in reducing our crises; therefore, it is recommended that House caucuses use House CATs to more effectively address these 23 national crises. In order to improve effectiveness of the caucuses and House CATs working to reduce our national crises, it is recommended all caucuses working on serving special interests be suspended until our national crises are eliminated.

To be effective, recommendations for improvements must be implemented, and therefore, the House of Representatives and the Senate need to *act* on House CAT recommendations, particularly the no- or low-cost recommendations.

The House committee on caucus rules should include House CATs and a common support for them.

Of the 23 national crises analyzed in this book, I could not find a caucus that addressed 6 of the 23 crises. Those six crises are:
- Wall Street and Corporate Debt
- Social Media
- Gun Violence
- Land, Air, and Fresh Water
- Defense Costs
- Government

The House should establish caucuses and House CATS to address these 6 crises.

REFERENCES

This book used 263 references as the basis of the analyses in this book. Thanks to the hard work of the research teams, authors, reporters, non-profits, and government agencies that provided the data and facts that were used to perform and support the analyses in this book.

Preface
Parker, Kim, Rich Morin, and Juliana Menasce Horowitz. 2019. "Looking to the Future, Public Sees an America in Decline on Many Fronts." *Pew Research Center*. March 21, 2019.
https://www.pewsocialtrends.org/2019/03/21/public-sees-an-america-in-decline-on-many-fronts/

Chapter 1 – Goals
Pew Research Center. 2019. "Public Trusts in Government: 1958-2019." April 11, 2019. https://www.people-press.org/2019/04/11/public-trust-in-government-1958-2019/

Harvard Kennedy School Institute of Politics (IOP). 2019. "Spring 2019 IOP Youth Poll." Accessed August 31, 2019. https://iop.harvard.edu/youth-poll/spring-2019-poll

Harvard Kennedy School Institute of Politics (IOP), n.d. "Nearly Two-thirds of Young Americans Fearful About the Future of Democracy in America, Harvard youth poll finds." Accessed September 30, 2019. https://iop.harvard.edu/about/newsletter-press-release/nearly-two-thirds-young-americans-fearful-about-future-democracy

American Psychological Association. 2017. "Many Americans Stressed about Future of our Nation." February 15, 2017.
https://www.apa.org/news/press/releases/2017/02/stressed-nation

American Psychological Association. 2018. "APA Stress in America Survey: Generation Z Stressed about Issues in the News but Least Likely to Vote." October 30, 2018.
https://www.apa.org/news/press/releases/2017/02/stressed-nation

Ray, Julie. 2019. "Americans' Stress, Worry and Anger Intensified in 2018." *Gallup World Poll*, April 25, 2019.
https://news.gallup.com/poll/249098/americans-stress-worry-anger-intensified-2018.aspx

Gupta, Sanjay. 2019. "One Nation Under Stress." HBO Documentary. March 25, 2019.
https://www.hbo.com/documentaries/one-nation-under-stress

Goodreads. n.d. "Dalai Lama, Quotable Quote." Accessed August 31, 2019.
https://www.goodreads.com/quotes/18432-if-a-problem-is-fixable-if-a-situation-is-such

National Archives. n.d. "Declaration of Independence: A Transcription." Accessed August 31, 2019.
https://www.archives.gov/founding-docs/declaration-transcript

National Archives. n.d. "The Constitution of the United States: A Transcription." Accessed 31, 2019.
https://www.archives.gov/founding-docs/constitution-transcript

DeSilver, Drew. 2019. "Despite global concerns about democracy, more than half of countries are democratic." *Pew Research Center,* May 14, 2019.
https://www.pewresearch.org/fact-tank/2019/05/14/more-than-half-of-countries-are-democratic/

Scanlan, Phillip M. 1998. *The Dolphins Are Back: A Successful Quality Model for Healing the Environment.* Portland, Or: Productivity Press.

Tuchman, Barbara. 1984. *The March of Folly.* New York: Alfred A. Knopf.

Chapter 2 – Crises

Kemp, Luke. 2019. "The lifespans of ancient civilisations." BBC Future, February 20, 2019.
http://www.bbc.com/future/story/20190218-the-lifespans-of-ancient-civilisations-compared

Diamond, Jared. 2006. *Collapse — How Societies Choose to Fail or Succeed.* London: Penguin Press.

Diamond, Jared. 2019. *Upheaval — Turning Points for Nations in Crisis.* New York: Little, Brown and Company.

Stockholm International Peace Research Institute. 2019. "World military expenditure grows to $1.8 trillion in 2018." April 29, 2019. https://www.sipri.org/media/press-release/2019/world-military-expenditure-grows-18-trillion-2018

World Population Review. n.d. "Debt to GDP ratio by country 2019." Accessed September 1, 2019 http://worldpopulationreview.com/countries/countries-by-national-debt/

Duffin, Erin. 2019. "United States' trade balance from 2000 to 2018." *Statista*, August 9, 2019. https://www.statista.com/statistics/220041/total-value-of-us-trade-balance-since-2000/

Pearce, Tim. 2019. "Rural America is going bust as farm bankruptcies soar." *Daily Caller*, February 17 2019. https://www.dailycaller.com/2019/02/17/farmers-bankruptcy-trade/

American Society of Civil Engineers. 2017. "2017 Infrastructure Report Card." March 13, 2017. https://www.infrastructurereportcard.org/

Cochrane, Emily, Alan Rappeport, and Jim Tankersley. 2019. "Federal Budget Would Raise Spending by $320 Million." The New York Times, July 22, 2019. https://www.nytimes.com/2019/07/22/us/politics/budget-deal.html

Student Loan Hero. 2019. "A Look at the Shocking Student Loan Debt Statistics for 2019." Last modified February 4, 2019. https://studentloanhero.com/student-loan-debt-statistics/

Centers for Disease Control and Prevention. 2017. "New CDC report: More than 100 million Americans have diabetes or prediabetes." July 18, 2017.
https://www.cdc.gov/media/releases/2017/p0718-diabetes-report.html

Rowley, William R.C., Clement Bezold, Yasemin Arikan, E.O. Byrne, and Shannon Krohe. 2017. "Diabetes 2030: Insights from Yesterday, Today, and Future Trends." *Population Health Management* 10, no. 10.
https://pdfs.semanticscholar.org/619c/8a3045a6903a595e5dac0f76d1b98faaba93.pdf?_ga=2.197611623.915666901.1567532981-29953732.1567532981

Gunnars, Kris. 2017. "11 Graphs That Show Everything That is Wrong with the Modern Diet." *Healthline,* June 8, 2017.
https://www.healthline.com/nutrition/11-graphs-that-show-what-is-wrong-with-modern-diet

Food Pyramid. 2015. "Which Country Consumes the Most Sugar Per Capita?" April 30, 2015.
http://www.foodpyramid.com/healthy-eating/which-country-consumes-the-most-sugar-per-capita-11894/

Centers for Disease Control and Prevention. n.d. "HPV Vaccination Coverage Data." Last reviewed August 23, 2018.
https://www.cdc.gov/hpv/hcp/vacc-coverage/

Gonzales, Selena and Bradley Sawyer. 2017. "How does infant mortality in the U.S. compare to other countries?" Peterson-Kaiser Health System Tracker, July 7, 2017.
https://www.healthsystemtracker.org/chart-collection/infant-mortality-u-s-compare-countries/

Murphy, Sherry L., Jiaquan Xu, Kenneth D. Kochanek, and Elizabeth Arias. "Mortality in the United States, 2017." Centers for Disease Control and Prevention: National Center for Health Statistics, no. 328, November 2018.
https://www.cdc.gov/nchs/data/databriefs/db328-h.pdf

Department of Homeland Security. 2017. "Efforts by DHS to Estimate Southwest Border Security between Ports of Entry." Department of Homeland Security, Office of Immigration Statistics, September 2017: 4. https://www.dhs.gov/sites/default/files/publications/17_0914_estimat es-of-border-security.pdf

Chapter 3 – Barriers, Follies and Values
El-Najjar, Ahmad. 2017. "Why the ACA is good for small businesses – and America." Small Business Majority, January 25, 2017. https://smallbusinessmajority.org/es/blog/why-aca-good-small-businesses%E2%80%94and-america

Giese, Catherine. 2019. "U.S. Small Business Employment and Growth: All the Statistics You Need to Know." *Fundera*, last modified July 5, 2019. https://www.fundera.com/blog/small-business-employment-and-growth-statistics

Paine, Thomas. *Common Sense*. Chicago: Otbebookpublishing, 2019.

U.S. Department of State. 2017. "Core Values." May 2017. https://2001-2009.state.gov/s/d/rm/rls/dosstrat/2007/html/82948.htm

Center for Civic Education. n.d. National Standards for Civics and Government. "D. What Values and Principles are Basic to American Constitutional Democracy?" Accessed September 3, 2019. http://www.civiced.org/standards?page=58erica

Bialik, Kristen. 2018. "How the world views the U.S. and its president in 9 charts." *Pew Research Center,* October 9, 2018. https://www.pewresearch.org/fact-tank/2018/10/09/how-the-world-views-the-u-s-and-its-president-in-9-charts/

Chapter 4 – Unfixing Washington
Mothers Against Drunk Driving (MADD). n.d. "Statistics." Accessed September 3, 2019. https://www.madd.org/statistics/?gclid=CjOKCQjwwb3rBRDrARIsALR3X eZOXrBeX-QNY-S1nJkncd3bAey1tOUZpNpKOjwyAdeZ92aivshODQoaAqqeEALw_wcB

Foundation for Advancing Alcohol Responsibility. n.d. "Drunk Driving Fatality Statistics." Accessed September 4, 2019. https://www.responsibility.org/alcohol-statistics/drunk-driving-statistics/drunk-driving-fatality-statistics/

United Nations, n.d. "International Day for the Preservation of the Ozone Layer, September 16." Accessed September 30, 2019. https://www.un.org/en/events/ozoneday/background.shtml

United Nations. 2000. "We The Peoples: The Role of the United Nations in the 21st Century" Presented to General Assembly by Secretary General. April 3, 2000. https://www.un.org/press/en/2000/20000403.ga9704.doc.html

National Institute of Standards and Technology (NIST). n.d. "Baldrige Performance Excellence Program: Self-assessing." Accessed September 3, 2019. https://www.nist.gov/baldrige/self-assessing

Robinson, Julian and AP. 2019. "Bono praises capitalism for rescuing people from poverty – but warns those it has 'chewed up' are driving politics 'towards populism'." *Daily Mail.* January 23, 2019. https://www.dailymail.co.uk/news/article-6622873/Bono-praises-capitalism-rescuing-people-poverty.html

Quote Investigator. n.d. Definition of Insanity. Accessed September 3, 2019. https://quoteinvestigator.com/2017/03/23/same/

Brainy Quote. n.d. "Margaret Mead Quotes." Accessed September 3, 2019. https://www.brainyquote.com/quotes/margaret_mead_100502

CNN. 2019. "State of the Union 2019: Read the Full Transcript." February 6, 2019. https://www.cnn.com/2019/02/05/politics/donald-trump-state-of-the-union-2019-transcript/index.html

Chapter 5 – Quality Approach

Vanderbilt University Center for Teaching. n.d. "Bloom's Taxonomy."
Accessed September 4, 2019.
https://cft.vanderbilt.edu/guides-sub-pages/blooms-taxonomy/

Weimer, Maryellen. 2013. "Moving up Bloom's Taxonomy in an
Introductory Course: What's Being Done." *Faculty Focus.* April 12, 2013.
https://www.facultyfocus.com/articles/teaching-and-learning/moving-
up-blooms-taxonomy-in-an-introductory-course-whats-being-done/

Chappelow, Jim. 2019. "Pareto Principle." *Investopedia.* Last updated
August 29, 2019.
https://www.investopedia.com/terms/p/paretoprinciple.asp

Chapter 6 – A Path of Reason for the World

Freedom House. n.d. "Democracy in Crisis." Accessed September 4, 2019.
https://freedomhouse.org/report/freedom-world/freedom-world-2018

Diamond, Larry. 2010. "Why Are There No Arab Democracies"? *Journal
of Democracy*, no. 1 (2010): 93 – 104.
https://www.journalofdemocracy.org/articles/why-are-there-no-arab-
democracies/

DeSilver, Drew. 2019. "Despite global concerns about democracy, more
than half of countries are democratic." *Pew Research Center*, May 14,
2019.
https://www.pewresearch.org/fact-tank/2019/05/14/more-than-half-
of-countries-are-democratic/

United Nations Office on Drugs and Crime. 2019. "Global Study on
Homicide 2019." July 8, 2019.
https://www.unodc.org/unodc/en/data-and-analysis/global-study-on-
homicide.html

Giffords Law Center. n.d. "Annual Gun Law Scorecard." Accessed
September 5, 2019.
https://lawcenter.giffords.org/scorecard/

Centers for Disease Control and Prevention/National Center for Health
Statistics. 2019. "Firearm Mortality by State." January 10, 2019

https://www.cdc.gov/nchs/pressroom/sosmap/firearm_mortality/firearm.htm

Stranger. 2012. "US' Violent Crime Rates Compared to Western Europe's." *Extrano's Alley*. August 25, 2012. http://extranosalley.com/us-violent-crime-rates-compared-to-western-europes/

Charlton, Emma. 2017. "These charts show where the world's refugees came from in 2017 – and where they're heading." *World Economic Forum*. June 20, 2018. https://www.weforum.org/agenda/2018/06/worlds-refugees-charts-2017-unhcr-global-trends/

Efron, Shira, Jordan R. Fischbach, and Giulia Giordano. n.d. "Gaza's Water and Sanitation Crisis: The Implications for Public Health." The Rand Corporation. Accessed September 5, 2019. https://www.rand.org/content/dam/rand/pubs/external_publications/EP60000/EP67494/EP-67494.pdf

Weisser, Mike. 2014. "What Does the New UN Small Arms Treaty Really Say?" *Huffington Post*, November 25, 2013. https://www.huffpost.com/entry/un-small-arms-treaty_b_4337810

Preface to the Second Half of the Book
Paine, Thomas. *Common Sense*. Chicago: Otbebookpublishing, 2019.

Scanlan, Phillip M. 1998. *The Dolphins Are Back: A Successful Quality Model for Healing the Environment*. Portland, Or: Productivity Press.

Near, Holly. n.d. "I Am Willing." *Song Lyrics*. Accessed July 11, 2019. http://www.songlyrics.com/holly-near/i-am-willing-lyrics/

Chapter 7 – Financial Crises
Schneeweiss, Zoe. 2019. "Eleven Euro Nations have a Debt Ratio Above 60% of GDP." *Bloomberg*, April 23, 2019. https://www.bloomberg.com/news/articles/2019-04-23/eleven-euro-nations-have-a-debt-ratio-above-60-of-gdp-chart

Diamond, Jared. 2006. *Collapse — How Societies Choose to Fail or Succeed.* London: Press.

Committee for a Responsible Federal Budget. 2018. "Interest Spending is on Course to Quadruple." March 15, 2018. http://www.crfb.org/blogs/interest-spending-course-quadruple?gclid=CjwKCAjwmZbpBRAGEiwADrmVXv3lBOqNecVH_LcE5x NCycU48qNnyFB86-I650XvCUbFhQRM7TH0SRoCygcQAvD_BwE

Caner, Mehmet, Thomas Grennes, Fritzi Koehler-Geib. 2010. "Finding the Tipping Point -- When Sovereign Debt Turns Bad." Accessed July 9, 2019. World Bank Group Open Knowledge Repository. https://openknowledge.worldbank.org/handle/10986/3875?locale-attribute=en

Torry, Harriet. 2019. "Growth Didn't Hit 3% Mark Last Year, Revised Data Show." Wall Street Journal, July 27, 2019 https://www.thestar.com/wsj/economy/2019/07/26/growth-didnt-hit-3-mark-last-year-revised-data-show.html

Amadeo, Kimberly. 2019. "National Debt by Year Compared to GDP and Major Events." *The Balance*, last updated June 25, 2019. https://www.thebalance.com/national-debt-by-year-compared-to-gdp-and-major-events-3306287

Chappell, Bill. 2019. "U.S. National Debt Hits Record $22 Trillion." *National Public Radio,* February 13, 2019. https://www.npr.org/2019/02/13/694199256/u-s-national-debt-hits-22-trillion-a-new-record-thats-predicted-to-fall

Richter, Wolf. 2019. "US Gross National Debt Jumps by $1.2 Trillion in Fiscal 2019, to $22.7 Trillion, Hits 106.5% of GDP." *The Daily Coin*, October 3, 2019. https://thedailycoin.org/2019/10/03/us-gross-national-debt-jumps-by-1-2-trillion-in-fiscal-2019-to-22-7-trillion-hits-106-5-of-gdp/

Congressional Budget Office. 2019. "The Budget and Economic Outlook: 2018 to 2028." April 9, 2019. https://www.cbo.gov/publication/53651

Trading Economics. n.d. "China Government Debt to GDP." Accessed July 9, 2019
https://tradingeconomics.com/china/government-debt-to-gdp

Keiser Report. 2018. "Think Trump's Economy is Booming? It's a Corporate Debt Bubble Blowing Up – RT's Keiser Report." September 25, 2018. Accessed July 10, 2019.
https://www.rt.com/business/439297-us-economy-bond-bubble/

Peter G. Peterson Foundation. n.d. "The Fiscal and Economic Challenge." Accessed September 5, 2019.
https://www.pgpf.org/the-fiscal-and-economic-challenge

Carter, Joe. 2018. "7 Figures: Trump's 2019 Budget Plan." February 13, 2018.
https://blog.acton.org/archives/100204-7-figures-trumps-2019-budget-plan.html

Amadeo, Kimberly. 2019. "Wall Street: How it Works, Its History, and Its Crashes." *The Balance*, last updated January 21, 2019.
https://www.thebalance.com/wall-street-how-it-works-history-and-crashes-3306252

Roberts, Lance. 2018. "How the Bubbles in Stocks and Corporate Bonds Will Burst." Real Estate Investment Advice, November 16, 2018.
https://realinvestmentadvice.com/how-the-bubbles-in-stocks-and-corporate-bonds-and-will-burst/

Investopedia. n.d. "Dodd-Frank Wall Street Reform and Consumer Protection Act." Last updated May 10, 2019.
https://www.investopedia.com/terms/d/dodd-frank-financial-regulatory-reform-bill.asp

Zingales, Luigi, Oliver Hart. 2019. "Curbing Risk on Wall Street." *National Affairs,* no. 40, Summer 2019.
https://www.nationalaffairs.com/publications/detail/curbing-risk-on-wall-street

Office of the Special Inspector General for the Troubled Asset Relief Program. 2014. "Quarterly Report to Congress." July 30, 2014.

https://www.sigtarp.gov/Quarterly%20Reports/July_30_2014_Report_t
o_Congress.pdf

Colombo, Jesse. 2019. "U.S. Household Wealth is Experiencing an
Unsustainable Bubble." *Forbes*, August 24, 2018.
https://www.forbes.com/sites/jessecolombo/2018/08/24/u-s-
household-wealth-is-experiencing-an-unsustainable-
bubble/#c8aabf26b932

Egan, Matt. 2019. "Despite Backlash, Stock Buybacks Keep Booming."
Microsoft News, February 21, 2019.
https://www.msn.com/en-us/money/markets/despite-backlash-stock-
buybacks-keep-booming/ar-BBTULxY

Turak, Natasha. 2018. "The Biggest Red Flag for the Next Recession?
Corporate Debt to Cash Ratios, Top Economist Says." *CNBC*, September
12, 2018.
https://www.cnbc.com/2018/09/12/the-biggest-red-flag-for-the-next-
recession-corporate-debt-to-cash-ratios-top-economist-says.html

Corporate Finance Institute. n.d. "Cash Flow to Debt Ratio." Accessed July
10, 2019.
https://corporatefinanceinstitute.com/resources/knowledge/finance/ca
sh-flow-to-debt-ratio/

Tankersley, Jim and Ana Swanson. 2019. "In Blow to Trump, America's
Trade Deficit in Goods Hits Record $891 Billion." *New York Times*, March
6, 2019.
https://www.nytimes.com/2019/03/06/us/politics/us-trade-deficit.html

Thaler, Robert, and Cass R. Sunstein. 2008. *Nudge: Improving Decisions
about Health, Wealth, and Happiness*. New Haven: Yale University Press.

American Society of Civil Engineers. 2017. "2017 Infrastructure Report
Card: Economic Impact." Accessed July 10, 2019.
https://www.infrastructurereportcard.org/the-impact/economic-
impact/

Brady, Joe. 2018. "Analysis of Federal Bridge Data Confirms ASCE Report Card Bridge Grade." American Society of Civil Engineers 2017 Infrastructure Report Card, February 2, 2018.
https://www.infrastructurereportcard.org/analysis-of-federal-bridge-data-confirms-asce-report-card-bridge-grade/

Chapter 8 – Worker Crises
Pelley, Scott. 2019. "Federal Reserve Chairman Jerome Powell: The 60 Minutes Interview." *60 Minutes*, March 10, 2019.
https://www.cbsnews.com/news/jerome-powell-federal-reserve-chairman-60-minutes-interview-2019-03-10/

Gorman, Sean. 2016. "Dave Brat: U.S. labor participation rate is lowest since '70s." *PolitiFact*, June 13, 2016.
https://www.politifact.com/virginia/statements/2016/jun/13/dave-brat/dave-brat-us-labor-participation-rate-lowest-70s/

Index Mundi. n.d. "Labor Force Participation Rate, Total Country Ranking." Accessed July 11, 2019.
https://www.indexmundi.com/facts/indicators/SL.TLF.CACT.ZS/rankings

Amadeo, Kimberly. n.d. "Current US Unemployment Rate Statistics and News." *The Balance.* Last modified August 2, 2019.
https://www.thebalance.com/current-u-s-unemployment-rate-statistics-and-news-3305733

Equal Justice Initiative. 2016. "United States Still Has Highest Incarceration Rate in the World." April 26, 2019.
https://eji.org/news/united-states-still-has-highest-incarceration-rate-world

Dixon, Lauren. 2018. "Labor Force Participation is Down: Who's on the Sidelines?" *Talent Economy*, January 26, 2018.
https://www.chieflearningofficer.com/2018/01/26/labor-force-participation-who-sidelines/

Pelley, Scott. 2019. "China's Greatest Natural Resource May Be its Data." *60 Minutes*, March 13, 2019.
https://www.cbsnews.com/news/60-minutes-ai-facial-and-emotional-recognition-how-one-man-is-advancing-artificial-intelligence/

Sawhill, Isabel. 2018. *The Forgotten Americans: An Economic Agenda for a Divided Nation*. New Haven: Yale University Press.

Robert Half. 2019. "Survey: 42 Percent of Job Applicants Don't Meet Skills Requirements, But Companies Are Willing to Train Up." *PR News Wire*, March 19, 2019.
https://www.prnewswire.com/news-releases/survey-42-percent-of-job-applicants-dont-meet-skills-requirements-but-companies-are-willing-to-train-up-300813540.html

Casselman, Ben and Satariano, Adam. 2019. "Amazon's Latest Experiment: Retraining Its Work Force." *New York Times*, July 11, 2019.
https://www.nytimes.com/2019/07/11/technology/amazon-workers-retraining-automation.html

Donnelly, Grace. 2017. "Top CEOs Make More in Two Days Than an Average Employee Does in One Year." *Fortune*, July 20, 2017.
https://fortune.com/2017/07/20/ceo-pay-ratio-2016/

Hembree, Diana. 2018. "CEO Pay Skyrockets to 361 Times That of the Average Worker." *Forbes*, May 22, 2018.
https://www.forbes.com/sites/dianahembree/2018/05/22/ceo-pay-skyrockets-to-361-times-that-of-the-average-worker/#37df2369776d

Driscoll, John. 2019. "We Froze the Salaries of 20 Executives – and It Improved the Lives of 500 Employees." The Guardian, May 15, 2019.
https://www.theguardian.com/commentisfree/2019/may/15/executive-pay-salaries-carecentrix-senior-team-employees

Bureau of Labor Statistics. 2017. "Characteristics of Minimum Wage Workers, 2016." April 2017.
https://www.bls.gov/opub/reports/minimum-wage/2016/home.htm

Massachusetts Institute of Technology (MIT). 2019. "Living Wage Calculator." Accessed September 5, 2019.
http://livingwage.mit.edu/

Jacksonville Times Union Editorial. 2019. "Will Voters Get a Chance to Raise Florida's Minimum Wage?" *Jacksonville Times Union*, January 31, 2019.

https://www.jacksonville.com/opinion/20190131/thursdays-editorial-will-voters-get-chance-to-raise-floridas-minimum-wage

U.S. Census Bureau. 2018. "Income and Poverty in the United States: 2017." Accessed July 11, 2019. https://www.census.gov/library/publications/2018/demo/p60-263.html

Schoenherr, Neil. 2018. "Childhood Poverty Costs U.S. $1.03 Trillion in a Year, Study Finds." Washington University in St. Louis, April 16, 2018. https://source.wustl.edu/2018/04/childhood-poverty-cost-u-s-1-03-trillion-in-a-year-study-finds/

McLaughlin, Michael and Mark Rank. 2018. "Estimating the Economic Cost of Childhood Poverty in the United States." *Social Work Research*, 42, no. 2 (June): 73-83. https://doi.org/10.1093/swr/svy007

R29 Brand Experiences. 2018. "How One Entrepreneur Learned to Budget as a Single Mom." April 4, 2018. https://www.refinery29.com/en-us/single-parent-budgeting-how-to-save

Van Pelt, Toni. 2019. "The Feminist Agenda is Rising – When Will Women's Pay?" *National Organization for Women*, April 2, 2019. https://now.org/media-center/press-release/the-feminist-agenda-is-rising-when-will-womens-pay/

United Way ALICE. n.d. "The ALICE Project." *United Way*. Accessed July 11, 2019. http://www.uwof.org/sites/uwof.org/files/14UW%20ALICE%20Report_FL_Lowres_11.21.14.pdf

Center on Budget and Policy Priorities. 2019. "Policy Basics: The Supplemental Nutrition Assistance Program (SNAP)." Last modified June 25, 2019. https://www.cbpp.org/research/food-assistance/policy-basics-the-supplemental-nutrition-assistance-program-snap

Student Loan Hero. n.d. "A Look at the Shocking Student Loan Debt Statistics for 2019." Last updated February 4, 2019. https://studentloanhero.com/student-loan-debt-statistics/

Indiviglio, Daniel. 2011. "Chart of the Day: Student Loans Have Grown 511% Since 1999." *The Atlantic*, August 18, 2011. https://www.theatlantic.com/business/archive/2011/08/chart-of-the-day-student-loans-have-grown-511-since-1999/243821/

CNBC. 2019. "Canceling Student Debt: The Costs and Benefits of a 2020 Plan." April 28, 2019. https://www.cnbc.com/video/2019/04/26/canceling-student-debt-costs-benefits-2020-democrat-plan.html

Value Colleges. n.d. "College Access and Affordability: USA versus the World." Accessed July 11, 2019. https://www.valuecolleges.com/collegecosts/

Nykiel, Teddy. 2019. "3 Colleges that Help You Handle Student Debt." *The Jacksonville Florida Times Union*. January 23, 2019. https://www.jacksonville.com/ZZ/business/20190123/3-colleges-that-help-you-handle-student-debt

Carnevale, Anthony, Nicole Smith, and Jeff Strohl. 2013. "Recovery: Job Growth and Education Requirements Through 2020." Georgetown Public Policy Institute, June 26, 2013. https://1gyhoq479ufd3yna29x7ubjn-wpengine.netdna-ssl.com/wp-content/uploads/2014/11/Recovery2020.FR_.Web_.pdf

College Board. 2018. "Trends in College Pricing 2018." https://trends.collegeboard.org/sites/default/files/2018-trends-in-college-pricing.pdf

Safier, Rebecca. 2018. "Study: How US College Costs Stack Up With the Rest of the World." Student Loan Hero, last updated August 13, 2018. https://studentloanhero.com/featured/study-college-costs-around-world/

Stahl, Lesley. 2019. "How the NYU School of Medicine is Going Tuition-Free." *60 Minutes*, April 7, 2019.

https://www.cbsnews.com/news/tuition-free-medical-school-how-the-nyu-school-of-medicine-is-going-tuition-free-60-minutes/

Erb, Kelly. 2019. "More Good News for Morehouse Grads: They Likely Won't Owe Taxes on Gift from Billionaire." *Forbes*, May 19, 2019. https://www.forbes.com/sites/kellyphillipserb/2019/05/19/billionaire-robert-f-smith-promises-to-pay-off-student-debt-worth-millions/#34737b9a59f5

National Foundation on American Policy. 2018. "Declining International Student Enrollment at U.S. Universities and its Potential Impact." February 2018. https://nfap.com/wp-content/uploads/2018/02/Decline-in-International-Student-Enrollment.NFAP-Policy-Brief.February-2018-2.pdf

Value Colleges. n.d. "College Access and Affordability: USA versus the World." Accessed July 11, 2019. https://www.valuecolleges.com/collegecosts/

Student Loan Hero. n.d. "A Look at the Shocking Student Loan Debt Statistics for 2019." Last updated February 4, 2019. Accessed July 11, 2019. https://studentloanhero.com/student-loan-debt-statistics/

U.S. Department of Education. 2018. "National Student Loan Cohort Default Rate Falls." September 26, 2018. https://www.ed.gov/news/press-releases/national-student-loan-cohort-default-rate-falls

Nielsen. 2018. "Time Flies: U.S. Adults Now Spend Nearly Half a Day Interacting With Media." July 31, 2018. https://www.nielsen.com/us/en/insights/article/2018/time-flies-us-adults-now-spend-nearly-half-a-day-interacting-with-media/

Franklin, Ben. 1726. "Thirteen Virtues." Accessed July 11, 2019. http://www.thirteenvirtues.com/

Pew Research 2019, "Social Media Fact Sheet." June 12, 2019.https://www.pewinternet.org/fact-sheet/social-media/

Sun, Carolyn. 2017. "How Do Your Social Media Habits Compare to the Average Person's?" Entrepreneur, December 14, 2017.
https://www.entrepreneur.com/slideshow/306136

Molina, Brett. 2018. "Too Much Screen Time For Kids Can Lead to Poor Health, American Heart Association Says." USA Today, August 8, 2018.
https://www.usatoday.com/story/tech/nation-now/2018/08/08/kids-screen-time-health-american-heart-association/933030002/

American Academy of Pediatrics. 2016. "American Academy of Pediatrics Announces New Recommendations for Children's Media Use." October 21, 2016.
https://www.aap.org/en-us/about-the-aap/aap-press-room/Pages/American-Academy-of-Pediatrics-Announces-New-Recommendations-for-Childrens-Media-Use.aspx

World Health Organization. 2019. "To Grow Up Healthy, Children Need to Sit Less and Play More." April 24, 2019.
https://www.who.int/news-room/detail/24-04-2019-to-grow-up-healthy-children-need-to-sit-less-and-play-more

Chapter 9 – Health Care Crises

Mukherjee, Sy. 2018. "U.S. Drug Overdose Deaths Rose to a Record 72,000 Last Year, CDC Says." Fortune, August 15, 2018.
http://fortune.com/2018/08/15/drug-overdose-deaths-cdc-record

Talbott Campus. n.d. "2018 Prescription Drug Abuse Statistics You Need to Know." Accessed June 25, 2019.
https://talbottcampus.com/prescription-drug-abuse-statistics/

Gusovsky, D. 2016. "Americans still lead the world in something: Use of highly addictive opioids." CNBC, April 27, 2016.
https://www.cnbc.com/2016/04/27/americans-consume-almost-all-of-the-global-opioid-supply.html

CBS News. December 16, 2018. "Opioid Crisis: The lawsuits that could bankrupt manufacturers and distributors."
https://www.cbsnews.com/news/opioid-crisis-attorney-mike-moore-takes-on-manufacturers-and-distributors-at-the-center-of-the-epidemic-60-minutes/

Spector, Mike and Jessica DiNapoli. 2019. "Purdue Pharma in Discussion on $10 billion - $12 billion Offer to Settle Opioid Lawsuits: Sources." *Reuters.* August 27, 2019. https://www.reuters.com/article/us-purdue-pharma-oxycontin-idUSKCN1VH26I

White House, November 20, 2017. "Council of Economic Advisers Report: the Underestimated Cost of the Opioid Crisis." Accessed June 26, 2019. https://www.whitehouse.gov/briefings-statements/cea-report-underestimated-cost-opioid-crisis/

Courtwright, David. 2001. *Dark Paradise: A History of Opiate Addiction in America.* Cambridge, Mass: Harvard University Press.

Massachusetts General Hospital. 2019. "Study predicts worsening of opioid overdose crisis, limits of focusing on prescription opioids." *Mass General News Release*, February 1, 2019. https://www.massgeneral.org/News/pressrelease.aspx?id=2351

Centers for Disease Control and Prevention. 2018. "National Drug Overdose Deaths: Figure 1." December 2018. https://d14rmgtrwzf5a.cloudfront.net/sites/default/files/national_drug _overdose_deaths_through_2017.pdf

Centers for Disease Control and Prevention. 2017. "New CDC report: More than 100 million Americans have diabetes or prediabetes." July18, 2017.   https://www.cdc.gov/media/releases/2017/p0718-diabetes-report.html

Hales, Craig, Margaret Carroll, Cheryl Fryar, and Cynthia Ogden. 2017. "Prevalence of Obesity Among Adults and Youth: United States, 2015-2016." Centers for Disease Control and Prevention: NCHS Data Brief No. 288, October 2017. https://www.cdc.gov/nchs/products/databriefs/db288.htm

Mayo Clinic. 2019. "Type 2 Diabetes." Accessed June 27, 2019. https://www.mayoclinic.org/diseases-conditions/type-2-diabetes/symptoms-causes/syc-20351193

National Heart, Lung, and Blood Institute. n.d. "Classification of Overweight and Obesity by BMI, Waist Circumference, and Associated Disease Risks." Accessed June 27, 2019
http://www.nhlbi.nih.gov/health/educational/lose_wt/BMI/bmi_dis.htm

Schnabel, Laure, Emmanuelle Kesse-Guyot, Benjamin Allès, Mathilde Touvier, Bernard Srour, Serge Hercberg, Camille Buscail, and Chantal Julia. *Journal of the American Medical Association (JAMA Intern Med.)* 2019; 179(4): 490-498.
https://jamanetwork.com/journals/jamainternalmedicine/article-abstract/2723626

Centers for Disease Control and Prevention. 2018. "Adult Obesity Facts." Last reviewed August 13, 2018.
https://www.cdc.gov/obesity/data/adult.html

Organization for Economic Co-operation and Development. 2017. "Obesity Update 2017."
https://www.oecd.org/els/health-systems/Obesity-Update-2017.pdf

World Health Organization. 2018. "Obesity and Overweight." February 16, 2018.
https://www.who.int/news-room/fact-sheets/detail/obesity-and-overweight

Centers for Disease Control and Prevention. 2017. "Obesity: United States 2017 Results." Accessed October 1, 2019
https://nccd.cdc.gov/youthonline/App/Results.aspx?

Infogram. n.d. "U.S. Adult Obesity Rates since 1960." Accessed July 5, 2019.
https://infogram.com/us-adult-obesity-rates-since-1960-1gzxop49on65mwy

World Health Organization. n.d. "Obesity and overweight." Accessed September 29, 2019.
https://www.who.int/dietphysicalactivity/media/en/gsfs_obesity.pdf

Centers for Disease Control and Prevention. n.d. "National Diabetes Statistics Report, 2017." Accessed June 27, 2019. https://www.cdc.gov/diabetes/pdfs/data/statistics/national-diabetes-statistics-report.pdf

Mozaffarian, Dariush and Dan Glickman. 2019. "Our Food is Killing Too Many of Us." *The New York Times,* August 26, 2019. https://www.nytimes.com/2019/08/26/opinion/food-nutrition-health-care.html?searchResultPosition=1

American Beverage Association. n.d. "Cutting Sugar in the American Diet." Accessed September 6, 2019. https://www.balanceus.org/industry-efforts/cutting-sugar-american-diet/

Yang, L., Cao, C., Kantor, E. D., Nguyen, L. H., Zheng, X., Park, Y., Giovannucci, E. L., Matthews, C. E., Colditz, G. A., Cao, Y. 2019. "Trends in Sedentary Behavior Among the US Population, 2001-2016." *Journal of the American Medical Association* 321, no. 16 (April): 1587-1597. https://doi:10.1001/jama.2019.3636

National Cancer Institute. 2018. "Cancer Statistics." Last update April 27, 2018. https://www.cancer.gov/about-cancer/understanding/statistics

National Institutes of Health. 2018. "Cancer Statistics." Last updated April 27, 2018. https://www.cancer.gov/about-cancer/understanding/statistics

World Cancer Research Fund, n.d. "Global Cancer Data by Country." Accessed September 30, 2019. https://www.wcrf.org/dietandcancer/cancer-trends/data-cancer-frequency-country

Simon, Howard. 2019. "Facing Florida's public health crisis: toxic blue-green algae." South Florida Sun Sentinel, April 16, 2019. https://www.sun-sentinel.com/opinion/commentary/fl-op-com-blue-green-algae-simon-20190410-story.html

U.S. Environmental Protection Agency. n.d. "Nutrient Pollution: Harmful Algal Blooms." Accessed October 1, 2019. https://www.epa.gov/nutrientpollution/harmful-algal-blooms

Centers for Disease Control and Prevention. 2018. "HPV Vaccination Coverage Data." Last reviewed August 23, 2018. https://www.cdc.gov/hpv/hcp/vacc-coverage/index.html

National Institutes of Health. 2019. "Annual Report to the Nation: Overall cancer mortality continues to decline." May 30, 2019. https://www.nih.gov/news-events/news-releases/annual-report-nation-overall-cancer-mortality-continues-decline

American Cancer Society. 2016. "Cancer Statistics Report." January 7, 2016. https://www.cancer.org/latest-news/cancer-statistics-report-death-rate-down-23-percent-in-21-years.html

Heid, Markham. 2014. "How Stress Affects Cancer Risk." The University of Texas M.D. Anderson Cancer Center, December 2014. https://www.mdanderson.org/publications/focused-on-health/how-stress-affects-cancer-risk.h21-1589046.html

American Cancer Society. n.d. "Survival Rates for Colorectal Cancer." Last modified February 1, 2019. https://www.cancer.org/cancer/colon-rectal-cancer/detection-diagnosis-staging/survival-rates.html

Centers for Disease Control and Prevention. 2019. "Deaths: Final Data for 2017." *National Vital Statistics Reports*, 68, no. 9 (June): 1-76. https://www.cdc.gov/nchs/data/nvsr/nvsr68/nvsr68_09-508.pdf

Vox. 2018. "America is one of 6 countries that make up more than half of gun deaths." August 29, 2018. https://www.vox.com/2018/8/29/17792776.us-gun-deaths-global

Gander, Kashmira. 2018. "U.S. Child Gun Deaths: Firearms Are Second Biggest Killer in America." *Newsweek*, December 19, 2018. https://www.newsweek.com/us-child-gun-death-firearms-2nd-biggest-killer-america-1264804

NBC News. 2018. "Guns kill twice as many kids as cancer does, new study shows." December 19, 2018.
https://www.nbcnews.com/health/health-news/guns-kill-twice-many-kids-cancer-does-new-study-shows-n950091

Kiesel, Laura, 2018. "Don't Blame Mental Illness for Mass Shootings; Blame Men." *Politico*, January 17, 2018.
Https://www.politico.com/magazine/story/2018/01/17/gun-violence-masculinity-216321

Centers for Disease Control and Prevention. 2019. "Deaths: Final Data for 2017." *National Vital Statistics Reports*, 68, no. 9 (June): 1-76.
https://www.cdc.gov/nchs/data/nvsr/nvsr68/nvsr68_09-508.pdf

Gun Violence Archive. n.d. "Mass Shootings 2019." Accessed June 29, 2019.
 https://www.gunviolencearchive.org/reports/mass-shooting?page=3

Newtown Action Alliance. 2018. "National Vigil on December 5th to Mark 6-Year Anniversary of Sandy Hook Shootings." November 29, 2018.
https://www.newtownactionalliance.org/naa-press-media/nationalvigil2018?rq=600%2C000

Santaella-Tenorio, Julian, Magdalena Cerda, Andres Villaveces, and Sandro Galea. 2016. "What do we know about the association between firearm legislation and firearm-related injuries?" *Epidemiologic Reviews* 38, no. 1. (Jan.)" 140-157
https://academic.oup.com/epirev/article/38/1/140/2754868

Singletary, Michelle. 2018. "The Enormous Cost of Gun Violence." *The Washington Post,* February 22, 2018.
https://www.washingtonpost.com/newssearch/?datefilter=All%20Since%202005&query=michelle%20singletary%20gun%20violence%20costs&sort=Relevance

Giffords Law Center. n.d. "Statistics on the Costs of Gun Violence." Accessed August 26, 2019.
https://lawcenter.giffords.org/costs-of-gun-violence-statistics/

Mothers Against Drunk Driving (MADD). n.d. "Statistics." Accessed September 3, 2019. https://www.madd.org/statistics/?gclid=CjOKCQjwwb3rBRDrARIsALR3X eZOXrBeX-QNY-S1nJkncd3bAey1tOUZpNpKOjwyAdeZ92aivsh0DQoaAqqeEALw_wcB

Peterson-Kaiser Health System Tracker. 2018. "How has U.S. spending on healthcare changed over time?" December 10, 2018. https://www.healthsystemtracker.org/chart-collection/u-s-spending-healthcare-changed-time/

CNBC. 2018. "Here's the Real Reason Health Care Costs so Much More in the US." March 22, 2018. https://www.cnbc.com/2018/03/22/the-real-reason-medical-care-costs-so-much-more-in-the-us.html

KFF Henry J. Kaiser Family Foundation. 2018. "An Overview of the Medicare Part D Prescription Drug Benefit." October 12, 2018. https://www.kff.org/medicare/fact-sheet/an-overview-of-the-medicare-part-d-prescription-drug-benefit/

Harvard T.H. Chan School of Public Health. 2018. "Prices of Labor, Prices of Pharmaceuticals, and Administrative Costs are the Key Drivers of High U.S. Healthcare Spending." March 13, 2018. https://hsph.harvard.edu/news/press-releases/labor-pharmaceuticals-administrative-costs-health-costs/

Brookings Institution. 2016. "Social Spending, not Medical Spending, is Key to Health." July 13, 2016. https://www.brookings.edu/opinions/social-spending-not-medical-spending-is-key-to-health/

Van Groningen, Nicole. 2017. "Big Pharma Gives Your Doctor Gifts. Then Your Doctor Gives You Big Pharma's Drugs." *Washington Post*, June 13, 2017. https://www.washingtonpost.com/opinions/big-pharma-gives-your-doctor-gifts-then-your-doctor-gives-you-big-pharmas-drugs/2017/06/13/5bc0b550-5045-11e7-b064-828ba60fbb98_story.html

U.S. Congresswoman Judy Chu. 2019. "Insulin Costs as Much as 32 Times More in San Gabriel Valley than Abroad." April 2, 2019. https://chu.house.gov/media-center/press-releases/new-report-insulin-costs-much-32-times-more-san-gabriel-valley-abroad

Centers for Disease Control and Prevention. 2018. "Births: Final Data for 2917." National Vital Statistics Reports 67, no. 8. November 7, 2018. https://www.cdc.gov/nchs/data/nvsr/nvsr67/nvsr67_08-508.pdf

World Health Organization. 2016. "WHO Statement on Caesarean Section Rates." Accessed September 29, 2019. https://apps.who.int/iris/bitstream/handle/10665/161442/WHO_RHR_15.02_eng.pdf;jsessionid=039FCEF6E8289FB37CAEE0FACAE87042?sequence=1

Penn Medicine OncoLink. 2018. "Protein Needs During Cancer Treatment." Last modified August 3, 2018. https://www.oncolink.org/support/nutrition-and-cancer/during-and-after-treatment/protein-needs-during-cancer-treatment

Chapter 10 – Environmental Crises

Centers for Disease Control and Prevention. n.d. "Infant Mortality." Last reviewed March 27, 2019. https://www.cdc.gov/reproductivehealth/maternalinfanthealth/infant mortality.htm

World Health Organization. 2016. "An Estimated 12.6 Million Deaths Each Year are Attributable to Unhealthy Environments." March 15, 2016. https://www.who.int/news-room/detail/15-03-2016-an-estimated-12-6-million-deaths-each-year-are-attributable-to-unhealthy-environments

National Institute of Environmental Health Sciences. 2019. "Conditions and Diseases." Health and Education. Last reviewed April 26, 2019. https://www.niehs.nih.gov/health/topics/conditions/index.cfm

National Institute of Environmental Health Sciences. 2019. "Environmental Agents." Health and Education. Last reviewed June 27, 2019. https://www.niehs.nih.gov/health/topics/agents/index.cf

Center for Public Integrity. 2011. "EPA Superfund Cleanup Costs Outstrip Funding." Last updated May 19, 2014.
https://publicintegrity.org/environment/epa-superfund-cleanup-costs-outstrip-funding/

Reuters. 2011. "Coal's Hidden Costs Top $345 Billion in U.S.-Study." February 16, 2011.
https://www.reuters.com/article/usa-coal-study/coals-hidden-costs-top-345-billion-in-u-s-study-idUSN1628366220110216

Green Car Congress. 2017. "Lancet Commission Report Estimates Pollution Responsible for 9 Million Premature Deaths Globally in 2015; 16% of Deaths." October 21, 2017.
https://www.greencarcongress.com/2017/10/20171021-lancet.html

U.S. Environmental Protection Agency, n.d. "Air Quality Improves as America Grows" and "Economic Growth with Cleaner Air." Accessed June 30, 2019.
https://gispub.epa.gov/air/trendsreport/2017/#home

BBC News. 2019. "Report: US 2018 CO2 emissions saw biggest spike in years." January 8, 2019.
https://www.bbc.com/news/world-us-canada-46801108

Keiser, David, Catherine L. Kling, and Joseph S. Shapiro. 2018. "The low but uncertain measured benefits of US water quality policy." *Proceedings of the National Academy of Sciences of the United States of America.* October 8, 2018.
https://www.pnas.org/content/116/12/5262

Gross, Samantha. 2019. "Ron DeSantis Names Florida Blue-Green Algae Task Force." *Tampa Bay Times,* April 29, 2019.
http://www.tampabay.com/florida-politics/buzz/2019/04/29/ron-desantis-names-florida-blue-green-algae-task-force/

United Nations Convention on the Law of the Sea. 1982. Article 61, 45-46. Accessed September 5, 2019.
https://www.un.org/Depts/los/convention_agreements/texts/unclos/unclos_e.pdf

Marine Protected Areas. n.d. "About Marine Protected Areas." Accessed June 30, 2019.
https://marineprotectedareas.noaa.gov/aboutmpas/

Marine Conservation Institute and Atlas of Marine Protection. 2017. "SeaStates 2017."
https://marine-conservation.org/seastates/us/2017/

Ocean Conservancy. n.d. "Sustainable Fisheries: Healthy Fish for a Healthy Ocean." Accessed June 30, 2019.
https://oceanconservancy.org/sustainable-fisheries/

TreeHugger. 2019. "Ocean Plastic Pollution Costs the Planet $2.5 Trillion a Year." April 19, 2019.
https://www.treehugger.com/plastic/ocean-plastic-pollution-costs-planet-25-trillion-year.html

Bryant, Miranda. 2019. "Fecal bacteria found at more than half of US beaches last year, report says." *The Guardian,* July 24, 2019.
https://www.theguardian.com/environment/2019/jul/23/fecal-bacteria-found-at-more-than-half-of-us-beaches-last-year-report-says

Microcosm Aquarium Explorer. n.d. "Baba Dioum." Accessed June 30, 2019.
http://en.microcosmaquariumexplorer.com/wiki/Baba_Dioum

Earth. 2019. "U.S. Carbon Emissions Increased in 2018 After a Three-Year Decline." January 9, 2019.
https://www.earth.com/news/us-carbon-emissions-increased-2018/

National Climate Assessment. 2018. Fourth National Climate Assessment: "Chapter 2: Our Changing Climate." Accessed July 1, 2019
https://nca2018.globalchange.gov/chapter/2/

Institute for Energy Research. 2019. "Fossil Fuels Dominate U.S. Energy Production, But Receive a Small Percentage of Federal Fuel Subsidies." January 9, 2019.
https://www.instituteforenergyresearch.org/renewable/fossil-fuels-dominate-u-s-energy-production-but-receive-a-small-percentage-of-federal-fuel-subsidies/

Hayhoe, Katharine. 2018. "Five Myths about Climate Change." *The Washington Post*, November 13, 2018. https://www.washingtonpost.com/outlook/five-myths/five-myths-about-climate-change/2018/11/30/9fba233a-f428-11e8-bc79-68604ed88993_story.html?noredirect=on&utm_term=.69e78627b564

National Geographic. 2017. "Hidden Costs of Climate Change Running Hundreds of Billions a Year." September 27, 2017. https://news.nationalgeographic.com/2017/09/climate-change-costs-us-economy-billions-report/

U.S. Department of Defense. 2018. "Climate-Related Risk to DoD Infrastructure: Initial Vulnerability Assessment Survey (SLVAS) Report." January 2018. https://climateandsecurity.files.wordpress.com/2018/01/tab-b-slvas-report-1-24-2018.pdf

Kennedy, John. 2019. "Florida Legislature to Look at Hurricane Michael Recovery." *The Jacksonville Times Union,* March 4, 2019. https://www.jacksonville.com/news/20190304/florida-legislature-to-look-at-hurricane-michael-recovery/1

Kossin, James. 2018. "A Global Slowdown of Tropical-Cyclone Translation Speed." *Nature—International Journal of Science,* June 6, 2018. https://www.nature.com/articles/s41586-018-0158-3

Brown, Matthew. 2019. "Trump rollbacks for fossil fuel industries carry steep cost." *Associated Press,* January 27, 2019. https://www.apnews.com/e38e8c16b610439db2273b8b35b4bc58

Mann, Michael. 2019. Interview by Katy Tur. MSNBC, February 5, 2019. https://www.msnbc.com/katy-tur/watch/the-state-of-the-climate-in-2019-1437702723950

Jacobson, Mark. 2017. "Roadmaps to Transition Countries to 100% Clean, Renewable Energy for All Purposes to Curtail Global Warming, Air Pollution, and Energy Risk." September 20, 2017. *Earth's Future 5*: 942-955. https://agupubs.onlinelibrary.wiley.com/doi/epdf/10.1002/2017EF000672

San Francisco Estuary Institute. 2019. "Working with Nature to Plan for Sea Level Rise Using Operational Landscape Units." April 2019. https://www.sfei.org/sites/default/files/biblio_files/SFEI%20SF%20Bay%20Shoreline%20Adaptation%20Atlas%20April%202019_medres_0.pdf

Chapter 11 – Security Crisis
United Nations Office for Disarmament Affairs. n.d. "Treaty on the Non-Proliferation of Nuclear Weapons." Accessed July 1, 2019. https://www.un.org/disarmament/wmd/nuclear/npt/

International Atomic Energy Agency. 2017. "Radioactive Waste Management: Workshop Highlights Flexibility of IAEA's ARTEMIS Review." April 24, 2017. https://www.iaea.org/newscenter/news/radioactive-waste-management-workshop-highlights-flexibility-of-iaeas-artemis-review

Stanford Earth. 2018. "The Steep Costs of Nuclear Waste in the U.S." July 3, 2018. https://earth.stanford.edu/news/steep-costs-nuclear-waste-us#gs.n6tp4g

Department of Homeland Security. 2018. "Cybersecurity Strategy." May 15, 2018. 1-35. https://www.dhs.gov/sites/default/files/publications/DHS-Cybersecurity-Strategy_1.pdf

National Institute of Standards and Technology. n.d. "National Vulnerability Database: Understanding Vulnerability." Accessed July 3, 2019. https://nvd.nist.gov/vuln

Vox. 2017. "America's Plan for Stopping Cyberattacks is Dangerously Weak." May 27, 2017. https://www.vox.com/the-big-idea/2017/3/27/15052422/cyber-war-diplomacy-russia-us-wikileaks

Perlroth, Nicole, David E. Sanger, and Scott Shane. 2019. *The New York Times*, May 6, 2019.

https://www.nytimes.com/2019/05/06/us/politics/china-hacking-cyber.html

U.S. Council of Economic Advisers. 2018. "Annual Report of the Council on Economic Advisers." February 2018, page 329, box 7-1. https://www.whitehouse.gov/wp-content/uploads/2018/02/ERP_2018_Final-FINAL.pdf

Statista.com. 2019. "Percentage change in the proposed 2018 federal budget of the United States from 2017 edition, by department or service." Accessed August 28, 2019. https://www.statista.com/statistics/687901/budget-2018-proposal-change-in-budget-by-department/

Doffman, Zak. 2019. "Chinese State Hackers Suspected of Malicious Cyber Attack on U.S. Utilities." August 3, 2019. https://fortunascorner.com/2019/08/04/chinese-state-hackers-suspected-of-malicious-cyber-attack-on-u-s-utilities/

Internet Protocol Video Marketing. n.d. "The Authority on Video Surveillance." Accessed August 29, 2019. https://ipvm.com/about

U.S. Customs and Border Protection. 2019. "Nationwide Illegal Alien Apprehensions Fiscal Years 1925-2018." March 2019. https://www.cbp.gov/sites/default/files/assets/documents/2019-Mar/bp-total-apps-fy1925-fy2018.pdf

Dickerson, Caitlin. 2019. "Border at 'Breaking Point' as More Than 76,000 Unauthorized Migrants Cross in a Month." *The New York Times*, March 5, 2019. https://www.nytimes.com/2019/03/05/us/border-crossing-increase.html

Sanchez, Tatiana. 2019. "Trump slashes 2020 refugee admissions nearly in half to 18,000, spurring outrage." *San Francisco Chronicle,* September 26, 2019. https://www.sfchronicle.com/nation/article/Trump-slashes-2020-refugee-admissions-nearly-in-14471501.php

Institute on Economic Taxation and Policy. 2017. "Undocumented Immigrants' State and Local Tax Contributions." March 2017. https://itep.org/wp-content/uploads/immigration2017.pdf

Substance Abuse and Mental Health Services Administration. 2015. "Behavioral Health Trends in the United: Results from the 2014 National Survey on Drug Use and Health." September 2015. https://www.samhsa.gov/data/sites/default/files/NSDUH-FRR1-2014/NSDUH-FRR1-2014.pdf

Unity Rehab. n.d. "Increase in NAS and Drug-Related Newborn and Mother Hospitalizations." Accessed July 1, 2019. https://www.unityrehab.com/blog/drug-related-newborn-mother-hospitalizations/

NIH National Institute on Drug Abuse. n.d. "Prescription Opioids and Heroin." Last updated January 2018. https://www.drugabuse.gov/publications/research-reports/relationship-between-prescription-drug-abuse-heroin-use/introduction

U.S. Drug Enforcement Agency. n.d. "Fentanyl." Accessed July 3, 2019. https://www.dea.gov/factsheets/fentanyl

Humor in America. 2014. "The Morphology of a Humorous Phrase: 'We have met the enemy and he is us'." May 19, 2014. https://humorinamerica.wordpress.com/2014/05/19/the-morphology-of-a-humorous-phrase/

Business Insider. 2018. "The 15 Countries with the Highest Military Budgets in 2017." May 2, 2018. https://www.businessinsider.com/highest-military-budgets-countries-2018-5

U.S. Department of Defense. 2019. "DOD Releases Fiscal Year 2020 Budget Proposal." March 12, 2019. https://dod.defense.gov/News/News-Releases/News-Release-View/Article/1782623/dod-releases-fiscal-year-2020-budget-proposal/

Pillsbury, James. 2015. *The Hundred-Year Marathon.* Henry Holt and Co.

Forbes. 2015. "The Biggest Military Budgets as a Percentage of GDP."
June 25, 2015.
https://www.forbes.com/sites/niallmccarthy/2015/06/25/the-biggest-military-budgets-as-a-percentage-of-gdp-infographic-2/#736c844c4c47

Chapter 12 –Democracy Crisis
Open Secrets. n.d. "Money in Politics Timeline." Accessed July 3, 2019.
https://www.opensecrets.org/resources/learn/timeline

Open Secrets. n.d. "2016 Outside Spending, by Super PAC." Accessed July
3, 2019.
https://www.opensecrets.org/outsidespending/summ.php?cycle=2016
&chrt=V&disp=O&type=S

Metrocosm. 2016. "What Trump and Hillary Spent versus Every General
Election Candidate Since 1960." November 7, 2016.
http://metrocosm.com/2016-election-spending/

Confessore, Nicholas and Karen Yourish. 2016. "$2 Billion Worth of Free
Media for Donald Trump." *The New York Times*, March 15, 2016.
https://www.nytimes.com/2016/03/16/upshot/measuring-donald-trumps-mammoth-advantage-in-free-media.html?searchResultPosition=1

Open Secrets. 2018. "Blue Wave of Money Propels 2018 Election to
Record-Breaking $5.2 Billion in Spending." October 29, 2018.
https://www.opensecrets.org/news/2018/10/2018-midterm-record-breaking-5-2-billion/

FiveThirtyEight. 2018. "How Money Affects Elections." September 10,
2018.
https://fivethirtyeight.com/features/money-and-elections-a-complicated-love-story/

Browder, Bill. 2015. *Red Notice, A true Story of High Finance, Murder, and
One Man's Fight for Justice.* New York: Simon and Schuster.

Chinni, Dante and Sally Bronston. 2018. "Democratic Voters Face off
Against Gerrymandered Districts." *NBC News*, October 7, 2018

https://www.nbcnews.com/politics/first-read/democrats-voters-face-against-gerrymandered-districts-n917511

Ballotpedia. n.d. "Independent Redistricting Commissions." Accessed August 29, 2019.
https://ballotpedia.org/Independent_redistricting_commissions
MacLeod, Alexander. 1997. "Strict Laws Keep British Campaign Short, Cheap – And No TV Ads." *The Christian Science Monitor*, April 7, 1997.
https://www.csmonitor.com/1997/0407/040797.intl.intl.5.html

Kurtzleben, Danielle. 2015. "Why are U.S. elections so much longer than other countries?" *NPR*, October 21, 2015.
https://www.npr.org/sections/itsallpolitics/2015/10/21/450238156/can
adas-11-week-campaign-reminds-us-that-american-elections-are-much-longer

Mount Vernon. n.d. "Center for Digital History – Quotes." Accessed July 5, 2019.
https://www.mountvernon.org/library/digitalhistory/quotes/article/ho
wever-political-parties-may-now-and-then-answer-popular-ends-they-are-likely-in-the-course-of-time-and-things-to-become-potent-engines-by-which-cunning-ambitious-and-unprincipled-men-will-be-enabled-to-subvert-the-power-of-the-people-and-to-usurp-for-th/

Democrats.　2016. "The 2016 Democratic Party Platform." Accessed August 30, 2019.
https://democrats.org/where-we-stand/party-platform/

US History. n.d. Historic Documents. Accessed July 5, 2019.
http://www.ushistory.org/documents/ask-not.htm

GLOSSARY of TERMS

This Glossary provides a definition of 47 terms that might help the reader who has not had training in the quality approach – an approach used to prevent problems, disasters and crises by eliminating root causes of problems.

American Dream	The opportunity for everyone to succeed through education and hard work, and pursue a better quality of life for yourself, your family, and your children.
Analytical	Relating to use of analysis and logical reasoning, based on facts.
Autocracy	A system of government in which one person has absolute power.
Barriers	Obstacles that prevent improvement.
Benchmarks	A standard of excellence that can be used to set performance standards and from which best practices can be learned.
Best Practices	Processes, procedures, or methods that are accepted and proven to have obtained the most efficient and effective results in addressing a particular problem or crisis.
Brainstorming	Group discussion to produce ideas or solve problems.
Carcinogens	Substances known to cause cancer.

Chronic Stress

Continuous, daily stress that can affect the lives of both children and adults; it impairs health and the ability to have a normal life.

Climate Change

Changes in the Earth's climate system that result in new weather patterns that are long lasting. The climate system is comprised of five interacting parts: the atmosphere (air), hydrosphere (water), cryosphere (ice), biosphere (living things, such as trees), and lithosphere (the earth's crust).

Climate Warming

A part of climate change that results from the sun providing more heat than the earth can give off. The presence of carbon dioxide in the atmosphere acts like a blanket in the atmosphere that holds heat in, creating climate warming. Ocean warming near the coasts causes increased intensity of hurricanes along the coast.

Confirmation bias

This is created when people make up their mind about an issue. They then put up a barrier to accepting any new information that might require a change in that predetermined belief or opinion.

Crisis

A condition of social, economic, or political instability or danger where a decisive change is impending; a point at which all future events are determined, and where the wrong decision can lead to disaster.

Critical Thinking

An approach to problem solving based on gathering and analyzing facts and data, determining root causes, and developing the most efficient and effective solutions to reduce the root causes of a problem or crisis.

Cybersecurity

Provides protection to prevent our IT systems from being penetrated by criminals, terrorists, and other countries' attempts to disrupt our IT infrastructure, which is relied upon by government, businesses, and citizens.

Decision of Folly

A decision of folly is one made to benefit the greed or selfish ambition of a few, in contrast to a decision of reason for the common good.

Disasters

Sudden events, both environmental and man-made, that cause great damage in the community, affect many lives, and have high costs. Disaster impacts exceed the ability of the community to cope with the disaster and result in enormous costs to individuals, communities, states, and the nation.

Folly

In contrast to its more normal definition, as a lack of good sense, the word in this book refers to decisions that are made based on greed and selfish ambition to benefit a few, instead of decisions of reason to benefit many.

Gross Crisis Cost
(GCC)

The total annual country's costs of its crises. It is a measure of the financial costs of crises.

Gross Domestic
Product (GDP)

The total annual country's expenditures of consumers and government, plus business investments, minus the trade deficit. A measure of the financial size of an economy.

Goals

Long-term, over-arching performance levels set in order to reduce a crisis or resolve a problem. Goals are achieved through a series of improvements made to achieve annual objectives.

Greed

Greed is an intense desire for wealth or power; a desire to possess more than one needs.

House CATs	Crisis Action Teams (CATs) would be drawn from members of the House of Representatives to create bipartisan teams working together, using a quality approach, to prevent or reduce our crises.
HPV	Human Papillomavirus (HPV) is a virus that has the potential to cause cancer.
IT	Information Technology consists of networks made of both communications and computing technologies to support various government, business, and consumer processes, transactions, and functions.
Oligarch(s)	One or more wealthy business or political leaders who rule through a power structure that allows them to control government decisions, in order to serve their special interests.
Objectives	Objectives are the short-term measurable improvements needed to obtain long-term goals in order to reduce a crisis.
Path of Reason	A Path of Reason refers to choosing the path of making decisions for the common good, over choosing a Path of Folly with decisions benefiting special interests.
Partisan	Biased, prejudiced, one-sided, discriminatory, unjust, unfair, and/or inequitable. Partisan politics support only the approaches of one political party platform's policies to solve a problem or crisis
Political	Relating to the strategies or campaigns of a political party; motivated by political interests rather than best interests of the country.

Prevention   Planning and improvement necessary to
                           prevent, or reduce, the crises that are the cause
                           of our disasters.

Quality Approach   Four improvement steps in a Plan, Do, Check, Act
                           (PDCA) cycle, along with appropriate quality
                           methods in each step, provide a common
                           approach to identify root causes of a crisis and to
                           develop the most efficient and effective
                           improvements to reduce the crisis.

Quality Check   An organizational assessment against high-
                           performance criteria. The U.S. Commerce
                           Department has developed excellent criteria and
                           approaches for assessing an organization's
                           performance using the Baldrige Criteria for
                           Performance Excellence.

Quality   Improvements that are the most efficient and
Improvements   effective actions taken to eliminate root causes
                           and to achieve the objectives and goals that
                           were set to reduce a crisis.

Quality Methods   Techniques to analyze data and develop
                           solutions to a problem or crises.

Quality Spiral   When the PDCA approach is continued year after
                           year, it can create an upward spiral of
                           continuous improvement which is needed to
                           reach long-term goals.

Rigged or   Washington has created a system that
Fixed System   facilitates implementation of decisions of folly
                           for the selfish ambition of a few, while rejecting
                           implementation of decisions of reason for the
                           many; creating a predetermined outcome no
                           matter what the input is.

Root Cause	The underlying cause(s) of a problem, disaster or crisis which must be uncovered and eliminated to prevent recurrence.
Second Responders	Second responders have been generally defined as those who support "first responders" by cleaning up physical sites after a disaster. In this book, I am extending the term "second responders" to also refer to those who prevent, or reduce, the crises that are the cause of our disasters; those who clean up the crises that are the causes of our disasters.
Special Interests	A group seeking to influence legislative or government policy to further their own narrowly defined interests, typically using lobbying and offering campaign donations to elected officials in order to obtain the own goals.
Speculation	Investment with substantial risk of loss, but also substantial opportunity for gain.
Super PACs	In 2010, the Supreme Court allowed unlimited special interest money from unidentified businesses to be used in election campaigns through Super Political Action Committees (Super PACs), which in turn influence politicians' decisions.
Superfund site	A toxic site that is contaminated with hazardous substances and pollutants, including carcinogens; typically created by businesses.
Values	Values are what are considered important in life and to the country. Values can help us decide what is right and wrong.

INDEX

2008 economic crash, 38, 70, 222

Addiction, 41, 87, 110, 143, 244, 245, 246, 247, 275, 336, 337

Amazon, 2, 215, 226, 418

American Dream, 1, 2, 5, 8, 19, 31, 65, 67, 102, 124, 126, 130, 140, 354, 357, 358, 367, 369, 370, 384, 385, 401, 439

American Society of Civil Engineers, 40, 205, 408, 417

Artificial intelligence, 27, 202

Asylum, 17, 61, 141, 142, 143, 246, 332, 333, 334, 335, 340, 341, 353

Barack Obama, 1, 68

Big Pharma, 45, 81, 90, 91, 276, 375, 429

Birmingham, 215

Bloom's Taxonomy, 7, 126, 215, 412

Border Security, 29, 30, 32, 33, 60, 63, 64, 69, 73, 151, 309, 332, 335, 339, 341, 342, 399, 410

Budget deficit, 4, 36, 39, 42, 74, 82, 102, 172, 173, 176, 186

Bush, George 20, 68, 170, 313, 345, 356, 361

Carbon dioxide, 300, 302, 440

Carbon emissions, 57, 298, 299, 302, 303, 305, 306, 390

Carcinogens, 45, 49, 153, 258, 261, 262, 390, 445396, 440

Centers for Disease Control and Prevention, 12, 47, 49, 243, 246, 249, 251, 252, 259, 265, 266, 275, 282, 337, 409, 410, 413, 423, 424, 425, 426, 427, 429, 430

Childhood poverty, 219, 227

China, 27, 36, 39, 42, 55, 63, 82, 124, 140, 168, 173, 176, 177, 200, 210, 212, 216, 217, 232, 233, 247, 252, 300, 311, 313, 326, 329, 345, 346, 347, 349, 415, 418

Chronic stress, 46, 50, 260, 261

Clean energy, 302, 303, 306, 378

Climate change, 24 30, 33, 53, 56, 69, 83, 90, 96, 98, 137, 151, 282, 283, 284, 286, 298, 300, 301, 304, 305, 306, 375, 378, 390, 397, 432, 440

Climate warming, 90, 91, 153, 285, 298, 299, 300, 302, 303, 376, 397, 440

Congressional Budget Office, 172, 187, 415

Corporate debt, 36, 38, 188,

189, 192, 193, 194, 195
Critical thinking skills, 5, 26, 79,
  85, 113, 123, 126, 127, 239,
  240, 389, 395
Cyber attack, 321, 324, 326,
  328, 329, 347
Cyber intrusions, 59, 320, 324,
  326, 328, 329

Cybersecurity, 30, 33, 58, 59,
  60, 63, 64, 69, 73, 137, 151,
  159, 184, 200, 309, 320, 321,
  322, 323, 324, 325, 326, 327,
  328, 329, 330, 341, 344, 347,
  348, 353, 390, 398, 399, 400,
  434, 441
Cyberspace, 320, 324
Dark web, 323, 326, 327, 328,
  329, 399
Debt-to-GDP ratio, 36, 37, 82,
  106, 159, 165, 166, 167, 168,
  169, 171, 172, 173, 177, 178,
  179, 181, 182, 183, 184, 185,
  186, 198, 200, 371, 384, 389,
  393
Decisions of folly, 2, 3, 4, 5, 7,
  20, 26, 28, 31, 34, 35, 64, 66,
  68, 72, 74, 75, 77, 85, 86, 87,
  89, 95, 101, 103, 107, 140,
  161, 171, 174, 183, 194, ,223,
  295, 352, 354, 355, 357, 358,
  360, 361, 374, 382, 383, 384,
  441, 444
Department of Defense, 27, 59,
  176, 301, 327, 344, 346, 347,
  349, 350, 433, 436
Department of Homeland
  Security, 59, 60, 321, 322,
  327, 333, 341, 344, 347, 399,
  410, 434

DeSantis, 285, 431
DHS, 60, 321, 322, 323, 324,
  325, 327, 333, 337, 341, 344,
  347, 348, 399, 400, 410, 434
Diamond, Jared, 25, 26, 139,
  165, 307, 408, 412, 414
Dodd-Frank Act, 190, 222
Donald Trump, 1, 68, 325, 359,
  361, 437
Drug epidemic, 45, 46, 250, 338
Drug overdose, 46, 49, 243,
  245, 246, 340
Drug smuggling, 61, 133, 332,
  336, 337, 338, 340, 341, 353
Environmental Protection
  Agency, 18, 49, 54, 71, 258,
  259, 285, 288, 302, 426, 431
FDA, 244, 246, 247, 339, 341,
  395, 399
Federal Reserve Bank, 170, 182,
  191, 192, 201, 210, 417
Fentanyl, 243, 245, 247, 338,
  436
GDP, 1, 4, 32, 34, 36, 52, 63, 70,
  80, 83, 102, 139, 150, 160,
  165, 166, 167, 168, 169, 170,
  173, 179, 180, 185, 189, 194,
  198, 200, 217, 240, 241, 242,
  274, 277, 278, 281, 284, 347,
  348, 349, 350, 408, 414, 415,
  436, 441
Gerrymandering, 105, 355, 359,
  360, 364, 365, 391, 400
Global Climate Treaty, 299, 300
Global warming, 299, 300
Government follies, 7, 8, 34, 66,
  72, 88, 184, 193, 201, 206,
  215, 226, 239, 246, 254, 260,
  271, 277, 286, 293, 304, 316,
  327, 339, 348, 363, 369, 374,

379, 383, 384, 392, 403

Gross Crisis Cost, 1, 4, 32, 34, 74, 83, 102, 121, 122, 150, 151, 152, 153, 380, 383, 384, 441

Gun violence, 13, 16, 45, 50, 51, 110, 121, 141, 142, 149, 243, 267, 268, 269, 271, 272, 275, 279, 335, 340, 341, 396

House Crisis Action Teams (CATs), 6, 84, 113, 370, 371, 380, 384, 387, 404

Human Papillomavirus, (HPV), 49, 259, 442

Illegal immigration, 60, 63, 332, 333, 334, 335, 338, 340, 341, 410

Immigrants, 17, 60, 108, 129, 142, 143, 332, 333, 335, 336, 341, 353, 390

Infant mortality rate, 54, 282

Internet, 27, 59, 239, 240, 267, 322, 323, 328, 329, 344

IT, 59, 115, 183, 321, 322, 323, 326, 327, 344, 441, 442

Kemp, Luke, 23, 24, 25, 26, 408

Kennedy, John F 10, 13, 262, 302, 385, 406, 433

Loss of hope, 1, 4, 5, 8, 14, 16, 18, 19, 21, 28, 66, 74, 75, 77, 86, 87, 95, 101, 102, 109, 119, 121, 124, 130, 160, 168, 198, 354, 357, 358, 374, 385

Marine Protected Areas (MPA), 291, 292, 294, 295, 390, 397, 431

Mass shooting, 11, 13, 50, 83, 120, 266, 267, 268, 270, 271, 272, 372

Minimum wage, 203, 211, 214,

216, 219, 221, 222, 223, 224, 226, 227, 228, 389

National debt,7, 16,30, 33, 36, 37, 41, 56, 65, 69, 73, 82, 90, 151, 164, 165, 166, 167, 168, 172, 174, 176, 184, 185, 209, 230, 367, 369, 371, 375, 392, 401

Non Proliferation Treaty (NPT),2, 58, 310, 311, 312, 314, 315, 316, 318

National Riffle Association (NRA), 16, 71, 142, 267, 268, 270

Nuclear arms, 58, 59, 309, 310, 315, 317, 318, 353

Nuclear disarmament, 311, 315, 317, 398

Nuclear energy, 310, 315, 319

Nuclear waste, 58, 59, 90, 137, 309, 310, 316, 317, 318, 319, 353, 375, 398

Nuclear weapons, 58, 91, 137, 309, 310, 311, 312, 313, 314, 316, 317, 318, 319, 344, 375, 398

Obesity, 2, 45, 46, 47, 249, 250, 251, 252, 253, 254, 256, 274, 424, 425

Ocean Conservancy, 4, 292, 295, 304, 431

Ocean pollution, 55, 296

Oil industry, 206, 315, 394

Opioid, 46, 81, 83, 90, 110, 244, 245, 246, 247, 248, 275, 338, 339, 372, 399, 423

Opioids, 211, 243, 244, 245, 247, 248, 337, 338, 339, 341, 389, 423

Overdose, 46, 243

OxyContin, 243, 244, 246, 247, 395

Pareto principle, 132

Pew Research Center, 1, 10, 140, 238, 370, 406, 407, 410, 412

Plan, Do, Check, Act (PDCA), 7, 2, 103, 127, 135, 148, 325, 443

Ports of Entry, 61, 133, 332, 334, 338, 339, 399, 410

Purdue Pharma, 244, 246, 395, 423

Quality approach, 2, 3, 4, 5, 6, 7, 8, 10, 18, 19, 20, 21, 23, 25, 29, 31, 71, 72, 74, 75, 77, 79, 86, 94, 96, 111, 118, 119, 122, 137, 138, 141, 144, 148, 149, 158, 162, 304, 309, 370, 371, 378, 384, 385, 404, 439, 442

Quality of life, 3, 15, 16, 41, 46, 124, 165, 168, 198, 386, 439

Russia 7, 59, 313, 321, 325, 327, 358, 359, 3991

Sea level rise, 159, 303, 304

Social media, 41, 44, 59, 80, 106, 211, 237, 239, 240, 241, 250, 255, 260, 344, 355, 363, 364, 365, 379, 402

Special interests, 2, 3, 5, 6, 7, 8, 21, 31, 34, 64, 66, 74, 75, 77, 83, 86, 87, 88, 89, 92, 95, 96, 98, 100, 103, 104, 105, 106, 107, 108, 109, 114, 119, 122, 125, 129, 133, 140, 154, 159, 160, 168, 268, 291, 349, 354, 357, 358, 361, 364, 367, 369, 370, 371, 372, 374, 376, 379, 380, 382, 383, 384, 385, 386,

387, 388, 391, 401, 402, 403, 404, 442

Speculation, 36, 37, 81, 134, 165, 171, 182, 188, 189, 190, 191, 193, 194, 195, 370, 371, 393, 394

Stress, 11, 12, 13, 407, 427, 440

Student debt, 43, 231, 232, 235, 236

Super PACs, 28, 65, 77, 101, 105, 114, 356, 357, 363, 364, 365, 391, 400, 436, 444

Supreme Court, 28, 65, 71, 77, 101, 109, 355, 357, 358, 444

Terrorism, 136, 333

The Swamp, 1, 6, 8, 23, 70, 95, 96, 103, 104, 105, 107, 108, 109, 111, 120, 122, 362, 367, *383, 385, 403*

Trade deficit, 38, 39, 42, 153, 173, 192, 197, 198, 199, 200, 201, 202, 203, 210, 216, 372, 441

Tuchman, Barbara, 20, 26, 77, 85, 88, 89, 138, 359, 372, 407

Unfixing Washington, 6, 9, 22, 72, 85, 108, 411

United Nations, 314

Wall Street, 7, 16, 33, 34, 36, 37, 38, 41, 42, 69, 70, 73, 81, 91, 134, 151, 165, 166, 171, 182, 188, 189, 190, 191, 193, 195, 375, 393, 404, 414, 415, 416

Workforce participation, 42, 199, 200, 202, 210, 211, 216, 240

Working poor, 16, 43, 149, 159, 218, 219, 220, 222, 223, 226, 227, 228, 231, 235, 395

Made in the USA
Lexington, KY
04 November 2019

56487114R00240